SECOND EDITION

ENVIRONMENTAL COMMUNICATION
and the Public Sphere

For my mother, Julia Bransford Cox,
and in memory of my father, James Robert Cox,
who taught me respect for nature and
kindness to living beings.

SECOND EDITION

ENVIRONMENTAL COMMUNICATION
and the Public Sphere

ROBERT COX
The University of North Carolina at Chapel Hill

Los Angeles | London | New Delhi
Singapore | Washington DC

For information:

SAGE Publications, Inc.
2455 Teller Road
Thousand Oaks, California 91320
E-mail: order@sagepub.com

SAGE Publications Ltd.
1 Oliver's Yard
55 City Road
London EC1Y 1SP
United Kingdom

SAGE Publications India Pvt. Ltd.
B 1/I 1 Mohan Cooperative Industrial Area
Mathura Road, New Delhi 110 044
India

SAGE Publications Asia-Pacific Pte. Ltd.
33 Pekin Street #02-01
Far East Square
Singapore 048763

Printed in the United States of America

Library of Congress Cataloging-in-Publication Data

Cox, Robert.
Environmental communication and the public sphere / Robert Cox. — 2nd ed.
    p. cm.
Includes bibliographical references and index.
ISBN 978-1-4129-7211-6 (pbk.)
    1. Communication in the environmental sciences—Textbooks. 2. Mass media and the environment—Textbooks. I. Title.

GE25.C69 2010
333.7201′4—dc22   2009006547

This book is printed on recycled, acid-free paper.

09   10   11   12   13   10   9   8   7   6   5   4   3   2

Acquisitions Editor:	Todd R. Armstrong
Editorial Assistant:	Aja Baker
Production Editor:	Astrid Virding
Copy Editor:	Pam Suwinsky
Typesetter:	C&M Digitals (P) Ltd.
Proofreader:	Dennis W. Webb
Indexer:	Mary Mortensen
Cover Designer:	Glenn Vogel
Marketing Manager:	Carmel Schrire

Brief Contents

Detailed Contents

Acknowledgments

Environmental communication continues to grow as a field of study and practice, and a book attempting to introduce this field could not have been written without the help of numerous individuals. In writing this second edition, I particularly thank the students in my environmental communication classes at the University of North Carolina at Chapel Hill whose intelligence and commitment to a more environmentally sane and just world inspires me every day. Once again, I am indebted to many friends and colleagues, especially Tarla and Marcus Petersen, Elizabeth Smith, Steve Depoe, Phaedra Pezzullo, and Renee Lertzman, who provided support and encouragement unselfishly.

Many other colleagues in the academy and the U.S. environmental movement responded to pleas for help, provided materials, and gently pointed out omissions and errors in earlier drafts. In particular, I thank Allison Aurelia Fisher, Carol Corbin, Helen Correll, Emily Plec, Melissa Yule, and many others from the Environmental Communication Network (ECN) for their invaluable help in many sections of the book.

The following reviewers are gratefully acknowledged:

Second edition:

Peter K. Bsumek, James Madison University

William Kinsella, North Carolina State University

Mark S. Meisner, The State University of New York College of Environmental Science and Forestry

R. J. Multari, University at Buffalo (SUNY)

Tarla Rai Peterson, Texas A&M University

Anne Marie Todd, San Jose State University

Wayne D. Woodward, University of Michigan-Dearborn

First edition:

Terence Check, St. John's University

Helen M. Correll, Metropolitan State University

Kevin DeLuca, University of Georgia

Steve Depoe, University of Cincinnati

Adrian Ivakhiv, University of Vermont

Dennis Jaehne, San Jose State University

Jennifer A. Peeples, Utah State University

Tarla Rai Peterson, Texas A&M University

Phaedra Pezzullo, Indiana University

Steve Schwarze, University of Montana

Susan L. Senech, The State University of New York College of Environmental Science and Forestry

Christina Zarcadoolas, Brown University

At SAGE Publications, my thanks go to Aja Baker for her generous help as editorial assistant throughout the writing process, and also to Astrid Virding's skillful work as project editor, and to Pam Suwinsky, whose discerning eye as copy editor saved me from many stumbles in the text. Although I have benefited from the suggestions and help of many, I am clearly responsible for any errors that have found their way into the text.

Most important, my writing and work with the U.S. environmental movement would not be possible without the wise counsel, support, and patience of my life partner and colleague, Julia Wood.

The way we communicate with one another about the environment powerfully affects how we perceive both it and ourselves and, therefore, how we define our relationship with the natural world.

Introduction

Speaking for and About the Environment

Communication about the environment has increased dramatically—from news about melting glaciers and a warming climate to "green" business headlines. Interest runs across all media—cable TV, online sites, films, YouTube, newspapers, public rallies, and in classrooms. A Website lists its "Top 10 Environmental Blogs," while *Time*, *Vanity Fair*, *Sports Illustrated*, and other popular magazines and e-zines showcase special environmental reports. Documentary films like the BBC's *Planet Earth* showcase the loss of biodiversity and warnings of a "Sixth Great Extinction." And online sites like 350.org and social networking sites such as climatecrossroads.org link us globally with daily news, opportunities to take action, and videos from across the world.

The *ways* we are talking about the environment are also changing. Concern over chemicals in our food, congested highways, global warming, and rising energy costs—food, gas, heating our homes—affect our daily lives. There is also a palpable sense of *urgency* in many public pronouncements about the environment. For example, Rajendra Pachauri, director of the UN Intergovernmental Panel on Climate Change (IPCC), warned world leaders, "If there's no action [on climate change] before 2012, that's too late. What we do . . . [now] will determine our future. This is the defining moment" (Rosenthal, 2007).

The increased public awareness also has prompted interest in the new field of **environmental communication,** the subject of this book. But, why *communication?* Legendary environmentalist David Brower, whom nature writer John McPhee (1971) called the "Archdruid," once told me, "We're fiddling while the earth burns. We need to *act!*" Yet, history remembers David Brower himself as a pioneer in communicating to public audiences about human threats to wild places. As one of the most innovative leaders of the modern environmental movement, David took out bold, full-page ads in U.S. newspapers that successfully rallied public opposition to the construction of two dams in the Grand Canyon. He introduced books of stunning nature photography, such as *In Wildness Is the Preservation of the World* (Porter, 1964), and captured the wild beauty of Glen Canyon on film, documenting this once-wild canyon in southern Utah (now dammed and flooded). He never separated his sense of urgency about a problem from the need to *communicate urgently to others*. Indeed, David's genius was to realize that somebody must speak for nature and rally others to add their own voices on behalf of threatened forests, wild rivers, and the wildlife they sustain.

Communication and Nature's Meaning

David Brower was a powerful advocate for the environment. But not everyone sees herself or himself as an environmental advocate or an environmental communication professional such as a journalist, science educator, or filmmaker. Some of you may be reading this book simply to learn more about environmental issues. Yet, it is impossible to separate our knowledge about environmental issues from communication itself. As environmental communication scholars James Cantrill and Christine Oravec (1996) make clear, the "environment we experience and affect is largely a product of how we come to talk about the world" (p. 2). That is, *the way we communicate with one another about the environment powerfully affects how we perceive both it and ourselves and, therefore, how we define our relationship with the natural world*. For example, Harvard University scientist E. O. Wilson (2002) uses the language of biology to describe the environment as "a membrane of organisms wrapped around Earth so thin it cannot be seen edgewise from a space shuttle, yet so internally complex that most species composing it remain undiscovered" (p. 3).

The images and information we receive from friends, blogs, the news media, Facebook, or popular films play a powerful role in influencing not only how we perceive the environment but also what actions we take. For example, when the massive Larson B ice shelf, in Antarctica, collapsed suddenly in February 2002, it sounded alarm bells among climate scientists over the pace of global warming. An ice shelf the size of Rhode Island simply disappeared. (See Figure I.1.) While scientists had known Larson B was a "hotspot of global warming" (Pearce, 2006, p. 92), the speed of the collapse (a short three weeks) fueled new concern and debate over global warming. Similarly, it was biologist Rachel Carson (1962), whose book *Silent Spring*, in describing the poisoning of birds, "contributed directly to society's ability to recognize and respond to the threat of dangerous agricultural chemicals" (Peterson, Peterson, & Peterson, 2007, p. 79).

Although images of a "silent spring" or drowning polar bears clearly communicate, we encounter these images through the labor of others—filmmakers, reporters, scientists—who focus our attention in dramatic ways. Indeed, it is scientists, Environmental Protection Agency (EPA) officials, environmental advocates, business lobbyists, and ordinary citizens who debate the meaning of environmental questions: Can the United States meet its energy needs through renewable sources like wind and solar power, or must it drill for oil in the Arctic National Wildlife Refuge? Is it safe for the U.S. Army to burn stores of chemical weapons near schools and residential neighborhoods? In engaging such questions, we rely on speech, symbols, art, persuasion, and debate to imagine, describe, debate, and celebrate our multiple relations with the natural world.

Figure I.1   "Larsen B ice shelf" collapse, in Antarctica, February 2002.

Image courtesy Landsat 7 Science Team and NASA GSFC.

That's one reason I wrote this book: I believe that communication about the environment matters. It matters in the ways we interact with our friends, at work, and in *naming* certain conditions in our environment as "problems." And it matters ultimately in the choices we make in response to these problems. This book, therefore, focuses on the role of communication in helping us negotiate the relationship between ourselves and the thin "membrane of organisms" that makes up our environment.

The purpose of *Environmental Communication and the Public Sphere* is threefold: (1) to increase your insight into how communication shapes our perceptions of environmental issues; (2) to acquaint you with some of the media and public forums that are used for environmental communication, along with the communication practices of scientists, corporate lobbyists, ordinary citizens, and others who seek to influence decisions about nature and the human environment; and (3) to enable you to join in conversations and debates that are already taking place locally and globally that may affect the environments where you yourself live, study, work, and play.

Why Do We Need to Speak for the Environment?

At first glance, there appears to be little need for persuasion and debate about environmental issues. Since the first Earth Day in 1970, U.S. opinion polls have reported that the public is concerned about environmental problems and strongly supports environmental values. On the 30th anniversary of Earth Day, a Gallup poll found that 83 percent of Americans "readily agreed with the broadest goals of the environmental movement" (Guber, 2003, p. 3). And, even with the U.S. economy in a slump, a poll by CNN/Opinion Research in 2008 revealed that a plurality of Americans say that "protection of the environment should be given priority, even at the risk of curbing economic growth" (Goldman, 2008).

Such support for environmental values is not surprising. Marine sciences professor Willett Kempton, along with anthropologists James S. Boster and Jennifer A. Hartley (1996), found a decade ago that "most Americans share a common set of environmental beliefs and values" (p. 211). Even radically divergent groups in U.S. society shared more agreement than one might expect. For example, workers who had been laid off from lumber sawmills in the Pacific Northwest and members of the radical environmental group Earth First! agreed on a range of questions about what they valued. More than two-thirds of respondents from the two groups agreed with such statements as·

- "We have to protect the environment for our children and for our grandchildren, even if it means reducing our standard of living today."
- "We have a moral duty to leave the earth in as good or better shape than we found it. . . ."
- "The reason politicians break their promises to the people to clean up our environment is the power of industry lobbyists." (pp. 204–205)

Although the public's concern for the environment is significant, considerable differences exist among individuals over how society should solve environmental problems. A good example is global warming. A poll conducted by the World Wildlife Fund found that 74 percent of the public felt that the problem of warming of the Earth's atmosphere was either "somewhat serious" or "extremely serious." Differences were revealed, however, when people were asked what actions the United States should take to reduce the major cause of global warming: "Do you think we should rely mainly on strict regulations to limit emissions of carbon dioxide, or do you think we should rely mainly on incentives that cause the free market to discourage carbon dioxide pollution?" Respondents were split almost evenly between those who favored government regulation (37%), those who supported free market options (32%), and those who felt they lacked enough information to choose (30%) (Guber, 2003, pp. 30–31).

The complexity of issues such as global warming makes the finding of a public consensus difficult. And as the different voices of climate scientists, Americans for Balanced Energy Choices (a group backed by the coal industry), and environmental groups such as the Sierra Club enter the public debate, widely divergent viewpoints compete for our support.

There exists, then, a dilemma. Although in one sense, nature is silent, others— politicians, business leaders, environmentalists, the media—claim the right *to speak for* nature, or for their own interests in the use of natural resources. Hence, the dilemma: If nature cannot speak, who has the right to speak on nature's behalf? Who should define the interests of society in relation to the natural world? Is it appropriate, for example, to drill for oil offshore or along fragile coastlines? Who should bear the cost of cleaning up abandoned toxic waste sites—the businesses responsible for the contamination or taxpayers? These questions illustrate the rhetorical nature of environmental communication. Only in a society that allows public debate can the public mediate among the differing voices and ways of understanding the environment–society relationship. That is one of my purposes in writing this book: I believe that you, I, and everyone in a democratic society have a pivotal role in speaking about these larger environmental issues.

Background and Perspective of the Author

After inviting you to join in conversations about the environment, perhaps it's time I described myself and my own involvement in the field. In recent years, I have been involved in a leadership role in the U.S. environmental movement while also teaching as a communication professor at the University of North Carolina at Chapel Hill. I also have served as president of the national Sierra Club, based in San Francisco, 2007–2008 and also 2000–2001 and 1994–1996. I continue to serve on its board of directors and also advise the Sierra Club on strategic challenges.

However, my interest in the environment arose long before I had heard of the Sierra Club. As a boy growing up in the Appalachian region of southern West Virginia, I fell in love with the wild beauty of the mountains near my home and the graceful flow of the Greenbrier River. However, as I grew older, I saw coal mining's devastating effects on the natural landscape and on the streams and water supplies of local communities. The awful curse of black lung disease also placed hardship on coal miners and their families. Later, in graduate school in Pittsburgh, I saw the health effects of air pollution from steel mills, and I began to realize how intimately people and their environments are bound together. Human beings and nature do not stand apart from each other.

As a professor at the University of North Carolina at Chapel Hill, I began to volunteer with environmental groups. Although I was motivated initially by my personal experiences, I soon became aware of the essential role of communication in the work of these organizations as they sought to educate public audiences and policymakers. I also spent much of my time as president of the Sierra Club communicating with the public in some form: briefing newspaper editorial boards, speaking at public rallies, testifying before Congress, organizing in communities, talking with reporters, and helping to design elements of advocacy campaigns.

As a result of these experiences and also as a result of my own research and teaching in environmental communication, I've become more firmly persuaded of several things:

1. Individuals and communities have a stronger chance to safeguard the environmental health and quality of their local environments if they understand some of the dynamics of and opportunities for communication about their concerns.

2. Environmental issues and public agencies do not need to remain remote, complex, or impenetrable. The environmental movement, legal action, and the media have helped to demystify governmental procedures and open the doors and computer files of government bureaucracies to greater public access and participation in environmental decisions.

3. As a consequence, individuals have opportunities to participate in meaningful ways in public debates about our environment, and, indeed, there is more urgency than ever in doing so. That is why I wrote *Environmental Communication and the Public Sphere.*

One other thing: Largely because of my work in the U.S. environmental movement, I cannot avoid a personal perspective on many of the issues discussed in this book, nor do I wish to. In this sense, I am clearly biased in favor of environmental values and certain approaches to environmental protection. I do three things, however, as I develop the topics in this book. First, when I introduce views or positions, I try to acknowledge any bias or personal experience that I might have. Second, I explain how I arrived at my perspective, based on my experience and my knowledge or research.

Finally, I include a brief "Another Viewpoint" in some chapters to alert you to important disagreements or debates. For example, because I believe that states and the federal government have an important role to play in protecting the environment, I also refer you to sources that favor a private-sector or market approach. My aim is not to set up false dichotomies but to introduce a multiplicity of perspectives. I also refer you to sources and URLs that challenge my own stance to allow you to learn about other views.

Distinctive Features of the Book

As its title suggests, the framework for *Environmental Communication and the Public Sphere* is organized around two core concepts:

1. The importance of human communication in shaping our perceptions of the environment and our relationships with it

2. The role of the **public sphere** in mediating or negotiating among the different voices seeking to influence decisions and the environment

I use the idea of the **public sphere** throughout this book to refer to the realm of influence that is created when individuals engage others in communication—through conversation, argument, debate, and questions—about subjects of shared concern or topics that affect a wider community. (I describe the idea of the public sphere more in Chapter 1.) Nor is communication limited to words: Visual and nonverbal symbolic actions such as photographs, flash videos, marches, Greenpeace banners, and documentary film have prompted discussion, debate, and questioning of environmental policy as readily as editorials, speeches, and TV newscasts. (See Figure I.2.)

| Figure I.2 | The "public sphere" arises when individuals engage others in communication—through conversation, argument, debate, and questions—about subjects of shared concern. |

Photo courtesy of Tony Bonanno.

Along with the focus on human communication and the public sphere, this second edition includes several distinctive features:

1. Practical ways that ordinary citizens can affect decisions about the environment, including a "right-to-know" and a right to comment publicly before certain actions are taken

2. Attention to new media—online sites, blogs, and social networking—as well as other less-studied forms of environmental communication such as citizen lawsuits, collaborative partnerships, social marketing, and advocacy campaigns of environmental groups

3. New emphasis on communicating about global warming and the movement for "climate justice," illustrating many of the principles of environmental communication

4. Discussion of the resources of language—metaphor and rhetorical genres— and the challenge of the "attitude-behavior gap" in social marketing campaigns

5. Use of personal experiences and cases studies to illustrate key points; also more visual and online resources such as films, blogs, and books to supplement ideas in each chapter

6. Opportunities to apply your knowledge of environmental communication on your campus or community through "Act Locally!" exercises in many chapters

7. International examples and applications of the principles of environmental communication in different regions of the world

Environmental communication is growing rapidly in many regions of the world. Although this book developed out of a U.S. context, the second edition attempts to do two things: (1) increase the potential for application and understanding of many of the concepts of environmental communication more globally; and (2) provide case studies and recognize recent developments in environmental communication in different nations. For example, many European nations, including the countries of Eastern Europe and the former Soviet Union, are making great strides in implementing the **Aarhus Convention**—a UN agreement ensuring access to environmental information and public participation in environmental decisions in Europe. (See Chapter 3.)

New Terrain/New Questions

I recognize that you probably bring a range of views and assumptions to the subject of the environment and to the study of environmental communication. Some of you may be a little suspicious of environmentalists, perhaps thinking they're somewhat strange (as in the popular image of "tree huggers"). Others of you may hope to work in the environmental field in the future or consider yourselves environmental activists. Many of you—perhaps the majority—may not label yourself environmentalists at all but nevertheless support recycling, clean air, and preserving more green space on your campus. And I suspect that some of you may have questions about your ability to affect any of the big problems, such as global warming, loss of tropical rain forests, or the safety of genetically modified organisms (GMOs) in our food chain.

In this book, I start at the beginning. I do not assume any special knowledge on your part about environmental science or politics. Nor do I assume that you know about particular theories of communication. For example, I use **boldface** type when I introduce and define an important communication or environmental term. I also include a list of these "Key Terms" at the end of each chapter. In some cases, an "FYI" feature provides background information to help you become familiar with theories or issues raised in a chapter.

In turn, I hope you'll be open to exploring what might be a new perspective: the role of human communication in shaping how we understand and respond to environmental problems. If you are, I think you'll find new possibilities for joining ongoing and urgent conversations about environmental problems, as well as discovering ways to be more effective in voicing your own concerns or influencing solutions.

I also hope you'll seriously reflect on material that may challenge your own assumptions or views, not only about environmentalists but also about the roles of science, the news media, television programming, corporations, and environmental groups in constructing our views of nature and the environment. For example, a common misconception is that people who espouse environmental values are an elite group, that they want to "turn back the clock" to an earlier, romanticized past (Hays, 2000, p. 23). Yet, there is little support for such views. As we'll see, some of the most environmentally engaged citizens of recent years have been residents of low-income, at-risk communities that are plagued by polluting industries, incinerators, and toxic waste landfills, as well as students concerned about climate change on their campuses.

In my own work, I've found that debates about environmental concerns have emerged as a kind of crucible for a participatory, democratic culture in the United States. As environmental goals broaden beyond wilderness and wildlife to include urban concerns about pollution and the quality of the places where people live and work, more and more people of diverse backgrounds—university faculty, students, neighborhood activists, scientists, residents of low-income communities, and affluent suburbanites—are increasingly working together to protect the health of their communities as well as the natural world.

SUMMARY

The study of environmental communication invites us to explore new paths and unfamiliar terrain. In some cases, those paths lead to local town hall meetings as citizens voice their concerns over permits for new coal-burning power plants. Other paths will take you inside the advocacy campaign of a southwestern indigenous tribe that sought to protect its sacred lands or behind the scenes of a social marketing campaign on global warming. Still other paths invite you to go online to the Toxic Release Inventory to check on pollution levels in your own community or to call a radio talk show to voice concerns about too many orange or red alerts on bad air days.

In traveling these new paths, we'll look especially for the ways in which language, symbols, discourse, and ideology shape our perceptions of nature and our own relationship with the environment. By becoming aware of some of the dynamics of human communication in constructing our response to environmental problems, we are able to join in public conversations about not only the fate of the Earth in the abstract, but urgent debates over the fate of the places where we live, work, and enjoy everyday life.

KEY TERMS

Aarhus Convention: Adopted in 1998 at the Danish city of Aarhus, this is one of five international environmental conventions of the United Nations Economic Commission for Europe. It addresses three areas: Access to Information, Public Participation in Decision-making, and Access to Justice in Environmental Matters.

Environmental communication: A study of the ways in which we communicate about the environment, the effects of this communication on our perceptions of both the environment and ourselves, and therefore on our relationship with the natural world. For a formal definition of environmental communication, see Chapter 1.

Public sphere: The realm of influence created when individuals engage others in communication—through conversation, argument, debate, questions, and nonverbal acts—about subjects of shared concern or topics that affect a wider community.

DISCUSSION QUESTIONS

1. Can nature speak? Or is the natural world silent? Can you understand, appreciate, or relate to the natural world without language?

2. Is it necessary for humans to speak for the natural world? Without communication, what happens to nature?

3. What are some of the urgent environmental problems in your community? In the United States? Around the globe? What changes do you believe you, society, business, or governmental institutions need to make to protect the natural and human environments?

4. Have you ever spoken publicly about the environment at a town meeting, called in to a radio talk show, participated in an Earth Day event? How did you feel about this experience? What was its impact on you and on others?

REFERENCES

Cantrill, J. G., & Oravec, C. L. (1996). Introduction. In J. G. Cantrill & C. L. Oravec (Eds.), *The symbolic earth: Discourse and our creation of the environment* (pp. 1–8). Lexington: University of Kentucky Press.

Carson, R. (1962). *Silent spring.* Boston: Houghton Mifflin.

Goldman, D. (2008, July 3). Environmental support dips vs. the economy—poll. CNNMoney.com, Retrieved August 28, 2008, from http://money.cnn.com.

Guber, D. L. (2003). *The grassroots of a green revolution: Polling America on the environment.* Cambridge: MIT Press.

Hays, S. P. (2000). *A history of environmental politics since 1945.* Pittsburgh: University of Pittsburgh Press.

Kempton, W., Boster, J. S., & Hartley, J. A. (1996). *Environmental values in American culture.* Cambridge, MA: MIT Press.

McPhee, J. (1971). *Encounters with the archdruid.* New York: Farrar, Straus & Giroux.

Pearce, F. (2006). *The last generation: How nature will take her revenge for climate change.* London: Eden Project Books.

Peterson, M. N., Peterson, M. J., & Peterson, T. R. (2007). *Environmental Communication: A Journal of Nature and Culture, 1,* 74–86.

Porter, E. (1967, 1974). *In wildness is the preservation of the world.* New York: Sierra Club/Ballantine.

Rosenthal, E. (2007, November 18). U.N. chief seeks more climate change leadership. *The New York Times,* http://www.nytimes.com/2007/11/18/science/earh/18climatenew, retrieved August 24, 2008.

Wilson, E. O. (2002). *The future of life.* New York. Knopf.

PART I

Conceptual Perspectives

Our actions toward the environment depend not only on ecological sciences but also on public education, news media, Websites, and even ordinary conversations.

CHAPTER 1

Studying Environmental Communication

Environmental communication seeks to enhance the ability of society to respond appropriately to environmental signals relevant to the well-being of both human civilization and natural biological systems.

—Cox, "Nature's 'Crisis Disciplines'" (2007)

Before I began to write this morning, I checked several online sites, as well as the morning's newspaper. All had news stories about environmental concerns: Efforts to restore Florida's magnificent Everglades had fallen behind schedule, and oil companies had called again to drill in Alaska's Arctic National Wildlife Refuge. And, both Grist.org and the *Washington Post* were reporting that "the rise in global carbon dioxide emissions last year outpaced international researchers' most dire projections," rising nearly 3 percent (Eilperin, 2008, p. A2). This news fueled online debate throughout the day about new urgency to reduce our carbon output to slow global warming.

Similar stories about the environment surround us daily. They appear when we tune into CNN or the *Daily Show*. We see such stories when we go online at sites like *Environment News Network* (www.enn.com), *Real Climate* (www.realclimate.org), or the award-winning science blog *Dot Earth* (http://dotearth.blogs.nytimes.com). We find them when we open the *New York Times* or the local newspaper, or read popular books such as Thomas Friedman's *Hot, Flat, and Crowded* (2008), and the list goes on.

Many years ago, when I first began my study of environmental communication, the news carried few stories like these. Few college classes about the environment existed on campuses. Today, environmental studies is one of the fastest-growing majors for students. The environment is also one of the most important areas of research and employment in the 21st century. Along with this trend, courses in environmental *communication* are also becoming popular on many campuses.

Chapter 1 describes environmental communication as a new, multidisciplinary field of study. As a growing number of people realize that our understanding of nature and our behavior toward the environment depend not only on ecological sciences but also on public debate, media representations, Websites, and even ordinary conversation, courses and research devoted specifically to environmental communication are emerging.

The first section of this chapter defines the term *environmental communication* and identifies seven principal areas of study in this emerging field. The second section introduces three themes that constitute the framework of this book: (1) human communication is a form of symbolic action; (2) as a result, our beliefs, attitudes, and behaviors relating to nature and environmental problems are *mediated* or influenced by communication; and (3) the public sphere (or spheres) emerges as a discursive space for communication about the environment. Finally, the third section describes some of the diverse voices that speak about the environment and whose communication practices we'll study in this book: the voices of local citizens, scientists, public officials, news media, online news services, environmental groups, and corporations.

After reading this chapter, you should have an understanding of environmental communication as an area of study. You should also be able to recognize the range of voices and communication practices through which environmental groups, ordinary citizens, and opponents of environmentalism discuss important questions about the environment. As a result, I hope that you'll not only become a more critical consumer of such communication but also discover opportunities to add your own voice to the vibrant conversations about the environment that are already in progress.

The Field of Environmental Communication

Along with the growth of environmental studies, courses devoted specifically to the role of human communication in environmental affairs also have emerged. These courses study environmental news media, methods of **public participation** in environmental decisions, environmental rhetoric, risk communication, environmental conflict resolution, advocacy campaigns, "green" marketing, and images of nature in popular culture.

On a practical level, the study of environmental communication helps to prepare you to enter many professional fields. Businesses, governmental agencies, law firms, public relations (PR) firms, and nonprofit environmental groups increasingly employ consultants and practitioners in environmental communication. Skills in environmental communication have become vital to a growing number of public and private organizations, from the Society of Environmental Journalists (www.sej.org) to the Environmental Protection Agency (EPA).

On a more conceptual level, the study of environmental communication contributes to theories about human communication itself. For example, its focus on the role of human speech, art, symbols, and so forth in defining the human–nature relationship is perhaps the clearest example of the thesis that human communication mediates or negotiates our relations to, and understanding of, the world beyond our minds. The study of environmental communication also reminds us of the *material* consequences of our communication choices. For example, citizens' comments in public hearings on an air quality permit or an advocacy campaign to close a hospital waste incinerator—and countless other modes of communication about environmental concerns—contribute to actions that protect, harm, nurture, sustain, alter, or otherwise change aspects of our material world.

Growth of the Field

Communication scholar Susan Senecah recently remarked, "Fields of inquiry do not simply happen by wishing them into existence. The field of [environmental communication] is no different" (2007, p. 22). In the United States, the field grew out of the work of a diverse group of communication scholars, many of whom used the tools of rhetorical criticism to study conflicts over wilderness, forests, farmlands, and endangered species, as well as the rhetoric of environmental groups (Cox, 1982; Lange, 1990, 1993; Moore, 1993; Oravec, 1981, 1984; Peterson, 1986; Short, 1991). Christine Oravec's (1981) study of the "sublime" in John Muir's appeals to preserve California's Yosemite Valley in the 19th century is considered by many to be the start of scholarship in what would become "environmental communication."

At the same time, the field of environmental communication began to widen to include the roles of science, media, and industry in responding to threats to human health and safety. Early studies investigated issues such as industry's use of public relations and mass-circulation magazines to construct an "ecological" image (Brown & Crable, 1973; Greenberg, Sandman, Sachsman, & Salamone, 1989; Grunig, 1989); the nuclear power industry's response to dramatic accidents at Three Mile Island and Chernobyl (Farrell & Goodnight, 1981; Luke, 1987); and risk communication in conveying the dangers of recombinant DNA experiments (Waddell, 1990). Scholars in the fields of journalism and mass communication began a systematic study of the influence of media depictions of the environment on public attitudes (Anderson, 1997; Shanahan & McComas, 1999, pp. 26–27). In fact, the study of environmental media has grown so rapidly that many now consider it a distinct subfield.

By the 1990s, a biennial "Conference on Communication and Environment" had begun to attract scholars from a range of academic disciplines in the United States and other nations. Also, a new Environmental Communication Network (www.esf.edu/ecn) provided an online resource for scholars, teachers, and practitioners. And, many nations host special conferences on environmental communication, including "Communicate Now," in the United Kingdom in 2008, and "The Media and the Environment—Between Complexity and Urgency," in Lisbon, Portugal, in 2009. And more recently, new journals in environmental communication, such as *Environmental Communication: A Journal of Nature and Culture* (2007), *Applied Environmental Education and*

Communication (2002), and the *International Journal of Sustainability Communication* (2007) have appeared on the scene.

As a result of these developments, scholars have expanded their research into nontraditional subjects, media, and forms of environmental communication. Recent topics include **toxic tours** conducted by members of poor and minority communities, who invite news reporters to witness their struggles against chemical pollution in their region (Pezzullo, 2007); warnings of "tipping points" in climate change communication (Russill, 2008); and wide-ranging studies of environmental public participation, including the mechanisms of different government agencies for public input and the public's influence on these agencies' decision making (Norton, 2007). Finally, scholars in political science, urban planning, sociology, and public health have begun to explore the intersections of the economy, power, and environmental problems. For example, Julian Agyeman, chair of Urban and Environmental Policy at Tufts University, has called for new attention to communicating **just sustainability**, the effort to fuse concerns for environmental sustainability and issues of race, class, gender, and social justice to ensure a "just" and sustainable future for all (Agyeman, 2007).

The sheer range of subjects makes defining environmental communication difficult. For example, environmental communication scholar Steve Depoe earlier (1997) defined the field as the study of the "relationships between our talk and our experiences of our natural surroundings" (p. 368). Yet, Depoe cautioned that environmental communication is more than simply "talk" about the environment.

Areas of Study

Although the study of environmental communication covers a wide range of topics, most research and public and professional practice fall into one of seven areas. We explore these areas more deeply in later chapters. For now, I identify the kind of concerns that environmental communication scholars currently are pursuing.

1. *Environmental rhetoric and discourse.* Rhetorical studies of the communication of environmental writers and campaigns emerged as an early focus of the new field. This is one of the broadest areas of study; it includes the rhetoric of environmental groups, nature writing, and business PR campaigns, as well as environmental media, and Websites. Generally, a **rhetorical focus** includes two subareas: (1) a study of the pragmatic modes of persuasion that individuals and groups use to communicate about the environment and (2) a study of critical rhetorics, or communication that questions or challenges the dominant discourses that define the relationship between nature and society.

In the first area, rhetorical scholars have studied the range of persuasion influencing our attitudes and behaviors toward the environment. For example, Marafiote (2008) has described the ways in which environmental groups reshaped the idea of "wilderness" to win passage of the 1964 Wilderness Act. In the second area, scholars studying critical rhetorics examine the role of communication in questioning or challenging society's values and assumptions about nature and our relationships to the environment. Studies of the rhetoric of radical environmental groups and the philosophies of deep ecology and ecofeminism are just some of the subjects of critical rhetoric studies. For example, scholars have studied Earth First! activists' questioning of the ideology of "progress" (Cooper, 1996) and debunked the myth that only humans have the ability to communicate (Rogers, 1998). More recent work by Taylor, Kinsella, Depoe, and Metzler (2008) investigates the rhetorical legacy of nuclear weapons production in the post–Cold War era and pose critical questions about the dispersed network of nuclear labs, test sites, factories, and cleanup sites and the communities that make up a "nuclear weapons production complex" (p. 2).

2. *Media and environmental journalism.* In many ways, the study of environmental media has become its own subfield. It focuses on the ways in which the news, advertising, commercial programs, and Internet sites portray nature and environmental problems. It is also the study of the *effects* of media on public attitudes. Traditional subjects include the **agenda-setting** role of the news media, its ability to influence which issues audiences think about; and also media **framing,** the way that stories guide readers' or viewers' sense making and evoke certain perceptions and values rather than others. (We cover this in more detail in Chapter 5.) For example, Wagner (2008) studied newspapers' re-framing of "Ecotage" (the destruction of property as a form of protest) as a form of "ecoterrorism," a more explicitly negative frame.

Other studies in environmental media have explored topics such as the rise of alternative media in reporting environmental news or events. These studies analyze the roles of independent media (for example, www.indymedia.org) and the emergence of "post-network television" such as TreeHugger.com, a "collection of online videos that explores how to create, consume, and live in environmentally friendly ways" (Slawter, 2008).

3. *Public participation in environmental decision making.* In a new study, the National Research Council found that "when done well, public participation improves the quality and legitimacy of a decision and . . . can lead to better results in terms of environmental quality" (Dietz & Stern, 2008). Still, in too many cases barriers prevent meaningful involvement of citizens in decisions affecting their communities or the natural environment. As a result, a number of environmental communication scholars have scrutinized government agencies in the United States and other nations to identify both the opportunities for—and barriers to—the participation of ordinary citizens, environmentalists, and scientists in an agency's decision making (Depoe, Delicath, & Aepli, 2004; Norton, 2007).

Environmental communication scholars' work in this area include the study of citizens' comments on national forest management plans (Walker, 2004), public access to information about sources of pollution in local communities (Beierle & Cayford, 2002), obstacles to meaningful public dialogue with the Department of Energy over the cleanup of nuclear weapons waste (Hamilton, 2008), and ways that public involvement in a hydropower (dam) project in India was compromised by communication practices that denied citizens' access to information and privileged technical discourse (Martin, 2007).

4. *Social marketing and advocacy campaigns.* A rapidly growing area of study is the role of public education and advocacy campaigns by environmental and health groups and, increasingly, climate scientists concerned about global warming. Sometimes called **social marketing,** these campaigns attempt to change public behavior to achieve an environmental or related social goal. These range from campaigns that mobilize the public to protect a wilderness area or raise the fuel efficiency on cars and sport utility vehicles (SUVs), to corporate accountability campaigns to persuade businesses to abide by strict environmental standards (for example, convincing building-supply stores to buy lumber that comes only from sustainable forests).

Scholars have used a range of approaches in the study of public education and advocacy campaigns. For example, many are devoting attention to the role of communication in alerting the public to the risks from global warming as well as barriers to the public's sense of urgency about the problem (Moser & Dilling, 2007). (I look more closely at social marketing and advocacy campaigns in Chapters 6 and 7.)

5. *Environmental collaboration and conflict resolution.* Dissatisfaction with adversarial forms of public participation and methods of settling environmental disputes has led practitioners and scholars alike to explore alternative models of resolving environmental conflicts. The search for alternatives draws inspiration from the success of local communities that have discovered ways to bring disputing parties together. For instance, groups that had been in conflict for years over logging in Canada's coastal Great Bear Rainforest reached agreement recently to protect 5 million forest acres (Krauss, 2006).

At the center of these modes of conflict resolution is the ideal of **collaboration**, a mode of communication that invites stakeholders to engage in problem-solving discussion rather than advocacy and debate. Such collaboration is characterized as "constructive, open, civil communication, generally as dialogue; a focus on the future; an emphasis on learning; and some degree of power sharing and leveling of the playing field" (Walker, 2004, p. 123).

6. *Risk communication.* Does the outbreak of mad cow disease in cattle on one farm pose an unacceptable risk for people who eat beef regularly? Should the EPA regulate the amount of the toxic chemical dioxide in sewage sludge that is used as fertilizer for agricultural crops? Do signs announcing a beach is "CLOSED" and warning that the water is "unsafe" (Figure 1.1) adequately inform the public of the risk of water pollution? These questions arise out of recent cases that illustrate a growing area of research in both public health and environmental communication. The study of risk communication includes two areas:

a. Traditionally, scholars have evaluated the effectiveness of particular communication strategies for conveying technical information about health risks to potentially affected populations, such as the methods that risk communicators use to alert the public after a biological weapons attack that unleashes the plague (Casman & Fischhoff, 2008) or the U.S. Army's plan for disposal of VX nerve gas (Simmons, 2007).

    b. Since the late 1980s, scholars also have begun to look at the impact of cultural understandings of risk on the public's judgment of the acceptability of a risk (Plough & Krimsky, 1987). For example, risk communication scholar Jennifer Hamilton (2003) found that sensitivity to cultural—as opposed to technical—understandings of risk influenced whether the residents living near the polluted Fernald nuclear weapons facility in Ohio accepted or rejected certain methods of cleanup at the site.

    7. *Representations of nature in popular culture and green marketing.* The use of nature images in popular music, television shows, photography, and commercial advertising is hardly new or surprising. What is new is the questioning of how such images of nature shape popular culture or influence our attitudes toward nature—from Hallmark greeting cards, SUV ads, and *The Simpsons* to supermarket tabloids and Loch Ness monsters (Meister & Japp, 2002). Scholars in cultural studies as well as environmental communication also are mapping some of the ways in which such images in popular media sustain attitudes of dominance and exploitation of the natural world rather than reduced consumption or preservation of wild lands.

Studies of popular culture have explored the representations of nature and the environment in Hollywood films particularly. For example, Brereton (2005) traced the evolution of images of nature in science fiction, westerns, nature, and road movies from 1950s to the present, films like *Emerald Forest, Jurassic Park, Easy Rider, Thelma and Louise, Invasion of the Body Snatchers,* and *Blade Runner.* Other scholars such as

Figure 1.1	Risk communication evaluates the effectiveness of different efforts to convey information to citizens about public health and environmental dangers.

© Kimberly White/Getty Images.

Retzinger (2002, 2008) have illustrated the ways in which Hollywood movies use food to depict images of nature and agrarian life, including the future on a post-apocalyptic Earth (in science fiction films). In subsequent chapters, we describe some of the ways in which nature is portrayed in other visual arts such as photography (Chapter 2), news and entertainment (Chapter 5), and corporate marketing (Chapter 10).

Defining Environmental Communication

With such a diverse range of topics, the field can appear at first glance to be confusing. If we define *environmental communication* as simply "talk," or the transmission of information about the wide universe of environmental topics—whether it's global warming or grizzly bear habitat—our definition will be as varied as the topics for discussion.

A clearer definition takes into account the distinctive roles of language, art, photographs, street protests, and even scientific reports as forms of **symbolic action**. The term comes from Kenneth Burke (1966), a 20th-century rhetorical theorist. In his book *Language as Symbolic Action,* Burke stated that even the most unemotional language is necessarily persuasive. This is so because our language and other symbolic acts *do* something as well as say something.

The view of communication as a form of symbolic action might be clearer if we contrast it with an earlier view, the **Shannon–Weaver model of communication**. Shortly after World War II, Claude Shannon and Warren Weaver (1949) proposed a model that defined human communication as simply the transmission of information from a source to a receiver. There was little effort in this model to account for *meaning* or for the ways in which communication acts on, or shapes, our awareness. Unlike the Shannon–Weaver model, symbolic action assumes that language and symbols do more than transmit information: *they actively shape our understanding, create meaning, and orient us to a wider world.* Burke (1966) went so far as to claim that "much that we take as observations about 'reality' may be but the spinning out of possibilities implicit in our particular choice of terms" (p. 46).

If we focus on symbolic action instead of taking a transmission view of human communication, then we can offer a richer definition. In this book, I use **environmental communication** to mean *the pragmatic and constitutive vehicle for our understanding of the environment as well as our relationships to the natural world; it is the symbolic medium that we use in constructing environmental problems and negotiating society's different responses to them.* Defined this way, environmental communication serves two different functions:

1. *Environmental communication is* **pragmatic**. It educates, alerts, persuades, mobilizes, and helps us to solve environmental problems. It is this instrumental sense of communication that probably occurs to us initially: the work of *communication-in-action*. It is a vehicle for problem solving and debate and is often part of public education campaigns. For example, a pragmatic function of environmental communication occurs when car manufacturers buy online ads opposing higher miles-per-gallon fuel standards or when an environmental group rallies support for protecting a wilderness area.

2. *Environmental communication is* **constitutive**. On a subtler level, environmental communication also helps to constitute, or compose, representations of nature and environmental problems themselves as subjects for our understanding. By shaping our perceptions of nature, environmental communication may invite us to perceive forests and rivers as threatening or as bountiful, to regard natural resources as for exploitation or as vital life support systems, as something to conquer or as something to cherish. For example, a campaign to protect wilderness may use instrumental means for planning a press conference, but at the same time, the words in the press statement may tap into cultural constructions of a pristine or unspoiled nature. (In Chapter 2, we look closely at the role of communication in shaping perceptions of a pristine American West in 19th-century art, photographs, and literature.)

Act Locally!

Pragmatic and Constitutive Communication in an Advertisement for "Clean Coal"

The group Americans for Balanced Energy Choices recently ran a multiple-million dollar series of television, print, and online ads promoting "Clean Coal" as an energy source. One of its TV ads, "Clean Coal: America's Power," shows an older couple on their front porch, a young woman driving her convertible, two workers going into a factory, kids waving, and a family at the beach. A (male) voice declares:

> We wish we could say farewell to our dependence on foreign energy. And we'd like to say "adios" to rising energy costs. But first, we have to say "so long" to our outdated perceptions about coal. And we have to continue to advance new clean coal technologies to further reduce emissions, including the eventual capture and storage of CO_2. If we don't, we may have to say "good-bye" to the American way of life we all know and love. Clean coal. America's power.

Watch the ad (www.youtube.com) and read Steven Mufson's (2008) review of this group at http://www.washingtonpost.com. Then answer these questions:

1. What "pragmatic" function does the "Clean Coal" ad serve? Who is its intended audience? What is the ad trying to persuade this audience to think or do?

2. Does this ad draw on "constitutive" functions in its use of certain words or images? For example, what is the connotation of the phrase *dependence on foreign energy*? How do the phrases *outdated perceptions about coal* and *new clean coal technologies* function to actively shape our understanding and create meaning? And how do images of smiling couples, children, and workers affect our response to this ad?

Americans for Balanced Energy Choices (ABEC) is funded by coal companies, railroads, and electric utilities and operates a Website, *America's Power* (www.americaspower.org). For background on ABEC, see Source*Watch*, at http://www.sourcewatch.org/index.php?title=Americans_for_Balanced_Energy_Choices.

Communication as "constitutive" also assists us in defining certain subjects as *problems*. For example, when climate scientists call our attention to "tipping points," they are naming a threshold beyond which warming "could trigger a runaway thaw of Greenland's ice sheet and other abrupt shifts such as a dieback of the Amazon rainforest" (Doyle, 2008). Such communication also associates particular *values* with these problems—health and well-being, caring, economic prosperity, and so forth. Finally, this shaping of our perceptions, in turn, invites *pragmatic* communication as we educate and rally the public to act on these problems and values.

Environmental communication as a pragmatic and constitutive vehicle serves as the framework for the chapters in this book. The book builds on the three core principles mentioned at the beginning of the chapter:

1. Human communication is a form of symbolic action.

2. Our beliefs, attitudes, and behaviors relating to nature and environmental problems are mediated by communication.

3. The public sphere emerges as a discursive space for communication about the environment.

These principles obviously overlap (see Figure 1.2). As I've noted, our communication (as symbolic action) actively shapes our perceptions when we see the natural world through myriad symbols, words, images, or narratives. And when we communicate publicly with others, we share these understandings and invite reactions to our views. For example, in the 1990s, when environmentalists sought to protect millions of acres in the California desert as wildlife sanctuaries and national parks, opponents argued that the desert was a "wasteland" and worthless. Yet, public discussion and debate introduced new information and perspectives

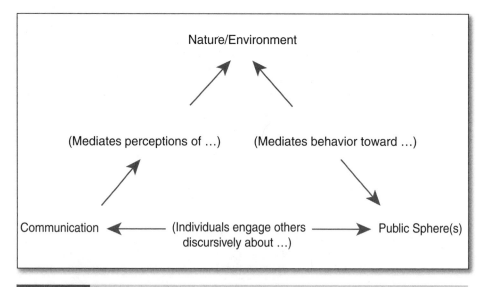

Figure 1.2   Nature, communication, and the public sphere

about this fragile area, its wildlife, and archeological and ecological values. As a result, in 1994 Congress enacted the California Desert Protection Act, setting aside nearly 8 million of the state's 25 million acres of desert, establishing a new Mojave National Preserve, and enlarging areas like Death Valley National Park and Joshua Tree National Park.

As we and others discuss, question, and debate this information and these differing viewpoints, we might reinforce our judgments or perhaps gain new understanding of a problem. In other words, as we engage others, our communication *mediates*, or shapes, our own and others' perceptions, beliefs, and behavior toward the environment.

Nature, Communication, and the Public Sphere

Let's return to the three basic themes that organize the chapters in this book: (1) communication is a form of symbolic action; (2) our beliefs, attitudes, and behaviors relating to nature and environmental problems are mediated by communication; and (3) the public sphere emerges as a discursive space for communication about the environment. I'll introduce and illustrate these themes briefly here and then draw on them in each of the remaining chapters.

Human Communication as Symbolic Action

Earlier, I defined environmental communication as a form of symbolic action. Our language and other symbolic acts *do something*. They create meaning and actively structure our conscious orientation to the world. Films, online sites, photographs, art, popular magazines, and other forms of human symbolic behavior act upon us. They invite us to view the world this way rather than that way; to affirm these values, and not those. Our stories and words warn us, but they also invite us to celebrate.

And language that invites us to celebrate also leads to real-world outcomes. Consider the American gray wolf. In late 2008, a federal judge restored protection to wolves in the Northern Rocky Mountains under the nation's Endangered Species Act (Brown, 2008). But, it was not always this way. Wolves had become almost extinct until the federal government initiated a restoration plan in the mid-1990s (see Figure 1.3).

At the end of 1995, former secretary of the interior Bruce Babbitt delivered a speech celebrating the return of wolves to Yellowstone National Park. Earlier that year, he had carried the first American gray wolf into the transition area in the national park where she would later mate with other wolves also being returned. After setting her down, Babbitt recalled, "I looked . . . into the green eyes of this magnificent creature, within this spectacular landscape, and was profoundly moved by the elevating nature of America's conservation laws: laws with the power to make creation whole" (para. 3).

Babbitt's purpose in speaking that day was to support the beleaguered Endangered Species Act, which was under attack in the Congress at the time. In recalling the biblical story of the Flood and Noah's ark, Babbitt evoked a powerful narrative for valuing

Figure 1.3	The gray wolf has been reintroduced to areas such as Yellowstone National Park.

Photo courtesy of and copyright © Greenpeace/Daniel Beltra.

wolves and other endangered species. In retelling this ancient story to his listeners at Yellowstone, he invited them to embrace a similar ethic in the present day:

> And when the waters receded, and the dove flew off to dry land, God set all the creatures free, commanding them to multiply upon the earth.
>
> Then, in the words of the covenant with Noah, "when the rainbow appears in the clouds, I will see it and remember the everlasting covenant between me and all living things on earth."
>
> Thus we are instructed that this everlasting covenant was made to protect the whole of creation. . . . We are living between the flood and the rainbow: between the threats to creation on the one side and God's covenant to protect life on the other. (Babbitt, 1995, paras. 34–36, 56)

Because communication provides us with a means of sense making about the world, it orients us toward events, experiences, people, wildlife, and choices that we encounter. And because different individuals (and generations) value nature in different ways, we find our voices to be part of a conversation about which meaning of nature is the best or the most useful. Secretary Babbitt invoked an ancient story of survival to invite the American public to appreciate anew the Endangered Species Act. So, too, our own communication mediates or helps us to make sense of the different narratives, ideologies, and appeals that people use to define what they believe is right, feasible, ethical, or just "common sense."

Human communication therefore is symbolic *action* because we draw upon language and other symbols to construct a framework for understanding and valuing and to bring the wider world to others' attention. We explore this aspect of communication more closely in Chapter 2.

Mediating "Nature"

It may seem odd to place "nature" in quotation marks. The natural world definitely exists: Forests are logged or left standing; this morning's air was definitely cold when I walked my dog near our mountain cabin; streams may be polluted or clean; and large glaciers in Antarctica definitely are calving into the ocean. So, what's going on? As one of my students asked me, "What does communication have to do with nature or the study of environmental problems?" My answer to her question takes us into the heart of this book.

Simply put, whatever else "nature" and "the environment" may be, they are also words and therefore *ideas*. And ideas have consequences. For instance, is "wilderness" a place of primeval beauty or a territory that is dark, dangerous, and alien to humans? Early settlers in New England saw North American forests as forbidding and dangerous. Michael Wigglesworth, a Puritan writer, described the region as "a waste and howling wilderness, / Where none inhabited / But hellish fiends, and brutish men / That Devils worshiped" (quoted in Nash, 2001, p. 36). Indeed, writers, scientists, business leaders, citizens, poets, and conservationists have fought for centuries over whether forests should be logged, rivers dammed, air quality regulated, and endangered species protected.

Consider again wolves. Once ranging in every region in North America, by the 19th and early 20th centuries the wolf had become a symbol of "monstrous cruelty and incredible cunning" (Fischer, 1995, pp. 10). Although ancient folklore nurtured fear and hatred of wolves, hostility toward them sharpened as farms, towns, and industries spread into the West. Historian Richard Bartlett (1985) noted that the punitive labels assigned to wolves in this era reached "pathological proportions" (p. 329). In 1914, Congress appropriated funds to eradicate wolves in the West. Fischer writes that within 12 years wolves had essentially disappeared from their historic habitat in wild places like Yellowstone National Park (p. 22).

Not everyone saw wolves in this light. The wildlife ecologist Aldo Leopold (1966/1949) described seeing a wolf die as he was hunting deer in the Southwest in the 1920s. He and his companions had spotted what they took to be a doe fording a turbulent river. When she reached the shore and shook her tail, they realized that she was a wolf. Suddenly, a half-dozen wolf pups sprang from the willows to greet her "in a welcoming mêlée of wagging tails and playful maulings" (p. 138). Leopold describes what happened next.

> In those days we had never heard of passing up a chance to kill a wolf. In a second we were pumping lead into the pack, but with more excitement than accuracy. . . . When our rifles were empty, the old wolf was down, and a pup was dragging a leg into impassable slide-rocks. We reached the old wolf in time to watch a fierce green fire dying in her eyes. I realized then, and have known ever since, that there was something new to me in those eyes—something known only to her and to the mountain. I was young then, and full of trigger itch; I thought that because fewer wolves meant more deer, that no wolves would mean a hunters' paradise. But after seeing the green fire die, I sensed that neither the wolf nor the mountain agreed with such a view. (pp. 138–139)

I suspect that others in your class will have differing views of wolves and wilderness as you discuss these concerns. My point is simply that, although nature inspires different responses in us, nature is ethically and politically silent. Ultimately, it is we who invest its seasons and species with meaning, significance, and value. Similarly, some problems become problems only when someone identifies a threat to important values we hold. Indeed, decisions to preserve habitat for endangered species or impose regulations on factories emitting air pollution seldom result from scientific study alone. Instead, a choice to take action arises from a crucible of debate and (often) public controversy. Even as Aldo Leopold, after seeing "something new" in the old wolf's dying eyes, felt a need to write about its meaning for him, so too are we led into the realm of human communication in our study of nature and environmental problems.

Public Sphere as Discursive Space

A third theme central to this book is the idea of the public sphere or, more accurately, public spheres. Earlier, in the Introduction, we defined the **public sphere** as the realm of influence that is created when individuals engage others in communication—through conversation, argument, debate, or questioning—about subjects of shared concern or topics that affect a wider community. The public comes into being both in our everyday conversations and in our more formal interactions with others when we sustain talk about the environment or other topics. And, as I pointed out, the public sphere is not just words: Visual and nonverbal symbolic actions, such as sit-ins, banners, photography, film, and Earth First! tree sits, also have prompted discussion, debate, and questioning of environmental policy as readily as editorials, speeches, and TV newscasts.

The German social theorist Jürgen Habermas (1974) offered a similar definition when he observed that "a portion of the public sphere comes into being in every conversation in which private individuals assemble to form a public body" (p. 49). As we engage others in conservation, questioning, or debate, we translate our private concerns into public matters and thus create spheres of influence, which affect how we and others view the environment and our relation to it. Such translations of private concerns into public matters occur in a range of forums and practices that give rise to something akin to an environmental public sphere—from a talk at a local ecology club to scientists' testimony before a congressional committee. In public hearings, newspaper editorials, Web alerts, speeches at rallies, street festivals, and countless other occasions in which we engage others in conservation, debate, or other forms of symbolic actions, the public sphere emerges as a potential sphere of influence.

But private concerns are not always translated into public action, and technical information about environmental subjects sometimes remains within scientific journals or specialized conferences. Therefore, it is important to note that at least two other spheres of influence exist parallel to the public sphere. Communication scholar Thomas Goodnight (1982) has called these the *personal* and the *technical* spheres. For example, two strangers arguing at an airport bar is a relatively private affair, whereas the technical findings of biology that influenced Rachael Carson's (1962) discussion of Dichloro-Diphenyl-Trichloroethane (DDT) in *Silent Spring* were originally limited to technical journals. Yet Carson's book presented this scientific information in a context that engaged the attention—and debate—of millions of readers and scores of public officials. In so doing, it gave rise to a sphere of influence that occurs when personal or technical concerns are translated into matters of public interest.

Goodnight cautioned that, in contemporary society, information needed for judgments about the environment and other technical subjects may cause both private and public conversations to defer to scientific or technical authority. The danger in such situations obviously is that *the public sphere can decline.* It can lose its relevance as a sphere of influence that exists in a democracy to mediate among differing viewpoints and interests. Goodnight himself feared that "the public sphere is being steadily eroded by the elevation of the personal and technical groundings of argument" (p. 223). In Chapter 9, I examine the tension that exists between one technical sphere—environmental science—and arguments in the public sphere over government regulation of industry.

Because the idea of the public sphere is easily misunderstood, I address briefly three common misconceptions about it here. These are the beliefs that the public sphere is (1) only an official site or forum for government decision making, (2) a monolithic or ideal collection of all citizens, and (3) a form of "rational" or technical communication. Each of these ideas is a misunderstanding of the public sphere.

First, the public sphere is not only, or even primarily, an official space. Although there are forums and state-sponsored spaces, such as public hearings that invite citizens to communicate about the environment, these official sites do not exhaust the public sphere. In fact, discussion and debate about environmental concerns more often occur outside government meeting rooms and courts. The early fifth-century Greeks (BCE) called these meeting spaces of everyday life **agoras**, the public squares or marketplaces where citizens gathered during the day to sell farm products, tools, clothes, and other items and also to exchange ideas about the life of their community. At the dawn of one of the first experiments in democracy, Greek citizens believed they needed certain essential skills to voice their concerns publicly and influence the judgment of others, skills they called the art of rhetoric. (I return to this background in Chapter 2.)

Second, the public sphere is neither monolithic nor a uniform assemblage of all citizens in the abstract. As the realm of influence that is created when individuals engage others discursively, a public sphere assumes more concrete forms: calls to a local talk radio show, letters to the editor, blogs, news conferences, or local meetings where residents question public health officials about possible risks to their health from contaminated well water. As Habermas (1974) noted, some form of the public sphere comes into existence whenever individuals question, converse, debate, collaborate, mourn, or celebrate with others about subjects of shared concern. Indeed, some have argued that environmental groups now have the ability to create an "alternative public realm" for environmental communication through their own publications and other ways of reaching supporters and journalists (Downing, 1988). In doing so, they articulate for themselves a space within society in which "their own discourse can be privileged and their own knowledge pursued" (p. 45).

Third, the definition of the public sphere as a space for popular or democratic communication is meant to counter the idea that communication in the public sphere is a kind of elite conversation or specialized or "rational" form of communication. Such a view of the public sphere unfairly and inaccurately ignores the diverse voices and communication styles that characterize a robust, participatory democracy. In fact, in this book I introduce the voices of ordinary citizens and the special challenges they face in gaining a hearing about matters of environmental and personal survival in their communities.

☞ **FYI** **Is Environmental Communication a "Crisis Discipline"?**

When launching the field's academic journal *Environmental Communication: A Journal of Nature and Culture* in 2007, scholars debated whether the new field was a **crisis discipline**. The term comes from other disciplines like conservation biology and cancer biology that are "defined by crisis, and driven by urgency" (Cox, 2007, p. 10), where researchers believe they have an ethical duty to bring their research to bear on important environmental and societal problems.

In an essay in the new journal, Cox (2007) argued that environmental communication is similar to these crisis disciplines. Like the disturbances in biological systems, "distortions, ineptitudes, and system pathologies occur in our communication about the environment" (p. 10). Since these failures can inhibit society's ability to respond to environmental dangers, Cox believes the field of environmental communication has an ethical premise:

> Environmental communication seeks to enhance the ability of society to respond appropriately to environmental signals relevant to the well-being of both human civilization and natural biological systems. [And that] scholars, teachers, and practitioners have a duty to educate, question, critically evaluate, or otherwise speak in appropriate forums when . . . communication practices are constrained or suborned for harmful or unsustainable policies toward human communities and the natural world. (pp. 15, 16)

While some scholars agree environmental communication is a "crisis discipline," other do not. Senecah (2007), for example, fears this definition narrows the field and moves it too closely to the environmental movement itself; such a definition "limits our communication practices and research to an *adversarial* dynamic" (p. 27). What is your view of the field of environmental communication?

Diverse Voices and Interests in a "Green" Public Sphere

The landscape of environmental politics and public affairs can be as diverse, serious, controversial, colorful, and complex as an Amazonian rain forest or the Galapagos Islands' ecology. The callers on talk radio who berate Earth Liberation Front activists for setting SUVs afire differ dramatically from the residents who complain of contaminated well water at a meeting in their community center. These groups, in turn, seem a world apart from scientists at the National Press Club who warned of a dangerous collapse of ocean marine life. Whether at press conferences, in community centers, on Internet list-servs, or outside the fenced barriers of a World Bank meeting, individuals and groups speaking about the environment appear today in diverse sites and public spaces.

In this final section of the chapter, I introduce seven of the major points of view, or voices, of environmental communication in the public sphere. I use Myerson and Rydin's (1991) concept of **voices** here to stress the "types" of concerns (for example, the "anxious citizen voice," "expert voice") that place certain "voices in relation to other voices" (pp. 5, 6). These include the voices of:

1. Citizens and community groups

2. Environmental groups

3. Scientists and scientific discourse

4. Corporations and business lobbyists

5. Anti-environmentalist groups

6. Media and environmental journalism

7. Public officials and regulators

Citizens and Community Groups

Local residents who question or complain to town officials and who organize their neighbors to take action are one of the most common and effective sources of environmental change. Some citizens are motivated by urban sprawl or development projects that destroy their homes as well as their "green spaces," the natural areas in cities and towns. Others who may live near an oil refinery or chemical plant may be motivated by noxious fumes or pollution to organize resistance to the industry's lax air quality permit.

In 1978, Lois Gibbs, resident of the working-class community of Love Canal in Niagara Falls, New York, and mother of two small children, grew concerned when her five-year-old son, Michael, complained of rashes and headaches after playing in the nearby elementary school yard. Gibbs had just read a newspaper report that Hooker Chemical Company, a subsidiary of Occidental Petroleum, had buried dangerous chemicals on land it later sold to the local school board. The report raised suspicions on the part of Gibbs and her neighbors, many of whom had noticed odors and oily substances surfacing in their yards and on the school's playground (Center for Health, Environment, and Justice, 2003).

Despite an initial denial of the problem by state officials, Lois Gibbs and her neighbors persisted. They organized media coverage, carried symbolic coffins to the state capital, marched on Mother's Day, and pressed health officials to take their concerns seriously. Then, on August 2, 1978, New York's Department of Health issued an order recommending that the school be closed and cautioning that pregnant women and children under the age of two needed to be evacuated from the area closest to the school (Center for Health, Environment, and Justice, 2003). In 1982, the citizens succeeded in persuading the federal government to relocate the residents of Love Canal who wanted to leave. Finally, the U.S. Justice Department prosecuted Hooker Chemical Company and imposed large fines on it (Shabecoff, 1993, pp. 234–235). Love Canal ultimately became a symbol, in the nation's consciousness, of abandoned toxic sites and fueled a citizens' anti-toxics movement in the United States.

Lois Gibbs's story is not unique. In rural towns in Louisiana, in inner-city neighborhoods in Los Angeles, on Native American reservations in New Mexico, and in communities throughout the country, citizens and community groups have launched campaigns to clean up polluting plants, protect green space, and halt mining operations on sacred tribal lands. As we learn in later chapters, local activists and residents face the challenges of finding a voice and securing the communication resources to express their concerns and to persuade others to join with them to demand accountability of public officials. Chapter 3 describes some legal guarantees of the public's right to know about polluting companies as well as opportunities to participate in federal and state decision making about environmental matters. On the other hand, in other chapters we examine communities that often are targeted as "sacrifice zones" for hazardous facilities and whose residents face subtle and not-so-subtle barriers to being heard. For example, in Chapter 8, we look more closely at the movement for environmental justice in many communities of color, in workplaces, and on Native American reservations.

Environmental Groups

U.S. environmental groups are a frequently encountered source of communication about the environment, as is the growing number of international conservation organizations. This diverse movement comprises a wide array of groups and networks, both online and on-the-ground. And each has its own focus and mode of communication. They range from thousands of grassroots and community groups to regional and national environmental organizations such as the Natural Resources Defense Council, the Sierra Club, the Audubon Society, and the National Wildlife Federation; and international groups such as Friends of the Earth, Conservation International, Greenpeace, World Wide Fund for Nature, and grassroots groups across the planet fighting toxics in their communities (Naquib, 2007). Online networks have proliferated by the tens of thousands, included global networks like 350.org, linking other groups in the fight against global warming.

These groups address a diversity of issues and often differ significantly in their modes of advocacy. For example, the Wilderness Society and the Sierra Club focus on the protection of public lands through public advocacy campaigns and lobbying of the U.S. Congress. On the other hand, the Nature Conservancy and hundreds of local land conservancy groups protect rare and endangered habitat on private lands by purchasing the properties. Still other groups, such as Greenpeace (see Figure 1.4) and Rainforest

Figure 1.4	Activists of the Alaska Wilderness League dressed as polar bears (background) look on as a Greenpeace activist (L) holds a sign reading "Global warming = Extinction" as U.S. Interior Secretary Dirk Kempthorne announces the listing of the polar bear as a threatened species under the Endangered Species Act at the Interior Department in Washington, DC, on May 14, 2008. According to the Interior Department, the loss of sea ice puts polar bears at risk of being endangered in the foreseeable future.

Action Network, have turned to image events (DeLuca, 1999) to shine the spotlight of media attention on concerns as diverse as global warming, illegal whaling, and the destruction of tropical rain forests. (For information on U.S. and international environmental groups, see Brulle, 2000, 2005; Doherty and Doyle, 2008; Karan and Suganuma, 2008; Kline, 2007; Shabecoff, 2003; Sonneborn, 2007; Taylor, 1995.)

Some regional and national groups actually are networks of hundreds of local organizations. For example, in the United States, the Center for Health, Environment, and Justice (started by Lois Gibbs) shares information with local groups that are struggling with hazardous facilities in their communities. Other regional networks, such as the Southern Utah Wilderness Alliance, the National Forest Protection Alliance, and Appalachian Voices (and its online action center, www.ilovemountains.org), help hundreds of wilderness protection groups and communities fighting harmful coal mining plan campaign strategy, from media events to legal challenges to national forest management plans. For example, the Clean Water Network coordinates the work of more than 1,000 local groups on water issues—such as soil erosion from logging that harms trout streams, and mountaintop removal, in which coal companies in West Virginia, Kentucky, and Tennessee blast the tops of mountains to expose coal seams, pushing the excess earth over the sides and clogging the streams in valleys below.

Act Locally!

Identify a representative from a local environmental group to interview for your class. Such a person can be helpful in describing some of the differences among the thousands of local and national groups that are concerned about the environment.

Ask this person to speak about these things:

- The nature of the organization: Is it local, regional, or an affiliate of a national environmental group? What is its mission? Is it member based?

- The forms of communication used by this group to pursue its mission: Public education? Political advocacy? Lobbying? Door-to-door canvassing? Newspaper, radio, or television ads? The effectiveness of this group's environmental communication: What is an example of its effectiveness? What does its representative see as the biggest barrier to success?

Scientists and Scientific Discourse

The widening hole in the Earth's ozone layer over Antarctica first was publicized in 1985 when scientists discovered that the chlorofluorocarbons (CFCs) used in air conditioning, aerosols, refrigerators, and other products were breaking down the protective ozone shield. The ozone layer filters harmful ultraviolet rays that damage crops and forests, cause skin cancer and other human diseases, and can damage the corneas of mammals, including humans. In 1987, the United States and 23 other nations signed the **Montreal Protocol**, an international treaty requiring signatory nations to phase out the production of CFCs.

As in the case of the ozone layer, scientific reports have led to important investigations of—and debate about—problems affecting human health and Earth's biodiversity. From asthma in children caused by air pollution to global warming and the spreading desertification in sub-Saharan Africa, scientific research and the alerts of scientists have contributed substantially to public awareness and to debate about environmental policy.

However, the link between scientific research and public policy is not always direct. Scientific findings in such areas as climate change, genetically modified organisms, HIV/AIDS research, or the use of stem cells in research, to name a few, often are not immediately accepted because they challenge long-held beliefs or ideologies. As we see in Chapter 9, the results of environmental science are sometimes disputed or ignored, its findings distorted by radio talk-show hosts, ideological "think tanks," and environmental skeptics. For example, the respected journal *Science* has described the campaign by political partisans to discredit the work of atmospheric scientists on ozone depletion in the 1990s (Taubes, 1993). And, more recently, Jacques, Dunlap, and Freeman (2008) discovered that 92 percent of the English-language books critical of environmental science published between 1972 and 2005 could be traced to conservative think tanks that espoused an anti-environmental skepticism.

Corporations and Business Lobbyists

Environmental historian Samuel Hays (2000) reports that, as the new environmental sciences began to document the environmental and health risks from industrial products, the affected businesses challenged the science "at every step, questioning both the methods and research designs that were used and the conclusions that were drawn" (p. 222). As part of this opposition, industries organized trade associations to defend their practices and to lobby against environmental regulations.

Organized, corporate opposition to environmental measures appears to be based on two factors: (1) resentment of restrictions on traditional uses of land (for example, mining or logging) and (2) threats to the economic interests of newer industries such as petrochemicals, energy, computers, transportation, automobile manufacturing, and electronics. Worried by the threat of tighter limits on air and water discharges from factories and refineries, many corporations have formed trade associations such as the Business Round Table and the Chemical Manufacturers Association to lobby the U.S. Congress on behalf of their industries (Hays, 2000). For example, the American Coalition for Clean Coal Electricity, a coal industry group, has been active online (www.americaspower.org) and on TV, airing extensive ads promoting coal as a "clean energy" source. Many businesses recently have begun to "green" or environmentally improve their operations, while others have opposed higher standards for fuel efficiency in cars and trucks as well as President Obama's initiatives on energy and global warming. We explore the role of "green marketing" as well as business opposition to certain forms of environmental protection in Chapter 10.

Anti-Environmentalist Groups

Although it may be difficult to conceive of groups that are opposed to protection of the environment per se (clean air, healthy forests, safe drinking water, and so on), a backlash against government regulations and even environmental science has arisen periodically in U.S. politics. This is often fueled by the perception that environmentalism harms economic growth and jobs. Additionally, Jennifer Switzer (1997), in her study of "green backlash," has identified an ideological challenge from individuals who feel marginalized or overlooked by environmental regulations. This is felt particularly by some who lived near public lands such as national parks and wilderness areas and who believed themselves limited in their use of these lands.

One early expression of this resentment was the **Sagebrush Rebellion** of the late 1970s and 1980s, an effort by traditional land users to take control of federal land and natural resources in the West. Environmental journalist Philip Shabecoff (2003) reported that "the [cattle] stockmen, miners, and other range users, long accustomed to treating the public lands as a private fiefdom, reacted angrily to what they perceived as a threat to their rights and their livelihood" (p. 155). In response, these sagebrush rebels

> evoked states' rights, the free market, and rugged cowboy individualism to assert their right to use the land for grazing, to mine coal and other materials, and to drill for oil. . . . They attacked, sometimes physically, and vilified federal land managers and sought to discredit conservationists as un-American left-wingers. (p. 155)

By the 1990s, offshoots of the Sagebrush Rebellion called themselves **Wise Use groups**, or property rights groups. These groups organize those who resent restrictions on the use of their property for such purposes as protection of wetlands or habitat for endangered species. They include groups like Ron Arnold's Center for the Defense of Free Enterprise (opposed to environmental regulations generally). Arnold, a controversial figure in the anti-environmentalist movement, once told a reporter, "Our goal is to destroy environmentalism once and for all" (Rawe & Field, 1992, in Helvarg, 2004, p. 7).

More recently, global warming "skeptics" have arisen to oppose the science and many of the policies being proposed to reduce greenhouse gases or enable communities to adapt to climate change. Using online sites, conferences, conservative think tanks (Jacques, Dunlap, & Freeman, 2008), and films like *The Great Global Warming Swindle,* such skeptics have fueled debate and sometimes stalled government action on climate change in the United States. The Union of Concerned Scientists (www.ucsusa.org) maintains a profile of many of these organizations, and we examine some of these groups and their campaigns in Chapter 9.

Media and Environmental Journalism

It would be difficult to overstate the impact of television, radio, print, and Internet news on environmental politics. News media act not only as voices in their coverage of issues and events but as conduits for other voices that seek to influence public attitudes. These voices range from scientists and corporations to radical environmentalists. The news media also are a constitutive force through their **agenda-setting** role. The term *agenda setting* refers to the effect of media on the public's perception of the salience or importance of issues. As early as 1963, journalism scholar Bernard Cohen (1963) explained that the news media filter or select issues for readers' or viewers' attention and set the public's agenda, telling people not what to think but what to think *about*. For example, the public's concern over the deaths of sea otters, shore birds, and salmon soared after extensive television coverage of the 11 million gallons of crude oil that spilled from the *Exxon Valdez* supertanker in Alaska's Prince William Sound in 1989.

Although the *Exxon Valdez* story focused on a single, dramatic event that fulfilled criteria for newsworthiness, most environmental topics, even quite serious ones, are less dramatic. As a result, media often have discretion in choosing *what* events or information to cover and also *how* to frame or package a news story. Indeed, the many voices and viewpoints in the media illustrate a wide range of approaches to environmental concerns, from conservative Websites like that of the Cooler Heads Coalition, a group that claims to dispel myths of global warming (www.globalwarming.org), to a scientific news story in the *New York Times* about the effects of shifting crops that could be used for food to use as a fuel substitute: "U.N. Says Biofuel Subsidies Raise Food Bill and Hunger" (Rosenthal, 2008, p. A13). In Chapter 5, we examine such issues as agenda setting, media frames, and the media's criteria for newsworthiness of environmental news stories.

Public Officials and Regulators

At the heart of debates over the environment are public officials at every level of government—those elected or appointed persons whose role is to shape or enforce local ordinances, enact state and national laws, develop and carry out regulations, and negotiate international agreements such as the Montreal Protocol (described earlier). Such individuals are at the heart of the political and legislative process because it is they who must reconcile the arguments and interests of the diverse "voices" speaking for, or against, specific measures. For legislators, particularly, this is "characteristically, a balancing act," since they must "reconcile a variety of contending forces [who are] affected in various ways" by a proposed law (Miller, 2009, p. 41). As we see throughout this book, public officials are, therefore, the *audience* for a range of environmental communication practices—for example, citizens testifying before state regulators about permits for a coal-fired power plant or industry campaigns to mobilize public opinion in hopes of persuading members of the Congress to preserve tax breaks for oil companies or extend tax credits for wind and solar energy.

Less visible to the public, but arguably as important as legislators, are environmental **regulators**. These are agency appointees and professional staff whose role is to ensure that laws are actually implemented and enforced. As political scientist Norman Miller (2009) explains, the federal Clean Air Act's goal of reducing harmful "pollutants" in the air is uncontroversial, but also unclear. After all, how clean is "clean"? The standards for each pollutant or the technologies industry must use to control their emissions "are all largely beyond the expertise of those who make the laws" (p. 37). Public officials, therefore, "must turn to engineers, scientists, land use planners, lawyers, economists, and other specialists . . . to set protocols, standards, methodologies, equipment specifications," and so on to ensure that a law can be carried out (p. 38). These are regulators.

While determining rules or standards (regulations) is a highly technical process, it is not a completely neutral or nonpolitical one. The language adopted for these rules often has powerful implications for industry, local communities, or public health. For example, the Office of Surface Mining recently proposed to change the language of the "stream buffer rule," which, if strictly enforced, would prohibit virtually all coal mining within 100 feet of a stream. Yet, for decades, mining companies have ignored this rule and covered over hundreds of miles of streams in the mountains of West Virginia and Tennessee in a practice called "mountaintop removal." This is the process whereby coal is mined by blasting off the tops of mountains to get at the coal seams beneath them. The excess soil and rocks are pushed over the sides of the mountains, filling valleys and streams below. The rule change would delete the strict language, requiring only that mining companies minimize the debris and cause the least environmental harm (Broder, 2007). If adopted, community activists believe, the rule change would allow hundreds of miles of mountain streams to be destroyed, along with the mountains of their region. We return to conflicts over public policy and environmental regulations in many chapters.

SUMMARY

This chapter introduced the emerging field of environmental communication by illustrating the diversity of areas that scholars study, from advocacy campaigns and public participation to environmental conflict resolution and the images of nature in popular culture. The study of environmental communication inquires into the dynamics of human communication—speech, art, symbols, street performances, media, and campaigns—that shape our understandings of nature and environmental problems. It also studies the occasions on which ordinary citizens, environmental groups, journalists, scientists, corporations, and others seek to influence decisions affecting the environment.

Although there is a considerable range of areas in the study of environmental communication, two basic functions underlie much of our talk about nature and environmental problems: (1) a pragmatic function, in which we educate, alert, mobilize, and persuade others, and (2) a constitutive function, in which language and other symbols themselves help to shape our perceptions about reality and the nature of environmental problems. These two functions are included in the basic definition of *environmental communication* as the pragmatic and constitutive vehicle for our understanding of the environment as well as our relationships to the natural world; it is the symbolic medium that we use in constructing environmental problems and in negotiating society's different responses to them.

Drawing on this definition of environmental communication, this book is organized around three basic themes: (1) human communication is a form of symbolic action, (2) our beliefs, attitudes, and behaviors relating to nature and environmental problems are mediated or influenced by communication, and (3) the public sphere emerges as a discursive space for communication about the environment. It is within these wider conversations and forums that citizens, environmental groups, media, scientists, and corporate lobbyists seek to influence others about environmental issues.

Now that you have learned what environmental communication is and how widely it is practiced, I hope you'll feel inspired to join (or to renew your commitment to) the public conversations already in progress about the environment. Also, I hope that you'll discover your own voice and develop personal efficacy in speaking on behalf of the natural world and your own communities.

KEY TERMS

Communication-Related Concepts

Agenda setting: The ability of media to affect the public's perception of the salience or importance of issues; in other words, news reporting may not succeed in telling people what to think, but it succeeds in telling them what to think *about.*

Agora: In ancient Greece, the public square or marketplace where citizens gathered during the day to sell produce and other products and to exchange ideas about their community.

Collaboration: A mode of communication that invites stakeholders to engage in problem-solving discussion rather than advocacy and debate.

Constitutive: A characteristic of environmental communication whereby representations of nature and environmental problems are composed as subjects for our understanding.

Environmental communication: The pragmatic and constitutive vehicle for our understanding of the environment as well as our relationships to the natural world; the symbolic medium that we use in constructing environmental problems and in negotiating society's different responses to them.

Framing: A way that **news** stories guide readers' or viewers' sense making and evoke certain perceptions and values rather than others. For a more detailed description, see Chapter 5, "Media and the Environment Online."

Pragmatic: Instrumental; a characteristic of environmental communication whereby it educates, alerts, persuades, mobilizes, and helps us to solve environmental problems.

Public participation: The involvement of the public in decisions by government agencies affecting the environment. For a more detailed description, see Chapter 3, "Public Participation in Environmental Decisions."

Public sphere: A realm of influence that is created when individuals engage others in communication—through conversation, argument, debate, or questioning—about subjects of shared concern or topics that affect a wider community.

Rhetorical focus: (a) The study of the sources and modes of persuasion that individuals and groups use to communicate about the environment. (b) The study of critical rhetorics, or communication that questions or challenges the discursive framing of the nature–society relationship itself.

Shannon–Weaver model of communication: A linear model that defined human communication as the transmission of information from a source to a receiver.

Social marketing: A communication campaign, often using commercial marketing tools, aimed at changing public behaviors to achieve an environmental or other goal.

Symbolic action: The property of language and other acts to *do something* as well as literally to say something; to create meaning and orient us consciously to the world.

Voices: Myerson and Rydin's (1991) concept about the "types" of concerns (for example, the "anxious citizen voice," "expert voice") that place certain "voices in relation to other voices" (pp. 5, 6).

Environment-Related Concepts

Crisis discipline: The term comes from disciplines like conservation biology and cancer biology that are "defined by crisis, and driven by urgency" (Cox, 2007, p. 10), where researchers believe they have an ethical duty to bring their research to bear on important environmental and societal problems.

Just sustainability: The effort to fuse concerns for environmental sustainability and issues of race, class, gender, and social justice to ensure a "just" and sustainable future for all.

Montreal Protocol: An international treaty requiring the United States and 23 other signatory nations to phase out the production of chlorofluorocarbons (CFCs).

Regulators: These are agency appointees and professional staff whose role is to ensure that laws are implemented and enforced by establishing the standards, methodologies, equipment specifications, and so on to ensure that a law can be carried out.

Sagebrush Rebellion: An effort in the late 1970s and 1980s by traditional land users to take control of federal land and natural resources in the West.

Toxic tours: Visits conducted by members of poor and minority communities, who invite news reporters to witness their struggles against chemical pollution in their region. See Chapter 7, "Environmental Justice Advocacy Campaigns."

Wise Use groups: Groups that organize individuals who oppose restrictions on the use of their own (private) property for purposes such as protection of wetlands or habitat for endangered species. Also called *property rights groups.*

DISCUSSION QUESTIONS

1. Is nature ethically and politically silent? What does this mean? If nature is politically silent, does this mean it has no value apart from human meaning?

2. The rhetorical theorist Kenneth Burke wrote, "Much that we take as observations about 'reality' may be but the spinning out of possibilities implicit in our particular choice of terms." What does he mean by this claim? Do you agree with him?

3. Are wolves intrinsically cruel? After looking into the eyes of a dying wolf, Aldo Leopold wrote, "There was something new to me in those eyes—something known only to her and to the mountain." What did he mean?

4. Is environmental communication a "crisis discipline"? What does this mean? Do scholars, teacher, and practitioners have an ethical duty to alert society to failures of communication that affect the environment?

5. In our society, whose voices are heard most often about environmental issues? Do you believe that ordinary citizens like yourself are likely to be heard by government officials or policymakers when they make decisions about environmental topics?

REFERENCES

Agyeman, J. (2007). Communicating "just sustainability." *Environmental Communication: A Journal of Nature and Culture, 1,* 119–122.

Anderson, A. (1997). *Media, culture, and the environment.* New Brunswick, NJ: Rutgers University Press.

Babbitt, B. (1995, December 13). Between the flood and the rainbow. Speech. Retrieved April 20, 2001, from www.fs.fed.us/eco/eco-watch.

Bartlett, R. A. (1985). *Yellowstone: A wilderness besieged.* Tucson: University of Arizona Press.

Beierle, T. C., & Cayford, J. (2002). *Democracy in practice: Public participation in environmental decisions.* Washington, DC: Resources for the Future.

Brereton, P. (2005). *Hollywood utopia: Ecology in contemporary American cinema.* Bristol, UK: Intellect Books.

Broder, J. M. (2007, August 23). Rule to expand mountaintop coal mining. *The New York Times.* Retrieved October 9, 2008, from http://www.nytimes.com/.

Brown, M. (2008, October 5). Molloy restores ESA protection for wolves. *The Missoulian.* Retrieved October 5, 2008, from http://www.missoulian.com.

Brown, W. R., & Crable, R. E. (1973). Industry, mass magazines, and the ecology issue. *Quarterly Journal of Speech, 59,* 259–272.

Brulle, R. J. (2000). *Agency, democracy, and nature: The U.S. environmental movement from a critical theory perspective.* Cambridge, MA: MIT Press.

Brulle, R. J. (2005). *Power, justice, and the environment: A critical appraisal of the environmental justice movement.* Cambridge, MA: MIT Press.

Burke, K. (1966). *Language as symbolic action.* Berkeley: University of California Press.

Carson, R. (1962). *Silent spring.* Boston: Houghton Mifflin.

Casman, E. A., & Fischhoff, B. (2008). Risk communication planning for the aftermath of a plague bioattack. *Risk Analysis: An International Journal, 28,* 1327–1342.

Center for Health, Environment, and Justice. (2003). *Love Canal: The journey continues.* Retrieved October 5, 2008, from http://www.chej.org/30thA_Love_Canal.htm.

Cohen, B. C. (1963). *The press and foreign policy.* Princeton: Princeton University Press.

Cooper, M. M. (1996). Environmental rhetoric in an age of hegemony: Earth First! and the Nature Conservancy. In C. G. Herndl & S. C. Brown (Eds.), *Green culture: Environmental rhetoric in contemporary America* (pp. 236–260). Madison: University of Wisconsin Press.

Cox, J. R. (1982). The die is cast: Topical and ontological dimensions of the *locus* of the irreparable. *Quarterly Journal of Speech, 6,* 227–239.

Cox, R. (2007). Nature's "crisis disciplines": Does environmental communication have an ethical duty? *Environmental Communication: A Journal of Nature and Culture, 1,* 5–20.

DeLuca, K. M. (1999). *Image politics: The new rhetoric of environmental activism.* New York: Guilford.

Depoe, S. (1997). Environmental studies in mass communication. *Critical Studies in Mass Communication, 14,* 368–372.

Depoe, S. P., Delicath, J. W., & Aepli, M. F. (Eds.). (2004). *Communication and public participation in environmental decision making.* Albany: State University of New York Press.

Dietz, T., & Stern, P. C. (2008). *Public participation in environmental assessment and decision making.* National Research Council. Washington, DC: National Academies Press.

Doherty, B., & Doyle, T. (Eds.). (2008). *Beyond borders: Environmental movements and transnational politics.* London: Taylor & Francis.

Doyle, A. (2008, February 4). "Tipping point" on horizon for Greenland ice. Reuters. Retrieved October 4, 2008, from http://www.reuters.com.

Downing, J. (1988). The alternative public realm: The organization of the 1980s anti-nuclear press in West Germany and Britain. *Media, Culture, and Society, 28,* 38–50.

Eilperin, J. (2008, August 26). Carbon is building up in atmosphere faster than predicted. *The Washington Post,* p. A2.

Farrell, T. B., & Goodnight, G. T. (1981). Accidental rhetoric: The root metaphors of Three Mile Island. *Quarterly Journal of Speech, 48,* 271–300.

Fischer, H. (1995). *Wolf wars.* Helena, MT: Falcon Press.

Friedman, T. L. (2008). *Hot, flat, and crowded: Why we need a green revolution—and how it can renew America.* New York: Farrar, Straus, & Giroux.

Goodnight, T. G. (1982). The personal, technical, and public spheres of argument: A speculative inquiry into the art of public deliberation. *Journal of the American Forensic Association, 18,* 214–227.

Greenberg, M. R., Sandman, P. M., Sachsman, D. B., & Salamone, K. L. (1989). Network television news coverage of environmental risk. *Risk Analysis, 9,* 119–126.

Grunig, L. (Ed.). (1989). *Environmental activism revisited: The changing nature of communication through organizational public relations, special interest groups, and the mass media.* Troy, OH: North American Association for Environmental Education.

Habermas, J. (1974). The public sphere: An encyclopedia article (1964). *New German Critique, 1*(3), 49–55.

Hamilton, J. D. (2003). Exploring technical and cultural appeals in strategic risk communication: The Fernald radium case. *Risk Analysis, 23,* 291–302.

Hamilton, J. D. (2008). Convergence and divergence in the public dialogue on nuclear weapons cleanup. In B. Taylor, W. Kinsella, S. Depoe, & M. Metzler (Eds.), *Nuclear legacies: Communication, controversy, and the U.S. nuclear weapons complex* (pp. 41–72). Lanham, MD: Lexington Books.

Hays, S. P. (2000). *A history of environmental politics since 1945.* Pittsburgh: University of Pittsburgh Press.

Helvarg, D. (2004). *The war against the greens: The "wise-use" movement, the new right, and the browning of America.* Boulder, CO: Johnson Books.

Jacques, P. J., Dunlap, R. E., & Freeman, M. (2008). The organization of denial: Conservative think tanks and environmental skepticism, *Environmental Politics, 17,* 349–385.

Karan, P. P. & Suganuma, U. (2008). *Local environmental movements: A comparative study of the United States and Japan.* Frankfurt: University Press of Kentucky.

Kline, B. (2007). *First along the river:* A brief history of the U.S. environmental movement. Lanham, MD: Rowman & Littlefield.

Krauss, C. (2006, February 7). Canada to shield 5 million forest acres. *The New York Times.* Retrieved October 8, 2008, from http://www.nytimes.com.

Lange, J. (1990). Refusal to compromise: The case of Earth First! *Western Journal of Speech Communication, 54,* 473–494.

Lange, J. I. (1993). The logic of competing information campaigns: Conflict over old growth and the spotted owl. *Communication Monographs, 60,* 239–257.

Leopold, A. (1966). *A Sand County almanac.* New York: Ballantine Books. (Original work published 1949 by Oxford University Press.)

Luke, T. W. (1987). Chernobyl: The packaging of transnational ecological disaster. *Critical Studies in Mass Communication, 4,* 351–375.

Marafiote, T. (2008). The American dream: Technology, tourism, and the transformation of wilderness. *Environmental Communication: A Journal of Nature and Culture, 2,* 154–172.

Martin, T. (2007). Muting the voice of the local in the age of the global: How communication practices compromised public participation in India's Allain Dunhangan environmental impact assessment. *Environmental Communication: A Journal of Nature and Culture, 1,* 171–193.

Meister M., & Japp, P. M. (Eds.). (2002). *Enviropop: Studies in environmental rhetoric and popular culture.* Westport, CT: Praeger.

Miller, N. (2009). *Environmental politics: Stakeholders, interests, and policymaking* (2nd ed.). New York: Routledge.

Moore, M. P. (1993). Constructing irreconcilable conflict: The function of synecdoche in the spotted owl controversy. *Communication Monographs, 60,* 258–274.

Moser, S. C., & Dilling, L. (2007). *Creating a climate for change: Communicating climate change and facilitating social change.* Cambridge, UK: Cambridge University Press.

Mufson, S. (2008, January 18). Coal industry plugs into the campaign. *The Washington Post,* p. D1. Retrieved October 4, 2008, from www.washingtonpost.com.

Myerson, G., & Rydin, Y. (1991). *The language of environment: A new rhetoric.* London: University College London Press.

Naquib, D. (2007). *Resisting global toxics: Transnational movements for environmental justice.* Cumberland, MD: Triliteral.

Nash, R. (2001). *Wilderness and the American mind* (4th ed.). New Haven: Yale University Press.

Norton, T. (2007). The structuration of public participation: Organizing environmental control. *Environmental Communication: A Journal of Nature and Culture, 1,* 146–170.

Oravec, C. (1981). John Muir, Yosemite, and the sublime response: A study of the rhetoric of preservationism. *Quarterly Journal of Speech, 67,* 245–258.

Oravec, C. (1984). Conservationism vs. preservationism: The "public interest" in the Hetch Hetchy controversy. *Quarterly Journal of Speech, 70,* 339–361.

Peterson, T. R. (1986). The will to conservation: A Burkeian analysis of dust bowl rhetoric and American farming motives. *Southern Speech Communication Journal, 52,* 1–21.

Pezzullo, P. C. (2007). *Toxic tourism: Rhetorics of pollution, travel, and environmental justice.* Tuscaloosa: University of Alabama Press.

Plough, A., & Krimsky, S. (1987). The emergence of risk communication studies: Social and political context. *Science, Technology, & Human Values, 12,* 4–10.

Rawe, A. L., & Field, R. (1992, Fall). Interview with a "wise guy." *Common Ground of Puget Sound, 1.*

Retzinger, J. P. (2002). Cultivating the agrarian myth in Hollywood films. In M. Meister & P. M. Japp (Eds.), *Enviropop: Studies in environmental rhetoric and popular culture* (pp. 45–62). Westport, CT: Praeger.

Retzinger, J. P. (2008). Speculative visions and imaginary meals. *Cultural Studies, 22,* 369–390.

Rogers, R. A. (1998). Overcoming the objectification of nature in constitutive theories: Toward a transhuman, materialist theory of communication. *Western Journal of Communication, 62,* 244–272.

Rosenthal, E. (2008, October 8). U.S. says biofuel subsidies raise food bill and hunger. *The New York Times,* p. A13.

Russill, C. (2008). Tipping point forewarnings in climate change communication: Some implications of an emerging trend." *Environmental Communication: A Journal of Nature and Culture, 2,* 133–153.

Senecah, S. L. (2007). Impetus, mission, and future of the environmental communication/ division: Are we still on track? Were we ever? *Environmental Communication: A Journal of Nature and Culture, 1*(1), 21–33.

Shabecoff, P. (1993). *A fierce green fire: The American environmental movement.* New York: Hill & Wang.

Shabecoff, P. (2003). *A fierce green fire: The American environmental movement* (Rev. ed.). Washington, DC: Island Press.

Shanahan, J., & McComas, K. (1999). *Nature stories: Depictions of the environment and their effects.* Cresskill, NJ: Hampton Press.

Shannon, C., & Weaver, W. (1949). *The mathematical theory of communication.* Urbana: University of Illinois Press.

Short, B. (1991). Earth First! and the rhetoric of moral confrontation. *Communication Studies, 42,* 172–188.

Simmons, W. M. (2007). *Participation and power: Civic discourse in environmental policy decisions.* Albany: State University of New York Press.

Slawter, L. D. (2008). TreeHuggerTV: Re-visualizing environmental activism in the post-network era. *Environmental Communication: A Journal of Nature and Culture, 2,* 212–228.

Sonneborn, L. (2007). *The environmental movement: Protecting our natural resources.* New York: Facts on File.

Switzer, J. V. (1997). *Green backlash: The history and politics of environmental opposition in the U.S.* Boulder, CO: Lynne Rienner.

Taubes, G. (1993). The ozone backlash. *Science, 260,* 1580–1583.

Taylor, B. R. (Ed.). (1995). *Ecological resistance movements: The global emergence of radical and popular environmentalism.* Albany: State University of New York Press.

Taylor, B. C., Kinsella, W. J., Depoe, S. P., & Metzler, M. S. (2008). *Nuclear legacies: Communication, controversy, and the U.S. nuclear weapons complex.* Lanham, MD: Lexington Books.

Waddell, C. (1990). The role of pathos in the decision-making process: A study in the rhetoric of science policy. *Quarterly Journal of Speech, 76,* 381–401.

Wagner, T. (2008). Reframing ecotage as ecoterrorism: News and the discourse of fear. *Environmental Communication: A Journal of Nature and Culture, 2,* 25–39.

Walker, G. B. (2004). The roadless area initiative as national policy: Is public participation an oxymoron? In S. P. Depoe, J. W. Delicath, & M.-F. A. Elsenbeer (Eds.), *Communication and public participation in environmental decision making* (pp. 113–135). Albany: State University of New York Press.

The natural world is clearly "out there," but it is through differing social and symbolic systems that we understand this world, infuse it with significance, and act toward it.

CHAPTER 2

Social/Symbolic Constructions of "Environment"

What could they see but a hideous & desolate wilderness, full of wild beasts & wild men?

—William Bradford, *Of Plymouth Plantation, 1620–1647* (1898/1952)

Here I can be the voice and face of this tree, and for the whole forest that can't speak for itself.

—Julia "Butterfly" Hill (2002), sitting in Luna, a 1,000-year-old redwood tree

Writing of settlers' hardships at Plymouth in 1620, William Bradford described the landscape beyond the colony as a "hideous and desolate wilderness." With that phrase, he began what environmental historian Roderick Nash (2001) called a "tradition of repugnance" for nature (p. 24). His account of the New England forests also would be the start of a long-running controversy over how to define and shape the meaning of the relationship between human society and the environment.

On the eve of the 21st century, activist Julia "Butterfly" Hill (2002) voiced a quite different view of humans' relationship with the environment while she lived for two years high in the branches of an ancient redwood tree (named Luna) to prevent loggers from cutting it down. (For more information, see "Julia Butterfly" at www.circleoflife.org.) Bradford's fears and Hill's desire illustrate two different views of nature, each of which has evoked wide-ranging passion, debate, imagination, and angst. Nash (2001) observed in his classic study, *Wilderness and the American Mind*, that the term *wilderness* "is *so* heavily freighted with meaning of a personal, symbolic, and changing kind as to resist easy definition" (p. 1).

The diverse meanings of *wilderness* as well as the term *environment* remind us that these are powerful and changing ideas, the meanings of which have consequences for our behavior toward them. For example, the designation of old-growth forests in the United States as "wilderness" under the 1964 Wilderness Act has had the effect of removing land from the timber base and restricting commercial development on it. Because differing views of the environment have serious economic, health, and social consequences, many individuals throughout history have "battled mightily and often" over the best ways to define humans' relation to the natural world (Warren, 2003, p. 1).

From a communication perspective, the history of human behavior toward the natural world is one of competing voices and interests that have sought to define, shape, or challenge societies' attitudes about the environment. What the term *environment* symbolizes at any particular time depends upon the communications of these differing interests. This chapter briefly traces this history and introduces a social/symbolic perspective that we use to describe these ongoing attempts to shape our relationships with the natural world.

The first section of this chapter traces the historical background of the environmental movement in the United States. We also look at four major junctures in this history, points at which individuals, movement activists, scientists, and media began to challenge different, societal attitudes about the environment. The second section introduces a *social/symbolic* perspective for the study of environmental communication. This builds on our definition of environmental communication in Chapter 1 as both "a pragmatic and constitutive vehicle" for our understanding of the environment as well as our relationships to the natural world. The third section extends this perspective to include visual media such as photographs, art, and film. Just as news reports and speeches can persuade others, so, too, can nonverbal images affect attitudes and behavior toward nature.

The U.S. Environmental Movement

By the start of the 21st century, respect for the environment had emerged as a "first tier" concern of citizens in the United States and many other regions of the world. Yet the roots of this achievement lay in centuries-old efforts to transform society's views by challenging its discourses about human dominion and the conquest of nature.

Important to transforming prevailing beliefs are **antagonisms.** In everyday language, *antagonism* means "conflict" or "disagreement." Here, I use the term more specifically to denote the recognition of the *limit* of an idea, a widely shared viewpoint, or ideology (Laclau & Mouffe, 2001). Recognition of a *limit* allows an opposing idea or belief to be voiced. A limit is recognized when questioning or criticism reveals a prevailing view to be inadequate or unresponsive to new demands. Recognizing this creates an opening for alternative voices and ideas to redefine what is appropriate, wise, or ethical—in this case, the relationship between the environment and society. In the history of the U.S. environmental movement, four major antagonisms define recognitions of ideological limits, at which point new voices and interests challenged the prevailing views of society:

1. Preservation and conservation of nature versus human exploitation of nature

2. Human health versus unregulated business and manufacturing activity

3. Environmental justice versus a vision of nature as "a place apart" from the places where people live and work

4. Health of the global commons (and climate) versus "business as usual" growth

One important note about histories of the U.S. environmental movement: Traditional accounts describe the 19th century as an era that focused on protection of wilderness and the post-1960s as a period of awakening to concerns about human health. As Gottlieb (1993b) observed, the problem with this historical divide in recounting the movement is "who is left out and what it fails to explain" (p. 1). Although I follow this standard account to some extent, I also try to bring in "who is left out"—figures such as Dr. Alice Hamilton, who urged a concern for the "dangerous trades" of urban environments as early as the 1920s. Also, in describing the post-1960s period, I highlight minority citizens' demands for environmental justice as well as new concerns for the global climate under "business as usual" economic growth.

Challenging the Exploitation of Nature

The first serious questioning of the exploitation of America's remaining wild areas began in the late 18th century. This was in sharp contrast to a centuries-old tradition of loathing wilderness and seeking to subdue wild nature. Puritans such as Michael Wigglesworth (1662) had described the dark forests as "a waste and howling wilderness" (p. 83, quoted in Nash, 2001, p. 36). And in his classic essay, "The Historical Roots of Our Ecological Crisis," historian Lynn White Jr. (1967) noted that Europeans and, later, early American settlers[1] inherited a specific religious injunction to "subdue" nature—a belief that it was "God's will that man [sic] exploit nature for his proper ends" (p. 1205).

Nevertheless, by the late 18th century the questioning of this tradition of repugnance for wild nature had begun. In art, literature, and on the lecture circuits, voices began to challenge the view of nature as alien or exploitable. Nash identifies three major sources of these challenges: (1) Romantic ideals in art and literature, (2) a search for U.S. national identity, and (3) transcendentalist ideals in writings of Henry David Thoreau and others.

The first source of resistance to aversion toward wilderness came through the influence of Romantic and primitivist ideals in art and literature. Nash (2001) writes that 18th- and early 19th-century English nature poets and aestheticians such as William Gilpin "inspired a rhetorical style for articulating [an] appreciation of uncivilized nature" (p. 46). These writers and poets, along with Edmund Burke, Jean-Jacques Rousseau, and others, fostered in American art and literature an ideal of sublimity in wild nature. The **sublime** was an aesthetic category that associated God's influence with the feelings of awe and exultation that some experienced in the presence of wilderness. "Combined with the primitivistic idealization of a life closer to nature, these ideas fed the Romantic movement which had far-reaching implications for wilderness" (Nash, 2001, p. 44).

A second challenge to the tradition of repugnance toward wilderness was the young nation's quest for a sense of national identity. Believing that America could not match Europe's history and soaring cathedrals, advocates of a uniquely American identity sought to champion the distinctive characteristics of the American landscape. "Nationalists argued that far from being a liability, wilderness was actually an American asset" (Nash, 2001, p. 67). Writers such as James Fenimore Cooper and artists of the Hudson River school such as Thomas Cole celebrated the wonders of the American wilderness by defining a national style in fiction, poetry, and painting. In his 1835 "Essay on American Scenery," Cole argued that the new nation did not need to feel inferior to "civilized Europe," for "American scenery . . . has features, and glorious ones, unknown to Europe. The most distinctive, and perhaps the most impressive, characteristic of American scenery is its wildness" (quoted in Nash, 2001, pp. 80–81).

Finally, the 19th-century emergence of **transcendentalism** as a major philosophical perspective proved to be an important impetus for the reevalution of wild nature. "The core of Transcendentalism was the belief that a correspondence or parallelism existed between the higher realm of spiritual truth and the lower one of material objects. . . . Natural objects assumed importance because, if rightly seen, they reflected universal spiritual truth" (Nash, 2001, p. 85). Among those who drew upon transcendentalist beliefs to challenge older discourses about wilderness was the writer and philosopher Henry David Thoreau. For Thoreau (1862/1893), wilderness was more valuable than urban areas because it more closely embodied the truth of this transcendental realm. He argued that "in Wildness is the preservation of the World," and that there exists "a subtle magnetism in Nature, which, if we unconsciously yield to it, will direct us aright" (1862/1893, pp. 251, 265; see also Cox, 1980). By the late 19th century, Thoreau's writings had influenced others to preserve remnants of the vanishing American wilderness.

John Muir and the Wilderness Preservation Movement

By the 1880s, key figures in California and elsewhere had begun to argue explicitly for the preservation of wilderness areas.[2] Arising out of these efforts were campaigns to protect coastal forests and spectacular regions of natural scenery such as Yosemite Valley in the Sierra Nevada Mountains. **Preservationism** sought to ban commercial use of these areas, to preserve wild forests and other natural areas for appreciation, study, and outdoor recreation. This movement also would be one of the two major forces of the early 20th century, along with *conservationism*, to challenge the rapacious exploitation of wild nature. (We return to this second challenge shortly.)

One of the leaders of the preservation movement was the Scottish immigrant John Muir, whose literary essays in the 1870s and 1880s did much to arouse national sentiment for preserving Yosemite Valley. Communication scholar Christine Oravec (1981) has observed that Muir's essays evoked a **sublime response** from his readers through his description of the rugged mountains and valleys of the Sierra Nevada. This response on the part of readers was characterized by (1) an immediate awareness of a sublime object (such as Yosemite Valley), (2) a sense of overwhelming personal insignificance and awe in the object's presence, and (3) ultimately a feeling of spiritual exaltation (p. 248). Typical of this style was Muir's depiction of the 2,425-foot Yosemite Falls, the world's fifth highest: "Gray cliffs, wet black rock, the white hill of ice, trees, . . . and the surging, roaring torrents escaping down the gorge in front, glorifying all, and proclaiming the triumph of Peace and eternal Harmony" (Oravec, 1981, p. 249). Muir's influence and the support of others such as Robert Underwood Johnson, editor of the literary magazine *Century,* led to a national campaign to preserve Yosemite Valley. By 1890, these efforts had resulted in the creation of Yosemite National Park by Congress, "the first successful proposal for preservation of natural scenery to gain widespread national attention and support" from the public (p. 256).

Logging of giant redwood trees along California's coast in the 1880s also fueled interest in the preservation movement. Laura White and the California Federation of Women's Clubs were among those who led successful campaigns to protect redwood groves in the late 19th century (Merchant, 2005). As a result of these early campaigns, groups dedicated to wilderness and wildlife preservation began to appear: John Muir's Sierra Club (1892), the Audubon Society (1905), the Save the Redwoods League (1918), the National Parks and Conservation Association (1919), the Wilderness Society (1935), and the National Wildlife Federation (1936). In the 20th century, these groups launched other preservation campaigns that challenged exploitation of these wild lands. (For a history of this period, see Merchant, 2005, and Warren, 2003.)

Conservation: Wise Use of Natural Resources

Muir's ethic of preservation soon clashed with a competing vision that sought to manage America's forests and other natural resources for efficient and sustainable use. Influenced by the philosophy of **utilitarianism,** the idea of "the greatest good for the greatest number," some in the early 20th century began to promote a new conservation ethic. Associated principally with Gifford Pinchot, President Theodore Roosevelt's chief of the Division of Forestry (now the U.S. Forest Service), the term **conservation** meant "the wise and efficient use of natural resources" (Merchant, 2005, p. 128). For example, in managing public forest lands as a source of timber, Pinchot instituted a sustained yield policy, according to which logged timberlands were to be reforested after cutting, to ensure future timber supplies (Hays, 1989; Merchant, 2005; for more about Pinchot, see Miller, 2004.)

The tension between Muir's ethic of preservation and Pinchot's conservation approach came to a head in the fierce controversy over the building of a dam in Hetch Hetchy Valley in Yosemite National Park. In 1901, the City of San Francisco's proposal to dam the river running through this valley as a source for its water sparked a multiyear dispute over the purpose of the new park. At the heart of the controversy were two differing views of the public interest (Oravec, 1984). As an ideal, the **public interest** is a symbolic marker of legitimacy for actions taken in the name of the nation's people or the common good.

The tension between the aesthetic and practical values of Hetch Hetchy Valley would continue to incite debate long after the dam was approved in 1913. In the following decades, Pinchot's conservation approach strongly influenced the management of natural resources by agencies such as the Forest Service and the Bureau of Land Management (BLM). Preservationists, too, won significant victories. One major accomplishment was the National Parks Act of 1916, which established a national system of parks that continues to expand today. Other designations of parks, wildlife refuges, and wild and scenic rivers would follow into the 21st century. Perhaps the preservationists' most significant victory was the 1964 Wilderness Act. The Wilderness Act authorizes Congress to set aside wild areas in national forests, national parks, and other strictly managed public lands to preserve such areas' "primeval character and influence" (Warren, 2003, p. 243). (For another viewpoint, see "The Trouble With Wilderness.")

Another Viewpoint: "The Trouble With Wilderness"

The idea of wilderness has been challenged in recent years from a viewpoint other than Pinchot's conservation ethic. Historian William Cronon (1996) has argued that wilderness "is quite profoundly a human creation" (p. 69) that diverts attention from the places nearby, where people live and work. Cronon argued:

> The trouble with wilderness is that it ... represents the false hope of an escape from responsibility, the illusion that we can somehow wipe clean the slate of our past and return to the tabula rasa that supposedly existed before we began to leave our marks on the world.... This, then, is the central paradox: [W]ilderness embodies a dualistic vision in which the human is entirely outside the natural. If we allow ourselves to believe that nature, to be true, must also be wild, then our very presence in nature represents its fall. The place where we are is the place where nature is not. (pp. 80–81)

Interestingly, Cronon is arguing not for the elimination of wild areas but for a questioning of the idea embraced in some understandings of the term *wilderness* as a place beyond human presence.

The tension between preservation and conservation continues to be central in current debates about U.S. environmental policies. As early as the 1980s, a split had developed in the movement as a result of the perceived failure of mainstream groups to preserve more wild lands. Disillusioned wilderness activists formed the radical group Earth First! to engage in **direct action,** physical acts of protests such as road blockades, sit-ins, and **tree spiking.**[3] Other groups, such as the Earth Liberation

Front, have turned to arson and property damage in a controversial move to protect endangered species and to protest society's material consumption.

Still other groups have voiced a more critical rhetoric, questioning many of society's core values from the perspectives of "Deep Ecology" (www.deepecology.org) and "ecofeminism." Ecofeminism is a broadly diverse social and political movement that sees parallels between oppression of women and the degradation of nature. (For an introduction, see www.feministezine.com/feminist/ecofeminism.) (We return to this idea of "critical rhetoric" in Chapter 7.) Overall, the contemporary movement to protect wild nature consists of a broad and diverse range of both voices and strategies for the protection of wild nature.

Public Health and Urban Pollution

By the 1960s, a second antagonism had developed that focused on the effects of environmental pollutants on human health. At a time when environmental standards for air and water pollution were weak or nonexistent, citizens began to question the effects of unregulated business and manufacturing activities. Their concerns included pollution by factories and refineries, abandoned toxic waste sites, exposure to pesticides used on agricultural crops, and radioactive fallout from above-ground nuclear testing.

Traditional accounts of the U.S. environmental movement credit biologist and writer Rachel Carson for voicing the first public challenge to business practices that affect the natural environment and human health (see Figure 2.1). In her eloquent book *Silent Spring,* Carson (1962) wrote, "We are adding a . . . new kind of havoc— the direct killing of birds, mammals, fishes, and indeed, practically every form of wildlife by chemical insecticides indiscriminately sprayed on the land" (p. 83). Fearful of the consequences for human health from insecticides like DDT, she warned that modern agribusiness had "armed itself with the most modern and terrible weapons, and that in turning them against the insects it has also turned them against the earth" (p. 262). (For more information on the significance of Carson's *Silent Spring,* see Craig Waddell's anthology, *And No Birds Sing* [2000]).

With her prescient writings, Rachel Carson is widely considered the founder of the modern environmental movement. Although *Silent Spring* did prefigure a popular movement, earlier voices from the 1880s through the 1920s had warned of dangers to human health from poor sanitation and occupational exposures to lead and other chemicals. Trade unions, "sanitarians," reformers from Jane Addams's Hull House in Chicago, and public health advocates had warned of hazards to both workplace and urban life: "contaminated water supplies, inadequate waste and sewage collection disposal, poor ventilation and polluted and smoke-filled air, [and] overcrowded neighborhoods and tenements" (Gottlieb, 1993a, p. 55).

Urban environmental historian Robert Gottlieb (1993a) has called attention particularly to the influence of Dr. Alice Hamilton, "a powerful environmental advocate in an era when the term had yet to be invented" (p. 51), who worked in the 1920s to reform the "dangerous trades" of urban workplaces. With the publication of

| **Figure 2.1** | Rachel Carson (1907–1964), marine biologist and author of *Silent Spring* |

© Alfred Eisenstaedt/Getty Images.

Industrial Poisons in the United States (1925) and her work with the Women's Health Bureau, Hamilton became "the country's most powerful and effective voice for exploring the environmental consequences of industrial activity," including the impacts of occupational hazards on women and minorities in the workplace (p. 51).

Still, until *Silent Spring* in 1962, there was no such thing as an environmental movement in the United States in the sense of a "concerted, populous, vocal, influential, active" force (Sale, 1993, p. 6). However, by the late 1960s, news coverage of air pollution, nuclear fallout, fires on the Cuyahoga River near Cleveland when its polluted surface ignited, and oil spills off the coast of Santa Barbara, California, fueled a public outcry for greater protection of the environment. By 1970, the U.S. Congress had enacted new laws such as the Clean Air Act and the Clean Water Act to begin cleanup of the nation's air and water. Another milestone was the **National Environmental Policy Act** (NEPA), signed into law by President Richard M. Nixon on

January 1, 1970. This would become the cornerstone of modern environmental law. The act requires every federal agency to prepare an environmental impact statement for any project that would affect the environment.

By the first Earth Day on April 22, 1970, students, public health workers, new activist groups, and urban workers had coalesced into a recognizable movement to champion environmental controls on industry and governmental activities. Drawing some 20 million people and involving protests, teach-ins, and festivals at schools, colleges, and universities throughout the country, the inaugural Earth Day was one of the largest demonstrations in American history. Its events involved "every strata of American society" (Flippen, 2003, p. 272). At the same time, new groups arose to address the relationship between human health and the environment. Among the earliest were the Environmental Defense Fund (1967), Environmental Action (1970), and the Natural Resources Defense Council (1970). Finally, the growing popularity of the "ecology movement"—the term used in the 1970s for the environmental movement—led lawmakers to enact new legislation to strengthen protections for air and water quality and to regulate production and disposal of toxic chemicals.

Whereas the ecology movement championed human health and environmental quality against industrial pollution, much of the initial focus of the new environmental groups was at the federal level (enacting new laws). However, by the end of the 1970s, the challenge arose at local levels as communities became increasingly worried by the chemical contamination of their air, drinking water, soil, and school grounds. For example, the small, upstate New York community of Love Canal became a symbol of the nation's widening consciousness of the hazards of chemicals in their economy. (See the brief description of the Love Canal case in Chapter 1.) Ordinary citizens felt themselves surrounded by what Hays (1989) termed this "toxic 'sea around us'" (p. 171) and began to organize in hundreds of community-based groups to demand cleanup of their neighborhoods and stricter accountability of corporate polluters.

Prompted by the toxic waste scandals at Love Canal and other places, such as Times Beach, Missouri, the U.S. Congress passed the **Superfund** law of 1980, which authorized the Environmental Protection Agency to clean up toxic sites and take action against the responsible parties. Local citizens also took advantage of new federal laws such as the Clean Water Act to participate in local decision-making venues, such as state agencies' issuance of air and water permits for businesses. (We describe these guarantees for public participation in Chapter 3.)

Environmental Justice: Challenging Nature as "a Place Apart"

Even as the environmental movement widened its concerns in the 1960s to include health and environmental quality along with wilderness preservation, there remained a language of the environment that provided "disjointed and at times contradictory" accounts of humans' place in nature and assumed a "long-standing separation of the social from the ecological" (Gottlieb, 2002, p. 5). However, by the 1980s new activists from minority and low-income communities had begun to challenge the view of nature as "a place apart" from the environments where people lived and worked, disclosing a third antagonism in prevailing views of the environment.

Rearticulating the Meaning of Environment

Despite some earlier efforts to bring environmentalists, labor, and civil rights and religious leaders together to explore common interests in the 1960s and 1970s[4], national environmental groups largely failed to recognize the problems of urban residents and minority communities. For example, sociologist Giovanna Di Chiro (1996) reported that in the mid-1980s residents in south central Los Angeles who were trying to stop a solid waste incinerator from being located in their neighborhood discovered that "these issues were not deemed adequately 'environmental' by local environmental groups such as the Sierra Club or the Environmental Defense Fund" (p. 299). Activists in communities of color were particularly vocal in criticizing mainstream environmental groups for being "reluctant to address issues of equity and social justice, within the context of the environment" (Alston, 1990, p. 23).

By the 1980s, residents and activists in some low-income neighborhoods and communities of color had started to take matters into their own hands. In a historically significant move, they proposed to rearticulate the word *environment* to mean the places "where we live, where we work, where we play, and where we learn" (Lee, 1996, p. 6). A key moment in the launching of this new movement occurred in 1982 with the protests by residents of the largely African American community of Warren County, North Carolina. Local residents and leaders of national civil rights groups tried to halt the state's plans to locate a toxic waste landfill in this rural community by sitting in roads to block 6,000 trucks carrying PCB (polychlorinated biphenol)-contaminated soil.[5] More than 500 protesters were arrested in what sociologists Robert Bullard and Beverly Hendrix Wright (1987) called "the first national attempt by blacks to link environmental issues (hazardous waste and pollution) to the mainstream civil rights agenda" (p. 32). (For more on the significance of this event as a "story of origin" in the movement, see Pezzullo, 2001.)

With similar struggles in other parts of the nation and reports of the heavy concentration of hazardous facilities in minority neighborhoods, some charged that these communities suffered from a form of **environmental racism** (Sandler & Pezzullo, 2007, p. 4) or more broadly as environmental injustice (Roberts, 2007, p. 289). Residents and critics alike began to speak of being poisoned and "dumped upon," and of certain communities targeted as "sacrifice zones" (Schueler, 1992, p. 45). Importantly for these critics, the term *environmental racism* meant not only threats to their health from hazardous waste landfills, incinerators, agricultural pesticides, sweatshops, and polluting factories, but also the disproportionate burden that these practices placed on people of color and the workers and residents of low-income communities.

Defining Environmental Justice

Emerging from these struggles was a pluralistic vision of **environmental justice.** For most activists, this term connected the safety and quality of the environments where people lived, worked, played, and learned with concerns for social and economic justice. Residents and movement activists insisted that *environmental justice* referred to the basic right of all people to be free of poisons and other hazards. At its core, environmental justice also was a vision of the democratic inclusion of people and communities in the decisions that affected their health and well-being. Many people criticized decision-making processes that failed to provide meaningful participation "for those most burdened by environmental decisions" and called for affected communities to share more fully in those decisions at all levels of government that adversely impact their communities (Cole & Foster, 2001, p. 16; Gerrard & Foster, 2008).

The demand for environmental justice received significant publicity in 1991, when delegates from local communities, along with national leaders of civil rights, religious, and environmental groups, convened in Washington, D.C., for the First People of Color Environmental Leadership Summit. For the first time, the different strands of the emerging movement for environmental justice came together to challenge mainstream definitions of environmentalism. The delegates to the summit also adopted a powerful set of 16 **Principles of Environmental Justice** that enumerated a series of rights, including "the fundamental right to political, economic, cultural, and environmental self-determination of all peoples" (*Proceedings,* 1991, p. viii). (For the "Principles of Environmental Justice," see http://www.ejnet.org/ej/principles.html.)

In 1994, the movement achieved an important political goal when President Bill Clinton issued an executive order directing each federal agency to "make achieving environmental justice part of its mission by identifying and addressing . . . disproportionately high and adverse human health or environmental effects of its programs, policies, and activities on minority populations and low-income populations in the United States" (Clinton, 1994, p.7629). Nevertheless, the movement continues to face real-world, on-the-ground challenges to building sustainable and healthy communities. Beyond the disproportionate burden of hazards on communities is the movement's insistence on the democratic inclusion of peoples and communities in the decisions affecting their lives, a vision that is still largely unrealized. (We describe the movement for environmental justice in more detail in Chapter 8.)

Defending the Global Commons (and Climate)

Over the past two decades, an enthusiastic and diverse "movement of movements" (Klein, 2000) has been growing in countries throughout the world to protect local communities and environments. In Europe, Asia, North and South America, Africa, Australia, and the Pacific Islands, tens of thousands of local and regional groups have challenged dominant practices in their societies. These challenges often are similar to the three antagonisms described earlier—protection of natural areas and human health, and a concern for social justice. In his remarkable account, *Blessed Unrest*, Paul Hawken (2007) describes these grassroots, global efforts:

> The movement grows and spreads in every city and country, and involves virtually every tribe, culture, language, and religion, from Mongolians to Uzbeks to Tamils. It is composed of families in India, students in Australia, farmers in France, the landless in Brazil, the Bananeras of Honduras, the "poors" of Durban, villagers in Irían Jaya, indigenous tribes of Bolivia, and housewives in Japan. . . . These groups defend against corrupt politics and climate change, corporate predation and the death of oceans, governmental indifference and pandemic poverty, industrial forestry and farming, and depletion of soil and water. (pp. 11, 164–165)

These and thousands of other efforts reflect diverse agendas and rely on different strategies and methods of communication. Yet, underlying them is a more basic development: the growing recognition of a "limit" or inadequacy in societies' economic systems.

This fourth antagonism is the concern that *the health of the global commons (and climate) is threatened by "business as usual" growth.* For climate scientists, **business as usual** (BAU) means the unrestrained growth of carbon-based economies. "Carbon based" is the energy source—primarily fossil fuels such as oil, coal, and natural gas—used by human societies to produce electricity and fuel transportation, agriculture, heating, and other basic dimensions of life. Identifying these energy sources is important because climate scientists believe there is an increased warming of the Earth due principally to the emissions (carbon dioxide) caused by combustion of fossil fuels, as well as other so-called greenhouse gases. That the Earth is warming is no longer in doubt. The United Nations Intergovernmental Panel on Climate Change ([IPCC], 2007) has determined that warming of the Earth's climate is now "unequivocal" (p. 30). Furthermore, it has publicly warned that such anthropogenic (human-caused) emissions are "very likely" the cause of the increase in global average temperatures since the mid-20th century (p. 39).

As a result, growing numbers of scientists, health officials, and environmentalists, as well as many grassroots groups, are questioning the "business as usual" approach to growth. This is principally because of the impacts of a rapidly warming climate on the global commons but experienced in local regions. Among the major, observed impacts of global warming are those listed here:

- Melting of mountain glaciers, Arctic sea ice cover, and permafrost
- Decline in snow-fed rivers and water sources in North America, the Himalayas, and other areas
- Migration of plant and animal species
- Disturbances in terrestrial systems: drought, decline of agricultural productivity, disease in forests
- Impacts on human health, including heat-related deaths in Europe
- Sea rises, coastal flooding, and losses of coastal wetlands
- Loss of coral reefs and alteration of water quality: higher water temperatures, increased salinity of oceans

And, with greater warming come more severe consequences: spreading disease, failures of land-based and marine food sources, rising seas and flooding of populated regions, and as a result, massive population migrations and regional conflicts over scare resources. (For further information, see the Intergovernmental Panel on Climate Change's *Climate Change 2007: Synthesis Report* at www.ipcc.ch/ipccreports.)

In response to these warnings, a global "climate justice" movement has emerged, urging local and world leaders to take immediate action. (For more details on this movement, see Chapter 8.) In the United States, student-led activism, TV and Web ads by the Alliance for Climate Protection, and campaigns by environmental organizations have raised the alarm and begun to mobilize public support for comprehensive changes in U.S. energy policy. Both in the United States and globally, tens of thousands of activists and local groups are connecting through new, social networking sites such as 350.org. And the international group Greenpeace has even built a replica of Noah's Ark on Mount Ararat, the biblical mountain, in Turkey to warn of impending climate disaster (see Figure 2.2). Even climate scientists, concerned about the slowness of governmental response, have spoken out publicly. Rajendra Pachauri, director of the IPCC, warned, "If there's no action before 2012, that's too late. What we do in the next two to three years will determine our future. This is the defining moment" (quoted in Rosenthal, 2007).[6]

| Figure 2.2 | Igdir, TURKEY: A Greenpeace activist releases a pigeon as the other hold a banner during Noah's Ark opening ceremony on Mount Ararat, Igdir, 31 May 2007. Greenpeace activists built a model of Noah's Ark on Mount Ararat to raise awareness over global warming and the dangers—floods, droughts and natural disaster—it poses for the world. |

As we've seen in the development of these four antagonisms, the concepts of nature and the environment are highly contingent. That is, they are subject to redefinition as new voices and interests contest prevailing understandings of our environments. The core of these challenges is a distinctly *rhetorical* process of human influence, questioning, and persuasion, and it is this perspective that we explore in the following section.

Social/Symbolic Approaches to the Environment

As we've just seen, few words have acquired the same social and symbolic currency of the terms *nature* or *environment*. Literary scholars Carl Herndl and Stuart Brown (1996) report that the richness of the term *environment* has nurtured "not one environmental discourse but many" (p. 4). From its origin in wilderness preservation campaigns of the 19th century to calls for environmental justice of the 21st century, the environmental movements in the United States and other countries have drawn on a rich variety of languages and symbols to shape public perceptions of nature. *Environment* now signifies a wide range of concerns, from wilderness, air and water pollution, and toxic wastes to urban sprawl, global climate change, and the quality of life where people live, work, play, and learn.

By the end of the 20th century, scholars such as Donna Haraway (1991), Neil Evernden (1992), Andrew Ross (1994), Klaus Eder (1996a), and Bruno Latour (1999/2004) also had begun to describe the social and discursive *constructions* that influence our understanding of nature. This **social/symbolic perspective** focuses on the sources which help to constitute or shape our perceptions of what we consider to be "natural" or an environmental "problem." For example, Herndl and Brown (1996) argue that "environment" is "a concept and an associated set of cultural values that we have constructed through the way we use language. *In a very real sense, there is no objective environment in the phenomenal world, no environment separate from the words we use to represent it*" (p. 3; emphasis added). This is not to suggest that there is no material world "out there." Of course there is. But it is through differing social and symbolic modes that we understand and engage this world, infuse it with significance, and act toward it. As I noted in Chapter 1, environmental communication is *constitutive,* that is, our communication "helps to constitute, or compose, representations of nature and environmental problems themselves as subjects for our understanding."

If the environment is something that we know partly through language and other symbols, then *different* linguistic and symbolic choices are possible, and these choices construct diverse meanings for the worlds we know. As a result, some scholars adopt a more specifically *rhetorical* perspective to study the different ways in which journalists, scientists, corporations, environmentalists, and citizens attempt to influence our perceptions and behavior toward the environment. A **rhetorical perspective** focuses on *purposeful and consequential efforts* to influence society's attitudes and behavior through communication, including public debate, protests, news stories, advertising, and other modes of symbolic action (Campbell & Huxman, 2003).

In this section of the chapter, I introduce the concepts of rhetoric and its pragmatic and constitutive roles. I also describe some of the rhetorical resources used by the environmental movement and its opponents, including metaphor and rhetorical genres of melodrama and apocalypse. And, I look at the idea of "discourse" more generally. Finally, in the last section, I explore *visual rhetorics*—art, photos, film, and other nonverbal, symbolic actions.

A Rhetorical Perspective

The study of rhetoric traces its origins to classical Greek philosopher-teachers such as Isocrates (436–338 BCE) and Aristotle (384–322 BCE), who taught the arts of citizenship to political leaders in democratic city-states such as Athens. The practice in these city-states was for citizens to speak publicly in law courts and the political assembly, where each citizen represented his own interests. (In Athens and other cities, civic speech was limited principally to male, property-owning citizens.) As a result, competency in public speaking, debate, and persuasion was vital for conducting civic business—war and peace, taxes, construction of public monuments, property claims, and so forth.

It was during this period that Aristotle summarized the teachings in the art of civic speaking when he defined **rhetoric** as the faculty or ability of discovering "in any given case the available means of persuasion" (Herrick, 2009, p. 77). This art of rhetoric rested not simply on skillful delivery but on the ability to discover the resources for persuasion that were available in a specific situation. This draws our attention to rhetoric as a *purposeful choice* among the available means of persuasion useful in accomplishing some effect or outcome.

In Chapter 1, we defined *environmental communication* in part as the pragmatic and constitutive vehicle for our understanding of the environment as well as our relationships to the natural world. As I just noted, rhetoric traditionally has been viewed primarily as a *pragmatic* or instrumental activity that enables individuals to choose from the available means of persuasion to affect a desired outcome. Let me briefly describe this pragmatic role and then suggest a second function in which rhetoric may also be viewed as a *constitutive* vehicle.

Rhetoric as a Pragmatic Vehicle: Metaphor and Rhetorical Genres

The pragmatic efforts of citizens, environmental groups, and others to *educate, alert, persuade,* or *mobilize* draw on the resources of language itself. Rhetorical scholars have explored a wide range of such resources—emotional appeals, tropes, narrative accounts, argumentation, and rhetorical genres—in the Websites, campaign materials, speeches, banners, and other communication in environmental controversies. Although such rhetorical appeals also have *constitutive* dimensions (see later), there is no denying the pragmatic purposes these uses of languages have helped to achieve. Let's look briefly at two of these resources: tropes and rhetorical genres.

Among the most ubiquitous rhetorical resources are **tropes**, sometimes called "figures of speech." Tropes refer to the uses of language that "turn" a meaning from its original sense in a new direction, for a persuasive purpose. They include such familiar figures as metaphor, irony, and synecdoche, or the "part" standing for the "whole," as in references simply to "melting glaciers" to signal the wider impacts on natural systems and human communities caused by global warming.

Metaphor, one of the major tropes, abounds in the landscape of environmental communication: "Mother Nature," "Spaceship Earth," "population bomb," and the "web of life" are just a few examples. A metaphor's function is to invite a comparison, by "talking about one thing in terms of another" (Jasinski, 2001, p. 550). (I just did this in talking about the field of environmental communication in terms of a "landscape.") Let's take another example: The practice of speaking of the Earth as a spaceship became widespread after astronauts took the first photos of it from space in the 1960s. The photos of the blue-green Earth, against a dark universe, invited a concern for the precarious existence of this small planet. U.S. Ambassador Adlai Stevenson famously evoked this metaphor when he addressed the United Nations on July 9, 1965. He spoke about UN delegates traveling as passengers on "a little space ship, dependent on its vulnerable reserves of air and soil" (quoted in Park, 2001, p. 99). The metaphor was further popularized in the late 1960s by architect Buckminster Fuller (1969) in his *Operating Manual for Spaceship Earth.*

Newer metaphors have arisen as scientists, environmentalists, and businesses bring attention to new problems or seek to allay concerns. For example, environmental scholar Chris Russill (2008) identified climate scientists' use of "tipping points" as a metaphor to forewarn the public about irreversible and catastrophic occurrences if global warming continues. And oil companies routinely use the metaphor of a "footprint" to frame news stories about the opening of the Arctic National Wildlife Refuge to oil drilling. In 2001, as a vote neared in the U.S. Congress, oil company officials evoked this image to suggest that the drilling would have little impact on the environment. Touting advances in technology, industry spokespeople insisted, "With sideways drilling and other advances, the oil beneath the 1.5 million-acre coastal plain can be tapped with a 'footprint' on the surface no larger than 2,000 acres" (Spiess & Ruskin, 2001, para. 1). The *Anchorage Daily News* reported that the oil industry's footprint metaphor "proved to be a potent piece of rhetoric," implying that drilling would affect less than 1 percent of the coastal plain (para. 18).

Second, environmental sources often rely on different rhetorical *genres* to influence perceptions of an issue or problem. **Rhetorical genres** are generally defined as distinct forms or types of speech that "share characteristics distinguishing them" from other types of speech (Jamieson & Stromer-Galley, 2001, p. 361). For example, we observed John Muir's use of the genre of the "sublime" in his nature writing in the 19th century to evoke a feeling of spiritual exaltation. More current examples of genres include *apocalyptic* rhetoric, the *jeremiad,* and what Schwarze (2006) has termed "environmental *melodrama.*" For example, Paul Ehrlich (1968) and Rachel Carson (1962), in their classic works, *The Population Bomb* and *Silent Spring,* appropriated an **apocalyptic narrative** literary style to warn of impending and severe ecological crises. Literary critics Jimmie Killingsworth and Jacqueline Palmer (1996) explained that "in depicting the end of the world as a result of the overweening desire to control nature, [these authors] have discovered a rhetorical means of contesting their opponents' claims for the idea of progress with its ascendant narratives of human victory over nature" (p. 21).

More recently, scientists such as James Lovelock (2006), as well as Climate Ark (2008) and other blogs, have evoked apocalyptic images in warning of the severe and potentially catastrophic effects of global warming on civilization. For example, Lovelock cautioned in a commentary in *The Independent* that "before this century is over billions of us will die and the few breeding pairs of people that survive will be in the Arctic where the climate remains tolerable" (2006, para. 7). Yet, reliance on apocalyptic rhetoric may generate skepticism or charges that its claims are exaggerated. Scientists therefore face a dilemma: how to raise awareness of future, serious effects from climate changes—rising sea levels, regional conflicts, and so on—without relying on visions of apocalypse?

Less familiar genres used in environmental controversies include the *jeremiad* and *melodrama*. For example, Wolfe (2008) draws on an older genre of the jeremiad to sound an environmental alarm in Dr. Seuss's *The Lorax*. The genre of the **jeremiad**, originally named for the "lamentations" of the Hebrew prophet Jeremiah, has been a recurring genre of American public address (Bercovitch, 1978). It refers to speech or writing that laments or denounces the behavior of a people or society and warns of future consequences if society does not change its ways. *The Lorax*, of course, is a fable, but one that is also a "jeremiad," in which the Lorax speaks for the trees, whose fate is imperiled by the *Once-ler*, a symbol of industrial society.

Finally, Steven Schwarze (2006), William Kinsella (2008), and others have used the idea of **environmental melodrama** to clarify issues of power and the ways advocates "moralize" an environmental conflict. As a genre, melodrama "generates stark, polarizing distinctions between social actors and infuses those distinctions with moral gravity and pathos" and is therefore "a powerful resource for rhetorical invention" (Schwarze, 2006, p. 239). For example, Schwarze says that melodrama, by identifying key social actors and where the "public interest" lies, can "remoralize situations" that have been obscured by inaccuracies and "the reassuring rhetoric of technical reason" (p. 250). He offers the example of Bill Moyers's PBS documentary *Trade Secrets* (2001), about the health dangers of the vinyl chloride chemical industry:

> *Trade Secrets* shuttles between images of confidential company memos describing toxic workplace exposure in scientific language, and episodes of workers on hospital beds or widows tearily recalling their spouse's suffering. These melodramatic juxtapositions offer a clear moral framework for interpreting the actions of company decision-makers. They characterize officials as being knowledgeable about toxic hazards in scientific terms, but utterly indifferent to the human suffering that resulted from those hazards. . . . Melodrama puts the inaccuracy of scientific language on display and highlights its potential blindspots. (p. 251)

As the example of *Trade Secrets* makes clear, the use of melodrama helps to advance pragmatic purposes: public education and criticism of the chemical industry. But, the example also discloses a second function, a reordering of public consciousness, specifically the restoration of a moral frame. And, it is to this *constitutive* role of rhetoric that I turn now.

Rhetoric as a Constitutive Force

Although traditional definitions of rhetoric emphasize its pragmatic role, recent definitions have broadened rhetoric's scope by noting its *constitutive* function. Steve Depoe (2006), editor of the new journal, *Environmental Communication: A Journal of Nature and Culture,* observes that "symbolic and natural systems are mutually constituted" (p. vii). That is, the natural world affects us, but our language and other symbolic action also have the capacity to affect or constitute our perceptions of nature itself. The literary theorist Kenneth Burke (1966) makes a similar point about language. He uses the metaphor of **terministic screens** to describe the way in which our language orients us to see certain things, some aspects of the world and not others: "If any given terminology is a *reflection* of reality, by its very nature as a terminology it must be a *selection* of reality; and to this extent it must function also as a *deflection* of reality" (p. 45). That is, our symbolic action ("terministic screens") powerfully shapes or mediates our experiences—what is selected for notice, what is deflected from notice, and therefore how we understand our world. As a result, whenever we speak or write, we actively participate in *constituting* our world.

A striking illustration of rhetoric's constitutive role comes from a recent dispute between environmentalists and the U.S. Department of Commerce over the meaning of "Dolphin Safe," which appears on the labels on cans of tuna fish. Since 1990, the government has prohibited companies from using "Dolphin Safe" to label tuna caught by fishing fleets that chase and encircle dolphins in order to catch tuna. The reason is that dolphins often swim above schools of tuna and are snared in the fleets' encircling nets when the tuna is hauled on board. However, in 2002 the Commerce Department ruled that trapping dolphins while using encirclement nets to catch tuna does not significantly harm dolphin populations. As a result of this ruling, exporters of tuna to the United States could use the label "Dolphin Safe" even though they fished with controversial nets, as long as their fleets employed observers on board to certify that they saw no dolphins killed (M., 2003).

In response to the new rule, Earth Island Institute, Defenders of Wildlife, and seven other environmental groups filed a lawsuit to prevent the use of "Dolphin Safe" labels on tuna caught with encirclement nets. They argued that, even with observers, these nets "deplete dolphin populations by separating calves from mothers and causing stress-related deaths" (M., 2003, p. 3). Meanwhile, tuna companies like StarKist realized that it would be "a PR [public relations] nightmare to anger legions of dolphin-loving school kids armed with lunch-pails" by using the relaxed standards. Therefore, many of these companies pledged to adhere to the older, stricter rules for use of the "dolphin safe" label (p. 3). In 2007, a U.S. Court of Appeals panel, in *Earth Island Institute v. Evans,* upheld the environmental groups, refusing to allow the weakening of the "Dolphin Safe" tuna label (Palmer, 2007).

The point is that, in this and other environmental disputes, the public becomes concerned as a result of the selective presentation of terms and information that name or *constitute* the issue or "problem" at hand. German sociologist Klaus Eder (1996b) explains that often it is "the methods of communicating [about] environmental conditions and ideas, and not the state of deterioration itself, which explain . . . the emergence of a public discourse on the environment" (p. 209). This is particularly important in communication that names an environmental *problem*. Political scientist Deborah Stone (2002) explains that "problems . . . are not given, out there in the world waiting for smart analysts to come along and define them correctly. They are created in the minds of citizens by other citizens, leaders, organizations, and government agencies" (p. 156). Rhetoric's constitutive force comes into play in this ability to characterize a set of facts or a condition in the world one way rather than another and therefore to name it as a problem or not. It is for precisely this reason that questions of "how and why certain environmental issues become identified as 'problems,' including contestation of such claims as problematic," are such an important part of environmental communication itself (Tindall, 1995, p. 49).

Discourses and Symbolic Legitimacy

Earlier, I referred to discourse that viewed wild nature as a commodity to be used. The concept of *discourse* reminds us that persuasive effects are present in sources of communication that are broader than any single speech or utterance. Instead, a **discourse** is a *recurring pattern* of speaking or writing that has developed socially, that is, from multiple sources; it functions to "circulate a coherent set of meanings about an important topic" (Fiske, 1987, p. 14). Such meanings often influence our understanding of how the world works or should work. For example, Gifford Pinchot's conservation discourse in the early 20th century helped to justify utilitarian uses of nature such as logging. And, in the late 20th century, activists calling for "environmental justice" criticized the prevailing discourse of environmentalism that overlooked the places where people lived, worked, played, and learned. Each of these discourses arose from multiple sources—essays, news reports, and other symbolic acts—that articulated a coherent view of nature and our relationships to the environment.

Dominant and Insurgent Discourses

When a discourse gains a broad or taken-for-granted status in a culture (for example, "Growth is good for the economy") or when its meanings help to legitimize certain practices, it can be said to be a **dominant discourse**. Often, these discourses are invisible, in the sense that they express naturalized or taken-for-granted assumptions and values about how the world is or should be organized. Perhaps the best example of a dominant environmental discourse is what biologists Dennis Pirages and Paul Ehrlich (1974) called the **Dominant Social Paradigm (DSP)**. Although they use the term *paradigm*, communication scholars would note that the DSP is a *discursive* tradition that has sustained attitudes of human dominance over nature. As expressed in literature, art, political speeches, advertising, photography, and so forth, the DSP affirms society's "belief in abundance and progress, our devotion to growth and prosperity, our faith in science and technology, and our commitment to a laissez-faire economy, limited government planning and private property rights" (quoted in Dunlap & Van Liere, 1978, p. 10). In everyday terms, the DSP is recognized in references to free markets as the source of prosperity and the wise use of natural resources to build a strong economy and so forth.

Other discourses may question society's dominant discourses. These alternative ways of speaking, writing, or portraying nature in art, music, and photographs illustrate **insurgent discourses.** These are modes of representation that challenge society's taken-for-granted assumptions and offer alternatives to prevailing discourses. In some ages, insurgent discourses are muted or absent, whereas in other periods they may be boisterous and widespread. In our own time, insurgent discourses have proliferated in mainstream media and online, questioning dominant assumptions about growth and the environment. For example, we observed (earlier) the emergence of a new antagonism, opening space for a discourse by climate scientists and environmentalists who are questioning the "business as usual" model of carbon societies.

Some also point to a wider insurgent discourse that emerged in popularity after Earth Day 1970, the **New Environmental Paradigm (NEP).** The NEP emphasizes beliefs and values such as "the inevitability of 'limits to growth,' . . . the importance of preserving the 'balance of nature,' and the need to reject the anthropocentric notion that nature exists solely for human use" (Dunlap & Van Liere, 1978, p. 10; see also Dunlap, Van Liere, Mertig, & Jones, 2000). More recently, a related discourse of "natural capitalism" has emerged (Hawken, Lovins, & Lovins, 1999). This is a view that attempts to "fuse capitalist and environmentalist ideologies with an eye toward sustainable relationships between peoples, societies, and the natural world" (Kendall, 2008, pp. 59–60). Finally, as newly emerging discourses coalesce around specific policies and institutions, they form symbolic boundaries that help to *legitimize* these policies. I describe this related concept next.

Symbolic Legitimacy Boundaries

In an important sense, the function of much communication is to help to establish—or challenge—the *legitimacy* of actions affecting the environment. **Legitimacy** is generally defined as the right to exercise authority. Yet such a right is not granted naturally. Instead, recognition of legitimacy depends upon a specifically *rhetorical* process. Communication scholar Robert Francesconi (1982) defines this rhetorical basis of legitimacy as "an ongoing process of reason-giving . . . which forms the basis of the right to exercise authority as well as the willingness [of audiences] to defer to authority" (p. 49). Importantly, legitimacy may be *claimed* by a person or group, but it is *granted by others*—voters, a group's members, or other constituencies.

One of the most persuasive ways to earn legitimacy is to link a policy with certain values. Sociologist Talcott Parsons (1958) originally defined *legitimation* (the granting of legitimacy) as "the appraisal of [an] action in terms of shared or common values" (p. 201). For example, proposals to protect old-growth forests may be seen as more or less legitimate, depending upon public perception of the values that are at stake: Is the nation experiencing a shortage of timber supply, or is it facing a loss of biodiversity?

Detailed knowledge of how a proposal works, while obviously important, may be only part of the story of its legitimacy.

One of the most rhetorically powerful claims to legitimacy in American political culture is that something is just **common sense**. The term is imprecise, but it generally refers to what people assume to be the views of "everybody"—what is generally agreed to be true. For example, the claim of "common sense" has been a source of legitimacy in recent debates over western wildfires and ways to safeguard nearby homes and communities. When former President George W. Bush rolled out his Healthy Forests Initiative to "thin" forests to prevent wildfires (that is, to selectively log trees), he told a crowd in Portland, Oregon:

> We need to make our forests healthy by using some *common sense.* . . . We've got to understand that it makes sense to clear brush. We've got to make sense—it makes sense to encourage people to make sure that the forests not only are healthy from disease, but are healthy from fire. . . . This is just common sense." (White House, 2002, emphasis added)

The president sought rhetorically to justify his proposal for selective logging of forests—described as clearing brush—in terms of values that his listeners presumably shared about the caution they take around their own homes, summed up as "common sense."

Because legitimacy is rhetorically constituted, it is also open to question and challenge. An appeal to common sense is usually an effective means of gaining legitimacy, since it purports merely to describe things "as they really are." However, part of its power is that it also may mask other meanings or alternatives. For example, environmental groups challenged the common sense of logging *old-growth trees* as well as brush—part of the president's plan—thus beginning a public debate over the legitimacy of the president's Healthy Forests plan.

Political scientist Charles Schulzke (2000) observes that the outcome of arguments over legitimacy turns only partly on facts. Equally important are **symbolic legitimacy boundaries**. Schulzke defines these as the symbolic associations that politicians, business, and the public attach to a proposal, policy, or person. The result of these associations is a kind of symbolic "boundary" providing legitimacy for a particular policy or idea, that is, defining them as reasonable, appropriate, or acceptable. Such a boundary also helps to establish a presumption of normalcy that comes from being in the political center.

On the other hand, the symbolic associations that make up a legitimacy boundary also name what or who is unreasonable, unwise, or unacceptable. For example, a recent study in the journal *Science* reported a "scientific consensus" that human activities are behind the observed warming of the atmosphere in the past 50 years (Oreskes, 2004, p. 1686). The study analyzed 928 abstracts of research published by climate scientists in refereed scientific journals between 1993 and 2003; it found that in no case did a researcher disagree with the consensus position. The question of what to *do* about climate change is still open, the author of the study, Dr. Naomi Oreskes, concluded. "But there is a scientific consensus on the reality of anthropogenic climate change" (p. 1686). The claim of a "scientific consensus" is a powerful symbolic legitimacy boundary, and it was no surprise therefore that Oreskes's study became a target of criticism by skeptics who assert that the science of global warming is still uncertain. (See, for example, Lindzen, 2006). Their resistance is explained in part by the rhetorical *consequences* of a claim to consensus: Public disputes over symbolic legitimacy boundaries tell us "what or who is included or excluded in a category. [They] define people in and out of a conflict or place them on different sides" (Stone, 2002, p. 34).

As with legitimacy itself, symbolic legitimacy boundaries are not granted automatically but are constituted in the rhetorical struggle that makes up public debate and controversy in our modern-day *agora,* or public sphere. Stone (2002) says that, in these struggles to create public support, "symbols, stories, metaphors, and labels are all weapons in the armamentarium (to use a metaphor). . . . By conveying images of good and bad, right and wrong, suffering and relief, these devices are instruments in the struggle over public policy" (p. 156). (In Chapter 9, we return to the rhetorical struggle over an important symbolic legitimacy boundary in environmental policy—the public's respect for scientific knowledge.)

Visual Rhetorics: Portraying Nature

As I noted earlier, rhetoric is not limited to speech or writing. Visual representations have been prominent in shaping Americans' perceptions of the environment at least since the early 18th and 19th centuries, in oil paintings and photographs of the American West. Since then, visual portrayals of nature have ranged from the stunning photographs of melting glaciers, flooding, and droughts from global warming (Braasch, 2007) to the dramatic cinematography of oceans, rain forests, wildlife, and the polar ice worlds in the TV series *Plant Earth.* More recently, community activists in Appalachia have posted traumatic photographs online (for example, www.ilovemountains.org) to protest "mountaintop removal" coal mining in West Virginia, Kentucky, Tennessee, and southwest Virginia.

As a result, rhetorical scholars have begun to look more closely at the significance of *visual images* in the public sphere. As Olson, Finnegan, and Hope (2008) point out in their study *Visual Rhetoric,* "public images often work in ways that are rhetorical; that is, *they function to persuade*" (p. 1; emphasis added). For example, Robert Hariman and John Louis Lucaites (2002) argue that the famous photograph of five Marines and a sailor raising the American flag on Iwo Jima in 1945 is symbolically powerful and illustrates the fact that visual media are "particularly good at activating aesthetic norms that can shape audience acceptance of political beliefs and historical narratives" (p. 366). Other scholars have looked at the importance of visual symbols in post–Cold War images of nuclear devastation (Taylor, 2003); the Vietnam War photograph of a young girl, screaming in pain from napalm (Hariman & Lucaites, 2003); and the shock waves produced by images of the severely mutilated face of the murdered Emmett Till in 1955 (Harold & DeLuca, 2005). So, I believe it's important to end our discussion of a rhetorical perspective by describing the function of **visual rhetorics** of the environment—the role that visual images and representations of nature play in influencing public attitudes toward the environment.

Images of Polar Bears and Global Warming

Visual images clearly evoke attitudes about nature, but they also help to frame a state of affairs as an environmental problem or add urgency to an already-defined problem. For example, Tim Flannery (2005), author of *The Weather Makers*, writes, "If anything symbolizes the Arctic, it is surely *nanuk*, the great white bear" (p. 100). Recently, visual images of polar bears struggling for survival have emerged as an iconic and powerful symbol of global warming. As early as 2005, scientists were finding evidence that polar bears have been drowning in the Arctic sea due to the melting of ice floes from climate change. Polar bears feed from these ice floes, and as they drift farther apart, the bears are being forced to swim longer distances. "Although polar bears are strong swimmers, they are adapted for swimming close to the shore. Their sea journeys leave them vulnerable to exhaustion, hypothermia or being swamped by waves" (Iredale, 2005, para. 3).

In the summer of 2008, observers flying for a whale survey over the Chukchi Sea spotted polar bears swimming in open water The bears were 15–65 miles off the Alaskan shore, "some swimming north, apparently trying to reach the polar ice edge, which on that day was 400 miles away" ("As Arctic Sea Ice Melts," 2008, p. A16).

Within the context of recent concerns over global warming, images of polar bears swimming in the open ocean function as a visual **condensation symbol** (see Figure 2.3.). Graber (1976) defined a condensation symbol as a word or phrase that "stirs vivid impressions involving the listeners' most basic values" (p. 289). Political scientist Murray Edelman (1964) stressed the ability of such symbols to "condense into one

Figure 2.3	Images of vulnerable polar bears are today's condensation symbol for our anxieties about the planet's warming.

symbolic event or sign" powerful emotions, memories, or anxieties about some event or situation (p. 6). Images of vulnerable polar bears are today's condensation symbol for our anxieties about the planet's warming.

Let's take two other examples to illustrate in more detail some of the ways visual rhetoric works to shape our understanding and/or evoke strong emotions about nature.

Refiguring Wilderness in Art and Photographs

Earlier, we saw that 18th- and 19th-century artists such as Thomas Cole, Albert Bierstadt, and the Hudson River School painters were a significant source of the public's awareness of the American West. Equally important were the artists and photographers who followed military expeditions and surveyors into western territories. Rhetorical critics Kevin DeLuca and Anne Demo (2000) have argued that landscape photographers such as Carleton Watkins, Charles Weed, and William Henry Jackson were among the first to portray the West to many people who lived in eastern cities and towns. Photographs of Yosemite Valley, Yellowstone, the Rocky Mountains, and the Grand Canyon not only popularized these sites but, as they became broadly available in the media, "were factors in building public support for preserving the areas" (p. 245).

With such popularization, however, came an embedded orientation and an ideological disposition toward nature and human relationships with the land. On the one hand, the paintings of the Hudson River School aided in constituting natural areas as pristine and as objects of the sublime. Yet, rhetorical scholars Gregory Clark, Michael Halloran, and Allison Woodford (1996) have argued that such portrayals of wilderness depicted nature as separate from human culture; the viewpoint of paintings distanced the human observer by viewing the landscape from above, or in control of nature. They concluded that, although expressing a reverence for the land, such depictions functioned "rhetorically to fuel a process of conquest" (p. 274).

More recently, DeLuca and Demo (2000) have argued that what was left out of landscape photographs of the West may be as important as what was included. They gave the example of early photos of Yosemite Valley taken in the 1860s by the photographer Carleton Watkins. DeLuca and Demo wrote that, when Watkins portrayed Yosemite Valley as wilderness devoid of human signs, he also helped to construct a national myth of pristine nature that was harmful. In a critique of the implicit rhetoric of such scenes, they argued that the "ability of whites to rhapsodize about Yosemite as paradise, the original Garden of Eden, depended on the forced removal and forgetting of the indigenous inhabitants of the area for the past 3,500 years" (p. 254). Writer Rebecca Solnit (1992) has pointed out, "The West wasn't empty, it was emptied—literally by expeditions like the Mariposa Battalion [which killed and/or relocated the native inhabitants of Yosemite Valley in the 1850s], and figuratively by the sublime images of a virgin paradise created by so many painters, poets, and photographers" (p. 56, quoted in DeLuca & Demo, p. 256).

Whether or not one agrees with DeLuca and Demo's claim about the impact of Watkins's photos, it is important to note that images often play pivotal roles in shaping perceptions of natural areas and—with recent visual awareness of the impacts of pollution and toxic waste—peoples and human communities. As DeLuca and Demo (2000) argue, *visual* portrayals often are "enmeshed in a turbulent stream of multiple and conflictual discourses that shape what these images mean in particular contexts"; indeed, in many ways such pictures *constitute* "the context in which a politics takes place—they are creating a reality" (p. 242).

A striking example of the capacity of photographs to construct a "context in which politics take place" occurred recently during debate about the opening of the Arctic National Wildlife Refuge to oil drilling.

Photography and the Arctic National Wildlife Refuge

In October 2000, a 33-year-old physicist named Subhankar Banerjee, a native of Calcutta, India, cashed his savings and left his job at the Boeing Company in Seattle, Washington, to begin a two-year project to photograph the seasons and the biodiversity of Alaska's Arctic National Wildlife Refuge. His project, which took him on a 4,000-mile journey by foot, kayak, and snowmobile through the wildlife refuge in winter as well as summer, culminated in a collection of stunning photographs that were published in his book *Arctic National Wildlife Refuge: Seasons of Life and Land* (2003). (For a sample of the photographs and description of Banerjee's project, see www .wwbphoto.com.)

Banerjee hoped that his book of photographs would educate the public about threats to the future of Alaska's remote refuge. The Smithsonian Museum in Washington, D.C., had scheduled a major exhibition of Banerjee's photos for spring 2003. However, the young scientist-photographer suddenly found his photos and the Smithsonian exhibit caught in the midst of a political controversy. During a March 18, 2003, debate in the U.S. Senate about oil drilling in the Arctic National Wildlife Refuge, Senator Barbara Boxer of California urged every senator to visit Banerjee's exhibit at the Smithsonian "before calling the refuge a frozen wasteland" (Egan, 2003, p. A20). The vote to open the refuge to oil drilling later failed by four votes—52 to 48.

Although Banerjee's photos were certainly not the only influence on the Senate's vote, the controversy over the photos caused a political firestorm and helped to create a context for debate over the refuge itself. *Washington Post* writer Timothy Egan (2003) reported that Banerjee had been told by the Smithsonian that "the museum had been pressured to cancel or sharply revise the exhibit" (p. A20). Documents from the museum give an idea of the changes. Egan reported:

> For a picture of the Romanzof Mountains, the original caption quoted Mr. Banerjee as saying, "The refuge has the most beautiful landscape I have ever seen and is so remote and untamed that many peaks, valleys and lakes are still without names." The new version says, "Unnamed Peak, Romanzof Mountains." . . . Shortly after the [failed] vote, the Smithsonian . . . sent a letter to the publisher, saying that the Smithsonian no longer had any connection to Mr. Banerjee's work. (p. A20)

After attorneys for the museum insisted that he remove all mention of the Smithsonian from his book, Banerjee spoke to reporters. "I was told that my work was just too political" (Bailey, 2003, p. 16). In fact, museum staff had objected that his photos and their captions constituted advocacy: "'We do not engage in advocacy,' said Randall Kremer, a museum spokesman. 'And some of the captions bordered on advocacy'" (Egan, 2003, p. A20).

In one important sense, Kremer's criticism of Banerjee's photographs was correct. Photographs may be powerful rhetorical statements and, as DeLuca and Demo (2000) argued, they can constitute a context for understanding and judgment. Especially when accompanied by captions that encourage a particular meaning, photos can embody a range of symbolic resources that sustain or challenge prevailing viewpoints. Some observers felt that Banerjee's photos of Alaska's wilderness had this potential. A book reviewer for the *Planet* in Jackson Hole, Wyoming, observed of these photos, "Sometimes pictures have a chance to change history by creating a larger understanding of a subject, thus enlightening the public and bringing greater awareness to an issue" (Review, 2003).

The images of drowning polar bears, 19th-century photographs of the "pristine" West, and Banerjee's scenes of Alaska's wildlife and indigenous peoples help to constitute a context of meaning and implicitly embody multiple streams of discourses. As a result, visual media's ability to affect contexts of understanding and appreciation exemplify well what I earlier described as the constitutive role of rhetorical agency.

SUMMARY

Over the centuries, people have described their relations to the environment in dramatically different ways—"a hideous and desolate wilderness," "pristine," and "the places where we live and work." These meanings have been the subject of political debate, art, advertising, scientific research, and fantasy. Whatever else they may be, *nature* and *environment* are powerful ideas whose meanings are always being defined and contested.

In the first section of this chapter, we described four historical periods in which individuals and groups challenged prevailing definitions of the environment. We called these *antagonisms*, which reveal limits of the prevailing views of society:

1. The late 19th- and early 20th-century questioning of nature as repugnant by advocates wishing to *preserve* the wilderness and others who articulated an ethic of *conservation* or efficient use of natural resources

2. The growth of an ecology movement in the 1960s and 1970s, which criticized a system of poorly regulated industrial behavior that contributed to human health problems from chemical contamination and other forms of air and water pollution

3. A community-based movement for environmental justice in the 1980s that challenged mainstream views of nature as "a place apart" from the places where people work, live, learn, and play

4. A growing, multinational movement to alter societies' "business as usual" model of economic growth in the face of global climate change

In the second section, we developed a rhetorical perspective by looking at the *pragmatic* and *constitutive* efforts by different forces to influence society through the distinctly human modes of communication available to us—persuasion, public debate, art, and other modes of symbolic action. Related to idea of the social/symbolic construction of environment are two other concepts: *discourse* and *symbolic legitimacy boundaries*. Discourses are the recurring patterns of speech or systems of representation that circulate a coherent set of meanings; they may achieve a dominant status in society when they coalesce around particular viewpoints and naturalize a way of behaving toward the environment. Closely related to the work of dominant discourses are *symbolic legitimacy boundaries*. These are the symbolic associations—words, metaphors, images, and other sources of meaning—that encourage perceptions of a policy, idea, or institution as reasonable or acceptable.

Finally, we explored some of the ways in which visual rhetoric such as art and photographs embody symbolic resources that can shape our perceptions of nature. As we saw in the photographs of polar bears, a "pristine" West, and scenes of Alaska, visual rhetorics may impart an ideological disposition toward specific definitions of nature and thereby help to constitute the context in which political decisions take place.

While the examples of communication in this chapter illustrate the social and discursive *constructions* of nature and the environment, they occur in concrete places and contexts. Therefore, in the next chapter we expand our view of environmental communication in the public sphere by looking at some of these contexts and the legal guarantees that empower ordinary citizens to speak for or about the environment.

KEY TERMS

Communication-Related Concepts

Antagonism: Recognition of the limit of an idea, a widely shared viewpoint, or an ideology that allows an opposing idea or belief system to be voiced.

Apocalyptic narrative: A literary style used by some environmental writers to warn of impending and severe ecological crises; evokes a sense of the end of the world as a result of the overweening desire to control nature.

Common sense: What people assume to be the views of "everybody," or what is generally agreed to be true; a source of legitimacy.

Condensation symbol: Graber (1976) defined a condensation symbol as a word or phrase that "stirs vivid impressions involving the listener's most basic values" (p. 289); political scientist Murray Edelman (1964) stressed the ability of such symbols to "condense into one symbolic event or sign" powerful emotions, memories, or anxieties (p. 6).

Discourse: A pattern of speaking, writing, or other symbolic action that results from multiple sources. Discourse functions to circulate a coherent set of meanings about an important topic.

Dominant discourse: A discourse that has gained broad or taken-for-granted status in a culture; for example, the belief that growth is good for the economy; its meanings help to legitimize certain policies or practices.

Environmental melodrama: A genre used to clarify issues of power and the ways advocates "moralize" an environmental conflict. As a genre, melodrama "generates stark, polarizing distinctions between social actors and infuses those distinctions with moral gravity and pathos," and is therefore "a powerful resource for rhetorical invention" (Schwarze, 2006, p. 239).

Insurgent discourse: Modes of representation that challenge society's taken-for-granted assumptions and offer alternatives to prevailing discourses.

Jeremiad: Originally named for the "lamentations" of the Hebrew prophet Jeremiah, the jeremiad refers to speech or writing that laments or denounces the behavior of a people or society and warns of future consequences if society does not change its ways.

Legitimacy: A right to exercise authority.

Metaphor: One of the major tropes; "Mother Nature," "Spaceship Earth," "population bomb," and the "web of life" are just a few examples. A metaphor's function is to invite a comparison by "talking about one thing in terms of another."

Public interest: The symbolic marker of legitimacy for actions that are taken in the name of the nation's people or the common good.

Rhetoric: The faculty (power) of discovering the available means of persuasion in the particular case.

Rhetorical genres: A distinct form or type of speech that share characteristics distinguishing them from other rhetorical genres.

Rhetorical perspective: A focus on purposeful and consequential efforts to influence society's attitudes and ways of behaving through communication, which includes public debate, protests, news stories, advertising, and other modes of symbolic action.

Social/symbolic perspective: Describes the social and discursive *constructions* that influence our understanding of nature; it focuses on the sources which help to constitute or shape our perceptions of what we consider to be "natural" or an environmental "problem."

Sublime: An aesthetic category that associates God's influence with the feelings of awe and exultation that some experience in the presence of wilderness.

Sublime response: Term used to denote (1) the immediate awareness of a sublime object (such as Yosemite Valley), (2) a sense of overwhelming personal insignificance and awe in its presence, and (3) ultimately a feeling of spiritual exaltation.

Symbolic legitimacy boundaries: The symbolic associations that politicians, businesses, and the public attach to a proposal, policy, or person; such boundaries define a particular policy, idea, or institution as reasonable, appropriate, or acceptable.

Terministic screens: The means whereby our language orients us to see certain things, some aspects of the world and not others. Defined by literary theorist Kenneth Burke (1966) to mean "if any given terminology is a *reflection* of reality; by its very nature as a terminology it must be a *selection* of reality; and to this extent it must function also as a *deflection* of reality."

Tropes: Sometimes called "figures of speech," tropes refer to the uses of language that "turn" a meaning from its original sense in a new direction.

Visual rhetoric: The capacity of visual images and representations to influence public attitudes toward objects such as the environment.

Environment-Related Concepts

Business as usual (BAU): The continued growth of carbon-based economies. "Carbon based" refers to the energy sources—primarily, fossil fuels or the burning of oil, coal, and natural gas—used to produce electricity, fuel transportation and heating, and power other dimensions of modern life.

Conservation: The term used by early 20th-century forester Gifford Pinchot to mean the wise and efficient use of natural resources.

Direct action: Physical acts of protest such as road blockades, sit-ins, and tree spiking.

Dominant Social Paradigm (DSP): A dominant discursive tradition of several centuries that has sustained attitudes of human dominance over nature. The DSP affirms society's belief in economic growth and its faith in technology, limited government, and private property.

Environmental justice: The basic right of all people to be free of poisons and other hazards. At its core, environmental justice also was a vision of the democratic inclusion of people and communities in the decisions that affected their health and well-being.

Environmental racism (and more broadly, environmental injustice): Refers not only to threats to communities' health from hazardous waste landfills, incinerators, agricultural pesticides, sweatshops, and polluting factories, but also the disproportionate burden that these practices placed on people of color and the workers and residents of low-income communities.

National Environmental Policy Act (NEPA): Requires every federal agency to prepare an environmental impact statement and invite public comment on any project that would affect the environment. Signed into law by President Richard M. Nixon on January 1, 1970, NEPA is the cornerstone of modern environmental law.

New Environmental Paradigm (NEP): An insurgent discourse emerging in popularity after Earth Day 1970, which emphasizes beliefs and values such as "the inevitability of 'limits to growth,' . . . the importance of preserving the 'balance of nature,' and the need to reject the anthropocentric notion that nature exists solely for human use" (Dunlap & Van Liere, 1978, p. 10).

Preservationism: The movement to ban commercial use of wilderness areas and to preserve wild forests and other natural areas for appreciation, study, and outdoor recreation.

Principles of Environmental Justice: Sixteen principles adopted by delegates at the First National People of Color Environmental Leadership Summit in 1991 that enumerated a series of rights, including "the fundamental right to political, economic, cultural, and environmental self-determination of all peoples."

Superfund: Legislation enacted in 1980 authorizing the Environmental Protection Agency to clean up toxic sites and hold the responsible parties accountable for the costs.

Transcendentalism: Belief that a correspondence exists between a higher realm of spiritual truth and a lower one of material objects, including nature.

Tree spiking: The practice of driving metal or plastic spikes or nails into trees in an area that is scheduled to be logged, to discourage the cutting of the trees.

Utilitarianism: Theory that the aim of action should be the greatest good for the greatest number.

DISCUSSION QUESTIONS

1. Is wilderness merely a symbolic construction? Does this matter?

2. Are *apocalyptic* warnings about global warming an effective form of pragmatic rhetoric, or does use of this genre create problems of credibility? How can scientists raise awareness of future, serious effects from climate changes—rising sea levels, regional conflicts, and so on—without relying on visions of apocalypse?

3. Do environmental problems exist before they are named as a problem? How do you explain the fact that not everybody agrees that global warming is a problem?

4. How would you characterize the dominant discourse about the environment today? Have popular discourses about the environment changed in recent years?

5. Do visual media function rhetorically to construct an ideological orientation toward nature or the environment? What examples can you give?

NOTES

1. This attitude of dominance was evident in the actions of officials in the U.S. government in their treatment of nature and Native Americans in the West. Helvarg (1994) recounts the strategy of elimination of Western tribes and animals they relied on: "Between 1600 and 1890 . . . more than two hundred major battles would be fought between indigenous groups and the settlers, some four hundred treaties signed and broken, and three-quarters of the Native American population destroyed. . . . [T]he Europeans' utilitarian approach to nature . . . included . . . resource denial ('Kill a buffalo, starve an Indian' was a motto favored by General George Crook's cavalry forces in the West). The near elimination of the buffalo was part of a strategic belief that it was "God's will that man [sic] exploit nature for his proper ends" (p. 1205). Such repugnance for nature provided fertile soil as it nurtured, along with the growth of commerce in a young nation, a dominant language that saw wild nature as a commodity to be conquered and exploited.

2. In 1872, President Ulysses S. Grant signed a law designating 2 million acres for Yellowstone National Park, the nation's first national park. And 13 years later, the state of New York set aside 715,000 acres for a forest preserve in its Adirondack Mountains. Still, these first acts were less motivated by an aesthetic or spiritual appreciation of wilderness than by a desire to protect against land speculation and, in the case of New York, a need to protect the forest watersheds for New York City's drinking water (Nash, 2001, p. 108).

3. Tree spiking is the practice of driving spikes or long nails into some trees in an area that is scheduled to be logged. (The metal—or, sometimes, plastic—spikes do not actually hurt the trees.) Tree spiking can discourage loggers from cutting the trees because of possible damage to their chain saws or, later, to the machinery in timber mills when saw blades strike the (hidden) spikes.

4. The 1971 Urban Environment Conference (UEC) was one of the first successful efforts to link environmental and social justice concerns. A coalition formed by Senator Philip Hart of Michigan, the UEC sought "to help broaden the way the public defined environmental issues and to focus on the particular environmental problems of urban minorities" (Gottlieb, 1993a, pp. 262–263; Kazis & Grossman, 1991, 247). I address this history in more detail in Chapter 8.

5. Although the State of North Carolina completed the landfill in Warren County in 1982, local activists persisted in calling for its detoxification. Two decades later, in 2004, their efforts finally paid off when the state cleaned up the landfill.

6. One of the pivotal moments for governments to act will occur shortly after this book goes to press, at the United Nations Climate Conference (www.cop15.dk/en) in Copenhagen, Denmark, in late 2009.

REFERENCES

Alston, D. (1990). *We speak for ourselves: Social justice, race, and environment.* Washington, DC: Panos Institute.

As arctic sea ice melts, experts expect new low. (2008, August 28). *The New York Times,* p. A16.

Axelrod, R. S., Downie, D. L., & Vig, N. J. (2004). *The global environment: Institutions law & policy* (2nd ed.). Washington, DC: CQ Press.

Bailey, H. (2003, May 5). Pictures of controversy: The Smithsonian. *Newsweek,* p. 16.

Banerjee, S. (2003). *Arctic National Wildlife Refuge: Seasons of life and land.* Seattle: Mountaineer Books.

Bercovitch, S. (1978). *The American jeremiad.* Madison: University of Wisconsin Press.

Braasch, G. (2007). *Earth under fire: How global warming is changing the world.* Berkeley: University of California Press.

Bradford, W. (1952). *Of Plymouth plantation, 1620–1647.* (S. E. Morison, Ed.). New York: Knopf. (Originally published 1898)

Bullard, R., & Wright, B. H. (1987). Environmentalism and the politics of equity: Emergent trends in the black community. *Midwestern Review of Sociology, 12,* 21–37.

Burke, K. (1966). *Language as symbolic action: Essays on life, literature, and method.* Berkeley: University of California Press.

Campbell, K. K., & Huxman, S. S. (2003). *The rhetorical act* (3rd ed.). Belmont, CA: Thomson Wadsworth.

Carson, R. (1962). *Silent spring.* Greenwich, CT: Fawcett Crest.

Clark, G., Halloran, M., & Woodford, A. (1996). Thomas Cole's vision of "nature" and the conquest theme in American culture. In C. G. Herndl & S. C. Brown (Eds.), *Green culture: Environmental rhetoric in contemporary America* (pp. 261–280). Madison: University of Wisconsin Press.

Climate Ark. (2008, April 23). *Apocalyptic climate and global ecological warnings justified.* Retrieved November 26, 2008, from http://www.climateark.org.

Clinton, W. J. (1994, February 16). Federal actions to address environmental justice in minority populations and low-income communities. Executive Order 12898 of February 14, 1996. *Federal Register, 59,* 7629.

Cole, L. W., & Foster, S. R. (2001). *From the ground up: Environmental racism and the rise of the environmental justice movement.* New York: New York University Press.

Cox, J. R. (1980). Loci communes and Thoreau's arguments for wilderness in "Walking" (1851). *Southern Speech Communication Journal, 26,* 1–16.

Cronon, W. (1996). The trouble with wilderness, or, getting back to the wrong nature. In W. Cronon (Ed.), *Uncommon ground: Rethinking the human place in nature* (pp. 69–90). New York: Norton.

DeLuca, K., & Demo, A. T. (2000). Imaging nature: Watkins, Yosemite, and the birth of environmentalism. *Critical Studies in Mass Communication, 17,* 241–260.

Depoe, S. P. (2006). Preface. In S. P. Depoe (Ed.), *The environmental communication yearbook* (Vol. 3, pp. vii–ix). London: Routledge.

Di Chiro, G. (1996). Nature as community: The convergence of environment and social justice. In W. Cronon (Ed.), *Uncommon ground: Rethinking the human place in nature* (pp. 298–320). New York: Norton.

Dunlap, R. E., & Van Liere, K. D. (1978). The "new environmental paradigm": A proposed instrument and preliminary analysis. *Journal of Environmental Education, 9,* 10–19.

Dunlap, R. E., Van Liere, K. D., Mertig, A. G., & Jones, R. E. (2000). Measuring enforcement of the new ecological paradigm: A revised NEP scale. *Journal of Social Sciences, 56,* 425–442.

Edelman, M. (1964). *The symbolic uses of politics.* Urbana: University of Illinois Press.

Eder, K. (1996a). *The social construction of nature.* London: Sage.

Eder, K. (1996b). The institutionalization of environmentalism: Ecological discourse and the second transformation of the public sphere. In S. Lash, B. Szerszynski, & B. Wynne (Eds.), *Risk, environment, and modernity: Towards a new ecology* (pp. 203–223). London: Sage.

Egan, T. (2003, May 3). Smithsonian is no safe haven for exhibit on Arctic Wildlife Refuge. *The New York Times,* p. A20.

Ehrlich, P. R. (1968). *The population bomb.* San Francisco: Sierra Club Books.

Evernden, N. (1992). *The social creation of nature.* Baltimore: Johns Hopkins University Press.

Fiske, J. (1987). *Television culture.* London: Methuen.

Flannery, T. (2005). *The weather makers: How man is changing the climate and what it means for life on earth.* New York: Grove Press.

Flippen, J. B. (2003). Richard Nixon and the triumph of environmentalism. In L. S. Warren (Ed.), *American environmental history* (pp. 272–289). Oxford, UK: Basil Blackwell.

Francesconi, R. A. (1982). James Hunt, the Wilmington 10, and institutional legitimacy. *Quarterly Journal of Speech, 68,* 47–59.

Fuller, B. (1963). *Operating manual for spaceship earth.* New York: Dutton.

Gerrad, M. B., & Foster, S. R. (Eds.). (2008). *The law of environmental justice* (2nd ed.). Chicago: American Bar Association.

Gottlieb, R. (1993a). *Forcing the spring: The transformation of the American environmental movement.* Washington, DC: Island Press.

Gottlieb, R. (1993b). Reconstructing environmentalism: Complex movements, diverse roots. *Environmental History Review, 17*(4), 1–19.

Gottlieb, R. (2002). *Environmentalism unbound: Exploring new pathways for change.* Cambridge, MA: MIT Press.

Graber, D. A. (1976). *Verbal behavior and politics.* Urbana: University of Illinois Press.

Hamilton, A. (1925). *Industrial poisons in the United States.* New York: Macmillan.

Haraway, D. (1991). *Simians, cyborgs, and women: The reinvention of nature.* New York: Routledge.

Hariman, R., & Lucaites, J. L. (2002). Performing civic identity: The iconic photograph of the flag raising on Iwo Jima. *Quarterly Journal of Speech, 88,* 363–392.

Hariman, R., & Lucaites, J. L. (2003). Public identity and collective memory in U.S. iconic photography: The image of "accidental napalm." *Critical Studies in Media Communication, 20,* 35–66.

Harold, C., & DeLuca, K. M. (2005). Behold the corpse: Violent images and the case of Emmett Till. *Rhetoric & Public Affairs, 8*(2), 263–286.

Hawken, P. (2007). *Blessed unrest: How the largest social movement in history is restoring grace, justice, and beauty to the world.* New York: Penguin Books.

Hawken, P., Lovins, A., & Lovins, L. H. (1999). *Natural capitalism: Creating the next industrial revolution.* New York: Back Bay Books.

Hays, S. P. (1989). *Beauty, health, and permanence: Environmental politics in the United States, 1955–1985.* Cambridge, UK: Cambridge University Press.

Helvarg, D. (1994). *The war against the greens: The "wise use" movement, the new right, and anti-environmental violence.* San Francisco: Sierra Club Books.

Herndl, C. G., & Brown, S. C. (1996). Introduction. In C. G. Herndl & S. C. Brown (Eds.), *Green culture: Environmental rhetoric in contemporary America* (pp. 3–20). Madison: University of Wisconsin Press.

Herrick, J. A. (2009). *The history and theory of rhetoric: An introduction.* Boston: Pearson.

Hill, J. (2002). *One makes the difference: Inspiring actions that change our world.* New York: HarperOne.

Intergovernmental Panel on Climate Change. (2007). *Climate change 2007: Synthesis report.* United Nations Environment Program. Retrieved November 2, 2008, from www. ipcc.ch/ipccreports.

Iredale, W. (2005, December 18). Polar bears drown as ice shelf melts. *The Sunday Times* (UK). Retrieved November 8, 2008, from http://www.timesonline.co.uk.

Jamieson, K. H., & Stromer-Galley, J. (2001). Hybrid genres. In T. O. Sloane (Ed.), *Encyclopedia of rhetoric* (pp. 361–363). Oxford, UK: Oxford University Press.

Jasinski, J. (2001). *Sourcebook on rhetoric: Key concepts in contemporary rhetorical studies.* Thousand Oaks, CA: Sage.

Kazis, R., & Grossman, R. L. (1991). *Fear at work: Job blackmail, labor and the environment* (New ed.). Philadelphia: New Society.

Kendall, B. E. (2008). Personae and natural capitalism: Negotiating politics and constituencies in a rhetoric of sustainability. *Environmental Communication: A Journal of Nature and Culture, 2,* 59–77.

Killingsworth, M. J., & Palmer, J. S. (1996). Millennial ecology: The apocalyptic narrative from *Silent Spring* to Global Warming. In C. G. Herndl & S. C. Brown (Eds.), *Green culture: Environmental rhetoric in contemporary America* (pp. 21–45). Madison: University of Wisconsin Press.

Kinsella, W. J. (2008). Introduction: Narratives, rhetorical genres, and environmental conflict: Responses to Schwarze's "environmental melodrama." *Environmental Communication: A Journal of Nature and Culture, 2,* 78–79.

Klein, N. (2000). *No logo: Taking aim at brand bullies.* New York: Picador.

Laclau, E., & Mouffe, C. (2001). *Hegemony and socialist strategy: Toward a radical democracy* (2nd ed.). London: Verso.

Latour, B. (2004). *Politics of nature: How to bring science into democracy.* (C. Porter, Tr.). Cambridge, MA: Harvard University Press. (Originally published 1999. Paris: Editions la Découverte)

Lee, C. (1996). Environment: Where we live, work, play, and learn. *Race, Poverty, and the Environment, 6,* 6.

Lindzen, R. (2006, April 12). Climate of fear: Global-warming alarmists intimidate dissenting scientists into silence. *The Wall Street Journal.* Retrieved February 28, 2009, from http://www.opinionjournal.com.

Lovelock, J. (2006, January 16). The earth is about to catch a morbid fever that may last as long as 100,000 years. [London] *The Independent.* Retrieved November 26, 2008, from http://www.independent.co.uk/opinion.

M., R. (2003, May/June). Tuna meltdown. *Sierra, 88*(3), 15.

Merchant, C. (2005). *The Columbia guide to American environmental history.* New York: Columbia University Press.

Miller, C. (2004). *Gifford Pinchot and the making of modern environmentalism.* Washington, DC: Island Press/Shearwater Books.

Nash, R. F. (2001). *Wilderness and the American mind* (4th ed.). New Haven: Yale University Press.

Olson, L. C., Finnegan, C. A., & Hope, D. S. (Eds.). (2008). *Visual rhetoric: A reader in communication and American culture.* Thousand Oaks, CA: Sage.

Oravec, C. (1981). John Muir, Yosemite, and the sublime response: A study in the rhetoric of preservationism. *Quarterly Journal of Speech, 67,* 245–258.

Oravec, C. (1984). Conservationism vs. preservationism: The "public interest" in the Hetch Hetchy controversy. *Quarterly Journal of Speech, 70,* 444–458.

Oreskes, N. (2004, December 3). Beyond the ivory tower: The scientific consensus on climate change. *Science, 306*(5702), 1686.

Palmer, M. J. (2007, Autumn). Court rejects bid to weaken the "Dolphin Safe" label. *Earth Island Journal.* Retrieved November 7, 2008, from http://findarticles.com/p/article.

Park, C. C. (2001). *The environment: Principles and applications.* London: Routledge.

Parsons, T. (1958). Authority, legitimation, and political action. In C. Friedrich (Ed.), *Authority* (pp. 197–221). Cambridge, MA: Harvard University.

Pezzullo, P. C. (2001). Performing critical interruptions: Rhetorical invention and narratives of the environmental justice movement. *Western Journal of Communication, 64,* 1–25.

Pirages, D. C., & Ehrlich, P. R. (1974). *Ark II: Social response to environmental imperatives.* San Francisco: Freeman.

Proceedings: The first national people of color environmental leadership summit. (1991, October 24–27). Washington, DC: United Church of Christ Commission for Racial Justice.

Review. (2003, June 5). Subhankar Banerjee, Arctic National Wildlife Refuge: Seasons of Life and Land. *Planet* (Jackson Hole, WY). Retrieved July 17, 2004, from www.mountaineersbooks.org.

Roberts, J. T. (2007). Globalizing environmental justice. In R. Sandler & P. C. Pezzullo (Eds.), *Environmental justice and environmentalism: The social justice challenge to the environmental* movement (pp. 285–307). Cambridge, MA: MIT Press.

Rosenthal, E. (2007, November 17). U.N. report describes risks of inaction on climate change. *The New York Times.* Retrieved November 3, 2008, from www.nytimes.com.

Ross, A. (1994). *The Chicago gangster theory of life: Nature's debt to society.* London: Verso.

Russill, C. (2008). Tipping point forewarnings in climate change communication: Some implications of an emerging trend. *Environmental Communication: A Journal of Nature and Culture, 2,* 133–153.

Sale, K. (1993). *The green revolution: The American environmental movement 1962–1992.* New York: Hill & Wang.

Sandler, R., & Pezzullo, P. C. (Eds.). (2007). *Environmental justice and environmentalism: The social justice challenge to the environmental movement.* Cambridge, MA: MIT Press.

Schueler, D. (1992). Southern exposure. *Sierra, 77,* 45–47.

Schulzke, E. C. (2000, March 26). *Policy networks and regulatory change in the 104th Congress: Framing the center through symbolic legitimacy conflict.* Paper presented at the meeting of the Western Political Science Association, San Jose, CA.

Schwarze, S. (2006). Environmental melodrama. *Quarterly Journal of Speech, 92*(3), 239–261.

Solnit, R. (1992). Up the river of mercy. *Sierra, 77,* 50, 53–58, 78, 81, 83–84.

Spiess, B., & Ruskin, L. (2001, November 4). 2,000-acre query: ANWR bill provision caps development, but what does it mean? *Anchorage Daily News.* Retrieved April 13, 2004, from www.adn.com.

Stone, D. (2002). *Policy paradox: The art of political decision making* (Rev. ed.). New York: Norton.

Taylor, B. C. (2003). "Our bruised arms hung up as monuments": Nuclear iconography in post-cold war culture. *Critical Studies in Media Communication, 20,* 1–34.

Thoreau, H. D. (1893). Walking. In *Excursions: The writings of Henry David Thoreau* (Riverside ed., Vol. 9, pp. 251–304). Boston: Houghton Mifflin. (Original work published 1862)

Tindall, D. B. (1995). What is environmental sociology? An inquiry into the paradigmatic status of environmental sociology. In M. D. Mehta & E. Ouellet (Eds.), *Environmental sociology: Theory and practice* (pp. 33–59). North York, Ontario, Canada: Captus Press.

Waddell, C. (Ed.). (2000). *And no birds sing: Rhetorical analyses of* Silent Spring. Carbondale: Southern Illinois University Press.

Warren, L. S. (Ed.). (2003). *American environmental history.* Oxford, UK: Basil Blackwell.

White House. (2002, August 22). *President announces Healthy Forest Initiative.* Office of the Press Secretary. Retrieved June 24, 2003, from www.whitehouse.gov.

White, L., Jr. (1967). The historical roots of our ecological crisis. *Science, 155,* 1203–1207.

Wigglesworth, M. (1662). God's controversy with New England. In *Proceedings of the Massachusetts Historical Society, 12* (1871), p. 83, in Nash (2001), p. 36.

Wolfe, D. (2008). The ecological jeremiad, the American myth, and the vivid force of color in Dr. Seuss's *The Lorax. Environmental Communication: A Journal of Nature and Culture, 2,* 3–24.

PART II

Citizen Voices
and Public Forums

WASHINGTON—August 4, 2008: The National Highway Traffic Safety Administration hears public comments on the environmental impacts of its proposed fuel economy standards for 2011–2015 model cars and light trucks.

© Chip Somodevilla/Getty Images.

CHAPTER 3

Public Participation in Environmental Decisions

Make diligent efforts to involve the public. . . .

—U.S. National Environmental Policy Act (1970)

The serious environmental . . . challenges faced by societies worldwide cannot be addressed by public authorities alone without the involvement . . . of a wide range of stakeholders, including individual citizens and civil society organizations.

—Aarhus Convention, Riga, Latvia (*Aarhus Parties,* 2008)

One of the most striking features of the political landscape since the 1990s has been the dramatic increase in participation by ordinary citizens, scientists, environmental groups, and others in decisions about the environment. Environmental historian Samuel Hays (2000) noted that people have been "enticed, cajoled, educated, and encouraged to become active in learning, voting, and supporting [environmental] legislation . . . as well as to write, call, fax, or e-mail decision makers at every stage of the decision-making process." Hays explained that all this has been "a major contribution to a fundamental aspect of the American political system—*public participation*" (p. 194; emphasis added). Such involvement by the public often has been the critical element in efforts to protect threatened wildlife habitats, achieve cleaner air and water, and ensure a safer workplace.

And not just in the United States: At its 2008 meeting in Latvia, European nations reaffirmed the goals of the Aarhus Convention, guaranteeing the rights of access to information and participation in decisions about the environment. Marek Belka, executive secretary of the UN Economic Commission for Europe, observed that the convention's core principles "empower ordinary members of the public to hold governments accountable and to play a greater role in promoting more sustainable forms of development" (Aarhus Parties, 2008). Similar moves to implement or strengthen the role of the public in decisions affecting the environment are actively underway in China and central Asia, as well as in many parts of Africa and South America.

Public participation is the belief that "those who are affected by a decision have a right to be involved in the decision-making process" ("Core Values," 2008). This has been especially true of environmental decisions in recent years. This chapter describes some of these legal guarantees and forums for communication that enable citizens to participate actively in decisions about the environment. Here, I define **public participation** more specifically as the ability of individual citizens and groups to influence environmental decisions through (1) access to relevant information, (2) public comments to the agency that is responsible for a decision, and (3) the right, through the courts, to hold public agencies and businesses accountable for their environmental decisions and behaviors.

In this chapter, I focus on developments in the United States and, to a lesser extent, other nations in strengthening the public's right to be involved in decisions about their environments. The first three sections of this chapter identify legal rights that embody these core principles and that have proved particularly important for citizen communication in the United States: (1) the right to know, (2) the right to comment publicly about proposed projects or rules, and (3) the right of **standing** to object to a government agency's actions. Standing is the legal status accorded a citizen who has a sufficient interest in a matter, whereby the citizen may appear in court to protect that interest.

These rights, in turn, reflect more basic, democratic principles of: (1) *transparency*, or openness of governmental actions to public scrutiny, (2) *direct participation* in official decisions, and (3) *accountability*, that is, the requirement that political authority meet agreed-upon norms and standards. (These principles are summarized in Table 3.1.) The fourth section describes in greater detail one of the most

Table 3.1	Modes of Public Participation in Environmental Decisions		
Legal Right	**Mode of Participation**	**Authority**	**Democratic Principle**
Right to Know	Written requests for information; access to documents online, etc.	Freedom of Information Act, Toxic Release Inventory, Clean Water Act, "Sunshine" laws	Transparency
Right to Comment	Testimony at public hearings, participation in advisory committees; written comment (letters, e-mail, etc.)	National Environmental Policy Act	Direct participation
Right of Standing	Plaintiff in lawsuit, *amicus* brief (third party) in legal case	Clean Water Act and other statutes; Supreme Court rulings (*Sierra Club v. Morton,* etc.)	Accountability

commonly used modes of public participation: citizen testimony in public hearings. In the final section, I describe recent developments in Europe and other nations to ensure greater public participation in environmental decisions.

A final note on the focus of this chapter: I describe *federal* law in the United States primarily because the Environmental Protection Agency (EPA) delegates to the states the administration of laws regulating clean air and water; still, these programs remain governed by federal laws ensuring the rights of citizen participation. Finally, information about local pollution sources is often available to any citizen through federal right-to-know laws.

Right to Know: Access to Information

One of the strongest norms of democratic society is the principle of **transparency**. Simply put, this is a belief in *openness* in government and *a right of citizens to know* about information important to their lives. Internationally, this principle gained recognition in the Declaration of Bizkaia, which proclaimed that transparency requires "access to information and the right to be informed. . . . Everyone has the right of access to information on the environment with no obligation to prove a particular interest" (1999). This recognition also illustrates the growing importance of *information*—and who controls it—in shaping environmental policies. As Hays (2000) noted, political power lies increasingly in an ability to understand the complexities of environmental issues, and "the key to that power is information and the expertise and technologies required to command it." As a result, the most interesting political drama of recent years has been "the continued struggle between the environmental community and the environmental opposition over the control of information" (p. 232).

By the late 20th century, moves to ensure transparency in government had begun to reshape public communication about U.S. environmental policy. New **sunshine laws**, intended to shine the light of public scrutiny on the workings of government, required open meetings of most government bodies. And the U.S. Congress threw open the doors to government records more generally. In environmental affairs, the Clean Water Act of 1972 for the first time required federal agencies to provide information on water pollution to the public. And, as we see later, the National Environmental Policy Act of 1970 required all federal agencies to provide environmental impact statements (EIS) about their proposed actions, such as the filling of wetlands, before making a final decision. These EIS reports proved critically important to groups who monitored government agencies.

Two laws in particular have provided important guarantees of the U.S. public's **right to know**—that is, their right of access to information about environmental conditions or actions of government that potentially affect the environment. These are the Freedom of Information Act of 1966 and the Emergency Planning and Community Right to Know Act of 1986, which established the Toxic Release Inventory.

Freedom of Information Act

The move toward greater transparency in government had its roots in an earlier law, the **Administrative Procedure Act (APA)** of 1946. In the 1940s, in response to charges of agency favoritism and corruption, the APA laid out new operating standards for U.S. government agencies. It required that all agency regulations that intended to implement a law be published in the *Federal Register* and that the public be given an opportunity to respond before the action took effect. Nevertheless, there was no accompanying requirement that these agencies make available to the public any records or documents related to their decisions.

As a result of growing public pressure for access to federal documents, Congress passed the **Freedom of Information Act (FOIA)** in 1966. FOIA provides that any person has the right to see the documents and records of any executive branch agency (but not the judiciary or Congress). Agencies whose records are typically requested by reporters, scholars, and environmental groups include the U.S. Forest Service, the Fish and Wildlife Service, the Bureau of Land Management, and the EPA, among others. Upon written request, an agency is required to disclose records relating to the requested topic, unless the agency can claim an exemption from disclosure as allowed by the act. (For a description of these exemptions, see http://www.usdoj.gov.)The FOIA also grants requesting parties who are denied their request the right to appear in federal court to seek the enforcement of the act's provisions.

In 1996, the Congress amended FOIA by passing the **Electronic Freedom of Information Amendments**. The amendments require agencies to provide public access to information in electronic form. This is done typically by posting a guide for making a FOIA request on the agency's Website. (See FYI: How to Make a Request Under FOIA.) Individual states have adopted similar procedures governing public access to the records of state agencies.

☞ FYI   How to Make a Request Under FOIA

For information on the Freedom of Information Act, consult the Reporters Committee for Freedom of the Press's booklet *How to Use the FOIA Act,* at http://www.rcfp.org. Also, see the Environmental Protection Agency's Website (www.epa.gov/foia) for requesting documents under the FOIA.

To request information from another agency, see the Website for that agency. For example, if you want to know what the U.S. Forest Service office in your area has done to enforce the Endangered Species Act in a recent timber sale, go to the Forest Service's Website for FOIA requests (www.fs.fed.us/im/foia/). There you will find instructions for submitting your request for information. The Forest Service site also includes a sample FOIA request letter (http://www.fs.fed.us) and details on FOIA procedures in the Forest Service.

For a list of contacts for all federal agencies, see: http://www.usdoj.gov.

Under the Freedom of Information Act, individuals, public interest groups, scientists, and others routinely gather information from public agencies in the course of monitoring their decisions and enforcement of permits. For example, a local "River Guardians" group might be interested in knowing what a mining company plans to do if its application to mine for gravel near a local river is approved by the Army Corps of Engineers. (The Corps is the federal agency responsible for permits under the Clean Water Act.) Although the application itself is public, the mining company's actual proposal may not be available; as a result, the River Guardians group can request this information by filing a FOIA request. Generally, individuals and environmental groups are interested in activities such as Forest Service management plans, U.S. Coast Guard data on mercury pollution in fish, Fish and Wildlife Service studies of endangered species, the U.S. Department of Defense plans to decommission military bases near a community, and more.

Citizens living in a community contaminated with toxic chemicals also may use the Freedom of Information Act to gather information for a "tort" or legal action against the polluter. An **environmental tort** is a legal claim for injury or a lawsuit, such as those depicted in the films *Erin Brockovich* and *A Civil Action*. In researching such a tort, a group may access information held by the EPA. Under federal law, the EPA is required to maintain records on any company that handles hazardous waste, including notices of permit violations and any legal actions taken against the company. As the group prepares its legal case, it can request all of these documents from the EPA under the agency's procedures for complying with the Freedom of Information Act.

Although an important tool for information, an FOIA request may not always be successful. Despite an executive order by the president in 2006 to speed up responses to FOIA requests by the public, federal agencies appear to be lagging. Recently, a 10-year study by the Coalition of Journalists for Open Government found a serious backlog of requests. Partly due to personnel cuts, "fewer people got all the information they sought than at any time since agency reporting began in 1998. The percent of requesters getting either a full or a partial [response] fell to 60% . . . a record low" (Coalition of Journalists, 2008). In an effort to improve the executive branch's performance in responding to FOIA requests, the U.S. Congress enacted the OPEN Government Act of 2007. This new law sets new standards for timely processing of requests and penalties for improperly withholding information in categories not otherwise exempted. (For the full text of the OPEN Government Act of 2007, see http://www.usdoj.gov.)

Restricting the Right to Know in the Post–9/11 Era

In the immediate aftermath of terrorist attacks on the United States in 2001, the U.S. Congress and the executive branch moved quickly to give new authority to federal law enforcement agencies and intelligence services. However, civil libertarians, public interest groups, and environmentalists soon learned that these actions had troublesome implications for civil society and the Bill of Rights. Historians Gerald

Markowitz and David Rosner (2002) reported that "in the wake of the September 11 attacks, the Bush administration acted to restrict public access to information about polluting industries and restricted journalists' and historians' access to government documents previously available through the Freedom of Information Act" (p. 303).

Scholars and individuals seeking information about environmental topics from sources that were available to the public before September 11, 2001, first noticed a shift in response by federal agencies. For example, *USA Today* reported:

> When United Nations analyst Ian Thomas contacted the National Archives . . . to get some 30-year-old maps of Africa to plan a relief mission, he was told the government no longer makes them public. When John Coequyt, an environmentalist, tried to connect to an online database where the Environmental Protection Agency lists chemical plants that violate pollution laws, he was denied access. (Parker, Johnson, & Locy, 2002, 1A)

In fact, in the eight months following the 9/11 attacks, the federal government removed hundreds of thousands of public documents from its Websites; in other cases, access to material was made more difficult. For example, documents reporting accidents at chemical plants, previously available online from the EPA, were now to be viewed only in government reading rooms (Parker, Johnson, & Locy, 2002).

The move to restrict public access to information gained a significant boost shortly after the first anniversary of the 9/11 attacks, when the U.S. Congress passed the **Homeland Security Act** of 2002. This law contains broad authority for the federal government to take steps to protect national security, including the right to restrict public access to any information that could be used to attack U.S. interests. Although differing political parties and interests agreed that national security measures were needed, the new law posed serious challenges to Americans' civil liberties. Certainly, the chief complaints against the law came from journalists, environmentalists, civil libertarians, and academics. Environmental groups focused particularly on provisions in the Homeland Security Act that permitted exemptions to the Freedom of Information Act.

The FOIA exemptions are in a key provision of the Homeland Security Act, called **Critical Infrastructure Information (CII)**. Wishing to shield information about vulnerabilities in the nation's energy and transportation infrastructure, such as electrical transmission lines, airlines, and oil and gas pipelines, the law authorizes a level of "extraordinary secrecy" (Bruggers, Ward, & Fagin, 2003, n.p.) from public scrutiny. Specifically, the CII section allows any federal agency to deny FOIA requests from journalists, environmental groups, and individuals for federal records of permit violations, fines, or other information about oil refineries, drinking water plants, oil and natural gas pipelines, and so forth. (The OPEN Government Act of 2007 does not restore these provisions.)

The rationale for the secrecy allowed by the Homeland Security Act seemed to make sense to many individuals in the aftermath of the 9/11 terrorist attacks. *USA Today* reporters seemed to capture the nation's mood: "Protecting maps and descriptions of nuclear power plants, hydroelectric dams, pipeline routes and chemical supplies seemed justified, for national security" (Parker, Johnson, & Locy, 2002, n.p.). Nevertheless, many reporters and environmentalists believed that an excessive secrecy also could undermine other vital interests, such as the need for transparency in alerting public agencies to potential safety problems. (For other concerns about the implications of the Homeland Security Act of 2002, see the Society of Environmental Journalists' Website, www.sej.org.)

In summary, the government's response to the attacks of September 11, 2001, although ensuring critical safeguards, also raises serious concerns about the public's access to information. Although intended to limit information useful to terrorists, some of the restrictions on information also limit the ability of journalists and environmental groups to address perceived problems or to publicize inadequate performance by government agencies or private businesses.

Emergency Planning and Community Right to Know Act

In 1984, thousands of people were killed when two separate plants released toxic chemicals—one a Union Carbide plant in Bhopal, India, the other a chemical plant in West Virginia. These two incidents fueled public pressure for accurate information about the production, storage, and release of toxic materials in local communities by such companies. Responding to this pressure, Congress passed the **Emergency Planning and Community Right to Know Act** in 1986, known simply as the Right to Know Act. The law requires industries to report to local and state emergency planners the use and location of specified chemicals at their facilities. (For the text of this law and description of its provisions, see http://www.epa.gov.)

The Toxic Release Inventory

The Right to Know Act also requires the Environmental Protection Agency to collect data annually on any releases of toxic materials into the air and water by designated industries and to make this information easily available to the public through an information-reporting tool, the **Toxic Release Inventory (TRI)**. The goal of the Toxic Release Inventory "is to empower citizens, through information, to hold companies and local governments accountable in terms of how toxic chemicals are managed" (Environmental Protection Agency, 2008). In the 23 years since the TRI debuted, the EPA has expanded its TRI reporting and now collects data on approximately 650 different chemicals (Environmental Protection Agency, 2008). The EPA regularly makes these data available through online tools such as its TRI Explorer (www.epa.gov/triexplorer), although the data tend to lag by two years. Other public interest groups also use the TRI database to offer more user-friendly e-portals for individuals wanting information about the release of toxic materials into the air or water in their local communities. (For an example, see "Act Locally: What Toxic Chemicals Are in Your Community?")

Act Locally!

What Toxic Chemicals Are in Your Community?

Use the Toxic Release Inventory to check for the presence of toxic chemicals in the air, soil, or water in the community where you or your family or friends live, work, or attend school.

To access the TRI database, use the EPA's TRI Explorer (www.epa.gov/triexplorer) or its Environfacts site (http://www.epa.gov/enviro), or the more user-friendly "Scorecard" at www.scorecard.org. Sponsored by Environmental Defense, Scorecard makes it possible for you to send faxes (free) to the polluters in your area or e-mail to state and federal decision makers. Scorecard also links you to volunteer opportunities and directories of environmental organizations in your area.

Also see the EPA's Enforcement and Compliance History Online (ECHO) at www.epa.gov/echo. This site allows you to know, for a specific facility, whether the EPA or state or local governments have conducted inspections at the facility, whether violations were detected or enforcement actions were taken, and whether penalties were assessed in response to environmental law violations.

More recently, the Bush administration eased the rules for industry in reporting their chemical releases into the air and water. The new rule, which became effective in 2007, allows industries to use a shorter, less-detailed form if they store or release less than 5,000 pounds of toxic chemicals. The old rules required full disclose for as little as 500 pounds of chemicals. The rule change ignited a firestorm of criticism from communities and state governments. In late 2007, twelve states sued the Environmental Protection Agency—the agency charged with implementing the Toxic Release Inventory—over the easing of these limits for chemical releases. (For the complete rule, see http://www.epa.gov.)

One reason for opposition to the weakening of the Toxic Release Inventory standards is that many community activists as well as city and state governments believe that TRI may be the single most valuable information tool for ensuring community and industry safety (see Figure 3.1). Indeed, sometimes the disclosure of information by itself may be enough to affect polluters' behavior. For example, Stephan (2002) found that public disclosure of information about a factory's chemical releases or violation of its air or water permit may trigger a **"shock and shame" response.** If community members found out that a local factory was emitting high levels of pollution, their "shock" could push the community into action. Furthermore, Stephan explained that the polluting facility itself (or those who work there) may feel shame from disclosure of its poor performance. However, he conceded another explanation might be that the company fears a backlash from citizens, interest groups, or the market (p. 194).

Calls for the Right of "Independent Expertise"

An important supplement to the Toxic Release Inventory is the right to *independent* expertise about toxic chemicals. Because the effects from exposure to

| Figure 3.1 | The Toxic Release Inventory gives citizens access to information about the presence of many toxic chemicals in their communities. |

Photo courtesy of Getty Royalty Free Images.

toxic chemicals involves complex issues, advocates from communities with toxic waste sites long have sought access to sources of expertise to aid them in understanding the effects of these chemicals. Often, there is a disparity in the expertise that is available to government agencies or industry, on the one hand, and that which is available to local citizens, on the other. That is, local citizens—in affected communities— lack training in toxicology or other environmental sciences that would allow them to assess the government's findings.

In response to this gap, Congress enacted the **Technical Assistance Grant (TAG) Program** in 1986. The TAG program is intended to help communities at **Superfund sites**. (Superfund sites are abandoned chemical waste sites that have qualified for federal funds for their cleanup.) Decisions about the cleanup of these sites are usually based on technical information that includes the type of chemical wastes and the technology available. The purpose of the TAG program is to provide funds for citizen groups to hire consultants; however, these consultants are limited to helping citizens to understand *the information provided by the EPA and the industries responsible for cleaning these sites,* not other sources.

As I learned in working with Superfund communities while I was president of the Sierra Club, the TAG program does not ensure that local citizens actually have a **right to independent expertise**. Such a right would allow the community to seek expertise from independent sources and to use this knowledge to assess the EPA or other government agencies' recommendations. For example, in working with the residents of a small town in Mississippi whose homes bordered an abandoned chemical plant, I learned that their requests to use funds from their TAG program to hire experts to analyze their well water had been denied. They had been dissatisfied with the EPA's plans for cleanup of the toxic waste site and distrusted the data supplied to them by the agency. When they asked for support to consult their own experts, they were told the TAG program did not allow funds for communities to generate *new* (independent) data (C. Keys, 1995, personal communication).

Dissatisfaction with the limits on the EPA funds for hiring experts has led community activists from toxic sites around the country to push for greater flexibility in the use of TAG program to secure independent experts to aid their efforts. (For more information about the EPA's Technical Assistance Grants program, see the "Frequently Asked Questions" about community involvement in decisions about local toxic waste sites at the EPA's Website, http://www.epa.gov.)

Overall, the public's access to information about their environments is an ongoing struggle—to restore access to important categories under the Freedom of Information Act, strengthen the reporting of the Toxic Release Inventory, and gain access to independent sources of expertise about hazards in their communities. Still, these laws have been a major advance for the principle of *transparency* as well as aiding communities in coping with environmental hazards in the United States.

Right of Public Comment

Town hall meetings are a long-standing tradition in the United States. When it comes to the environment, that tradition received a significant boost in 1970, the year millions of citizens first celebrated Earth Day. The National Environmental Policy Act (NEPA) guaranteed that the public would have an opportunity to comment directly to federal agencies such as the Forest Service before the agencies could proceed with any actions affecting the environment. At its core, the new law promised citizens that a kind of "pre-decisional communication" would occur between them and the agency responsible for any decision that affected the environment; the agency must solicit and hear citizens' views before acting (Daniels & Walker, 2001, p. 8).

Public comment typically takes the form of testimony at public hearings, exchanges of views at open houses and workshops, written communications (e-mails, letters, faxes, and research reports), and participation on citizen advisory panels (see Figure 3.2). In this section, I focus on the *right to comment,* provided under the

| Figure 3.2 | Public comment typically takes the form of citizens' testimony at public hearings, exchanges of views at open houses and workshops, and written communications (e-mails and letters). |

© Oleg Prikhodko/istockphoto.

National Environmental Policy Act and under the continuing Executive Order for Environmental Justice, originally issued by President Bill Clinton in 1994. We'll also examine the characteristics—and the limitations—of one of the most common forums for public participation, the "public hearing." I describe the role of citizens' advisory panels and more informal "collaboration" approaches for resolving environmental conflicts in Chapter 4.

National Environmental Policy Act

The core authority for the public's right to comment or participate directly in federal environmental decision making comes from the **National Environmental Policy Act,** commonly referred to as NEPA. Passed by Congress in 1969 and signed into law by President Richard M. Nixon on January 1, 1970, NEPA was the first effort to involve the public in environmental decision making in a comprehensive manner. Political scientists Matthew Lindstrom and Zachary Smith (2001) explained that NEPA's sponsors wanted the public not only to be aware of and informed about projects that might be environmentally damaging but also to have an active role in commenting on alternative actions that an agency had proposed. Thus, NEPA and its regulations "act like other 'sunshine' laws . . . in that they require full disclosure to the public as well as extensive public hearings and opportunities for comment on the proposed action" (p. 94).

Two NEPA requirements are intended to give members of the public an opportunity to communicate about a proposed federal environmental action: (1) a detailed statement of any environmental impacts must be made public, and (2) concrete procedures for public comment must be implemented.

Environmental Impact Statements

As implemented by the Council on Environmental Quality, the National Environmental Policy Act requires federal agencies to prepare a detailed **environmental impact statement (EIS)** for any proposed legislation or major actions "significantly affecting the quality of the human environment" (Council on Environmental Quality [CEQ], 1997, Sec. 102 [1][c]). Such actions range from constructing a highway to adopting a forest management plan. Regardless of the specific action that is proposed, all EISs must describe three things: (1) the environmental impact of the proposed action, (2) any adverse environmental effects that could not be avoided should the proposal be implemented, and (3) alternatives to the proposed action (Sec. 102 [1][c]). (In some cases, a less detailed environmental assessment may be substituted.) Furthermore, NEPA requires that an EIS clearly communicate its meaning to the public:

> Environmental impact statements shall be written in plain language and may use appropriate graphics so that decision makers and the public can readily understand them. Agencies should employ writers of clear prose or editors to write, review, or edit statements, which will be based upon the analysis and supporting data from the natural and social sciences and the environmental design arts. (Sec. 1502.8)

When federal agencies neglect NEPA requirements for an Environmental Impact Statement, they may be subject to legal action. For example, when the U.S. National Park Service recently released an EIS, along with its plan to allow 540 snowmobiles a day into Yellowstone and Grand Teton National Parks in the winter, environmental groups took the agency to court, complaining that its EIS was inadequate. In 2008, a federal judge in Washington, D.C., threw out the plan, agreeing with the groups that allowing 540 snowmobiles into the parks would increase air pollution and disturb wildlife. As a result, the National Park Service must conduct another EIS before deciding how many of the machines can enter the parks (Associated Press, 2008).

Public Comment on Draft Proposals

NEPA also requires that, before an agency completes a detailed statement of environmental impact, it must "make diligent efforts to involve the public" (CEQ, 1997, Sec. 1506.6 [a]). That is, the agency must take steps to ensure that interested groups and members of the public are informed and have opportunities for involvement prior to a decision. As a result, each federal agency must implement specific procedures for public participation in any decisions made by that agency that affect the environment. For example, citizens and groups concerned with natural resource policy ordinarily follow the rules for public comment developed in accordance with NEPA by the U.S. Forest Service, the National Park Service, the Bureau of Land Management, or the Fish and Wildlife Service. Community activists who work with human health and pollution issues are normally guided by Environmental Protection Agency and state rules. The states are relevant because the EPA delegates to them the authority to issue air and water pollution permits for plants and construction permits and rules for managing waste programs (landfills and the like).

The requirements for public comment or communication under NEPA typically occur in three stages: (1) notification, (2) scoping, and (3) comment on draft decisions. These steps are guided by the rules adopted by the Council on Environmental Quality to ensure that all agencies comply with basic requirements for public participation that are implied in the NEPA statute itself. (See "FYI: Requirements for Public Involvement in NEPA.")

☞ **FYI**   **Requirements for Public Involvement in NEPA**

Public Involvement (Section 1506.6): Agencies shall:

(a) Make diligent efforts to involve the public in preparing and implementing their NEPA procedures.

(b) Provide public notice of NEPA-related hearings, public meetings, and the availability of environmental documents so as to inform those persons and agencies who may be interested or affected. . . .

(c) Hold or sponsor public hearings or public meetings whenever appropriate or in accordance with statutory requirements.

Inviting Comments (Section 1503.1 [a] [4]):

(a) After preparing a draft environmental impact statement and before preparing a final environment impact statement, the agency shall . . . (4) Request comments from the public, affirmatively soliciting comments from those persons or organizations who may be interested or affected.

SOURCE: Council on Environmental Quality (http://ceq.hss.doe.gov) and Walker (2004, p. 116).

The process normally starts with publication of a **Notice of Intent (NOI)**, which states the agency's intent to prepare an EIS for a proposed action. The NOI is published in the *Federal Register* and provides a brief description of "the proposed action and possible alternatives" (CEQ, 2007). The NOI may also be announced in the media and in special mailings to interested parties. Typically, a notice describes the proposed regulation, management plan, or action and specifies the location and time of a public meeting or the period during which written comments will be received by the agency. The notice will also "contain an agency point of contact who can answer questions about the proposed action and the NEPA process" (CEQ, 2007, p. 13).

The Notice of Intent also describes the agency's proposed **scoping** process. Scoping is a preliminary stage in an agency's development of a proposed rule or action, including any meetings and how the public can get involved. It involves canvassing interested members of the public about some interest—for example, a plan to reallocate permits for water trips down the Colorado River in the Grand Canyon—to determine what the concerns of the affected parties might be (CEQ, 2007). Such scoping might involve public workshops, field trips, letters, and agency personnel speaking one on one with members of the public.

Finally, NEPA rules require agencies to actively solicit public comment on the draft proposal. Public comments on the draft proposal or action usually occur during public hearings and in written comments to the agency in the form of reports, letters, e-mails, postcards, or faxes. The public also may use this opportunity to comment on the adequacy of any environmental impact statement accompanying the proposal, or it may use the information in the EIS to assess the proposal itself. (For an example of a request for public comment, see: "FYI: Proposed Rule to List the Polar Bear as Threatened.")

 FYI **Proposed Rule to List the Polar Bear as Threatened**

DEPARTMENT OF THE INTERIOR

Fish and Wildlife Service

50 CFR Part 17

RIN 1018–AV19

Endangered and Threatened Wildlife and Plants; 12-Month Petition Finding and Proposed Rule To List the Polar Bear (Ursus maritimus) as Threatened Throughout Its Range

AGENCY: Fish and Wildlife Service, Interior.

ACTION: Proposed rule and notice of 12-month finding.

SUMMARY: We, the U.S. Fish and Wildlife Service (Service), announce a 12-month finding on a petition to list the polar bear (*Ursus maritimus*) as threatened with critical habitat under the Endangered Species Act of 1973, as amended (Act). After review of all available scientific and commercial information, we find that listing the polar bear as a threatened species under the Act is warranted. Accordingly, we herein propose to list the polar bear as threatened throughout its range pursuant to the Act. This proposed rule, if made final, would extend the Act's protections to this species. Critical habitat for the polar bear is not determinable at this time. The Service seeks data and comments from the public on this proposed listing rule.

DATES: We will consider all comments on this proposed rule received by the close of business (5 p.m.) Alaska Local Time on April 9, 2007. Requests for a public hearing must be received by the Service on or before close of business (5 p.m.) Alaska Local Time on February 23, 2007.

SOURCE: *Federal Register*, "Proposed Rules," Vol. 72, No. 5 (January 9, 2007), p. 1064.

In response, the agency is required to assess and consider comments received from the public. It must then respond in one of several ways: (1) by modifying the proposed alternatives, (2) by developing and evaluating new alternatives, (3) by making factual corrections, or (4) by "explain[ing] why the [public] comments do not warrant further agency response" (Sec. 1503.4).

The success of NEPA's public participation process obviously depends on how well agencies comply with the law's original intent. For example, in its study of NEPA's effectiveness, the Council on Environmental Quality observed that

> the success of a NEPA process heavily depends on whether an agency has systematically reached out to those who will be most affected by a proposal, gathered information and ideas from them, and responded to the input by modifying or adding alternatives throughout the entire course of a planning process. (CEQ, 1997, p. 17)

A successful illustration of NEPA's effectiveness occurred in 2001 when the Clinton administration announced its sweeping "roadless rule." The rule, adopted by the U.S. Forest Service, prohibited road building and restricted commercial logging on nearly 60 million acres of U.S. national forest lands in 39 states, including Alaska's Tongass National Forest. The final rule was adopted on January 5, 2001, after a year and a half of public review and comment. (Here, I must admit a personal interest, having participated as president of the national Sierra Club in helping to mobilize individuals to participate in the public comment process. A more critical review of the process used in the roadless rule can be found in Walker, 2004).

By the end of the process, the U.S. Forest Service had held more than 600 public meetings and had received an unprecedented 2 million comments from members of the public, environmentalists, businesspeople, sports groups and motorized recreation associations, local residents, and state and local officials. As a result of the public's review and comment on successive drafts, the rule grew stronger, expanding the amount of protected forest land. After the final rule was adopted, Forest Service chief Mike Dombeck reflected, "In my entire career, this is the most extensive outreach of any policy I've observed" (Marston, 2001, p. 12, in Walker, 2004, p. 114). (For the final roadless rule, see http://roadless.fs.fed.us.)

Following its adoption, the Clinton roadless rule has been both praised and criticized for its public participation process, and its implementation initially was delayed by court challenges from logging interests and western state officials. (In May 2005, the Bush administration dropped the roadless rule altogether after a hasty NEPA process. Environmental groups have challenged this ruling, and the case continues to be argued in the federal courts; they are also urging President Barack Obama to implement the roadless rule fully, as this book goes to press.) At the heart of the controversy has been a fierce debate over the meaning of public participation and the goals it is intended to serve. Walker asks, "Does the number of public meetings and amount of comment letters received provide sufficient evidence of meaningful public participation?" (p. 115). I take up this question more generally in the next chapter by describing some of the criticisms of public comment in environmental decision making.

The Executive Order on Environmental Justice

A less successful source for the right of public comment is President Clinton's 1994 **Executive Order on Environmental Justice.** Shortly after entering office, the president directed all federal agencies to "study the impact of proposed actions [permits for plants, and so forth] related to the environment and public health on minority communities and to implement an agency 'strategy' for public participation" (Clinton, 1994, p. 7629). The executive order specifically directed each agency to develop an agencywide environmental justice strategy that included opportunities for public participation and access to information. (See "FYI: The Executive Order on Environmental Justice.")

☞ FYI The Executive Order on Environmental Justice

President Clinton's executive order may be found at http://www.epa.gov/fedreg. The American Bar Association maintains a Website for news related to environmental justice, including official government statements and pending cases of enforcement of President Clinton's Executive Order on Environmental Justice. See www.abanet.org/environ.

See also the Environmental Protection Administration's *Environmental Justice Public Participation Checklist* at www.epa.gov. This checklist lays out ways to identify, inform, and involve stakeholders from communities of color.

Finally, the Office of Inspector General's report, *EPA Needs to Consistently Implement the Intent of* the Executive Order on Environmental Justice, is at http://www.epa.gov.

Although the Bush administration left the Clinton-era executive order in place, the administration's follow-through proved to be somewhat inconsistent. In fact, the Office of Inspector General for the U.S. Environmental Protection Agency—the agency chiefly responsible for implementing the executive order—reported that the EPA had "not fully implemented Executive Order 12898 nor consistently integrated environmental justice into its day-to-day operations" and had neither defined nor developed criteria for determining when a community was "disproportionately impacted" (Office of Inspector General, 2004, p. ii). Moreover, when the new administration entered office in 2001, the EPA "restated its commitment to environmental justice in a manner that does not emphasize minority and low-income populations, the intent of the Executive Order" (ibid.). The future of the original Clinton Executive Order on Environmental Justice now lies in the hands of President Barack Obama.

The effectiveness of an executive order may be somewhat limited. On the other hand, there is no doubt that the National Environmental Policy Act has proved to be one of the most empowering laws passed by the U.S. Congress. In terms of its scope and involvement of members of the public, NEPA has been the cornerstone of the principle of direct participation in governance through the right of citizens to comment directly to agencies responsible for decisions affecting the environment. There remains one other right of public participation, to which I now turn.

Right of Standing in Courts: Citizen Suits

Beyond the right to know and public comment is a third route for citizen participation in environmental decisions: the right of standing. A right of standing is based on the presumption that an individual having a sufficient interest in a matter may "stand" before legal authority to speak and seek protection of that interest in court. In both common law and provisions under U.S. environmental law, citizens— under specific conditions—may have standing to object to an agency's failure to enforce environmental standards or to hold a violator directly accountable.

Standing and Citizen Suits

The right of citizens to standing developed originally from common law, wherein individuals who have suffered an **injury in fact** to a legally protected right could seek redress in court. The definition of *injury* under common law normally meant a concrete, particular injury that an individual had suffered due to the actions of another party. One of the earliest cases of standing in an environmental case involved William Aldred, who in 1611 brought suit against his neighbor Thomas Benton. Benton had built a hog pen on an orchard near Aldred's house. Aldred complained that "the stench and unhealthy odors emanating from the pigs drifted onto [his] land and premises" and were so offensive that he and his family "could not come and go without being subjected to continuous annoyance" (9 Co. Rep. 57, 77 Eng. Rep. 816 [1611], in Steward & Krier, 1978, pp.117–118). Although Benton argued that "one ought not have so delicate a nose, that he cannot bear the smell of hogs," the court sided with Aldred and ordered Benton to pay for the damage caused to Aldred's property.

Aldred was able to pursue his claim before the court as a result of his and his family's injury in fact from the offensive odors. But in the 20th century, the principle of injury in fact would be expanded in ways that allowed wider access to the courts by environmental interests. Two developments modified the strict common-law requirement of concrete, particular injury, allowing a greater opening for citizens to sue in behalf of environmental values.

First, the 1946 Administrative Procedure Act broadened the right of judicial review for persons "suffering a legal wrong because of agency action, or adversely affected or aggrieved by agency action" (5 U.S.C. A7 702, in Buck, 1996, p. 67). This was so because, under the APA, the courts generally have held that an agency must "weigh all information with fairness and not be 'arbitrary and capricious'" in adopting agency rules (Hays, 2000, p. 133). Thus, when an agency's actions depart from this standard, they are subject to citizen complaints under the APA; that is, because citizens have suffered from an "arbitrary and capricious" action, they have standing to seek protection in the courts. In succeeding years, this provision of the

Administrative Procedures Act would be an important tool enabling environmental groups to hold agencies accountable for their actions toward the environment.

The second expansion of standing came in the form of **citizen suits** in major environmental laws. The provision for such lawsuits enables citizens to go into a federal court to ask that an environmental law be enforced. For example, the Clean Water Act confers standing on any citizen or "persons having an interest which is or may be adversely affected" to challenge violations of clean water permits if the state or federal agency fails to enforce the statutory requirements ("Clean Water Act," 2007). Using this provision, for example, citizens in West Virginia invoked their right of standing by filing citizen suits against the practice of mountaintop removal, in which coal companies literally push earth from the tops of mountains into nearby valleys, filling streams, in their search for coal. (For more information on the status of citizen suits against mountaintop removal, see Appalachian Center for the Economy and the Environment at http://www.appalachian-center.org.) Other environmental laws that allow citizen suits include the Endangered Species Act, the Clean Air Act, the Toxic Substances Control Act, and the Comprehensive Environmental Response Compensation and Liability Act (the Superfund law).

The purpose of a citizen suit is to challenge an agency's lack of enforcement of environmental standards; local citizens and public interest groups are empowered to sue the agency directly to enforce the law. Jonathan Adler (2000), a senior fellow at the Competitive Enterprise Institute, explained the rationale behind this. When federal regulators "overlook local environmental deterioration or are compromised by interest group pressure, local groups in affected areas are empowered to trigger enforcement themselves" (para. 48). This is especially important in cases of **agency capture**, in which a regulated industry pressures or influences officials to ignore violations of a corporation's permit for environmental performance (for example, its air or water discharges).

Landmark Cases on Environmental Standing

Citizens' claims to the right of standing are subject not only to the provisions of specific statutes (for example, the Clean Water Act), but also to judicial interpretations of the **cases and controversies clause** in Article III of the U.S. Constitution. Despite its arcane title, this requirement serves an important purpose. The cases and controversies clause "ensures that lawsuits are heard only if the parties are true adversaries, because only true adversaries will aggressively present to the courts all issues" (Van Tuyn, 2000, p. 42).

To determine if a party is a "true adversary," the U.S. Supreme Court uses three tests: (1) persons bringing a case must be able to prove an injury in fact, including a legal wrong as allowed by the APA; (2) this injury must be "fairly traceable" to an action of the defendant; and (3) the Court must be able to redress the injury through a favorable ruling (p. 42). Although environmental statutes grant a right of standing, citizens still must meet these three constitutional tests before proceeding.

The main question in granting standing in environmental cases is the meaning of "injury in fact." What qualifies as injury where individual citizens seek to enforce the provisions of an environmental law? The Supreme Court has worked out an uneven and, at times, confusing answer to this question in several landmark cases.

Sierra Club v. Morton

The Supreme Court's 1972 ruling in *Sierra Club v. Morton* provided the first guidance for determining standing under the Constitution's cases and controversies clause in an environmental case. In this case, the Sierra Club sought to block plans by Walt Disney Enterprises to build a resort in Mineral King Valley in California. Plans for the resort included the building of a road through Sequoia National Park. In its suit, the Sierra Club argued that a road would "destroy or otherwise adversely affect the scenery, natural and historic objects, and wildlife of the park for future generations" (Lindstrom & Smith, 2001, p. 105). Although the Supreme Court found that such damage could constitute an injury in fact, it noted that the Sierra Club did not allege that any of its members themselves had suffered any actual injury, and therefore they were not true adversaries. Instead, the Sierra Club had asserted a right to be heard simply on the basis of its interest in protecting the environment. The Court rejected the group's claim of standing in the case, ruling that a long-standing interest in a problem was not enough to constitute an injury in fact (Lindstrom & Smith, 2001, p. 105).

Despite its ruling in *Sierra Club v. Morton,* the Supreme Court spelled out a liberal standard for what might constitute a successful claim of standing. It observed that in the future, the Sierra Club need only allege an injury to its *members' interests*—for example, that its members would no longer be able to enjoy an unspoiled wilderness or their normal recreational pursuits. The Sierra Club immediately and successfully amended its suit against Disney Enterprises, arguing that such injury would occur to its members if the road through Sequoia National Park were to be built. (Subsequently, Mineral King Valley itself was added to Sequoia National Park, and Disney Enterprises withdrew its plans to build the resort.)

An interesting footnote to legal history occurred in a famous dissent in the original *Morton* case. Arguing for a more expansive standard, Justice William O. Douglas argued that even trees and rivers should have standing. He noted that U.S. law already gave standing to some inanimate objects and that environmental goals would be enhanced if citizens could sue on behalf of natural objects:

> The critical question of "standing" would be simplified . . . if we fashioned a federal rule that allowed environmental issues to be litigated before federal agencies or federal courts in the name of the inanimate object about to be despoiled, defaced, or invaded by roads and bulldozers and where injury is the subject of public outrage. . . .
>
> Inanimate objects are sometimes parties in litigation. A ship has a legal personality, a fiction found useful for maritime purposes. . . .
>
> So it should be as respects valleys, alpine meadows, rivers, lakes, estuaries, beaches, ridges, [and] groves of trees. . . . The river, for example, is the living symbol of all the life it sustains or nourishes—fish, aquatic insects, water ouzels, otter, fisher, deer, elk, bear, and all other animals, including man, who are dependent on it or who enjoy it for its sight, its sound, or its life. The river as plaintiff speaks for the ecological

unit of life that is part of it. Those people who have a meaningful relation to that body of water—whether it be a fisherman, a canoeist, a zoologist, or a logger—must be able to speak for the values which the river represents and which are threatened with destruction. . . . (*Sierra Club v. Morton,* 1972; see also the classic essay, "Should Trees Have Standing," Stone, 1996)

The Court's liberal interpretation of the test for injury in fact in *Sierra Club v. Morton* and other cases, along with the right of standing in many environmental laws, produced a 20-year burst of environmental litigation by citizens and environmental groups. This trend continued until the Supreme Court issued a series of conservative rulings that narrowed the basis for citizens' standing.

Lujan v. Defenders of Wildlife

In the 1990s, the U.S. Supreme Court handed down several rulings that severely limited citizen suits in environmental cases. In perhaps the most important case, **Lujan v. Defenders of Wildlife** (1992), the Court rejected a claim of standing by the conservation group Defenders of Wildlife under the citizen suit provision of the Endangered Species Act (ESA). The ESA declares that "any person may commence a civil suit on his own behalf (A) to enjoin any person, including the United States and any other governmental instrumentality or agency . . . who is alleged to be in violation of any provision" of the Act (ESA, 1973, A71540 [g] [1].) In its lawsuit, Defenders of Wildlife argued that the secretary of the interior (Lujan) had failed in his duties to ensure that U.S. funding of projects overseas—in this case, in Egypt—did not jeopardize the habitats of endangered species, as the law required (Stearns, 2000, p. 363).

Writing for the majority, Justice Antonin Scalia stated that Defenders had failed to satisfy constitutional requirements for injury in fact that would grant standing under the ESA. He wrote that the Court rejected the view that the citizen suit provision of the statute conferred upon "*all* persons an abstract, self-contained, noninstrumental 'right' to have the Executive observe the procedures required by law" (Lujan, 1992, p. 573). Rather, he explained, the plaintiff must have suffered a tangible and particular harm not unlike the common-law requirement (Adler, 2000, p. 52). This ruling overturned *Sierra Club v. Morton,* in which Sierra Club members needed only to prove injury to their interests— that is, that they couldn't enjoy their recreational pursuits or enjoyment of wilderness.

Consequently, courts began to limit sharply citizen claims of standing under citizen suit provisions of environmental statutes. Writing in the *New York Times,* Glaberson (1999) reported that the Court's rulings in the 1990s were one of the most "profound setbacks for the environmental movement in decades" (p. A1).

Friends of the Earth, Inc. v. Laidlaw Environmental Services, Inc.

In a more recent case, the Supreme Court appeared to reverse its strict Lujan doctrine, holding that the knowledge of a possible threat to a legally recognized interest (clean water) was enough to establish a "sufficient stake" by a plaintiff in enforcing the law (Adler, 2000, p. 52).

In 1992, Friends of the Earth and CLEAN, a local environmental group, sued Laidlaw Environmental Services in Roebuck, South Carolina, under the Clean Water Act citizen suit provision. Their lawsuit alleged that Laidlaw had repeatedly violated its permit limiting the discharge of pollutants (including mercury, a highly toxic substance) into the nearby North Tyger River. Residents of the area who had lived by or used the river for boating and fishing testified that they were "concerned that the water contained harmful pollutants" (Stearns, 2000, p. 382).

The Supreme Court's majority in *Friends of the Earth, Inc. v. Laidlaw Environmental Services, Inc.* (2000) ruled that Friends of the Earth and CLEAN did not need to prove an actual (particular) harm to residents. Writing for the majority, Justice Ruth Bader Ginsburg stated that injury to the plaintiff came from lessening the "aesthetic and recreational values of the area" for residents and users of the river due to their knowledge of Laidlaw's repeated violations of its clean water permit (Adler, 2000, p. 56). In this case, the plaintiffs were not required to prove that Laidlaw's violations of its water permit had contributed to actual deterioration in water quality. It was sufficient that they showed that residents' knowledge of these violations had discouraged their normal use of the river.

Massachusetts et al. v. Environmental Protection Agency

The right of standing arose as a pivotal issue again in *Massachusetts et al. v. Environmental Protection Agency et al.* (2007), the Supreme Court's first-ever ruling on global warming. Twelve states, including Massachusetts and the territory of American Samoa, and a number of environmental groups petitioned the Supreme Court to direct the EPA to regulate tailpipe emissions of greenhouse gases from motor vehicles under the Clean Air Act. In a 5–4 ruling, the Court sharply rebuked the Bush administration's claim that the EPA lacked this authority or, if it had the authority, could choose not to exercise it.

The central issue in this case was whether carbon dioxide and other greenhouse gases met the definition of an "air pollutant" under the broad meaning of this term in the Clean Air Act: "any air pollution agent . . . including any physical, chemical . . . substance or matter which is emitted into or other wise enters the ambient air" (7602[g]). While the majority ultimately agreed that carbon dioxide did meet this definition, the Justices first had to decide the question of the plaintiffs' standing to argue before the Court. In a strategic move, the petitioners decided to list the coastal state of Massachusetts first, as the lead plaintiff. (Only one plaintiff is required to be a true adversary for the case to proceed on its merits.) This proved to be important. Justice John Paul Stevens delivered the opinion of the Court on the question of standing:

> Massachusetts has a special position and interest here. It is a sovereign State and not, as in *Lujan*, a private individual, and it actually owns a great deal of the territory alleged to be affected. The sovereign prerogatives to force reductions in greenhouse gas emissions . . . are now lodged in the Federal Government. Because congress has ordered EPA to protect Massachusetts (among others) by prescribing applicable

> standards . . . and has given Massachusetts a . . . procedural right to challenge the rejection of its rulemaking petition as arbitrary and capricious, . . . petitioners' submissions as they pertain to Massachusetts have satisfied the most demanding standards of the adversarial process. EPA's steadfast refusal to regulate greenhouse gas emissions presents a risk of harm to Massachusetts that is both "actual" and "imminent," *Lujan,* 504 U.S., . . . and there is a "substantial likelihood that the judicial relief requested" will prompt EPA to take steps to reduce that risk. (*Mass. v. EPA,* 2007, p. 3)

Responding to the EPA's objection that a favorable ruling for the plaintiffs would not solve the problem, Justice Stevens wrote, "While regulating motor-vehicle emissions may not by itself *reverse* global warming, it does not follow that the Court lacks jurisdiction to decide whether EPA has a duty to take steps to *slow* or *reduce* it" (p. 4).

With these rulings, the Supreme Court reaffirmed the rationale of citizen suits that citizens, as well as states, have an interest in the enforcement of environmental quality under the provisions of specific laws such as the Clean Water Act or the Clean Air Act. However, disagreement over the criteria for citizen standing in environmental cases is likely to continue. At stake are differing interpretations of injury in fact and the rights of citizens of standing to compel the government to enforce environmental laws.

Citizens' Communication and Public Participation

Access to information, public comment, and the right of standing are basic procedural rights of public participation in U.S. environmental decision making, but they shed little light on the communication that occurs as individuals pursue these rights. Here and in the following chapter, I'll describe some of the characteristics of this communication. The most frequently used modes of individual citizen communication on environmental matters are (1) comments to agencies, including testimony at public hearings, (2) participation on advisory panels, and (3) collaboration with other parties with an interest in an environmental decision. This section of the chapter focuses on citizen testimony in public hearings. Chapter 4 explores the increasing use of citizen advisory panels and informal collaboration by citizens, businesses, agencies, and environmental groups to mediate disputes in environmental conflicts.

Public Hearings and Citizen Testimony

Public hearings, workshops, and meetings are the more common modes of participation by ordinary citizens in environmental decision making at both the federal and state levels. Typically, these are forums for public comments to an agency before it takes action that might significantly affect the environment. As we saw earlier, the National Environmental Policy Act requires federal and some state agencies to actively solicit public comment at this stage. In doing so, the agency normally conducts scoping sessions (workshops or open houses) and public hearings to establish a record of public comment. At the state and local levels, public hearings typically are held before an agency issues a permit for a company to discharge pollutants into the air or water, or to gather input before a town acts on a strictly local matter—for example, deciding the location of a municipal solid waste site, issuing a permit to widen a street, or approving funds to purchase land for a park.

The public hearings and meetings to address environmental questions usually involve an exchange of information. Typically, an agency will inform citizens about its proposed action, and citizens are then provided an opportunity to express their opinions about the proposal. This occurred recently when I attended a public hearing on a permit to construct a new coal-burning power plant in my state. Because of the recent interest in global warming, the hearing room was crowded with interested citizens—young professionals, religious leaders, student activists, officials from environmental groups, mothers with their young children, and many others. As usual, there were sign-in sheets for those of us wishing to speak. Before inviting comment from the public, the presiding official called on agency staff to testify and provide technical information on the proposed permit. Then, members of the audience were given three minutes each to comment orally or to read a statement. Some individuals read from a prepared statement; others spoke extemporaneously. Both supporters and opponents of a proposal may attend, and both sides speak, at such public meetings. In the public hearing that I attended, the comments were overwhelming in opposition to the permit for the power plant.

The communication at public meetings may be polite or robust, restrained or angry, as well as informed, opinionated, and emotional. The range of comments reflects the diversity of opinion and interests of the community itself. Officials may urge members of the public to speak to the specific issue that is on the agenda, but the actual communication often departs from this, ranging from individuals' calm testimony, emotionally charged remarks, and stories of their family's experiences to criticism of opponents or public officials.

Some people may denounce the actions of the agency or respond angrily, even theatrically, to plans that affect their lives or community. At one particularly intense public hearing, I witnessed residents of a rural community place bags of garbage on the stage of the auditorium where elected officials were presiding to protest plans to allow an out-of-state company to build a hazardous waste incinerator near their homes. The atmosphere in this public hearing was electric, with angry parents and other community members noisily confronting defensive and harried officials on the stage. On the other hand, an individual's quiet testimony may be emotionally powerful. At the public hearing on the coal plant in my state, a young mother told of her and her husband's borrowing money to install a solar panel, so concerned were they for their children's future; weeping quietly, she pleaded with the officials to deny the permit for the power plant.

The communication in public hearings also can be affected by factors other than personal emotions or concerns about an issue. Ordinary citizens find themselves apprehensive about having to speak in front of large groups, perhaps with a microphone, to unfamiliar officials. They may face opponents or others who are hostile to their views. Sometimes, they must wait hours for their turns to speak. Those with jobs or small children face additional constraints because they must take time from work or find (and often pay) someone to watch their children. I return to these and other constraints in Chapter 8 when I describe some of the barriers to citizen participation in public hearings in low-income communities.

Act Locally!

Attend a Local Public Hearing on the Environment

Investigate the procedures and types of communication that occur in a local public hearing on the environment in your city, county, or state.

1. Identify one local agency or committee and the environmental issue it is considering. What committee or body in your local government deals with environmental problems? Are there upcoming meetings to consider proposals for bike paths? A permit to operate a medical waste incinerator near your campus? A vote to approve funds to purchase green space? Are its meetings publicly announced? Is the public invited to attend its meetings?

2. Attend one of the public meetings, and observe the procedures for public comment. Is the public welcome to comment publicly during the proceedings? Who gets to speak? For how long? What do individuals testifying include in their remarks? Do they present facts? Are they sometimes emotional? Do agency officials treat members of the public respectfully?

3. Interview two or three members of the public who spoke at the public meeting, as well as an official who presided. Did members of the public feel that their comments made a difference? Did the officials listen to them? How did the presiding official feel about the quality of communication at the meeting? What effects, if any, did you observe as a result of the public meeting?

As I noted in Chapter 1, the National Research Council has found that "when done well, public participation improves the quality and legitimacy of a decision and. . . . can lead to better results in terms of environmental quality" (Dietz & Stern, 2008). Still, many believe that public hearings are not an effective form of public participation due to the conditions that are typically imposed by crowded hearing rooms, limited time, volatile emotions, and long waiting times for speaking. Daniels and Walker (2001) go further when they contend that some public lands management agencies such as the Forest Service exhibit a "Three-'I' Model . . . inform, invite, and ignore." For example, agency officials will inform the public about a proposed action, such as a timber sale, then "invite the public to a meeting to provide comments on that action, and ignore what members of the public say" (p. 9). As a result, some have called for a more **authoritative involvement** in environmental policymaking (Foreman, 1998). Such a shift would include citizens' input in an agency's initial framing or definition of a problem, as well as the range of solutions and criteria by which officials and the public jointly reach a decision (Katz & Miller, 1996; Lynn, 1986). For example, should communities be able to require, as a condition of a company's air permit, that it contribute to an independent monitoring service for future air pollution and a health fund to support local health clinics and hospitals?

Although adversarial and impolite at times, public meetings and hearings do reflect the diverse and messy norms of democratic life. At their best, meetings that invite wide participation by members of the public may generate comments and information that help agencies to shape or modify important decisions affecting the environment. Although they occasionally may be confrontational, such hearings provide many citizens their only opportunity to speak directly to government authority about matters of concern to them, their families, or their community.

Restricting Public Involvement in Forest Planning

Concern for national security has not been the only source of restrictions on the public's rights of public participation in the years since the 9/11 attacks. A second catalyst has been the shift in management by some federal environmental agencies. This shift was apparent very early in the second Bush administration when the President's Healthy Forests Initiative became public. The Healthy Forests Restoration Act, which became law in 2003, exempted some 10 million acres of forest land from the requirements under the National Environmental Policy Act for an environmental impact statement and public comment period. In other cases, the White House requested expedited environmental reviews of transportation and energy projects such as highway construction and oil and gas exploration on public lands.

Perhaps the most far-reaching shift in environmental management that affects public participation occurred in the U.S. Forest Service. In late 2004, the Forest Service announced sweeping new rules to implement the **National Forest Management Act** (NFMA). The U.S. Congress enacted the NFMA in 1976 to reform management of the nation's 155 national forests. Specifically, it required that each forest "insure that land management plans be prepared in accordance with the National Environmental Policy Act of 1969" (16 USC 1604[g][1]). As I noted earlier in this chapter, NEPA requires an environmental impact statement and an opportunity for public comment prior to any action that may significantly impact the environment. Yet, the *New York Times* reported that the new Forest Service rules relax these "long-standing provisions on environmental reviews and the protection of wildlife on 191 million acres of forests and grasslands . . . [and] also cut back on requirements for public participation in forest planning decisions" (Barringer, 2004, p. 1A). (Subsequent court decisions have struck down these regulatory changes under the NFMA.)

Many forest advocates believed at the time that the rule changes meant that the Forest Service could avoid public scrutiny for failures to respect laws like the Endangered Species Act—for example, to allow logging in sensitive habitats of endangered species. In its review of the new rules, the nonprofit forest law firm Wildlaw (2005) explained that the new Forest Service regulations eliminated the requirement to prepare an environmental impact statement pursuant to NEPA "whenever a forest plan is revised or significantly amended. Instead, forest plans 'may be categorically excluded from NEPA documentation' [219.4(b)], which means that the Forest Service can entirely bypass the NEPA process whenever it revises or amends a forest plan" (para. 9).

The attempt by the Bush administration to alter the National Forest Management Act illustrates the recurring tension between governmental agencies, on the one hand, to plan in an efficient manner, free of "interference" by others, and the need, on the other hand, of journalists and environmental groups to scrutinize the work of a public agency to ensure its compliance with environmental standards and public safety. As a result of such conflicts, a trend has emerged in recent years, exploring alternatives to the adversarial and one-way communication modes that characterize environmental public meetings.

Growth of Public Participation Internationally

In the past decade, more and more nations have begun to guarantee public access to information and implement various forms of public participation in governmental decisions about the environment. Clearly, the European Union, the UN Economic Commission for Europe (UNECE), and many of the former nations of the Soviet Union have taken the lead in this area. For example, UNECE has successfully negotiated five environmental treaties, governing trans-boundaries environmental protections in Europe for air pollution and watercourses and lakes, and extending guarantees for environmental impact assessments. Of these five treaties, the Convention on Access to Information, Public Participation, and Access to Justice in Environmental Matters—often called the Aarhus Convention—is unprecedented for its guarantees of public participation. (See "FYI: What Is the Aarhus Convention?")

☞ **FYI**   **What Is the Aarhus Convention?**

The UN Economic Commission for Europe *Convention on Access to Information, Public Participation, and Access to Justice in Environmental Matters* (the Aarhus Convention) was adopted on 25 June 1998 in the Danish city of Aarhus (Århus) at the Fourth Ministerial Conference as part of the "Environment for Europe" process. It entered into force on 30 October 2001. The Aarhus Convention provides for:

- the right of everyone to receive environmental information that is held by public authorities (**"access to environmental information"**)...Applicants are entitled to obtain this information...without having to say why they require it. In addition, public authorities are obliged, under the Convention, to actively disseminate environmental information in their possession;

- the right to participate in environmental decision-making. Arrangements are to be made by public authorities to enable the public affected and environmental non-governmental organisations to comment on...proposals for projects affecting the environment..., these comments to be taken into due account in decision-making, and information to be provided on the final decisions and the reasons for it (**"public participation in environmental decision-making"**);

- the right to review procedures to challenge public decisions that have been made without respecting the two aforementioned rights or environmental law in general (**"access to justice"**).

SOURCE: UN Economic Commission for Europe, "What Is the Aarhus Convention?" March 12, 2008. For the text of the Aarhus Convention, see http://www.unece.org.

Adopted in 1998 in the Danish city of Aarhus, the **Aarhus Convention** is a "new kind" of agreement, linking environmental rights and human rights (UNECE, 2008). Article 1 clearly announces its objective:

> In order to contribute to the protection of the right of every person of present and future generations to live in an environment adequate to his or her health and well-being, each party shall guarantee the rights of access to information, public participation in decision-making, and access to justice in environmental matters. . . . (UNECE, 2008, para. 13)

These three principles—access to information, public participation, and access to justice—are developed in detail, with concrete procedures for ensuring citizen access to these rights.

In many ways, the approach of the Aarhus Convention goes further than U.S. environmental law under NEPA by granting a "right" to public information and to review by public authorities. For example, the right of *access to justice* ensures that "any person who considers that his or her request for information . . . has been ignored, [or] wrongfully refused . . . has access to a review procedure before a court of law or another independent and impartial body" (Article 9).

The idea of transparency, particularly, is gaining in popularity internationally. For example, in addition to the Aarhus Convention, the UN Economic Commission for Europe also tracks changes in the U.S. Toxic Release Inventory for programs in Europe and nations of the former Soviet Union. And programs similar to the TRI have been established or are being implemented not only in Europe, but Asia, Australia, Canada, and some counties in South America and Africa. These TRI-like initiatives range from "emission inventories," which collect data on specific chemical releases, to more comprehensive programs known as **Pollutant Release and Transfer Register** (PRTR) that expand on this data collection. Like the Toxic Release Inventory, PRTR programs require not only the collection of data, but mandatory reporting of a facility's chemical releases, as well as public access to this data. PRTR programs also differ in some nations. For example, Japan collects information of automobile emissions, while Mexico's PRTR is voluntary for industries.

Clearly, demands for public participation in environmental matters are increasing worldwide. For example, in early 2008, the Carter Center in Atlanta convened an International Conference on the Right to Public Information. More than 125 representatives from 40 nations gathered to "identify the necessary steps and measures to ensure the effective creation, implementation, and exercise of the right of access to public information" (Carter Center, 2008, para. 2). Elsewhere, new initiatives for public participation are emerging in Asia, Africa, and Latin America, with a vigorous movement for environmental protection and public access to information growing in China, particularly. (For updates on recent initiatives to strengthen public participation guarantees in China, see the Greenlaw blog at www.greenlaw.org; Greenlaw is a joint project of the Natural Resources Defense Council and the China Environmental Culture Promotion Association.)

SUMMARY

In this chapter, I've identified some of the legal rights and forums that enable you and other citizens to participate directly and publicly in decisions about the environment. Basic to effective participation is a *right to know*—to have access to information. One of the more powerful tools for citizens is the Freedom of Information Act, which makes available (with some exceptions) any information held by agencies of the executive branch of government. An even more powerful information tool for investigating sources of pollution where you live is the Toxic Release Inventory.

Second, the ability of citizens to question, comment, or testify publicly before governmental officials has expanded dramatically since the passage of the National Environmental Policy Act in 1969. The requirements of NEPA to solicit the public's involvement before a proposed action may be the most important development in the past half-century for democratizing the process of environmental decision making. Along with citizen suits and the right of standing to enforce major environmental laws in court, these requirements give greater meaning and significance to the ideals of direct participation and accountability.

We also looked at the communication that typically occurs at public hearings, including the opportunity for any citizen to speak freely to governmental officials. Many citizens in communities affected by environmental hazards are pushing for a greater level of public access and direct participation—a right to know more, a right to independent expertise, and a right to more authoritative participation in public meetings.

Finally, even as new restrictions since September 11, 2001, have been imposed in the United States on the right to know, new initiatives to strengthen public participation are occurring in Europe and other nations. New "rights-based" approaches like the Aarhus Convention are encouraging signs as the rights of access to information, public comment on environmental matters, and review by the courts are expanding internationally.

KEY TERMS

Communication-Related Concepts

Aarhus Convention: Adopted in 1998 in the Danish city of Aarhus, this agreement guarantees the rights of access to information, public participation in decision making, and access to justice in environmental matters (right of standing).

Administrative Procedure Act (APA): Enacted in 1946; laid out new standards for the operation of U.S. government agencies; required that proposed actions be published in the *Federal Register* and that the public be given an opportunity to respond; also broadened the right of judicial review for persons "suffering a legal wrong" resulting from "arbitrary and capricious" actions on the part of agencies.

Agency capture: The pressuring or influencing of officials by a regulated industry to ignore violations of a corporation's permit for environmental performance (for example, its air or water discharges).

Authoritative involvement: An approach to public participation that includes citizens' input to an agency's initial framing or definition of a problem and to the development of a range of solutions and criteria by which officials and the public jointly reach a decision.

Cases and controversies clause: The portion of Article III of the U.S. Constitution that ensures that lawsuits are heard by true adversaries in a dispute, on the assumption that only true adversaries will represent to the courts the issues in a case; an important test of true adversary status is whether persons bringing the action are able to prove an injury in fact.

Citizen suits: Action brought by citizens in federal court asking that provisions of an environmental law be enforced. The right to bring such suits is a provision of major environmental laws.

Critical Infrastructure Information (CII): A section of the Homeland Security Act of 2002 that allows any federal agency to deny FOIA requests for federal records of permit violations, fines, or other information about oil refineries, drinking water plants, oil and natural gas pipelines, and so forth; also protects from public scrutiny and prosecution any information voluntarily submitted to federal agencies by corporations.

Electronic Freedom of Information Amendments: Amendments to FOIA that require federal agencies to provide public access to information in electronic form. This is done typically by posting a guide for making a freedom of information request on the agency's Website.

Freedom of Information Act (FOIA): Enacted in 1966; provides that any person has the right to see documents and records of any federal agency (except the judiciary or Congress).

Friends of the Earth, Inc., v. Laidlaw Environmental Services, Inc.: A 2000 case in which the Supreme Court reversed its strict Lujan doctrine, ruling that plaintiffs did not need to prove an actual (particular) harm; rather, the *knowledge* of a possible threat to a legally recognized interest (clean water) was enough to establish a sufficient stake in enforcing the law.

Homeland Security Act: Passed in 2002 shortly after the first anniversary of the September 11, 2001, terrorist attacks, this law contains broad authority for the federal government to take steps to protect national security, including the right to restrict public access to any information that could be used to attack U.S. interests.

Injury in fact: Under common law, this normally meant a concrete, particular injury that an individual had suffered due to the actions of another party. Currently, it is one of three tests used by U.S. courts to determine a plaintiff's standing or right to seek redress in court for a harm to a legally protected right; criteria for defining injury in fact have varied from the denial of enjoyment or use of the environment to a concrete, tangible harm to the plaintiff.

Lujan v. Defenders of Wildlife: A 1992 case in which the Supreme Court rejected a claim of standing by the group Defenders of Wildlife under the citizen suit provision of the Endangered Species Act, ruling that the Defenders had failed to satisfy constitutional requirements for injury in fact because plaintiffs had not suffered a tangible and particular harm. Overturned the more liberal standard established in *Sierra Club vs. Morton.*

Notice of Intent (NOI): A statement of the agency's intent to prepare an EIS for a proposed action. The NOI is published in the *Federal Register* and provides a brief description of the proposed action and possible alternatives.

Public comment: Required of federal agencies under the National Environmental Policy Act; public input solicited by a federal agency on any proposal significantly affecting the environment; usually takes place at public hearings and in written reports, letters, e-mails, or faxes to the agency.

Public hearing: The common mode of participation by ordinary citizens in environmental decision making at both the federal and state levels; a forum for public comment to an agency before the agency takes any action that might significantly impact the environment.

Public participation: The ability of individual citizens and groups to influence environmental decisions through (1) access to relevant information, (2) public comments to the agency that is responsible for a decision, and (3) the right, through the courts, to hold public agencies and businesses accountable for their environmental decisions and behaviors.

Right to independent expertise: A right demanded by advocates from communities with toxic waste sites to access sources of expertise that are independent of governmental agencies, to understand the effects of chemicals from these waste sites on the health of community residents.

Right to know: The public's right of access to information about environmental conditions or actions of government that potentially affect the environment.

Scoping: A preliminary stage in an agency's development of a proposed rule or action, including any meetings and how the public can get involved; it involves canvassing interested members of the public to determine what the concerns of the affected parties might be.

"Shock and shame" response: If community members found out that a local factory was emitting high levels of pollution, their "shock" could push the community into action. In some cases, the polluting facility itself may feel "shame" from disclosure of its poor performance.

Sierra Club v. Morton: A 1972 case that established the first guidance for determining standing under the Constitution's cases and controversies clause in an environmental case; the Supreme Court held that the Sierra Club need only allege an injury to its members' interests—for example, that its members could not enjoy an unspoiled wilderness or their normal recreational pursuits.

Standing: The legal status accorded a citizen who has a sufficient interest in a matter, whereby the citizen may appear in court to protect that interest.

Sunshine laws: Laws intended to shine the light of public scrutiny on the workings of government, requiring open meetings of most governmental bodies.

Transparency: Openness in government; citizens' right to know information that is important to their lives. In regard to the environment, the United Nations has declared that the principle of transparency "requires the recognition of the rights of participation and access to information and the right to be informed. . . . Everyone has the right of access to information on the environment with no obligation to prove a particular interest" ("Declaration of Bizkaia on the Right to the Environment," 1999).

Environment-Related Concepts

Emergency Planning and Community Right to Know Act (the Right to Know Act): Enacted in 1986; requires industries to report to local and state emergency planners the use and location of specified chemicals at their facilities.

Environmental impact statement (EIS): Required by the National Environmental Policy Act for proposed federal legislation or actions significantly affecting the quality of the environment, an EIS must describe (1) the environmental impact of the proposed action, (2) any adverse environmental effects that could not be avoided should the proposal be implemented, and (3) alternatives to the proposed action.

Environmental tort: A legal claim for injury or a lawsuit related to an environmental harm.

Executive Order on Environmental Justice: President Bill Clinton's 1994 order directing federal agencies to "study the impact of proposed actions (permits for plants, and so on) related to the environment and public health on minority communities and to implement an agency 'strategy' for public participation" (Clinton, 1994).

National Environmental Policy Act (NEPA): Enacted in 1970; involves the public in environmental decision making by federal agencies through (1) a detailed, public statement of any environmental impacts of a proposed action and (2) concrete procedures for public comment.

National Forest Management Act (NFMA): Enacted in 1976; required, among other things, that management plans for the nation's 155 national forests be prepared in accordance with the National Environmental Policy Act of 1969.

Pollutant Release and Transfer Register (PRTR). Like the U.S. Toxic Release Inventory, international PRTR programs require mandatory reporting of specific chemical releases into the air, water, or land; and public access to these data.

Superfund sites: Abandoned chemical waste sites that have qualified for federal funds for their cleanup under the Comprehensive Environmental Response Compensation and Liability Act (commonly called the Superfund law).

Technical Assistance Grant (TAG) Program: A program initiated in 1986 to help communities at Superfund sites by providing funds for citizen groups to hire consultants who can help them understand and comment on information provided by EPA and the industries responsible for cleaning these sites.

Toxic Release Inventory: An information-reporting tool established under the Emergency Planning and Community Right to Know Act (1986) that enables the Environmental Protection Agency to collect data annually on any releases of toxic materials into the air and water by designated industries and to make this information easily available to the public.

DISCUSSION QUESTIONS

1. Have you ever thought of requesting information from the federal government under the Freedom of Information Act? How would you go about doing that?

2. Have you ever attended a public hearing or spoken publicly about an environmental concern? Were you nervous? Did you think you made a difference?

3. Should trees have standing? That is, should citizens be able to seek legal remedies in court on behalf of trees and other environmental subjects (rivers, wildlife, and so on)?

4. In *Lujan v. Defenders of Wildlife,* Justice Antonin Scalia stated that citizen suits do not confer upon "all persons an abstract, self-contained, non-instrumental 'right' to have the Executive observe the procedures required by law." Why not? Must a person demonstrate a concrete, personal harm in order to gain standing? Or should the test of injury allow for a public purpose, that is, an interest in ensuring the enforcement of laws such as the Clean Water Act or the Endangered Species Act?

5. Does the executive branch of government have a right to restrict the public's access to information under the Freedom of Information Act on the grounds, for example, that release of information about vulnerabilities at chemical plants or oil refineries might aid terrorists?

REFERENCES

Aarhus Parties commit to strengthening environmental democracy in the UNECE region and beyond. (2008, June 11–13). UN Economic Commission for Europe. Retrieved August 31, 2008, from http://www.unece.org.

Adler, J. H. (2000, March 2–3). *Stand or deliver: Citizen suits, standing, and environmental protection.* Paper presented at the Duke University Law and Policy Forum Symposium on Citizen Suits and the Future of Standing in the 21st Century. Retrieved August 20, 2003, from www.law.duke.edu/journals.

Associated Press (AP). (2008, October 2). Montana: New study of snowmobiles. *The New York Times,* p. A20.

Barringer, F. (2004, December 23). Administration overhauls rules for U.S. forests. *The New York Times,* pp. A1, A18.

Bruggers, J., Ward, K., Jr., & Fagin, D. (2003, March 14). *Letter to senators.* Society of Environmental Journalists. Retrieved March 1, 2009, from http://www.sej.org/foia/senators.

Buck, S. J. (1996). *Understanding environmental administration and law.* Washington, DC: Island Press.

Carter Center. (2008, February 27–29). *International Conference on the Right to Public Information.* Retrieved December 30, 2008, from http://www.cartercenter.org.

Clean Water Act–Citizen Suits. (2007, July 30). Washington, DC: U.S. Environmental Protection Agency. Retrieved September 5, 2008, from http://www.epa.gov.

Clinton, W. J. (1994, February 16). Federal actions to address environmental justice in minority populations and low-income communities. Executive Order 12898 of February 14, 1994. *Federal Register 59,* p. 7629.

Coalition of Journalists for Open Government. (2008, July 3). *An opportunity lost.* Retrieved September 1, 2008, from http://www.cjog.net/documents.

Core values for the practice of public participation. (2008). The International Association for Public Participation. Available at http://www.iap2.org.

Council on Environmental Quality (CEQ). (1997, January). *The national environmental policy act: A study of its effectiveness after twenty-five years.* Washington, DC: Council on Environmental Quality, Executive Office of the President. Available at http://ceq.eh .doe.gov.

Council on Environmental Quality (CEQ). (2007, December). *A citizen's guide to the NEPA: Having your voice heard.* Retrieved December 29, 2008, from http://ceq.hss.doe.gov.

Daniels, S. E., & Walker, G. B. (2001). *Working through environmental conflict: The collaborative learning approach.* Westport, CT: Praeger.

Declaration of Bizkaia on the Right to the Environment. (1999, February 10–13). International Seminar on the Right to the Environment, held in Bilbao, Spain, under the auspices of UNESCO and the United Nations High Commissioner for Human Rights. Available at http://unesdoc.unesco.org.

Dietz, T. & Stern, P. C. (2008). *Public participation in environmental assessment and decision making.* National Research Council. Washington, DC: National Academies Press.

Environmental Protection Agency. (2008, March 31). *What is the Toxics Release Inventory (TRI) program?* Retrieved September 3, 2003, from http://www.epa.gov.

Foreman, C. H., Jr. (1998). *The promise and perils of environmental justice.* Washington, DC: Brookings Institution Press.

Glaberson, W. (1999, June 5). Novel antipollution tool is being upset by courts. *The New York Times*. Retrieved March 1, 2009, from http://query.nytimes.com.

Hays, S. P. (2000). *A history of environmental politics since 1945*. Pittsburgh: University of Pittsburgh Press.

Katz, S. B., & Miller C. R. (1996). The low-level radioactive waste siting controversy in North Carolina: Toward a rhetorical model of risk communication. In C. G. Herndl & S. C. Brown (Eds.), *Green culture: Environmental rhetoric in contemporary America* (pp. 111–140). Madison: University of Wisconsin Press.

Lindstrom, M. J., & Smith, Z. A. (2001). *The national environmental policy act: Judicial misconstruction, legislative indifference, & executive neglect*. College Station: Texas A&M University Press.

Lujan v. Defenders of Wildlife, 504 U.S. 555 (1992).

Lynn, Frances M. (1986). Citizen involvement in hazardous waste sites: Two North Carolina success stories. *Environmental Impact Assessment Review, 7*, 347–361.

Markowitz, G., & Rosner, D. (2002). *Deceit and denial: The deadly politics of industrial pollution*. Berkeley: University of California Press.

Marston, B. (2001, May 7). A modest chief moved the Forest Service miles down the road. *High Country News, 33*(9). Retrieved August 25, 2003, from www.hcn.org.

Massachusetts et al. v. Environmental Protection Agency et al. (2007). Supreme Court of the United States. Retrieved December 30, 2008, from www.supremecourtus.gov.

National Environmental Policy Act (NEPA). 42 U.S.C.A. A7 4321 *et seq.* (1969).

Office of Inspector General. (2004). *Evaluation report: EPA needs to consistently implement the intent of the Executive Order on environmental justice*. Report No. 2004-P-00007. Washington, DC: U.S. Environmental Protection Agency. Retrieved September 5, 2008, from http://www.epa.gov/oigearth.

Parker, L., Johnson, K., & Locy, T. (2002, May 15). Post-9/11, government stingy with information. *USA Today*, p. 1A. Retrieved March 12, 2005, from www.usatoday.com/news/nation.

Sierra Club v. Morton, 405 U.S. 727. (1972). FindLaw. Retrieved December 29, 2008, from http://caselaw.lp.findlaw.com.

Society of Environmental Journalists. (2002, November 14). *Comments of the Reporters Committee for Freedom of the Press and the Society of Environmental Journalists to proposed rules re: public access to critical energy infrastructure information*. Retrieved March 23, 2005, from www.sej.org/foia.

Stearns, M. L. (2000, March 2–3). *From Lujan to Laidlaw: A preliminary model of environmental standing*. Paper presented at the Duke University Law and Policy Forum Symposium on Citizen Suits and the Future of Standing in the 21st Century. Retrieved from www.law.duke.edu/journals.

Stephan, M. (2002). Environmental information disclosure programs: They work, but why? *Social Science Quarterly, 83*(1), 190–205.

Steward, R. B., & Krier, J. (Eds.). (1978). *Environmental law and public policy*. New York: Bobbs-Merrill.

Stone, C. (1996). *Should trees have standing? And other essays on law, morals and the environment* (Rev. ed.). Dobbs Ferry, NY: Oceana.

UN Economic Commission for Europe (UNECE). (2008, March 12). *Text of the [Aarhus] convention*. Retrieved December 31, 2008, from http://www.unece.org.

Van Tuyn, P. (2000). "Who do you think you are?" Tales from the trenches of the environmental standing battle. *Environmental Law, 30*(1): 41–49.

Walker, G. B. (2004). The roadless areas initiative as national policy: Is public participation an oxymoron? In S. P. Depoe, J. W. Delicath, & M.-F. A. Elsenbeer (Eds.), *Communication and public participation in environmental decision making* (pp. 113–135). Albany: State University of New York Press.

Wildlaw. (2005, January 20). *Review of the new NFMA planning regulations.* Retrieved March 30, 2005, from www.wildlaw.org.

White "spirit bear" in the Great Bear Rainforest of British Columbia, Canada.

CHAPTER 4

Conflict Resolution and Collaboration in Environmental Disputes

The New York Times, February 7, 2006

Canada to Shield 5 Million Forest Acres: Coalition of Natives, Loggers and Environmentalists Join Hands

HARTLEY BAY, British Columbia . . . In this sodden land of glacier-cut fjords and giant moss-draped cedars, a myth is told by the Gitga'at people to explain the presence of black bears with a rare recessive gene that makes them white as snow . . . "spirit bears" . . . a reminder to future generations that the world must be kept pristine.

On Tuesday, an improbable assemblage of officials from the provincial government, coastal Native Canadian nations, logging companies and environmental groups will announce an agreement that they say will accomplish that mission in the home of the spirit bear, an area that is the world's largest remaining intact temperate coastal rain forest.

A wilderness of close to five million acres . . . in what is commonly called the Great Bear Rain Forest or the Amazon of the North will be kept off limits to loggers. . . . "There's a new era dawning . . . ," said Gordon Campbell, the province's premier. "You have to establish what you value, and work together. This collaboration is something we have to take into the future, and it is something the world can learn from." (Krauss, 2006, p. A10)

NOTE: Used by permission.

Many citizens, scientists, environmentalists, industry groups, and government officials have become frustrated with public hearings and other traditional forms of public participation. In the past 20 years, many have begun to turn to alternative ways to manage environmental conflicts. For example, as I write, an agreement on western wilderness—the Idaho "Owyhee" initiative—is before the U.S. Congress, the result of "an unusual coalition of cattlemen, environmentalists and enthusiasts of off-road vehicles, who often clash over land issues" (Eilperin, 2004, p. A2). The agreement's designation of 511,000 acres of wilderness, if passed, would be one of the largest additions in recent years to the U.S. wild and scenic river system. Among those praising the groups' work was Idaho's Senator Michael Crapo, who said the initiative "should set a standard for collaborative decision-making that should be a model" (quoted in Eilperin, p. A2).

In hundreds of communities across the country, citizens, environmentalists, business leaders, and public officials are experimenting with new approaches to public participation in environmental disputes. They are talking with their opponents across the table, working through their differences, and in many cases resolving conflicts that have festered for years. These innovative forms of conflict management have been called by different names: partnerships, community-based collaboration, citizen advisory boards, consensus decision making, and alternative dispute resolution models. Usually, they involve a form of communication called **collaboration**. *Collaboration* has been defined generally as "constructive, open, civil communication, generally as dialogue; a focus on the future; an emphasis on learning; and some degree of power sharing and leveling of the playing field" (Walker, 2004, p. 123). In many cases, participants will strive to reach agreement by **consensus**, which usually means that discussions will not end until everyone has had a chance to share his or her differences and find common ground.

The purpose of this chapter is to describe the adoption by many communities, environmentalists, and businesses of some form of collaboration to resolve environmental disputes. In the first section of the chapter, I begin with some background—the growing dissatisfaction with traditional forms of public participation, such as public hearings. I then identify a range of collaborative alternatives for resolving environmental disputes.

In the second section, I ask, When is collaboration appropriate? What communication skills are required for successful collaboration? I also look at several case studies of collaboration—some quite successful and one that has served as a cautionary tale for many environmental groups. And I introduce a key term that is important to the idea of collaboration: **stakeholder**. Stakeholders are those parties in a dispute who have a real or discernible interest (a stake) in the outcome. Finally, in the third section, I consider criticisms of collaboration and identify some of the circumstances in which collaboration may *not* be appropriate for resolving environmental conflicts.

When you've finished this chapter, you should be familiar with the benefits of collaborative approaches to resolving environmental disputes and with the communication skills needed for successful collaboration. You should also be aware of barriers to effective collaboration and circumstances under which collaborative approaches may not be appropriate. Indeed, in the end, disputes over deeply held values about the environment at times require collaboration with opponents; at other times, such disputes may call for advocacy and resistance to compromise.

New Approaches to Environmental Disputes

In the four decades since the passage of the National Environmental Policy Act (NEPA), the public's right to comment on government actions affecting the environment has been widely recognized; hence, forums for public involvement have proliferated. As we learned in the previous chapter, public comment on an environmental proposal typically takes the form of public hearings, citizen testimony, and written comments. Yet, citizens and public officials alike feel that these processes sometimes produce more frustration and division than they do reasoned decision making. Officials and consultants often speak in technical jargon, using such phrases as "parts per billion" of chemical substances, and nonexpert members of a community sometimes feel that their concerns do not matter, that their efforts to speak are dismissed by public officials and experts. In this section, I examine some of the criticisms of traditional public hearings and identify some of the emerging alternatives for public involvement.

Criticism of Public Hearings

Several years ago, public officials in a town near mine announced a public hearing after they had decided informally to build a hazardous waste facility near residential homes and a hospital. Many of the town's residents and patients' advocates understandably were upset at this. At the public hearing, they voiced their anger at officials who sat stone-faced in the front of the auditorium. While some testified, other members of the audience shouted at the officials. One young man rushed to the front of the auditorium and dumped a bag of garbage in front of the officials to dramatize his objection to hazardous waste. Area TV stations and news editorials denounced the "irrational" behavior of residents and the heavy reliance on emotion.

Are ordinary citizens really irrational? Or are public officials insensitive to the concerns of ordinary citizens, dismissing citizens' fears because they lack technical expertise? Certainly, some officials feel that the behavior of citizens is "overdramatized and hysterical" and that they must endure "the public gauntlet" of angry, shouting, sign-waving protesters (Senecah, 2004, pp. 17, 18). Yet, environmental communication scholar Susan L. Senecah (2004) poses the question differently: Are public hearings sometimes divisive or unproductive because of the way the public acts, or *is there something wrong with the process itself*? She suggests that, in many local conflicts, "a significant incongruity exists between the expectations for public participation raised by the laws . . . and the actual experiences of participants in these processes" (p. 18). Although NEPA procedures require officials to solicit the views of the public, formal mechanisms for public participation too often are simply ritualistic processes that give members of the public little opportunity to influence decisions. It's no surprise, then, that ordinary citizens so often experience "frustration, disillusionment, skepticism, and anger" (Senecah, 2004, p. 18).

What has gone wrong? Stephen Depoe, director of the University of Cincinnati's Center for Environmental Communication Studies, and John Delicath (2004) of the

U.S. General Accounting Office have surveyed the extensive literature on the shortcomings of traditional modes of public participation, such as written comments and public hearings. They identify five primary shortcomings:

1. Public participation typically operates on technocratic models of rationality, in which policymakers, administrative officials, and experts see their roles as educating and persuading the public of the legitimacy of their decisions.

2. Public participation often occurs too late in the decision-making process, sometimes even after decisions have already been made.

3. Public participation often follows an adversarial trajectory, especially when public participation processes are conducted in a "decide–announce–defend" mode on the part of officials.

4. Public participation often lacks adequate mechanisms and forums for informed dialogue among stakeholders.

5. Public participation often lacks adequate provisions to ensure that input gained through public participation makes a real impact on decisions' outcomes. (pp. 2–3)

Although formal mechanisms for citizens' involvement in influencing environmental decisions have been effective on some occasions, on others they have fallen far short of citizens' expectations. Too often, disputes over local land use or the cleanup of communities contaminated by chemical pollution linger for years. In such cases, citizens, businesses, government agencies, and environmentalists have turned to alternatives to public hearings to resolve conflicts over environmental problems.

Emergence of Alternative Forms of Public Participation

In the 1990s, new forms of public involvement in environmental decisions began to emerge, from local, neighborhood initiatives to Environmental Protection Agency (EPA)-sponsored collaborations with cities over new standards for safe drinking water.[1] As citizens, public officials, businesses, and some environmentalists have grown frustrated with traditional forms, they have begun to experiment with new ways of organizing public participation: scoping meetings, focus groups, listening sessions, advisory committees, blue-ribbon commissions, citizen juries, negotiated rule making, consensus-building exercises, working groups, and professional facilitation, among others (Dietz & Stern, 2008). For example, former President George W. Bush issued a "Facilitation of Cooperative Conservation" Executive Order, requiring federal agencies like the Environmental Protection Agency and the Departments of Interior and Agriculture to collaborate with private landowners and local governments when formulating environmental rules that impact these parties. Additionally, the EPA provides "consensus-building," "conflict prevention," and "alternative dispute resolution" services to assist its staff, managers, and external parties resolve environmental problems through its Conflict Prevention and Resolution Center (Bush, 2004).

At the heart of these experiments is some version of community or place-based collaboration among the relevant parties. Earlier, we defined *collaboration* as "constructive, open, civil communication, generally as dialogue; a focus on the future; an emphasis on learning; and some degree of power sharing and leveling of the playing field" (Walker, 2004, p. 123). Later in the chapter, I identify characteristics of collaboration that help to explain its success or failure. But first, let's look at three forms that collaboration about environmental conflicts can take: (1) citizen advisory committees, (2) natural resource partnerships, and (3) community-based collaborations.

Citizens' Advisory Committees

One of the commonest types of citizen collaboration about environmental concerns is the **citizens' advisory committee.** Also called *citizens' advisory panels* or *boards*, these usually are groups that a government agency appoints to solicit input from diverse interests in a community—citizens, businesses, environmentalists— about a project or problem. (See Figure 4.1.) For example, the Department of Defense uses Restoration Advisory Boards (RABs) to advise military officials on the social, economic, and environmental impacts of military base closings and the restoration of military lands. The purpose of RABs, which were initiated in 1994, is to "achieve dialogue between the installation and affected stakeholders; provide a

| Figure 4.1 | One of the commonest types of citizen collaboration about environmental concerns is the citizens' advisory committee. |

vehicle for two-way communication; and provide a mechanism for earlier public input" (Santos & Chess, 2003, p. 270; for more information on RABs, see http://www.epa.gov). One typical RAB is composed of interested parties in collaboration on the Department of Defense's plans to convert the Rocky Mountain Arsenal, a former chemical weapons facility, into a wildlife refuge (Johnson, 2004).

The impetus for involving communities in the work of federal agencies was one result of the Federal Advisory Committee Act of 1972. Its impact can be seen in other agencies that also use citizen advisory panels. For example, the Environmental Protection Agency uses citizen advisory panels to involve citizens in ongoing projects to clean up abandoned toxic waste sites. Similarly, the Department of Energy relies on site-specific advisory boards to involve nearby residents during the cleanup of toxic waste at former energy sites such as the nuclear weapons production facility in Fernald, Ohio. (For case studies of the collaboration between citizens and the DOE at the Fernald nuclear site, see Depoe, 2004; Hamilton, 2004, 2008.)

For most citizen advisory committees, the government agency selects participants to represent various interests or points of view or to be "representative, that is, a microcosm of the socioeconomic characteristics and the issue orientation of the public in [a] particular area" (Beierle & Cayford, 2002, pp. 45–46). The committee's work normally takes place over time in meetings of the participants. The committee's decision-making process may or may not assume that consensus will be achieved, although that is often the stated objective. Typically, the outcome of collaboration is a set of recommendations to the agency (Beierle & Cayford, 2002).

Natural Resource Partnerships

Particularly in western states, the idea of collaboration has taken off as diverse groups seek ways to manage differences over the uses of public lands and natural features. As early as the 1990s, Colorado's *High Country News* reported, "Coalitions of ranchers, environmentalists, county commissioners, government officials, loggers, skiers, and jeepers are popping up as often as wood ticks across the Western landscape" (Jones, 1996, p. 1). Sometimes called **natural resource partnerships**, these coalitions include private landowners, local officials, businesses, environmentalists, and state and federal agencies. They are organized around an identifiable region—such as a watershed, forest, or rangeland—with natural resource concerns (for example, water quality, timber, agriculture, wildlife). Such partnerships operate collaboratively to integrate their differing values and approaches to the management of natural resource issues.

Organized in 1992, the Applegate Partnership is one of the longest-running models of natural resource collaboration. It was formed after years of conflict among ranchers, local government, loggers, environmentalists, and the Bureau of Land Management (BLM) in the watershed of southwestern Oregon and northern California. Feuding parties finally decided to take a different approach. Local BLM official John Lloyd explained, "We got to the point where we just had to sit down and start talking" (Wondolleck & Yaffee, 2000, p. 7).

As they talked, it became apparent that conservationists, loggers, and community leaders all shared a love of the land and a concern for the sustainability of local communities. At its first meeting, a group of 60 people from all sides of the controversy, the partnership agreed on a vision statement that foreshadowed a model later adopted by other communities in the West:

> The Applegate Partnership is a community-based project involving industry, conservation groups, natural resource agencies, and residents cooperating to encourage and facilitate the use of natural resource principles that promote ecosystem health and diversity.
>
> Through community involvement and education, the partnership supports the management of all lands within the watershed in a manner that sustains natural resources and that will, in turn, contribute to economic and community stability within the Applegate Valley. (Wondolleck & Yaffee, 2000, pp. 140–141)

While the Applegate Partnership has encountered its share of obstacles, particularly as local farmers, businesses, environmentalists, and different federal agencies attempt to work together, it has succeeded on numerous fronts—for example, altering the terms for timber sales to promote healthier forests, initiating projects to protect local communities from fire, and restoring streams allowing salmon to return to spawning grounds. (For an evaluation of the Applegate partnership, see http://www.fs.fed.us.)

Collaboration in natural resource partnerships differs somewhat from the agency-appointed citizen advisory committee. Partnerships usually are voluntary and focus on a geographical region and a wider range of ecological concerns. Unlike a citizen advisory committee, a partnership usually works on an ongoing basis to respond to new challenges and concerns about natural resources in its region.

Community-Based Collaboration

Occasions for local disputes over the environment are numerous: loss of green space, traffic planning, contamination of well water, pollution from manufacturing plants, lead paint in older buildings, tensions between automobile drivers and bicyclists, and so forth. Increasingly, local government, courts, and civic groups are encouraging the use of collaborative processes to avoid long, contentious conflicts that can drain resources, divide groups, and weaken community relationships. Such **community-based collaboration** usually involves individuals and representatives of affected groups, businesses, or other agencies in addressing a specific or short-term problem in the local community. Often operating by consensus, this kind of collaborative group identifies goals and issues of concern, forms subgroups to investigate alternatives, and seeks support for specific solutions. Besides being court-appointed or agency-sponsored associations, these community-based groups may be voluntary associations without legal sanction or regulatory power.

Although they have some features in common with natural resource partnerships, community-based collaborations tend to focus on specific, local problems that involve a shorter time frame; partnerships, on the other hand, usually require ongoing involvement with natural resource management. For example, in Sherman County, Oregon, a conflict arose over a proposal by Northwest Wind Power (NWWP) to locate a 24-megawatt wind farm in the community. A farming community with a population of 1,900, Sherman County lies directly in the path of relentless winds from the Pacific Ocean; for this reason, the area was proposed as a site for harvesting wind energy. In other communities, proposals for wind farms had generated considerable conflict—powerful, 200-foot-tall turbines can affect aviation, bird populations, cultural and historical sites, weed control, and other ecological matters (Policy Consensus Initiative, 2004b).

In the face of potential controversy, Oregon's governor invited local farmers, citizens' groups, landowners, the Audubon Society, and representatives from local, state, and federal agencies, NWWP, and other business concerns to engage in a collaborative process to decide the fate of the proposed wind farm. Working together, the group identified possible wind-farm sites and related issues of concern, then formed subteams to address each issue. Their efforts eventually led to an agreement on a site that would have "minimal negative impacts on the community and environment" (Policy Consensus Initiative, 2004b, n.p.).

Each of these forms of participation—citizen advisory committees, natural resource partnerships, and community-based collaboration—share certain characteristics that contribute to their eventual success (or failure). Therefore, in the next section of this chapter, I identify some of the conditions that must be in place for successful collaboration, as well as the requirements for building trust among the participants and sustaining open, civil dialogue.

☞ FYI Case Studies of Successful Collaboration in Environmental Disputes

- *The Fire Next Time:* www.pbs.org/pov

  A film about the way residents in the Flathead Valley, Montana, came together to resolve conflicts over loss of jobs and the environment that threatened to tear their community apart. For a copy of this film for local showing and discussion, see http://www.pbs.org/pov.

- *Cultivating Common Ground:* www.youtube.com

  The participants in the Lakeview Stewardship Group, a natural resource partnership, tell their story of successful collaboration to restore the 500,000-acre Lakeview Federal Stewardship Unit in the Fremont-Winema National Forest in Oregon, in this brief YouTube video. For more information, see http://rlch.org.

- *A River Reborn: The Restoration of Fossil Creek:* www.mpcer.nau.edu/riverreborn

  A film documenting environmental conflict and collaboration in an Arizona community as it struggled to protect Fossil Creek by removing a 100-year old hydro-electric dam in the high desert country. The DVD, narrated by actor Ted Danson, is available at http://www.mpcer.nau.edu/riverreborn.

- National Policy Consensus Center (NPCC): www.policyconsensus.org

  For more case studies of successful resolution of environmental conflicts, see the NPCC's Policy Consensus Initiative's archive of case studies at http://www.policyconsensus.org/casestudies.

Collaborating to Resolve Environmental Conflicts

As we saw in the previous examples, collaboration clearly differs from the more traditional forms of public hearings and written comments. In their survey of successful cases of collaboration among governmental agencies and environmental groups, citizens, and business, Wondolleck and Yaffee (2000) observed that most of the successful collaborations

> fostered two-way, interactive flows of information, and decision making occurred through an open, interactive process rather than behind closed agency doors. Such efforts actively involved people throughout a planning or problem-solving process so that they learned together, understood constraints, and developed creative ideas, trust, and relationships. (p. 105)

In this section, I build on Wondolleck and Yaffee's observations to describe some of the characteristics of successful collaboration and distinguish it from traditional forms of public participation. However, before going further, it may be helpful to distinguish collaboration from two other, closely related forms of conflict resolution: arbitration and mediation. **Arbitration** is usually court ordered and involves the presentation of opposing views to a neutral, third-party individual or panel that in turn renders a judgment about the conflict. **Mediation** is a facilitated effort entered voluntarily or at the suggestion of a court, counselors, or other institution. Most important, this form of conflict management involves an active mediator who helps the disputing parties find common ground and a solution on which they agree. Whereas collaboration may use a mediator on occasion, it requires active contributions from all participants.

Collaboration is also sharply distinguished from more adversarial forms of managing environmental conflict, such as litigation, advocacy campaigns, or contentious public hearings. One of the field's leading scholars in **collaborative learning**, Gregg Walker (2004, p. 124) identifies eight attributes that distinguish collaboration from traditional forms of public participation:

1. Collaboration is less competitive.

2. Collaboration features mutual learning and fact finding.

3. Collaboration allows underlying value differences to be explored.

4. Collaboration resembles principled negotiation, focusing on interests rather than positions.

5. Collaboration allocates the responsibility for implementation across many parties.

6. Collaboration's conclusions are generated by participants through an interactive, iterative, and reflective process.

7. Collaboration is often an ongoing process.

8. Collaboration has the potential to build individual and community capacity in such areas as conflict management, leadership, decision making, and communications.

Walker's list helps us understand collaboration as a process that is distinct from more adversarial forms of public participation in environmental decisions. With these distinctions in mind, let's look at the core conditions that are typically present when collaboration succeeds.

Requirements for Successful Collaboration

Most scholars and those who have participated in effective collaborations cite a number of conditions and participant characteristics that must be present for collaboration to succeed. (See Table 4.1.)

Relevant stakeholders are at the table. A collaborative process begins when the relevant stakeholders agree to participate in a collective effort to address some problem. As we noted earlier, stakeholders are those parties to a dispute who have a real or discernible interest (a stake) in the outcome. Sometimes, they're selected by a sponsoring agency to "sit at the table," usually to represent certain interests or constituents, such as local businesses, residents, environmental groups, the timber industry, and so forth. In other cases, stakeholders self-identify and volunteer to participate. In most collaborations, stakeholders are place based; that is, they live in the affected community or region. As we shall see later, this last condition constructs a potential barrier to participation by more distant but interested parties, such as national environmental groups. (For more information about the concept of the stakeholder in environmental decision making, see Dietz & Stern, 2008.)

Participants adopt a problem-solving approach. Communication among participants strives to solve problems instead of being adversarial or manipulative. Problem solving uses discussion, conversation, and information, seeking to define the concrete problem, the relevant concerns, the criteria for appropriate solutions, and finally a solution that addresses the concerns of all parties. Although conflict is expected in the discussion, collaboration keeps the focus on the issues rather than on people. It discourages adversarial or overtly persuasive stances and instead favors listening, learning, and trying to agree on workable solutions.

All participants have access to necessary resources and opportunities to participate in discussions. In a collaborative effort, solutions cannot be imposed. If agreement is to

---

Table 4.1   Requirements of Successful Collaboration

1. Relevant stakeholders are at the table.

2. Participants adopt a problem-solving approach.

3. All participants have access to necessary resources and opportunities to participate in discussions.

4. Decisions usually are reached by consensus.

5. Relevant agencies are guided by the recommendations of the collaboration.

be reached by all parties, all participants must have an opportunity to be heard, to challenge others' views, to question, and to provide input to the solution. If an individual stakeholder represents other individuals or groups, it is also important that the concerns of these constituencies be expressed to other stakeholders in the collaboration. Finally, the group must guard against the effects of different levels of power or privilege among the participants, to ensure that all voices are respected and have opportunities to contribute and influence the solution.

Decisions usually are reached by consensus. Most collaborative groups aim to reach decisions by *consensus,* which usually means that discussions will not end until everyone has had a chance to share their differences and find common ground. Consensus often means that all participants agree with the final decision. Daniels and Walker (2001) note, however, that the Oregon Department of Land Conservation and Development uses a definition of *consensus* that leaves room for some differences of opinion. In this use, consensus is an agreement that tries to identify the interests of all stakeholders and craft a decision that addresses as many of these concerns as possible (p. 72).

Consensus can be distinguished usefully from *compromise,* another form that groups use to reach decisions. As interpersonal communication scholar Julia Wood (2009) observes, in consensus, "members may differ in how enthusiastically they support a decision, but everyone agrees to it"; whereas in a **compromise**, "members work out a solution that satisfies each person's minimum criteria but may not fully satisfy all members" (pp. 270, 271). In either case, a decision assumes some form of cooperation, requiring opposing interests to work together, a process that can take the form of "internal negotiations among participants" (Beierle & Cayford, 2002, p. 46).

Most successful collaborations go to considerable effort to avoid deciding by anything less than consensus, because support of all parties usually is necessary for solutions to work. When participants disagree, discussion typically continues until an agreement is reached or until all objections have been explored thoroughly. If the disagreement continues, groups may drop the matter, perhaps returning later, or may decide by majority vote. For these reasons, Wood (2009) advises that consensus is "inappropriate for trivial decisions, emergency issues, or decisions on which members cannot agree even after extended discussion" (p. 308).

Relevant agencies are guided by the recommendations of the collaboration. The results of a collaborative effort usually are advisory to the agency that appointed the group, for example, the report of a citizens' advisory committee to the governmental agency handling the cleanup of a toxic waste site. The recommendations are not legally binding in most cases. However, in some cases an agency may agree to implement the results of a consensus-based process. The prospect of their solution's implementation is a powerful incentive for participants to invest the time and work required for successful collaboration. When a group's recommendations are not implemented, those who participated in the collaboration often feel frustrated or angry at the energy wasted in a process the outcome of which was ignored. (For an excellent case study illustrating this problem and the requirements for successful collaboration, see Depoe, 2004.)

Successful collaboration among parties with diverse interests is not always possible, particularly in environmental disputes where the stakes are high or the parties are too deeply divided by a history of discord or entrenched opposition. This proved to be the case when the Bush administration sought to impose collaboration in U.S. Forest Service planning in 2003 and again in 2005, in lieu of the public's rights to an environmental impact statement and to appeal forest plans or activities in roadless areas and other wild forests. (Environmental groups filed lawsuits against these rule changes, and federal courts eventually overturned the new regulations.[2]) Guy Burgess and Heidi Burgess (1996), co-directors of the Conflict Research Consortium at the University of Colorado at Boulder, observed, "While consensus building can be very effective in low-stakes disputes . . . , it does not work as well when the issues involve deep-rooted value differences, very high stakes, or irreducible win-lose confrontations" (p. 1). Those who have worked with environmental conflicts generally agree that collaboration succeeds only when the adversaries come to feel that "something must change" and can identify a shared vision of the future.

Collaborating About Water Quality and the Port of Savannah

It may be helpful to look at two case studies of collaboration—a natural resource partnership and a citizen advisory committee. The first is a successful case in Ohio that resolved a dispute over water quality standards. The second case illustrates a failed collaboration over plans to deepen the Port of Savannah in Georgia. In each case, we identify the presence or absence of the core requirements for effective collaboration and illustrate the importance of these to a successful outcome.

Reaching Consensus on Consensus on Water Quality in Ohio

The state of Ohio borders on Lake Erie and is therefore one of eight states subject to a stringent agreement called the Great Lakes Water Quality Initiative. For years, large portions of the Great Lakes have been dying biologically. Pollution runoff from factories, agricultural fields, and urban sources surrounding the Great Lakes has contaminated the water and led to high levels of toxins in fish. Starting in 1995, the Environmental Protection Agency issued a far-reaching Great Lakes Water Quality Initiative, requiring the states to adopt strict standards for waste disposal and discharge into the lakes. Although the EPA gave states such as Ohio two years to come up with rules to implement the new standards, the initiative caused considerable controversy among affected industries, environmentalists, and the states' governors (Policy Consensus Initiative, 2004a).

In an attempt to reach an agreement, Ohio's governor appointed a group of 25 diverse stakeholders as a citizen advisory committee. The members included representatives of business and industry, environmental groups, universities, local and state government, and the Ohio EPA. The charge to this external advisory group

(EAG) was to seek consensus on the new water quality rules that would satisfy the requirements of the Great Lakes Water Quality Initiative.

The task before the advisory group was daunting. In addition to the diverse interests among the 25-member group, the EAG had to resolve a total of 99 issues, many technically complicated. For example, they had to establish the numerical levels, or "parts per billion," of chemicals that could be present in waters discharged into Lake Erie (Policy Consensus Initiative, 2004a, para. 1), as well as the mix of aquatic species that would indicate a healthy recovery of the Great Lakes. The director of the Ohio EPA gave the EAG a strong incentive: "If the group achieved consensus on an issue, and if the recommendation was consistent with state and federal law, [the Ohio EPA] would implement it. If the group could not reach consensus, [the director] would make a decision," taking into account the recommendations of both the agency's technical staff and the majority of the advisory group (Policy Consensus Initiative, 2004a, para. 1).

As they started, EAG members agreed on the ground rules to guide their deliberations and encourage consensus. At first, the level of trust among participants was not high enough to make progress on the 99 issues facing them. As a result, they formed subcommittees, each with its own facilitator, to begin discussions. As the subcommittees made progress, they reported their recommendations to the full group, and when agreement was reached with the Ohio EPA staff on a specific issue, the issue was crossed off the list. As progress continued, the relationships among group members improved. In the end, the State of Ohio adopted new rules for waste disposal and discharge into the Great Lakes. One facilitator summed up the two-year process: "All perspectives had been thoroughly aired, and the interest groups were confident that they had been heard" (Policy Consensus Initiative, 2004a, n.p.).

The conditions for successful collaboration clearly were present in the Ohio experience. At the outset, all parties were aware of the need to reach agreement on rules. If they failed, the state EPA office would choose the rules. The right people were present, along with authority to recommend rules to the Ohio EPA. The two-year deadline also served to motivate the search for agreement. In addition, the requirements for effective collaboration were satisfied:

1. Relevant stakeholders were invited to the table (and nonrelevant people were absent).

2. EAG members agreed to use a problem-solving approach rather than advocacy. They agreed early on ground rules for discussion and had the assistance of "impartial, skilled facilitators" (Policy Consensus Initiative, 2004a, para. 2).

3. As a result of these ground rules, the presence of facilitators, and use of subcommittees in the early period, the participants learned to work with one another and felt they had an equal opportunity to participate in discussions.

4. Most of the recommendations of the EAG were reached by consensus.

5. The relevant agency, the Ohio EPA in this case, honored its pledge to implement the committee's recommendations.

The Port of Savannah and Failed Collaboration

A less successful case of collaboration occurred recently in Savannah, Georgia, over a controversial plan to deepen the Savannah River to allow large container ships to enter the city's harbor. The Georgia Ports Authority's (GPA) plan to increase the harbor's depth by 8 feet brought opposition from many in the community. City officials were concerned that deepening the Savannah River could puncture the underlying aquifer and cause saltwater contamination of the area's source of fresh water. Local conservationists and the EPA feared that increased salinity (saltwater) and a decrease in the level of dissolved oxygen in the river would cause a "catastrophic collapse" of local fisheries and "the loss of over half of the tidal freshwater marsh which forms the centerpiece of the Savannah National Wildlife Refuge" (quoted in Toker, 2004, p. 183). As a result of this opposition, the GPA created a citizens' advisory committee called the Stakeholder Evaluation Group (SEG). It consisted of representatives of local government, business, and the citizenry, whose role would be to examine the proposal's environmental impacts and to develop a plan for alleviating them. However, as environmental communication scholar Caitlin Wills Toker (2004) concluded in her study of the controversy, the communication in the SEG meetings failed to meet this vision for resolving the dispute.

When it created the Stakeholder Evaluation Group in 1999, the Georgia Ports Authority announced that the group would be a mechanism to ensure two-way communication between the GPA and representatives of the local citizenry, businesses, and government in developing "an environmentally acceptable mitigation plan" (quoted in Toker, 2004, p. 184). In the second meeting of the SEG, the facilitator reaffirmed the ideal of collaboration, "characterizing all stakeholders as equal with 'everybody' having the 'chance to speak up and be heard'" (Toker, 2004, p. 186). Nevertheless, Toker discovered that, as the actual process unfolded, inconsistencies between the ideal and the practice surfaced in two areas: (1) unequal relationships, in which the GPA had greater authority and voice than the local stakeholders participating in the collaboration, and (2) disagreement over the meaning of *stakeholder*, specifically the inability of SEG members to attend certain meetings.

The first problem arose when SEG representatives asked for a list of concerns about the deepening of the harbor that had been expressed during the earlier public comment period. They argued that these comments had revealed impacts other than those identified by the Georgia Ports Authority for the group's deliberation, and that "these comments were the very basis for the SEG's existence" (Toker, 2004, p. 187). However, the GPA representatives insisted that these concerns already had been adequately addressed and that they were "historical issues" (p. 187). Toker notes that by defining certain topics as historical issues, the GPA representative "worked to set the agenda for the SEG rather than allowing members to begin with a list of all issues" (p. 187).

A second inconsistency between the ideal of collaboration and actual practice occurred when some stakeholders were prohibited from attending the meetings of a technical group that the Georgia Ports Authority had created. The purpose of this group was to model the impacts of the deepened harbor on fisheries and the environment, a task directly related to the announced purpose of the stakeholders' group. When a business representative in the Stakeholder Evaluation Group asked to attend these meetings, he was told that everyone was already represented because the technical group was committed to "outreach" through e-mail, hard copies of materials, and Web page postings (Toker, 2004, pp. 193, 194).

Throughout the Savannah collaboration, it became clear that some SEG participants, such as the EPA and other agencies involved in the technical research, were considered "primary agencies" with "significant interests" (Toker, 2004, p. 194). In order to accommodate the "busy schedules" of these stakeholders, the GPA's consultant explained that the technical review meetings would be held in Atlanta, Georgia—four hours' drive—because two agencies were located there, and "they're really the two important agencies that really have to get involved" (quoted in Toker, 2004, p. 194).

In the end—and despite claims of an open, equal process—some in the Stakeholder Evaluation Group discovered that they lacked the ability to address certain topics and that they were prohibited from attending important technical meetings about impacts of the proposed deepening of the Savannah harbor. Toker (2004) concludes that although the Georgia Ports Authority continued to use a vocabulary that spoke favorably of a collaborative process for decision making, in practice it gave more authority to "primary agencies" and "scientific folks" and excluded "less knowledgeable stakeholders from the technical deliberations" (p. 197). (In many ways, this problem illustrates the clash between the technical sphere and the public sphere mentioned in Chapter 1.) In order to finish its work by the deadline, the Stakeholders Evaluation Group "ultimately transformed itself from an egalitarian, consensus-based group into an exclusive and efficient decision-making group" (p. 198). But in the process, it moved away from the principles of collaboration.

Limits of Collaboration and Consensus

As we've just seen, not all attempts at collaboration and consensus-based solutions are successful. Following, we examine a case that initially appeared to be a very successful experiment in bringing together loggers, environmentalists, and local business and community leaders but that was criticized almost immediately for excluding relevant stakeholders. However, before we look at this case, it may be helpful to identify some benchmarks by which to evaluate collaborative efforts and assess the reasons for their failures, where these occur.

Evaluating Collaboration and Consensus-Based Decisions

In recent years, environmental scholars have begun to address some of the recurring problems of the traditional forums for public participation and the newer models of consensus-based decisions. For example, Daniels and Walker (2001) have proposed a modification of the collaborative process that recognizes that environmental conflicts are inevitable, often irresolvable, but manageable. Rather than taking conflict resolution as the goal, their model of collaborative learning is more modest in viewing collaboration as a process of conflict management. As environmental decisions almost always involve controversy and conflict, Daniels and Walker propose that "our task is to learn how to *manage* their conflict dimensions so that rancor does not begin to dominate the discussion and diminish the possibility of substantive improvements" (p. 16).

Recently, Senecah (2004) has offered a three-part model for assessing the different forms of public participation in environmental decisions, called the **Trinity of Voices (TOV).** The TOV builds on the importance of the stakeholder and on many of the characteristics we identified earlier for effective collaboration. Therefore, I believe it can be used as a guide to plan and assess collaboration and consensus-based approaches. Overall, the model holds that the key to an effective participation process is "an ongoing relationship of trust building to enhance community cohesiveness and capacity [to reach] good environmental decisions" (p. 23).

Specifically, the TOV model refers to three elements that most effective participatory processes seem to share and that empower a stakeholder: access, standing, and influence. Senecah (2004) explains that **access** refers to the minimum resources that citizens need to exercise fully their opportunity to participate, including convenient times and places, readily available information and technical assistance to help them understand the issues, and continuing opportunities for public involvement. By **standing**, Senecah does not mean the right to bring a legal complaint in court (see Chapter 3). Instead, she explains, standing is "the civic legitimacy, the respect, the esteem, and the consideration that all stakeholders' perspectives should be given" (p. 24). Finally, **influence** is the element felt by many to be most often missing in traditional models of public participation. Influence refers to participants' opportunity to be part of a "transparent process that considers all alternatives, opportunities to meaningfully scope alternatives, opportunities to inform the decision criteria, and thoughtful response to stakeholder concerns and ideas" (p. 25).

Let's use Senecah's TOV model to evaluate one of the most highly touted examples of collaboration, a high-profile effort by a local community to develop a consensus approach for managing national forest lands in northern California. The effort ended by moving in a different, more adversarial direction, a move that appears to have undercut its initial goals. The **Quincy Library Group** experience is a provocative case of community-based collaboration that is worth examining in some detail.

The Quincy Library Group: Conflict in the Sierra Nevada Mountains

The rural town of Quincy (fewer than 50,000 residents) is located 100 miles northeast of Sacramento, California. More important, it lies in the geographical center of the "timber wars" in the Plumas, Lassen, and Tahoe National Forests of the Sierra Nevada Mountains. Although logging increased from the 1960s through the 1980s in the three national forests around Quincy, the timber cut fell sharply in the 1990s due to shifting market demands and to Forest Service restrictions that protected old-growth trees and habitat for spotted owls and other endangered species.

As logging declined and local sawmills shut down, the area began to experience sharp conflicts between timber interests and environmentalists. For example, loggers and their families blamed the Forest Service for restricting the level of timber cuts and organized the Yellow Ribbon Coalition to lobby for their interests. Charges and counter-charges also flew between the coalition and environmentalists over instances of tree spiking (see Chapter 2) and the use of nail clusters embedded on forest roads to stop logging trucks (Wondolleck & Yaffee, 2000, p. 71). Plumas County Supervisor Bill Coates expressed the fears of many in local communities: "Our small towns were already endangered. This [decline in logging] was going to wipe them out" (Wondolleck & Yaffee, 2000, p. 71).

Initial Success: Collaboration in Quincy

Despite the controversy, some in the community began to suggest that the different camps might share a larger set of interests and values. Michael Jackson, an environmental attorney and member of Friends of Plumas Wilderness, was one of the earliest. In 1989, he wrote a letter to the local newspaper, the *Feather River Bulletin,* "arguing that environmentalists, loggers, and business needed to work together for 'our mutual future'" (quoted in Wondolleck & Yaffee, 2000, p. 71). In his letter, Jackson invited loggers to work with environmentalists toward a set of common goals:

> What do environmentalists believe we have in common with the Yellow Ribbon Coalition? We believe that we are all honest people who want to continue our way of life. We believe that we all love the area in which we live. We believe that we all enjoy beautiful views, hunting and fishing and living in a rural area. We believe that we are being misled by the Forest Service and by large timber, which controls the Forest Service, into believing that we are enemies when we are not. (quoted in Wondolleck & Yaffee, 2000, pp. 71–72)

By 1992, a few individuals in each of the warring camps—forest industry, community and business leaders, and environmentalists—began to talk about the effects of declining timber production on the community. Initially, three men agreed to talk among themselves: Bill Coates (Plumas County supervisor and a business owner who supported the timber industry), Tom Nelson (a forester for Sierra Pacific Industries), and Michael Jackson, the environmental attorney and a passionate environmentalist (see Figure 4.2). The three "found more common ground than they had expected, and decided to try to build at least a truce, maybe even a full peace treaty, based upon that common ground" (Terhune & Terhune, 1998, para. 8).

Soon other people joined the discussions of Coates, Nelson, and Jackson. Later observers recalled that these "early meetings had some very tense moments, and some participants were very uncomfortable at times" (Terhune & Terhune, 1998, p. 8). Meeting in the public library, they began calling themselves the Quincy Library Group. "Some only half-jokingly [noted] that meeting in a library would prevent participants from yelling at each other" (Wondolleck & Yaffee, 2000, p. 72).

Figure 4.2	Quincy Library Group founders Michael Jackson, Bill Coates, and Tom Nelson

Photo by Jane Braxton Little.

By 1993, members of the Quincy Library Group (www.qlg.org) had agreed among themselves on the Community Stability Plan, which the group hoped would guide management practices in the Plumas, Lassen, and Tahoe National Forests. Although this plan had no official status—the Forest Service was not involved in the discussions—it reflected the group's belief that "a healthy forest and a stable community are interdependent; we cannot have one without the other" (Terhune & Terhune, 1998, p. 11). The purpose of the Community Stability Plan was to integrate these values into a common vision: "to promote the objectives of forest health, ecological integrity, adequate timber supply, and local economic stability" (Wondolleck & Yaffee, 2000, p. 72). The group's plan set forth a series of recommendations to the Forest Service for implementing its vision:

> The plan would . . . prevent clear-cutting on Forest Service land or in wide protection zones around rivers and streams and would require group and single tree selection [logging] intended to produce an "all-age, multi-storied, fire-resistant forest approximating pre-settlement conditions." Under the plan, local timber mills would process all harvested logs. The plan also included provisions to reduce the amount of dead or dying plant material, which the group believed was posing a significant threat of fire to the area. (Wondolleck & Yaffee, 2000, p. 72)

The Community Stability Proposal was the result of many meetings, difficult conversations, and the desire of all participants to reach consensus where possible. Their agreement was unusual among the (previously) contentious parties in Quincy and its surrounding communities. Nevertheless, the Quincy Library Group confronted resistance from others that would shift it to a more adversarial process. Most important, the Forest Service—which had not participated in the collaborative process—refused to entertain the group's Community Stability Proposal.

Frustrated by resistance from the Forest Service and criticisms from other environmentalists, QLG members turned to the legislative process in Washington, D.C. After successive lobbying trips in 1998, they persuaded Congress to enact a version of the Community Stability Proposal. In an unprecedented move, the new Herger-Feinstein *Quincy Library Group* Forest Recovery Act directed the Forest Service to include this version in its management planning for the three national forests in the Quincy area.

Although I return to some of the criticisms of this experience, it is important to note that initially the Quincy Library Group received considerable praise for its collaborative work. Prompted by the feeling that "something had to change," individuals in Quincy believed that conditions were ripe for some alternative mechanism for resolving the long-simmering dispute over logging in the area's national forests. Using Senecah's (2004) TOV model, we can assess favorably the group's effort to find consensus: Participants felt they had full *access* to all meetings, information, and ongoing opportunities to participate. Despite their initial suspicions, business and community leaders, timber industry personnel, and local environmentalists learned to respect and work with each other. In Senecah's (2004) term, they had acquired *standing* in one another's eyes. And, throughout the process, participants themselves exercised *influence* in determining the vision, the criteria to be used in their deliberations, and the final set of recommendations in the Community Stability Plan.

As they looked at their work, Quincy Library Group members Pat and George Terhune (1998) admit they weren't sure why their collaboration worked or whether it could be exported to other communities. Nevertheless, their assessment closely mirrored many of the characteristics we've identified for effective collaboration. They offered these five reasons for why they believed the Quincy group worked:

1. A project of great importance was taken on. . . .

2. Convergence of attention on the issues chosen [that is, "tight focus" on a short list of issues out of the larger problem] . . .

3. Decision by true consensus . . .

4. Maintaining "unofficial" status . . . QLG has found much greater power in having complete flexibility to choose when and where to put pressure on the system. . . .

5. And . . . the luck of having the right size community or having the right people show up. (pp. 32–33)

Terhune and Terhune (1998) stressed that it is hard to overstate the importance of consensus in keeping the group together and focused. "Votes are not taken until the group is pretty well convinced that the decision will be unanimous. If it isn't, then more discussion takes place, and if anybody is still opposed, the decision is either dropped or postponed for still more discussion" (p. 32).

Criticisms of the Quincy Library Group

Not everyone was pleased with the Quincy Library Group's process or with its vision for management of the national forests. "Although the group attracted widespread public participation at first, most outsiders who had offered new ideas said they got the cold shoulder and stopped attending. When the QLG chose to go the legislative route, others dropped out" (Red Lodge, 2008). Environmentalists were upset that the QLG's proposal would double the levels of logging in the Lassen, Plumas, and Tahoe National Forests (Brower & Hanson, 1999). Others objected that the process used by the Quincy group excluded key stakeholders—particularly environmental groups concerned with the national forests—therefore evading the NEPA process (Chapter 3) and allowing local interests to set national standards for managing natural resources. (See "Another Viewpoint: A Skeptic Looks at Collaboration.")

Indeed, by 2009, it has become clear that the QLG has been frustrated in its aims. Environmental groups have continued to block implementation of many projects by filing lawsuits as well as appeals with the Forest Service. (The QLG has developed a set of "responses" to the environmental concerns on its Website; see http://www.qlg.org.)

Based on these criticisms, community-based collaborations such as the Quincy Library Group would seem to violate the principle of access in Senecah's (2004) TOV model: Certain citizens (outside the local area) were not a part of the process for setting standards for these natural resources. Such exclusions can lead to mistrust of the collaboration's outcomes by those excluded, as well as prevent access to the resources that these other (outside) citizens can provide. For example, environmentalists David Brower and Chad Hanson (1999) charged that the QLG had allowed industry interests to capture the decision process: "The Quincy plan is based on the premise of letting industry groups in rural timber towns dictate the fate of federally owned lands, essentially transferring decision-making power from the American people and into the hands of extractive industries" (p. A25). Similar criticism came from other environmentalists, editorials, and scholars studying collaborative processes. For example, Wondolleck and Yaffee (2000) observed that, instead of being "a model collaborative effort, the QLG suddenly became the focus of an acrimonious debate" (p. 265).

Another Viewpoint: A Skeptic Looks at Collaboration

In a highly publicized article printed in the western *High Country News,* the Sierra Club's former executive director, Michael McCloskey (1996), argued that collaborative processes such as the Quincy Library Group give small local groups "an effective veto" over entire national forests. McCloskey cited two shortcomings of local or place-based collaboration:

1. Placed-based collaboration excludes key stakeholders. They ignore "the disparate geographical distribution of constituencies" (p. 7). That is, those who are sympathetic to environmental values often live in urban areas; therefore, they are not invited to participate in collaborative processes in the communities near the national forests where there is a dispute.

2. Placed-based collaboration undermines national standards for managing natural resources such as national forests. By transferring the power to decide the direction for public lands to small, local groups, local collaboration evades the need to hammer out "national rules to reflect majority rule in the nation" (p. 7).

As a result, McCloskey argued, such models are an abdication of the role of government to represent the national (public) interest.

The Red Lodge Clearinghouse (2008), a project of the Natural Resources Law Center at the University of Colorado, summarized the Quincy Library Group collaboration this way:

> It is as a collaborative that the Quincy Library Group is troubling. Many who have tried to participate have felt ostracized. And although it is developing policy for managing federal lands, the coalition has demonstrated little concern for involving the broader public in its process. . . .
>
> No one knows what would be happening now if QLG had stuck with consensus and insisted on trying to include everyone. Instead, . . . the QLG took a top-down, federally mandated approach that has limited participation in the program.
>
> . . . So far, at least, that shortcut hasn't gotten the Quincy Library Group much beyond widespread name recognition. The stronger sense of community it fostered is limited to those who subscribe to its program. (Red Lodge, 2008)

The charge by Brower and Hanson (1999) that local groups can capture the decision-making process affecting U.S. public lands also illustrates a dilemma posed by *place-based* collaboration. To what extent do such models provide a mechanism for resolving contentious disputes, and to what extent do they exclude key stakeholders and ignore national standards? The Quincy experience is not encouraging in this regard.

Common Criticisms of Collaboration

Although community-based collaborations have many advantages, Daniels and Walker (2001) have observed that they have not been universally accepted as a model for handling conflicts over natural resources. In closing, it may be useful to review some of the common criticisms of the use of collaboration and consensus decision making in environmental conflicts. (For a discussion of the limits of consensus-based approaches in wildlife conservation conflicts, see Peterson, Peterson, & Peterson, 2005.) Environmental scholars and facilitators who work with such disputes have found seven complaints or occasions on which collaboration may not be appropriate:

1. *Stakeholders may be unrepresentative of wider publics.* Some scholars have suggested that the "more intensive" modes of alternative participation, such as citizen advisory councils and consensus-seeking groups, may be able to reach agreement, but they often do so only by excluding wider publics. For example, Beierle and Cayford (2002) report that "the exclusion of certain groups, the departure of dissenting parties, or the avoidance of issues ultimately made consensus possible—or at least easier—in 33%" of the cases they studied involving consensus-based efforts in which conflict was reported (p. 48). Environmental communication scholar William Kinsella (2004) also observes that highly involved individuals who serve on citizen advisory boards "do not necessarily represent the larger public"; furthermore, as they serve for long time periods, "they may lose contact with the communities and values that they are presumed to represent" (p. 90). In other situations, the questions of who is a stakeholder and who should set environmental policy lie at the heart of many local, national, and global environmental controversies.

2. *Place-based collaboration may encourage exceptionalism or a compromise of national standards.* As we witnessed in the Quincy Library Group case, the exclusion of the representatives of national environmental groups gave local interests greater control over the management of national resources. Daniels and Walker (2001) reported that such cases may "preclude meaningful opportunities for non-parties to review and comment on proposals" (p.274), encouraging a kind of **exceptionalism,** or the view that because a region has unique or distinctive features it is exempt from the general rule. The concern by some critics is that, if place-based decisions reached at the local level in one area become a precedent for exempting other geographical areas, they may compromise more uniform, national standards for environmental policy.

3. *Power inequities may lead to co-optation.* One of the most common complaints about collaboration and consensus approaches is that power inequities among the participants may lead to the co-optation of environmental interests. The greater resources in training, information, and negotiation skills often brought to collaboration processes by industry representatives and government officials may make it harder for ordinary citizens and environmentalists to defend their interests. Environmentalists such as McCloskey (1996) are especially critical of such inequities in power and resources: "Industry thinks its odds are better in these forums [place-based collaboration]. . . . It believes it can dominate them over time and relieve itself of the burden of tough national rules" (p. 7).

4. *Pressure for consensus may lead to the "lowest common denominator."* As we saw in cases of successful collaboration, groups striving for consensus may drop contentious issues or defer them until later. However, some critics fear that this tendency can go too far, that vocal minorities are given an effective veto over the process. "Any recalcitrant stakeholder can paralyze the process. . . . Only lowest common denominator ideas survive the process" (McCloskey, 1996, p. 7). Instead of a win–win solution, agreement on the least contentious parts is simply a deferral of the real sources of conflict to other forums or other times.

Conversely, a pressure for conformity among the group's members can lead to what psychologist Irving Janis (1977) called **groupthink**, that is, excessive cohesion that impedes critical or independent thinking. Indeed, in a broad survey, Robert S. Baron (2005) found that the symptoms of groupthink are widespread, the result of groupthink often being an uninformed consensus. One tragic example is the admission by FBI director Robert Mueller after the September 11, 2001, terrorist attacks on the United States that the attacks were not inevitable. Mueller said FBI agents had not exercised critical thinking and "had fallen prey to the illusion that they and America were invulnerable" (Wood, 2008, p. 244).

5. *Consensus tends to delegitimize conflict and advocacy.* Conflict can be unpleasant. For many people, civil dialogue in forums where collaboration is the rule may be a safe harbor from controversy. The desire to avoid disagreement is closely related to groupthink and may lead to a premature compromise in a collaborative setting, thus postponing the search for long-term solutions. As a result some charge that the desire for consensus "may serve to de-legitimize conflict and co-opt environmental advocates" (Daniels & Walker, 2001, p. 274).

6. *Collaborative groups may lack authority to implement their decisions.* In the Ohio water quality standards case discussed earlier, the state pledged to implement any recommendation that the Great Lakes External Advisory Group reached by consensus. But this is not always the case. Many citizens' advisory committees deliberate for extended periods without the assurance that their decisions will be accepted or implemented by federal agencies. The Quincy Library Group ran into immediate resistance from the Forest Service when it presented its proposal. The simple fact is that most collaborative groups are composed of nonelected citizens and other individuals whose authority—when present—is contingent upon the very governmental agency they are seeking to influence.

7. *Irreconcilable values may hinder agreement.* I suggested earlier that collaborative approaches do not work well when the issues involve deep-rooted value differences, very high stakes, or irreducible, win–lose confrontations. Each of us has values that we believe we cannot or should not compromise—for example, the health of our children, liberty, biodiversity, private property rights, or the right of people to be safe from industrial poisons. For example, many wilderness advocates believe that the natural environment has been compromised enough. For them, further compromises presumably are nonnegotiable.

In a larger sense, efforts to move toward consensus on environmental values confront what social theorist Chantal Mouffe (2009) has called the **democratic paradox**. This paradox results from the core tension within liberal democracy itself: the tradition of respect for individual liberties (for example, freedom of speech and property rights) and the democratic tradition of equality and the respect for the will of the majority. This "intrinsic conflict" between individual liberty and democratic majorities thus prevents an ideal solution in some environmental conflicts (Peterson, Allison, Peterson, Peterson, & Lopez, 2004, p. 744). One example is the conflict that sometimes exists between private property owners and democratic majorities that support restrictions on property in order to protect habitat for endangered species.

Most successful instances of collaboration assume that not all conflict is bad and not all controversy should be avoided in group deliberations. Indeed, what communication scholar Thomas Goodnight and others have called "dissensus" may serve an important communication role (Fritch, Palczewski, Farrell, & Short, 2006; Goodnight, 1991). **Dissensus** is a questioning of, refusal of, or disagreement with a claim or a premise of a speaker's argument. Rather than bringing a discussion to a halt, dissensus can be generative. If properly handled, it may invite more communication about the areas of disagreement between the differing parties. In summary, the attractiveness of collaboration and consensus models for managing environmental conflicts should not overshadow the difficulties these processes may involve. For example, even when all parties with a stake in the conflict are involved, it may not be possible to level the playing field between citizens and the skilled representatives of industry or to identify solutions to conflicts between different or deeply rooted values.

SUMMARY

A s a result of their frustration with public hearings and other traditional forms of public participation, many communities, environmentalists, business leaders, and government agencies have begun to turn to alternative forms for addressing environmental conflicts. In the 1990s, alternative forums for public involvement in environmental decisions began to emerge, such as citizens' advisory committees, natural resource partnerships, and community-based collaborations. At the heart of these experiments is some version of *collaboration* among the relevant parties, which we defined as a "constructive, open, civil communication, generally as dialogue; a focus on the future; an emphasis on learning; and some degree of power sharing and leveling of the playing field" (Walker, 2004, p. 123).

Although successful collaborations on environmental matters have varied widely, they generally have been seen as requiring five conditions: (1) that all relevant stakeholders are at the table; (2) that the participants adopt a problem-solving approach; (3) that all participants have equal access to resources and opportunities to participate in discussions; (4) that decisions usually are reached by consensus; and (5) that the relevant agencies are guided by the recommendations of the collaborating group.

Although the collaboration and consensus approaches have been helpful in resolving numerous disputes, those who have helped to facilitate such groups or who have participated in them also have reported a number of recurring complaints and problems. These range from failure to include key stakeholders to pressure toward the lowest common denominator in order to reach consensus. Indeed, we found that collaboration may not always be possible, especially when a conflict involves deep differences over values or irreducible win–lose confrontations.

Our ability to manage the conflicts that arise in human relationships with the environment may require us to listen to one another and perhaps learn new ways to narrow the scope of our differences. As we've seen in the successful cases of collaboration in this chapter and also in the failures, our communication behaviors have consequences—whether we choose to listen to certain voices and not others, speak up for a different perspective, or find common ground with others. Neither collaboration nor the more adversarial forms of communication provide a magic answer to the difficulties that arise from the complex human–environment relationship. Indeed, in the end, disputes over deeply held values about the environment may require both conflict and conversation—collaboration with opponents and, at other times, advocacy of values that cannot or should not be compromised. Collaboration—like advocacy—has a place in managing environmental conflicts, but no single mode is always the most appropriate or effective path to a solution.

KEY TERMS

Communication-Related Concepts

Access: The minimum resources that citizens need to exercise fully their opportunity to participate, including convenient times and places, readily available information and technical assistance to help them understand the issues, and continuing opportunities for public involvement.

Arbitration: The presentation of opposing views to a neutral, third-party individual or panel that, in turn, renders a judgment about the conflict; usually court ordered.

Citizens' advisory committee: Also called a citizens' advisory panel or board, a group appointed by a government agency to solicit input from diverse interests in a community—for example, citizens, businesses, and environmentalists—about a project or problem.

Collaboration: "Constructive, open, civil communication, generally as dialogue; a focus on the future; an emphasis on learning; and some degree of power sharing and leveling of the playing field" (Walker, 2004, p. 123).

Collaborative learning: An approach to collaboration that recognizes that environmental conflicts are inevitable, often irresolvable, but manageable; rather than taking conflict resolution as the goal, this approach is more modest in enabling participants to learn how to manage their conflicts so that rancor does not dominate the discussion and diminish the possibility of substantive improvements.

Community-based collaboration: An approach to problem solving that involves individuals and representatives of affected groups, businesses, and other agencies in addressing a specific or short-term problem defined by the local community. Like natural resource partnerships, collaborative groups are usually voluntary associations without legal sanction or regulatory powers.

Compromise: An approach to problem solving in which participants work out a solution that satisfies each person's minimum criteria but may not fully satisfy all.

Consensus: The assumption that discussions will not end until everyone has had a chance to share differences and find common ground; often means that all participants agree with the final decision.

Democratic paradox: Term used by social theorist Chantal Mouffe (2009) to refer to the tension between two different traditions in Western societies: the liberal tradition of respect for individual liberty, and the democratic tradition of equality and respect for the will of the majority.

Dissensus: Term coined by communication scholar Thomas Goodnight (1991), meaning a questioning of, refusal of, or disagreement with a claim or a premise of a speaker's argument.

Exceptionalism: The view that, because a region has unique or distinctive features, it is exempt from the general rule. Some critics are concerned that place-based decisions reached at the local level in one area can become a precedent for exempting other geographical areas and thus compromise more uniform, national standards for environmental policy.

Groupthink: Term coined by psychologist Irving Janis (1977) referring to an excessive cohesion in groups that impedes critical or independent thinking, often resulting in uninformed consensus.

Influence: In Senecah's Trinity of Voices model, a term referring to participants' opportunity to be part of a "transparent process that considers all alternatives, opportunities to meaningfully scope alternatives, opportunities to inform the decision criteria, and thoughtful response to stakeholder concerns and ideas" (Senecah, 2004, p. 25).

Mediation: A facilitated effort, entered into voluntarily or at the suggestion of a court, counselors, or other institution, that involves an active mediator who helps the disputing parties find common ground and a solution upon which they can agree.

Stakeholders: Those parties to a dispute who have a real or discernible interest (a stake) in the outcome.

Standing: A term in Senecah's Trinity of Voices model that refers to the civic legitimacy—the respect, esteem, and consideration that all stakeholders' perspectives should be given; in this context, the term does not refer to legal standing in a court of law.

Trinity of Voices (TOV): Senecah's model for assessing the quality of public participation processes; holds that the key to an effective participation process is an ongoing relationship of trust building to enhance community cohesiveness and the capacity to reach good environmental decisions. The model poses three elements—access, standing, and influence—that empower stakeholders and are shared by most effective participatory processes.

Environment-Related Concepts

Natural resource partnerships: Informal working groups organized around regions with natural resource concerns such as the uses of rangelands, forests, and water resources for timber, agriculture, grazing, off-road motorized recreation, as well as concerns for protection of forests, wildlife, and watersheds. Partnerships operate collaboratively to integrate their differing values and approaches to the management of natural resource issues.

Quincy Library Group: A high-profile effort by a local community to develop a consensus approach for managing national forest lands in northern California. The effort ended by moving in a different, more adversarial direction, a move that appears to have undercut its initial goals.

DISCUSSION QUESTIONS

1. Would you feel comfortable speaking up or disagreeing with the majority in a collaborative process? Would you still support a group consensus even if your preferred solution was not adopted, as long as you felt that the group had fairly considered your views before it reached its decision?

2. McCloskey (1996) is critical of the inequities in power and resources between representatives of industry and others in consensus groups. "Industry thinks its odds are better in these forums. . . . It believes it can dominate them over time" (p. 7). Do you agree? In consensus groups, can ordinary citizens and industry representatives truly have equal access to resources and equal influence on decisions?

3. Is compromise or consensus possible in environmental conflicts over logging in national forests, over oil drilling in times of energy crisis in wilderness areas like the Arctic National Wildlife Refuge, or overprotecting critical habitat for endangered species on private property?

NOTES

1. President Bill Clinton's administration (1993–2001) sponsored several collaboration projects, including the Environmental Protection Agency's Project XL (a national pilot program that invited state and local governments, businesses, and federal agencies to develop innovative strategies for achieving environmental protection and public health). In 1995, in his Reinventing Government Initiative, President Clinton also identified consensus and the inclusion of stakeholders as the preferred method of public participation (Toker, 2004).

2. In 2005, a federal appeals court overturned the Bush administration's rule reducing the public's right to review and appeals procedures under the National Forest Management Act by allowing federal agencies to "categorically exclude" the entire forest planning process from NEPA requirements for an environmental impact statement (EIS) and public participation requirements (*Defenders of Wildlife v. Johanns*). And in 2007, the courts similarly invalidated the new regulations that excluded the public's right to appeal of categorical exclusions of proposed "hazardous fuels reduction activities" in the National Forests (*Sierra Club v. Bosworth*).

REFERENCES

Beierle, T. C., & Cayford, J. (2002). *Democracy in practice: Public participation in environmental decisions.* Washington, DC: Resources for the Future.

Baron, R. S. (2005). So right it's wrong: Groupthink and the ubiquitous nature of polarized group decision making. In M. P. Zanna (Ed.), *Advances in experimental social psychology* (Vol. 37, pp. 219–253). San Diego. Elsevier Academic.

Brower, D., & Hanson, C. (1999, September 1). Logging plan deceptively marketed, sold. *The San Francisco Chronicle,* p. A25.

Burgess, G., & Burgess, H. (1996). *Consensus building for environmental advocates.* Working Paper #96–1. Boulder: University of Colorado Conflict Research Consortium.

Bush, G. W. (2004, August 26). Executive Order 13352, Facilitation of cooperative conservation. Washington, DC: The White House, Office of the Press Secretary.

Daniels, S. E., & Walker, G. B. (2001). *Working through environmental conflict: The collaborative learning approach.* Westport, CT: Praeger.

Depoe, S. P. (2004). Public involvement, civic discovery, and the formation of environmental policy: A comparative analysis of the Fernald citizens task force and the Fernald health effects subcommittee. In S. P. Depoe, J. W. Delicath, & M-F. A. Elsenbeer (Eds.), *Communication and public participation in environmental decision making* (pp. 157–173). Albany: State University of New York Press.

Depoe, S. P., & Delicath, J. W. (2004). Introduction. In S. P. Depoe, J. W. Delicath, & M-F. A. Elsenbeer (Eds.), *Communication and public participation in environmental decision making* (pp. 1–10). Albany: State University of New York Press.

Depoe, S. P., Delicath, J. W., & Elsenbeer, M-F. A. (Eds.). (2004). *Communication and public participation in environmental decision making.* Albany: State University of New York Press.

Dietz, T., & Stern, P. C. (Eds.). (2008). *Public participation in environmental assessment and decision making.* National Research Council of the National Academies. Washington, DC: National Academies Press.

Eilperin, J. (2004, April 14). Groups unite behind plan to protect Idaho wilderness. *Washington Post,* p. A2.

Fritch, J., Palczewski, C. H., Farrell, J., & Short, E. (2006). Disingenuous controversy: Responses to Ward Churchill's 9/11 essay. *Argumentation and Advocacy, 42*(4), 190–205.

Goodnight, G. T. (1991). Controversy. In D. Parson (Ed.), *Argument in controversy* (pp. 1–12). Annandale, VA: Speech Communication Association.

Hamilton, J. D. (2004). Competing and converging values of public participation: A case study of participant views in Department of Energy nuclear weapons cleanup. In S. P. Depoe, J. W. Delicath, & M-F. A. Elsenbeer (Eds.), *Communication and public participation in environmental decision making* (pp. 59–81). Albany: State University of New York Press.

Hamilton, J. D. (2008). Convergence and divergence in the public dialogue on nuclear weapons cleanup. In B. C. Taylor, W. J. Kinsella, S. P. Depoe, & M. S. Metzler (Eds.), *Nuclear legacies: Communication, Controversy, and the U.S. nuclear weapons complex* (pp. 41–72). Lanham, MD: Lexington Books.

Janis, I. L. (1977). *Victims of groupthink.* Boston: Houghton Mifflin.

Johnson. K. (2004, April 19). Weapons moving out, wildlife moving in. *The New York Times,* p. 15.

Jones, L. (1996, May 13). "Howdy, Neighbor!" As a last resort, Westerners start talking to each other. [Colorado] *High Country News, 28,* pp. 1, 6, 8.

Kinsella, W. J. (2004). Public expertise: A foundation for citizen participation in energy and environmental decisions. In S. P. Depoe, J. W. Delicath, & M-F. A. Elsenbeer (Eds.), *Communication and public participation in environmental decision making* (pp. 83–95). Albany: State University of New York Press.

Krauss, C. (2006, February 7). Coalition of natives, loggers and environmentalists join hands. *The New York Times,* p. A10.

McCloskey, M. (1996, May 13). The skeptic: Collaboration has its limits. [Colorado] *High Country News, 28,* p. 7.

Mouffe, C. (2009). *The democratic paradox.* London: Verso.

Peterson, M. N., Allison, S. A., Peterson, M. J., Peterson, T. R., & Lopez, R. R. (2004). A tale of two species: Habitat conservation plans as bounded conflict. *Journal of Wildlife Management, 68*(4), 743–761.

Peterson, M. N., Peterson, M. J., & Peterson, T. R. (2005). Conservation and the myth of consensus. *Conservation Biology, 19,* 762–767.

Policy Consensus Initiative. (2004a). Reaching *consensus in Ohio on water quality standards.* Retrieved September 4, 2004, from http://www.policyconsensus.org.

Policy Consensus Initiative. (2004b). *State collaboration leads to successful wind farm siting.* Retrieved September 6, 2004, from http://www.policyconsensus.org.

Red Lodge Clearinghouse. (2008, April 11). *Quincy library group.* A project of the Natural Resources Law Center at the University of Colorado Law School. Retrieved November 22, 2008, from http://rlch.org.

Santos, S. L., & Chess, C. (2003). Evaluating citizen advisory boards: The importance of theory and participant-based criteria and practical implications. *Risk Analysis, 23,* 269–279.

Senecah, S. L. (2004). The trinity of voice: The role of practical theory in planning and evaluating the effectiveness of environmental participatory processes. In S. P. Depoe, J. W. Delicath, & M-F. A. Elsenbeer (Eds.), *Communication and public participation in environmental decision making* (pp. 13–33). Albany: State University of New York Press.

Terhune, P., & Terhune, G. (1998, October 8–10). *QLG case study.* Prepared for workshop "Engaging, Empowering, and Negotiating Community: Strategies for Conservation and Development." Sponsored by the Conservation and Development Forum, West Virginia University, and the Center for Economic Options. Retrieved August 12, 2004, from http://www.qlg.org/pub.

Toker, C. W. (2004). Public participation or stakeholder frustration: An analysis of consensus-based participation in the Georgia Ports Authority's stakeholder evaluation group. In S. P. Depoe, J. W. Delicath, & M-F. A. Elsenbeer (Eds.), *Communication and public participation in environmental decision making* (pp. 175–200). Albany: State University of New York Press.

Walker, G. B. (2004). The roadless area initiative as national policy: Is public participation an oxymoron? In S. P. Depoe, J. W. Delicath, & M-F. A. Elsenbeer (Eds.), *Communication and public participation in environmental decision making* (pp. 113–135). Albany: State University of New York Press.

Wondolleck, J. M., & Yaffee, S. L. (2000). *Making collaboration work: Lessons from innovation in natural resource management.* Washington, DC: Island Press.

Wood, J. T. (2009). *Communication in our lives* (5th ed.). Boston: Wadsworth Cengage Learning.

Wood, J. T. (2008). *Communication mosaics: An introduction to the field of communication* (5th ed.) Belmont, CA: Thompson Wadsworth.

PART III

Media Coverage
of the Environment

Former Vice President Al Gore's Alliance for Climate Protection uses a range of media—TV ads, Websites, news conferences, and ad placements on blogs—to educate the public about solutions to global warming.

© Paul Chinn/San Francisco Chronicle/Corbis.

CHAPTER 5

Media and the Environment Online

Most of what society learns about the environment is from news. . . . [Yet] news is not an objective presentation of political reality, but an interpretation of events and issues from the perspective of reporters, editors, and selected sources. . . .

—Travis Wagner (2008, p. 27)

People sense the weather is weird, but it's incredibly rare to hear the phrase "global warming" spoken by your local TV meteorologist. This is an opportunity to teach people about climate, just like we did with weather.

—Dr. Heidi Cullen, Weather Channel climatologist
(quoted in Friedman, 2008, p. 136)

B y now, we've seen that our perceptions and attitudes toward nature and environmental problems are mediated by many sources—popular culture, news, scientific reports, films, political debate, and so forth. Among the important sources of information about the environment are news media and representations of "environment" online. In describing "news media," however, it is important to distinguish between traditional, *mainstream* media and newer, online media. By **mainstream media**, I mean network television and cable news, newspapers, news magazines, and radio news and shows. And, in this chapter, I refer to online media specifically to mean Internet news services, blogs, Web TV, and other online sources that have arisen to challenge the mainstream media's control of information about the environment.

It is important to differentiate mainstream and online media, for at the heart of mainstream environmental journalism is a dilemma. Journalism professor Sharon

Friedman (2004) observed that environmental journalists working in traditional media today must deal with a "shrinking news hole while facing a growing need to tell longer, complicated and more in-depth stories" (p. 176). In journalistic parlance, a **news hole** is the amount of space that is available for a newspaper or TV news story, relative to other demands for the same space. Friedman argues that competition for shrinking news space increases pressure on journalists to simplify or dramatize issues to ensure that a story gets out. As a result, we are witnessing a rapid growth in alternative (online) media, offering greater freedom and news "space."

In this chapter we explore the constraints on environmental journalists and, to a lesser extent, commercial programming in mediating our perceptions, attitudes, and behavior regarding the environment. The first section looks at the ways nature is depicted in traditional news media and entertainment programs. The second section identifies some of the constraints on mainstream news production, such as media frames and the requirements for newsworthiness that influence the way stories are composed. The third section traces the influence of new (online) media—from the proliferation of blogs and online news services to online forums such as the *Yale Forum on Climate Change and the Media*—in expanding news and analyses about environmental issues. Finally, I present some of the research on *media effects* and the debate about the importance of the media in influencing attitudes and behavior related to the environment.

When you have finished this chapter, you'll be aware of some of the factors that influence the production of news about the environment, as well as the media's rhetorical construction of nature and environmental problems. You should also be able to raise questions about the possible influence of media in shaping our perceptions, attitudes, and behavior, as well as media's potential for public education about important environmental concerns.

Media Depictions of Nature

The mainstream media's portrayal of nature is hardly uniform. Images of polar bears and melting glaciers clash with ads depicting popular sports utility vehicles climbing rugged mountain ridges. *National Geographic* filmmakers capture hungry lions stalking gazelles even as television ads for Caribbean islands portray a more innocent nature. In this section, I explore the diverse, even conflicting depictions of nature in mainstream news and entertainment programs, even as the frequency of media stories about the environment periodically rise and fall over the years.

Media Representations of Nature

By the 1960s, news stories and visual images of environmental concerns began to appear prominently in the mainstream media, from the photo of the Earth taken by astronauts on *Apollo 8* in 1968 to TV film of an oil spill off the coast of Santa Barbara, and *Time* magazine's story of the Cuyahoga River in Ohio bursting into flames from pollution in 1969. During the next four decades, mainstream media's interest in environmental themes would periodically expand and wane, portraying nature and the environment in rich, multi-dimensional, and conflicting ways.

Frequency of References to the Environment

In the years after Earth Day 1970, mainstream media's interest in the environment continued to be strong, reaching a high point in 1989, the year of the *Exxon Valdez* oil spill in Alaska. Film of oil-soaked birds and otters and oil-blackened coast lines of Alaska's Prince William Sound filled nightly TV screens (see Figure 5.1). The Tyndall Report, which tracks network news minutes, reported that in 1989, environmental stories saw an unprecedented 774 minutes, combined, on the *CBS Evening News, NBC Nightly News,* and *ABC World News Tonight* (Hall, 2001). With the election of an environmentally friendly administration in Washington, D.C., in 1992, many media analysts expected continued interest in environmental stories.

The years following the *Exxon Valdez* oil spill, however, would see a marked difference. Shabecoff (2000) reports that not only did environmental stories not grow in the 1990s during President Bill Clinton's administration, but the total number of news stories about the environment carried by newspapers and television networks declined substantially. The Tyndall Report tracked a low of 174 minutes in 1996 for the major TV news reports and 195 minutes in 1998 (Hall, 2001). By the end of the 1990s decade, environmental reporters in New England were citing shrinking news holes as one of the most frequent barriers to coverage of environmental news (Sachsman, Simon, & Valenti, 2002).

| Figure 5.1 | After the *Exxon Valdez* oil spill in 1989, images of oil-soaked birds, otters, and oil-blackened coastlines of Alaska's Prince William Sound filled nightly TV screens. |

© Ben Osborne/Getty Images.

Similarly, in their study of fictional and non-news entertainment television shows, media scholars Katherine A. McComas, James Shanahan, and Jessica S. Butler (2001) found that attention to environmental themes decreased in the 1990s. They looked at programs on local affiliates of ABC, CBS, NBC, and (in 1997) Fox TV in the study period of 1991 to 1997. Out of 510 programs, McComas and her colleagues found a total of 72 environmental episodes. Furthermore, each episode itself was very brief: "Forty-seven of the 72 episodes lasted less than 15 seconds, most actions were over in less than 1 minute, and only 6 episodes lasted longer than 6 minutes" (p. 538). In short, the total time devoted to environmental themes—positive *or* negative—in prime-time television entertainment programs is glaringly low. McComas and colleagues concluded, "If all of the episodes were played back to back as one long episode, the 2 hours and 22 minutes of environmental references would not outlast one Monday Night Football game" (p. 539).

A resurgence in environmental coverage began briefly after President George W. Bush came into office in January 2001. Hall (2001) observed that the controversial policies of the Bush administration—such as the relaxing of rules for arsenic levels in drinking water—apparently put the environment back on page 1. This new trend, however, was interrupted with the events of September 11, 2001, when news coverage turned sharply to focus on terrorism and the war in Iraq. Friedman (2004) reports that nearly all the environmental journalists with whom she consulted during this period agreed that "the events of September 11 have shrunk the [environmental] news hole even further" (p. 179).

Since 2006, however, coverage of the environment has dramatically expanded across all media—newspapers, TV, online blogs and news sites, and "green" business stories. For example, in the past three years, popular magazines like *Glamour, Time, Vanity Fair,* and *Sports Illustrated* have flooded newsstands with special "green" cover issues, such as "The Green Issue," "The 10 Easiest Things You Can Do to Help the Planet," and "Sports and Global Warming," as well as *Time* magazine's April 3, 2006, cover warning, "Be Worried. Be Very Worried." And readers are responding: *Outside*'s 2008 green issue, for example, sold 30 percent more newsstand copies than the year before (Wilson, 2008, p. 1).

Newspaper stories about the environment are also expanding at unprecedented rates. Newspaper reporting on global warming, particularly, "has spiked over the last few years" (Brainard, 2008, para. 10). Roger Cohn, editor of the new *Yale Environment 360* online magazine, explained that the increased coverage of environmental issues is "strictly a reflection of heightened interest based on the implications of climate change" (quoted in Juskalian, 2008, para. 5). Similarly, there has been a dramatic rise in "green" business stories. Indeed, the number of environmentally related business news stories more than doubled in 2007 from the previous year, and "nearly seven times greater than . . . the year before that" ("'Green' Reporting," 2007, p. 4).

Down's Issue-Attention Cycle

An intriguing variation of the trend in media coverage is the different accounts of public support for environmental concerns over time. Has support among the public steadily increased, declined, or been uneven over time? A somewhat skeptical account is Anthony Downs's (1972) classic model of the **issue-attention cycle** and what is termed the "natural decline" of the public's concern with environmental issues (Dunlap, 1992, p. 90). Writing shortly after Earth Day in 1970, Downs predicted that the public's attention to environmental issues would go through the same stages as most social problems, from the public's lack of awareness to active engagement to disinterest. Dunlap summarizes Downs's five-stage progression:

1. The pre-problem stage

2. Alarmed discovery and euphoric enthusiasm

3. Realization of the cost of significant progress (the stage in which public support wanes)

4. A gradual decline in intense public interest

5. The post-problem stage, in which the issue moves into "a twilight of lesser attention" (Downs, 1972, p. 40).

In fact, research indicates that public interest in environmental problems has neither disappeared nor remained constant over the years. Rather, the public's environmental concern seems to go through bursts of support as well as periods of lesser interest, "at times shifting around definitive peaks and troughs" (Guber, 2003, p. 57). Political scientists Norman Vig and Michael Kraft (2003) conclude that, although developments such as 9/11 may divert the public's interest from environmental issues for a short term, over time "one can see the continuity of strong public support for environmental protection and expanding environmental authority" (p. 10).

Differing Views of Nature in Media

Beyond the frequency of environmental stories in news and entertainment programs, what is actually said or shown about nature itself? Do these depictions invite concern for environmental values or a desire to dominate or manage nature for our purposes? In Chapter 2, we saw that, rhetorically, nature can be presented in different ways, from the fearsome sermons of early colonial preachers to the passion for wild areas of preservationists such as John Muir. In her book *What Is Nature?* British philosopher Kate Soper (1995) observed that mainstream media construct contradictory images of nature—treacherous and sublime, and more:

> Nature is both machine and organism, passive matter and vitalist agency. It is represented as both savage and noble, polluted and wholesome, lewd and innocent, carnal and pure, chaotic and ordered. Conceived as a feminine principle, nature is equally lover, mother and virago: a source of sensual delight, a nurturing bosom, a site of treacherous and vindictive forces bent on retribution for her human violation. Sublime and pastoral, indifferent to human purposes and willing servant of them, nature awes as she consoles, strikes terror as she pacifies, presents herself as both the best of friends and the worst of foes. (p. 71)

If popular media images depict nature as both "the best of friends and the worst of foes," does this mean that there are no problems in the media's representations of nature? Or are there stable and recurring trends in media's depictions?

The research is somewhat mixed, as might be expected. For example, in their study of television entertainment programs noted earlier, McComas, Shanahan, and Butler (2001) rated 46 percent of the episodes from these shows "neutral," 40 percent "concerned," and 13 percent "unconcerned" about the environment (p. 538). More recently, Meisner (2005) surveyed images of nature in a comprehensive study of Canadian media that included newspapers, magazines, and prime-time television shows (news, drama, documentaries, comedy, science fiction, and current affairs). He reported that the most prominent representations of nature found in these media could be classified according to four major themes: (1) nature as a victim, (2) nature as a sick patient, (3) nature as a problem (threat, annoyance, and so forth), and (4) nature as a resource.

Meisner found that, not unlike Soper's account, these themes offered two competing views of nature: "Sometimes there seems to be a strong admiration and desire for Nature. At other times there is a hatred. Sometimes there is a strong injunction to connect with or care for Nature. At other times the injunction is to fight or exploit it" (p. 432). Overall, however, he found that the frequency of images valuing nature positively outweighed negative images by a ratio of 3 to 1.

Although the themes in this study appear contradictory at times, Meisner argues that there is an overarching theme: a "symbolic domestication of nature" (p. 434). By **symbolic domestication**, he means the rhetorical construction of nature as something tame and useful but also fragile and in need of human care and protection. He observes that these depictions invite a narrow range of possible human relationships with nature that are consistent with symbolic domestication. The relationships included Care for Nature, Protect Nature, Control Nature, Manage Nature, Use Nature, and Enjoy Nature (p. 431). Overall, Meisner concludes, these relationships suggest that a strong technological optimism guides human relations with nature, and this optimism cultivates in us the view of nature as something to protect, control, use, or enjoy. Indeed, he suggests that media that reproduce these images are "promoting an **anthropocentric and resourcist ideology of Nature**," that is, they primarily "serve the interests of those who benefit the most from the exploitation of Nature" (p. 435).

A related example of such cultural representations of nature from prime-time entertainment media might be *The Simpsons Movie* (2007) and the long-running *The Simpsons* cartoon television show. *Entertainment Weekly* has called *The Simpsons* television series "guerrilla TV, a wicked satire masquerading as a prime-time cartoon" (Korte, 1997, p. 9). We could also say that from the perspective of environmental communication, the show borrows themes in news and public debate about the environment for its satiric commentary, embodied in its key episodes. This is the view of communication critic Anne Marie Todd (2002) in her critical study of *The Simpsons.* Todd argues that the show "presents a strong ideological message about nature as a symbol—as an object for human exploitation" (p. 77).

In particular, Todd singles out the character of Lisa, the brainy daughter whose concern for the environment often emerges as a humorous counterpoint to the anthropocentricism of her father, Homer. (As used by many environmentalists, **anthropocentricism** is the belief that nature exists solely for the benefit of humans.) For example, "When Lisa bemoans the crashing of an oil tanker on Baby Seal Beach, Homer comforts her. . . . 'It'll be okay, honey. There's lots more oil where that came from'" (Appel, 1996, in Todd, 2002, p. 78). Todd notes that Homer's only concern about the oil tanker's wreck is whether there will be enough oil left for his and his family's usual lifestyle.

But why certain portrayals of nature and not others? One influence on media is the ease with which reporters can convey the subject's importance to viewers or readers who may know or care little about it. The challenge is that many environmental problems are both complex and *unobtrusive;* that is, it is not easy to link their relevance concretely to our lives. This makes it difficult to fit these concerns into the media's conventions for reporting and entertaining. Let's examine this further.

Unobtrusive Environmental Threats

In 1979, reports of a possible meltdown of the reactor core at the Three Mile Island nuclear plant became breaking news and captured headlines worldwide. The movie *The China Syndrome,* about a threatened nuclear plant meltdown, had just appeared in theaters, fueling the public's imagination about the horrors of an accident at a nuclear plant. But most environmental threats are usually far less dramatic. Chemical contamination, the loss of biodiversity, climate change, and other threats to human health and ecological systems are less visible and often go unnoticed for years or decades. These are **unobtrusive events** because they are remote from one's personal experience. Because many toxic chemicals are invisible and their effects on us delayed, we rarely notice such toxins in our everyday lives. Such contamination also may be a nonissue for government officials and the media because of this invisibility and lack of immediate impact.

As a result of the unobtrusiveness of many environmental concerns, the mainstream media have difficulty covering these issues and often report or represent issues in sensational ways. For example, Wilkins and Patterson (1990) found that newspapers frequently cover "slow-onset hazards," such as ozone depletion or global warming, in the same ways as traditional news stories, as *specific events* rather than as longer term developments. I recall learning of scientists' discovery of the gradual warming of the Earth's atmosphere many years ago by seeing a news story, "The Dunes of Durham," on a local television station in North Carolina. The news segment showed a reporter standing atop a sand dune (several hundred miles from the television station). I remember the reporter excitedly announcing that a new study warned that the Earth's temperature was rising and that melting polar ice caps would flood our coastal areas. If true, he predicted, Durham residents wouldn't have to travel quite as far to enjoy the state's beaches!

"The Dunes of Durham" was probably more sensational than many news media accounts of unobtrusive concerns. Still, news stories about the loss of biodiversity often focus not on moss or insects but on threats to charismatic fauna (the polar bear, the panda, the bald eagle), whereas stories about the pollution of the oceans may focus not on the cumulative effects of multiple industrial sources but on a dramatic oil spill or discharges from a well-known cruise liner. To cover unobtrusive events, news media often must find an event to link to the story, and such event-centered stories usually attribute the problem to one-time actions by individuals or corporations rather than to longer term social and economic developments (Wilkins & Patterson, 1990).

I don't mean to suggest that there is little or no value in mainstream news reporting on environmental problems. Clearly, that is not the case. Awareness of global warming has increased, and the dangers of chemical contamination have become part of our national consciousness. For example, recent coverage of mercury contamination from old, coal-fired power plants and its effects on human health has been exemplary. Yet, even in these cases, the effects observed by Wilkins and Patterson can be seen in stories that center on specific people and events rather than on the less visible, less immediate sources of mercury contamination. For example, in a *USA Today* article, "Mercury Damage 'Irreversible,'" scientists at Harvard found that "methyl mercury contamination of fish can cause heart damage and irreversible impairment to brain function in children, both in the womb and as they grow" (Weise, 2004a, para. 1). While the story foregrounds the horrible impacts on children, it offers no explanation of how mercury gets into fish in the first place, nor does it mention steps that public authorities are taking (or not taking) to reduce the source of mercury emissions from aging power plants.

The difficulty of reporting unobtrusive environmental and health effects, as the *USA Today* story about mercury suggests, raises important questions about the forces that shape the production of news. Therefore, it is important for us to look at influences on the reporting of environmental subjects and also at the effects of these constraints on viewers' and readers' perceptions and behavior.

News Production and the Environment

Representations of nature and of environmental problems such as toxic levels of mercury in pregnant women are shaped by an array of forces that influence and often limit the way these topics are covered by mainstream media. In her study of environmental journalism, *Media, Culture, and the Environment,* Anderson (1997) reports that the production of mainstream news is influenced by a range of factors, from the need to sell papers or garner market share for TV viewers to editorial policy and ownership and the constraints of a "shrinking news hole." In this section, we look at five factors that constrain news production generally and environmental news in particular: (1) media political economy, (2) gatekeeping and the environmental beat, (3) newsworthiness, (4) media frames, and (5) norms of objectivity and balance.

Political Economy

The term **media political economy** refers to the influence of ownership and the economic interests of the owners of newspapers and television networks on the news content of these media sources. In her critical study of corporate influence on the media, Australian environmental scholar Sharon Beder (2002) noted that most commercial media organizations are owned by multinational corporations with financial interests in other businesses—such as forestry, energy companies, pulp and paper mills, oil wells, real estate, electric utilities, and so forth—that are often affected by environmental regulations. With increasing consolidation of media ownership, some media managers and editors may feel pressure from owners to choose (or avoid) stories and to report news in ways that ensure a favorable political climate for these business concerns. In turn, such editors and managers "become the proprietor's 'voice' within the newsroom, ensuring that journalistic 'independence' conforms to the preferred editorial line" (McNair, 1994, p. 42).

Consider the example of General Electric (GE), one of the world's largest corporations and owner of NBC television and its business channel CNBC. Beder (2002) found that General Electric is by no means a hands-off owner of its networks. Instead, she reported, GE officials regularly insert the business's interests into network editorial decisions. Although GE has had environmental problems, "NBC journalists have not been particularly keen to expose GE's environmental record" (p. 224). For example, when the Environmental Protection Agency (EPA) found GE responsible for discharging more than a million pounds of polychlorinated biphenols (PCBs) into New York's Hudson River and proposed that GE pay for a massive cleanup, "the company responded with an aggressive campaign aimed at killing the plan," spending, by its own estimates, $10–15 million on advertising (Mann, 2001, para. 2). And, while the president of its NBC television network lobbied government officials in New York City urging them to oppose the EPA's plan, NBC news programs "offered little national coverage of the Hudson cleanup" (para. 4).

A more subtle form of ideological influence also may be present in some reporters. Corbett (2006) points out that media research have found a form of "social control" in newsrooms. This control sometimes takes the form of a "conditioned belief" where "a reporter does not realize that he or she is submitting to the organization's norms" (p. 225). In this sense, media political economy also determines the size of the news hole available for certain kinds of stories.

Gatekeeping and the Environmental Beat

The decisions of editors and media managers to cover or not to cover certain environmental stories illustrates what has been called the **gatekeeping** role of news production. Simply put, the metaphor of gatekeeping is used to suggest that certain individuals in newsrooms decide what gets through the "gate" and what stays out. White's classic study "The 'Gatekeeper': A Case Study in the Selection of News" (1950) launched the tradition in media research of tracking the structure and routines of the newsroom and the informal forces that set priorities for and help shape news stories. Gatekeeper studies thus focus on the routines, habits, and informal relationships among editors and reporters and among reporters' background, training, and sources.

Many editors and newsrooms find it particularly difficult to deal with the environmental beat (or assignment) for two reasons: First, as we saw earlier, the unobtrusive nature of many environmental problems makes it hard for reporters to fit these stories into conventional news formats. Second, environmental news can be difficult to report because few reporters have training in science or knowledge of complex environmental problems such as groundwater pollution, animal waste, urban sprawl, genetically modified crops, or cancer and disease clusters. Few news organizations have the financial means to hire such talent. As a result, Corbett (2006) observes, "Newsrooms may be at a loss as to how to best fit stories about the environment into newsroom organizations and routines" (p. 217).

Reporters and editors, therefore, face a dilemma: "As the public becomes increasingly aware of and worried about the environment, editors and reporters cannot rely on a 'seat-of-the-pants' approach when reporting on environmental issues. Stories must be technically accurate. . . . Yet few newspapers or broadcast stations can assign a full-time reporter to environmental stories" (West, Lewis, Greenberg, Sachsman, & Rogers, 2003, p. vii). For example, "on any given day, an environmental story may be assigned to a science specialist, a health reporter, a general assignment reporter, or even a business reporter" (Corbett, 2006, p. 217).

As a result of these constraints, reporters and editors have begun to turn to Internet news wires for information, such as *Greenwire* (www.greenwire.com) and the *Environmental News Network* (www.enn.com), as well as databases maintained by the Society of Environmental Journalists. Finally, the rise of independent media online as well as reporters' blogs has allowed journalists to bypass the "gatekeeper" restrictions of editors. (I discuss these newer sources later in the chapter.)

Newsworthiness

One of the most important of the gatekeeper practices that affect environmental news reporting is what editors describe as the news value, or **newsworthiness**, of a story. Newsworthiness is the ability of a news story to attract readers or viewers. In their popular guide to reporting, *Reaching Audiences: A Guide to Media Writing*, Yopp and McAdams (2007) identify the conventions, found in most U.S. media guidelines, that determine newsworthiness. Reporters and editors are likely to draw on one or more of these traditional criteria for selecting, framing, and reporting environmental news: (1) prominence, (2) timeliness, (3) proximity, (4) impact, (5) magnitude, (6) conflict, (7), oddity, and (8) emotional impact.

As a result, editors feel they must strive to fit or package environmental problems according to these news values. For example, a *New York Times* front-page story headline,

"Tennessee Ash Flood Larger than Initial Estimate," in late 2008 foreground the *magnitude* of a disaster from a coal-fired power plant. This frame was reinforced immediately in the lead paragraph: "A coal ash spill in eastern Tennessee that experts were already calling the largest environmental disaster of its kind in the United States is more than three times as large as initially estimated, according to an updated survey by the Tennessee Valley Authority" (Dewan, 2008, p. A8). Later in the story, a frame of "conflict" emerged to guide the story's narrative: "'We're terribly frustrated,' said Donald Smith, 58, a laboratory facilities manager who lives in the affected area. 'It seems like T.V.A. is just throwing darts at the problem, and they don't have a clue how to really fix it'" (p. A8).

Conflict is an especially influential factor in news production about the environment. Environmentalists versus loggers, climate scientists versus global warming skeptics, angry residents versus chemical company officials, and so forth. Conflict may also account for the front-page placement of stories. For example, stories about global warming are usually not on the front page of the *New York Times;* however, "the global warming stories that do make it onto the front page tend to concern the most contentious aspects of climate science" (Brainard, 2008, para. 13). *New York Times* reporter Andrew Revkin noted that, unfortunately, reserving the front page for stories exhibiting conflict or "hot conclusions" can lead to a glossing over of the climate science behind the controversy (quoted in Brainard, 2008, para. 13).

Overall, Anderson (1997) found that environmental news coverage tends to feature stories that are (1) event centered (for example, oil spills and publicity stunts), (2) characterized by strong visual elements (pictures or film), and (3) closely tied into a 24-hour daily cycle. An event-centered approach focusing on disasters such as the Bhopal chemical accident in India and the *Exxon Valdez* oil spill seemed to characterize environmental news coverage in the 1970s and 1980s in particular. However, Friedman (2004) suggested that this pattern may be changing as "the obvious stories [give] way to more complex issues like particulate air pollution, climate change, endocrine disruption, and non-point water pollution" (p. 179). (See "Another Viewpoint: Media Coverage of Climate Change at a Crossroads.")

Another Viewpoint: Media Coverage of Climate Change at a Crossroads

There is evidence of a move away from simplistic or dramatic news coverage of more complex, unobtrusive environmental issues. Christine Russell (2008), writing in the *Columbia Journalism Review,* reports, for example, that "media coverage of climate change is at a crossroads, as it moves beyond the science of global warming into the broader arena of what governments, entrepreneurs, and ordinary citizens are doing about it. Consider these recent examples:

- [A] decade from now, Abu Dhabi hopes to have the first city in the world with zero carbon emissions. In a windswept stretch of desert, developers plan to build Masdar City, a livable environment for fifty thousand people that relies entirely on solar power and other renewable energy. Science correspondent Joe Palca reported from Masdar's construction site as part of National Public Radio's yearlong project "Climate Connections." ...

(Continued)

(Continued)

• Dot Earth . . . [is] the innovative blog started by Andrew C. Revkin, the *New York Times* environment reporter. Having traveled the globe to cover global warming, Revkin now posts and exchanges ideas on Dot Earth about climate and sustainability issues, particularly the energy, food, and water demands on a planet that may house nine billion people by mid-century (para. 2–3).

These reporters are in the advance guard of an army of journalists around the world who are covering what *Time* magazine has dubbed the "War on Global Warming." Journalists will play a key role in shaping the information that opinion leaders and the public use to judge the urgency of climate change, what needs to be done about it, when and at what costs. It is a vast, multifaceted story whose complexity does not fit well with journalism's tendency to shy away from issues with high levels of uncertainty and a time-frame of decades, rather than days or months (para. 3).

Anderson emphasizes that a bias toward visual elements and the 24-hour news cycle still characterizes environmental news coverage and can be a particular challenge for reporting environmental stories on television. She cites the example of a BBC News correspondent who complained, "We're about pictures. . . . Above all environment stories need good pictures. . . . Global warming is very difficult because you can't actually see global warming" (pp. 121–122). Most environmental problems do not naturally fit these requirements for newsworthiness, because they involve slower, more diffuse and drawn-out processes or because they lack visual quality.

On the other hand, mainstream media's heavy reliance on visual images also provides an opening for environmentalists and journalists alike to fulfill the newsworthiness standard through the coverage of dramatic visual events. Environmental communication scholar Kevin DeLuca (2005) has called these **image events**. Image events fully take advantage of television's hunger for pictures, such as footage of large banners draped from a corporate headquarters proclaiming, "End clear-cutting of rain forests!" DeLuca quotes a veteran Greenpeace campaigner who explained that such image events succeed by "reducing a complex set of issues to symbols that break people's comfortable equilibrium, get them asking whether there are better ways to do things" (p. 3).

Despite the occasional success of image events, the traditional standards for newsworthiness of environmental news itself periodically comes under fire: Why must environmental stories meet standards like conflict, oddity, and emotional impact when these seem more relevant to entertainment than to news? One reason is that many editors and station owners insist there is little or no interest among the public in environmental stories. Yet, recent evidence, as I reported earlier, suggests otherwise. If there is such interest, why does coverage of environmental news vary over the decades? The answer lies partly in Vig and Kraft's (2003) finding that, while the public supports environmental protection over time, short-term developments often divert the public's interest from environmental issues. Editors are acutely aware of this, and such shifting interest is reflected in the size of the news hole. In the end, many journalists believe that the challenge of environmental journalism remains to make environmental news both accurate and newsworthy in the face of other pressures for news space.

Media Frames

In his classic study, *Public Opinion* (1922), Walter Lippmann was perhaps the first to grasp a basic dilemma of news reporting when he wrote:

> The real environment is altogether too big, too complex, and too fleeting for direct acquaintance. We are not equipped to deal with so much subtlety, so much variety, so many permutations and combinations. And although we have to act in that environment, we have to reconstruct it on a simpler model before we can manage it. *To traverse the world men [sic] must have maps of the world.* (p. 16, emphasis added)

As a result, journalists have sought ways to simplify, frame, or make "maps of the world" to communicate their stories.

The term **frame** was first popularized by Erving Goffman in his book *Frame Analysis: An Essay on the Organization of Experience* (1974). Goffman defined *frames* as the cognitive maps or patterns of interpretation that people use to organize their understanding of reality. Building on Goffman's insight, Pan and Kosicki (1993) defined **media frames** as the "central organizing themes . . . that connect different semantic elements of a news story (headlines, quotes, leads, visual representations, and narrative structure) into a coherent whole to suggest what is at issue" (Rodríguez, 2003, p. 80). By providing this coherence, media frames help people cope with new or problematic experiences, relating them to familiar ideas and assumptions about the way the world works.

A similar set of facts may be perceived quite differently when editors choose dramatically different media frames for stories. A striking example occurred several years ago when two stories about mercury poisoning appeared in the newspaper *USA Today*. The first story, "Mercury Damage 'Irreversible'" by reporter Elizabeth Weise, appeared on February 8, 2004. (I referred to this story earlier.) The headline and lead paragraph clearly frame the study as an *event,* the release of a new study by Harvard scientists who found that "mercury contamination of seafood can cause heart damage and irreversible impairment to brain function in children, both in the womb and as they grow" (para. 1). The second story, appearing April 7, 2004, carried the headline, "Pregnant Women Eating Too Much Fish" (Weise, 2004b, p. 3A). The opening paragraph in this second story reinforced a frame that appeared to blame mothers for poisoning their children: "Of the 4 million babies born in the USA in 2000, more than 300,000 of them—and as many as 600,000—may have been exposed to 'unacceptable' levels of methyl mercury *because their mothers ate a diet rich in fish*, a study finds" (p. 3A; emphasis added). The two *USA Today* stories—by the same reporter—orient readers in dramatically different ways to studies about mercury in seafood.

Choosing the right frame is especially important with the surge of complex news stories about environmental topics such as climate change. Recently, news stories have begun to turn away from "Be Worried" frames, such as *Time*'s 2006 cover showing a polar bear on a melting ice floe, to more positive frames like "'environmental stewardship," "public health," or, most important, a "solutions' frame" for dealing with climate change (Brainard, 2008, para. 19; see also Nisbet, 2008).

Because different frames orient us to different meanings, the parties to an environmental controversy—environmentalists, property owners, citizens, corporations, scientists, and so forth—sometimes *compete* to influence the framing of a news story. Miller and Riechert (2000) explain that opposing stakeholders try to gain public support for their positions, often "not by offering new facts or by changing evaluations of the facts, but *by altering the frames or interpretive dimensions for evaluating the facts*" (p. 45, emphasis added). An example of industry's success in reframing an important news story occurred in debates over the opening of the Arctic National Wildlife Refuge to oil drilling. As I said in Chapter 2, oil industry sources used the image of a "footprint" to suggest the drilling would have little impact on the environment. Touting advances in technology, industry spokespeople insisted, "With sideways drilling and other advances, the oil beneath the 1.5 million-acre coastal plain can be tapped with a 'footprint' on the surface no larger than 2,000 acres" (Spiess & Ruskin, 2001, para. 1). The *Anchorage Daily News* reported that the oil industry's footprint metaphor "proved to be a potent piece of rhetoric," implying that drilling would affect less than 1 percent of the coastal plain (para. 18).

On the other hand, opponents of the plan to drill in the Arctic National Wildlife Refuge objected to the footprint metaphor and countered with their own metaphor and media frame: "Oil extraction, much like open heart surgery, is a very messy business" (Ferris, 2001, para. 3). The critics' argument was that the figure of 2,000 acres for the impact from oil drilling was misleading because it did not count the large area covered by roads, connecting pipelines, worker housing, garbage dumps, water use, and other intrusions. And, like open heart surgery, the result of such drilling could be "messy."

Finally, some scholars have observed that media frames often function rhetorically to sustain dominant discourses about the economy, nature, or environmentalists. For example, in *Image Politics,* DeLuca (2005) argues that commercial news programs such as *ABC World News Tonight* tend to negatively frame—and thus marginalize—radical environmental groups such as Earth First! that criticize timber and mining interests and challenge the U.S. Forest Service. News frames may also work to cast certain issues or persons in a more negative light. Similarly, environmental sciences professor Travis Wagner (2008) argues that national newspapers have successfully reframed acts of "ecotage" through the frightening lens of "terrorism" (p. 25). **Ecotage** is controversial in itself, of course. It refers to acts such as vandalism and arson that are undertaken by activists for the purpose of protecting nature or certain species; yet, while clearly illegal, these acts are not intended to harm human beings. In his study of six newspapers, from 1984 to 2006, Wagner found "a marked shift in framing ecotage as terrorism starting in 2001"; although the volume of stories using the ecoterrorist frame increased afterward, the number of incidences of ectoage steadily declined during this same period (p. 25). This reframing, Wagner reports, helped to construct a "discourse of fear," a kind of "moral panic . . . that a widespread threat to society exists" (p. 28).

DeLuca suggests that, even in such negative media framing, there remain possibilities for insurgent discourses as well. For example, at the height of the cold war, Greenpeace activists in small Zodiac boats confronted Russian whaling ships in

Figure 5.2	A Greenpeace Zodiac maneuvers itself between two Russian whaling ships. Harpooned whales are being transferred from catcher vessels to the factory processing ship.

© Greenpeace/Rex Wyler.

attempts to disrupt the Russians' harpooning of whales (see Figure 5.2). In the television news reports of these confrontations on the high seas, it would have been easy to dismiss Greenpeace as extreme or strange, but DeLuca points to the larger frame of the cold war ideology of the United States versus the evils of communism. In that frame, "Greenpeacers are embraced as heroes, intrepid individuals (thirteen people against a Russian fleet) who went to war against the Soviet Union and returned victorious" (p. 96). Although framed in terms of cold war politics, "Greenpeace performs and gets favorably aired [on television] an image event that is a radical critique of industrialism [and] nature as a storehouse of resources" (p. 100).

Clearly, the choice of a frame in a story matters. Indeed, the recent history of environmentalism in the United States can be understood partly to be a struggle over quite different but powerful frames for nature and our relationship to the environment: Media now refer more often to "rain forests," instead of "jungles," and to "wetlands," instead of "swamps," for example.

Norms of Objectivity and Balance

The values of **objectivity and balance** have been bedrock norms of journalism for almost a century. In principle, these are the commitments by news media to provide information that is accurate and without reporter bias and, where there is uncertainty or controversy, to balance news stories with statements from all sides of the issue. The latter is especially valued when a reporter lacks the technical expertise or training, or time, to determine where "truth" lies in a story (Cunningham, 2003).

Objectivity

In practice, however, these norms run into difficulty. Particularly in environmental journalism, reporters struggle to maintain genuine objectivity. For example, although a story on deforestation may be accurate, a kind of bias already has occurred in the selection of *this* story versus others; this occurs also in its framing, and in the choice of sources that have been interviewed. As Lee and Solomon (1990) point out, "Value judgments infuse everything in the news media," ranging from the choice of which stories out of an infinite number to cover and which facts to include in the story, to what prominence to give it (whether on the front page or buried inside) (p. 16).

Some critics have suggested that what passes for objectivity is merely the prevailing consensus about what is real in a given time and society. For example, Craig L. LaMay (1991), the former editor of the *Gannett Center Journal*, noted that news reports of the nation's consumption—how much we spend on certain products—are taken to be an objective measure of its social and economic health. In contrast, why not measure the nation's health in terms of other variables, such as the literacy rate, the number of people in poverty, or the amount of energy conserved? LaMay explains that measures such as consumption "are objective only in the sense that they represent society's dominant values, largely agreed upon by government, commerce and other institutions—including the media. Objectivity as consensus . . . is a kind of Orwellian notion in which consensus belongs to those with the power to make it" (p. 108).

Balancing Different Views

When environmental issues are controversial, or when reporters lack the expertise to judge conflicting claims, the tendency in journalism has been to "balance" stories by quoting multiple or differing sources. This refers to the practice of balancing a controversial report or statement with an opposing viewpoint. For example, balance was a common practice in much of the early coverage of global warming. Boykoff and Boykoff (2004) cite the following example from a Los Angeles article in 1992:

> The ability to study climatic patterns has been critical to the debate over the phenomenon called "global warming." *Some scientists believe*—and some ice core studies seem to indicate—that humanity's production of carbon dioxide is leading to a potentially dangerous overheating of the planet. *But skeptics contend* there is no evidence the warning exceeds the climate's natural variations. (Abramson, 1992, p. A1; emphasis added)

In recent years, however, the norm of balance also has been sharply criticized. Some media critics have challenged the assumption that there are always two sides of an issue, particularly when empirical data or scientific research strongly supports one "side." As a result, balance sometimes can be misleading. For example,

Boykoff and Boykoff (2004) have argued that the norm of balancing in the reporting of global warming in major U.S. newspapers has actually led to "biased coverage" of the science of climate change and the findings of anthropogenic (human) contributions to global warming (p. 125).

The Boykoff and Boykoff study examined articles in the U.S. "prestigious press"—that is, the *New York Times, Washington Post, Los Angeles Times,* and *Wall Street Journal*—from 1988 to 2002. During this period, scientific institutions such as the U.S. National Oceanic and Atmospheric Administration (NOAA) and United Nations Intergovernmental Panel on Climate Change (IPCC) began to report an increasingly strong probability that human activities were an important variable in global climate change (IPCC, 1996, 2007). Nevertheless, the practice of balancing the scientific findings with skepticism appeared to introduce more uncertainty than the reports themselves contained. Overall, Boykoff and Boykoff found that "balanced accounts prevailed" in the 1988–2002 period and that these articles "gave 'roughly equal attention' to the view that humans were contributing to global warming, and the other view that exclusively natural fluctuations could explain the earth's temperature increase" (p. 129). Such balancing, they concluded, "can often lead to a form of informational bias" (p. 129).

The trend of balancing science and skepticism in reports of global warming may be changing. Brainard (2008), for example, reports that the news media seem to be "slowly but surely eliminating false balance when addressing human activity's role in global warming" (para. 6). Boykoff (2007) also has found that "balanced" coverage of global warming science has tapered off in recent years in major U.S. newspapers. Although such media representations of the role of anthropogenic contributions to climate change "diverged significantly from the scientific consensus in 2003 and 2004," this was no longer true by 2005 and 2006 (p. 474).

The constraints on news production that we've reviewed—political economy, gatekeepers, newsworthiness, media frames, and norms of objectivity and balance—limit mainstream media in different ways. One consequence of this is the growth of so-called new media and the environment online.

New Media and the Environment Online

Along with mainstream media, an alternative public sphere of "new media" has arisen in the past decade to report and comment on environmental issues—blogs, online news sites, listservs, forums, and research centers, as well as an increasing convergence of reporters' blogs and online readers. A foreshadowing of this trend was clear a decade ago, when Shanahan and McComas (1999) observed that, despite an elite control of the commercial media, outlets in other media for environmental opposition have been growing. They drew upon Downing's (1988) idea of an **alternative public sphere** for environmental communication, by which they mean that environmental and other groups have the ability to articulate for themselves a space within society in which "their own discourse can be privileged and their own knowledge pursued" (p. 45).

One of the reasons for the growth of alternative news sources, particularly online, is that environmentalists, science advocacy groups, working journalists, and readers themselves have grown frustrated with the insufficient depth, range, and accuracy of commercial media, along with the "shrinking news hole" of mainstream journalism. Indeed, with the erosion of mass circulation newspapers and network news, more and more individuals are seeking the kinds of information not found in traditional media. As a result, a wide range of information and analyses have proliferated online, with environmental news services and blogs, as well as the Websites of environmental groups and scientists.

In this section, I look at two sources of independent news and commentary about environmental topics: (1) online environmental news services and independent blogs and (2) professional societies for environmental journalists.

The Environment Online

The post-network era is defined largely by the proliferation of new media—blogs, online news services, listservs, and other Web-based sources of news and analyses. New media also are redefining the traditional roles of both news sources and readers in what Technorati (2008) has called the "active Blogosphere," the "interconnected community of bloggers and readers at the convergence of journalism and conversation" (para. 7).

The Environmental Blogosphere

The fastest growing source for online news and analyses of environmental topics has been the blogosphere, including personal blogs, newspapers and professional journalists' blogs, scientists' blogs, and even corporate blogs. There have been a number of studies attempting to characterize the size and types of sites generally in the Blogosphere, "but all studies agree that blogs are a global phenomenon that has hit the mainstream" (Center for Media Research, 2008, para. 2). Technocrati (2008), which tracks blogs, includes these estimates in its *State of the Blogosphere 2008:*

- 22.6 million bloggers in the United States with 94.1 million U.S. blog readers in 2007 (50% of all Internet users in the United States)

- Worldwide, an estimated 184 million who have started a blog and 346 million blog readers (para. 3)

A number of blogs, both in the United States and worldwide, have emerged as particularly relevant for environmental news and analyses. Recently, Environmental Graffiti (2007) came up with a list of what it concluded were the "Top 10 Best Environmental Blogs." (See "FYI: Top 10 Environmental Blogs.")

☞ FYI   Top 10 Environmental Blogs

Environmental Graffiti (2007) lists these Top 10 environmental blogs, based on "authority points" and other criteria. (See http://www.environmentalgraffiti.com.) Here are its Top 10 blogs:

1. Treehugger (http://www.treehugger.com)

   The big daddy of environmental blogs, Treehugger is one of the most-read blogs on any subject. It covers most everything environmental, from green news to eco-design and green products. . . .

2. Inhabitat (http://www.inhabitat.com)

   As its title would suggest, Inhabitat is one of the foremost blogs on green architecture and design. They frequently cover articles on sustainable architecture, green living, and green design. . . .

3. EcoGeek (http://www.ecogeek.org)

   EcoGeek specializes in writing about environmentally friendly technology. If you're looking for info on anything from solar iPods to electric cars, this is the place.

4. Real Climate (http://www.realclimate.org)

   Real Climate specializes in climate science news. . . . Most of its content is written by actively working climate scientists. . . .

5. World Changing (http://www.worldchanging.com)

   World Changing's articles cover tools and ideas to help build a better future. Their content is very future oriented, and runs the gamut from eco and future friendly housing to urban planning. . . .

6. Green Options (http://greenoptions.com)

   This general environmental blog is based in Berkeley, California. The blog has a large community and is dedicated to environmental education and discussion. . . .

7. The Oil Drum (http://www.theoildrum.com)

   The Oil Drum is a community discussing—you guessed it—oil and energy issues. They Environmental Graffiti cover peak oil, sustainable development, renewable energy, and pretty much anything else you can think of related to energy and the environment. . . .

8. Environmental Graffiti (http://www.environmentalgraffiti.com)

   Environmental Graffiti covers everything from Politics to Green Living, but specializes in Ecology and Offbeat news for the environmental community. . . .

9. Gristmill (http://gristmill.grist.org)

   Gristmill is a part of Grist Magazine. The blog provides a daily environmental news feed.

10. EcoStreet (http://www.ecostreet.com)

    EcoStreet is a green community, blog, and directory that aims to raise green consciousness.

Other blogs, while less cited, span the field of environmentally related topics. Here is just a sampling of the incredible range:

- *Green Citizenship* (http://greencitizenship.blogspot.com) is media scholar Toby Miller's blog, which focuses on e-waste.

- Sightline's *The Daily Score* (http://daily.sightline.org/daily_score), a smart and insightful blog, is focused on Cascadia (the Pacific Northwest).

- *Minh Bien* (www.minhbien.org), a Vietnamese/English-language blog, focuses on China–Vietnam transboundary resource management and is reportedly an open forum for discussion despite censorship in other media in the region.

Environmental blogs are no longer stand-alone, personal journals. In fact, as the Blogosphere grows, "the lines between what is a blog and what is a mainstream media site become less clear. Larger blogs are taking on more characteristics of mainstream sites and mainstream sites are incorporating styles and formats from the Blogosphere" (Technorati, 2008, para. 5). Many are posting videos and news feeds from other online sources, and some have launched Web TV sites. (For an analysis of Treehugger TV, for example, see Slawter, 2008.)

Newspapers themselves are migrating online with versions of their daily print editions. And many reporters are launching their own blog sites as well. In fact, 95 percent of the top 100 U.S. newspapers now have reporters' blogs (Technorati, 2008, para. 5). One of the most prominent reporter blogs is *New York Times* journalist Andrew Revkin's "Dot Earth" (http://dotearth.blogs.nytimes.com). Revkin, who received the prestigious John Chancellor Award for Excellence in Journalism, is recognized for his insightful reporting on climate change and energy. Launched in 2007, Dot Earth allows Revkin to expand on his stories in the *New York Times,* post breaking news and content from other Websites, share videos, and generally sustain a growing conversation about climate change among readers worldwide.

Finally, environmental and climate change groups have dramatically expanded online with blogs, news feeds, and social networking sites. Both local and national green groups now routinely have Websites that feature news and information about their organizations, campaigns, and resources for members and the general public (see Figure 5.3). And some groups have started their own blogs—Natural Resources Defense Council's *Switchboard* (http://switchboard.nrdc.org) and the Sierra Club's blog, *Taking the Initiative* by Carl Pope (http://sierraclub.typepad.com/carlpope) are two widely read green blogs. More recently, environmental social networks— modeled on popular sites but now taken to the realm of climate change activism, are starting to appear. (Check out 350.org and ClimateCrossroads.org, for example.)

Online News Services

Newer online news sources offer the widest access to both working journalists and readers looking for more in-depth environmental news and information. Friedman (2004) observes that many of the changes related to improved sources for environmental

| Figure 5.3 | New media allow climate scientists like Ian Bartholomew to record measurements in the field as part of a study to measure the speed of glaciers in Greenland. The study is looking at how increasing quantities of melt water caused by climate change are affecting the glacier's speed, which like most glaciers in Greenland has speeded up considerably in the past 20 years. |

© Ashley Cooper/Corbis.

journalists can be traced to these sources. One senior environmental reporter claimed that the Internet "drastically changed the way journalists do their job" (p. 183).

The first of this new genre was the Environmental News Service (ENS), the original daily, international wire service reporting environmental news. Established in 1990, ENS is an independently owned and Web-based service with more than 100,000 subscribers to its news stories. (See ENS's news service at http://www.ens-newswire.com.) ENS covers news stories from countries around the world on such topics as environmental politics, lawsuits, international agreements, and demonstrations, plus a range of environmental subjects—science and technology, air quality, public health, drinking water, oceans and marine life, land use, wildlife, natural disasters, toxics, nuclear issues, recycling, transportation, and environmental economics.

ENS was soon followed by other news services, listservs, and specialty coverage of subareas of environmental policy. Specialty coverage is of particular interest to environmental and business groups, policymakers, and others who follow environmental legislation in the U.S. Congress. One of the most prominent of these news sites is Environment and Energy (E&E) Publishing (www.eenews.net). It offers online newsletters, a wire service, E&E TV, and special reports, providing detailed coverage of energy, public lands issues, climate change, and other issues before the courts or Congress. Its *Land Letter* (www.eenews.net), for example, specializes in natural resources (wilderness, oil and gas drilling on public lands, and so forth), while *Environment and Energy Daily* (www.eenews.net/eed) focuses on air, water, and energy issues. E&E Publishing also sponsors *Greenwire* (www.eenews.net/gw), which many journalists consider the leading daily news source for environmental stories.

More recently, E&E Publishing launched *Climate Wire* (www.eenews.net/cw), featuring daily news reports on energy and climate-related stories. And, a new nonprofit science and media organization, Climate Central (www.climatecentral.org), is initiating an online news source for "high quality climate information" available for print media, television, and the Web. It describes its mission as "a unique hybrid linking science and media: a think tank with a production team" (Climate Central, 2009, para. 2).

Other general purpose environmental news and analysis Websites are available free to anyone online. The choices are wide ranging and seemingly endless. Here are just a few:

- *Environmental News Network* (www.enn.com) is a broad online service whose mission since its inception in 1993 has been "to publish information that will help people understand and communicate the environmental issues and solutions that face us and hopefully inspire them to get involved" (www.enn.com/static). It offers a variety of resources for online users from environmental news and commentary, video reports, and forums for debate.

- *EnviroLink Network* (www.envirolink.org) is a nonprofit organization that provides access online to a comprehensive set of environmental news and information. For example, a headline about orcas (so-called killer whales) boosting their calls to each other in order to be heard above boat noise might direct the user to the British Broadcasting Channel for the breaking story, or those interested in organic gardening might find links to dozens of nonprofit groups for resources, new ideas, and information.

- *Grist* magazine (www.grist.org) features biting commentary, analyses of developments within the environmental movement, and breaking news.

- *Rachel's Environment & Health News* (www.rachel.org), named for Rachel Carson, is known for its incisive reports on toxic chemicals, environmental justice, and worker health and safety.

In many ways, alternative media—online sites such as the Environmental News Service, Web forums, and blogs—are challenging conventional media theory about such topics as political economy and the gatekeeper function. With the unlimited availability and interconnectivity of Internet sites, scholars will need to rethink who—if anyone—controls access to news and information and what determines newsworthiness. Indeed, environmental issues may be "paving the way for the restructuring of the political economy of the news and information media" (S. Depoe, personal communication, March 9, 2005).

Professional Societies for Environmental Journalists

Journalists in particular have felt the need for more accurate sources of information and timelier briefings about environmental topics. In the United States, the main source of support for working journalists and editors is the Society of Environmental Journalists (SEJ). Its primary goal is "to advance public understanding of critically important environmental issues" by providing the resources for a network of professional journalists and editors who cover environment-related issues. (See SEJ's homepage at http://www.sej.org.) For example, SEJ maintains the Integrity in Science Database for journalists who want to investigate possible conflicts of interest on the part of scientists who publish on controversial environmental topics such as global warming. The database lists scientists' affiliations with principal funding sources, including chemical, gas, oil, food, drug, and other companies. It also lists nonprofit groups and universities that receive industry funding.

Recently, academic and media organizations have begun to provide online resources for journalists and others about the way news media are covering environmental stories, particularly the growth of news about climate change. For example, the Yale Forum on Climate Change and the Media (www.yaleclimatemediaforum.org), a project of Yale University, was launched in 2007. The site is emerging as an important source for the intersections of science, media, and global warming. As an online publication and forum, its purpose is "to foster dialogue on climate change among scientists, journalists, policymakers, and the public," and seeks "to provide print, broadcasting, and online reporters and editors timely and credible information on one of the most important and complicated issues of our time" (www.yaleclimatemediaforum.org/aboutus).

Internationally, similar networks for environmental journalists exist. The most prominent network is the Asia Pacific Forum of Environmental Journalists (APFEJ) (http://www.oneworld.org/slejf), constituted in 1988. APFEJ is the oldest and the largest world organization of professional environmental journalists. It coordinates the work of environmental journalists in 91 countries, including journalists working for newspapers, magazines, and radio and TV broadcast media, as well as environmental groups and government departments and agencies. Another is the International Federation of Environmental Journalists (IFEJ), an umbrella group of member associations from 40 nations (www.ifej.org).

Ultimately, the growth of news online and the role of environmental media generally presume that the news media and commercial programming affect us in certain ways. Do media have effects? Does exposure to media influence readers' and viewers' attitudes and behavior toward the environment? It is to this question that we now turn.

Media Effects

Earlier, in Chapter 1, I said that our understanding and behavior toward the environment depend not only on ecological science but also on media representations and public debate, as well as ordinary conversation. Nevertheless, there is also intense controversy about the possibility of **media effects**. By this phrase, I mean the influence of different media content, frequency, and forms of communication on audiences' attitudes, perceptions, and behaviors. In particular, there is doubt whether we can pinpoint particular media content as the cause of specific opinions or behavior (Bryant & Oliver, 2008; Shanahan & McComas, 1999).

We enter the debate over the impact of environmental media by reviewing three broad theories of the effects of news and media programming on the public's attitudes and behavior. These theories are (1) the direct transmission model, (2) agenda setting, and (3) narrative framing and cultivation theory. Overall, these approaches provide little evidence of direct, causal effects on audiences' beliefs and behaviors; rather, they suggest that media's impact is both cumulative and a part of a wider context of social influence that helps to construct our interest in and understanding of the environment.

Direct Transmission ("Hypodermic Effects Theory")

Early theories of media effects operated from a model that assumed that communication is a direct transmission. The **direct transmission model** described media effects as the result of the direct transmission of information from a sender (source) to a receiver. This early theory viewed audiences as highly susceptible to manipulation and typically viewed people "as a homogenous mass of damp sponges, uniformly soaking up messages from the media" (Anderson, 1997, pp. 18–19). Direct transmission, sometimes called the "magic bullet theory" and the **hypodermic effects theory**, likened the media to a syringe that "injected" messages into an audience, assuming that individuals would respond in predictable ways (p. 19).

Although there is little evidence of a direct transmission effect, the early communication model served practical needs. It encouraged researchers to ask whether specific campaigns to impart information or change attitudes or behavior have the desired effects. For example, do public information campaigns succeed in teaching farmers important information about soil conservation? Do pleas to the public to recycle change people's behavior? Generally, such research has failed to find evidence of direct, causal effects on audiences. For example, Allen and Weber (1983) reported that President Jimmy Carter's 1979 television campaign to persuade the public to turn down their thermostats and conserve energy was largely ineffective (p. 104). In other cases, information campaigns may succeed in encouraging positive attitudes about conservation—for example, strengthening the public's *intentions* to recycle—but such campaigns may not necessarily alter people's actual behavior.

Because the direct transmission model has not proved particularly useful in explaining the influence of environmental media, other accounts have emerged. These accounts move beyond the study of specific effects on individuals to broader influences of media in shaping perceptions of issues and in constructing social narratives about the environment. We turn now to the first of these, the agenda-setting theory.

Agenda Setting

Perhaps the single most influential theory of media effects that applies to environmental news is **agenda setting**. Cohen (1963) first suggested the idea of agenda setting to distinguish between individual opinion (*what* people believe) and the public's perception of the salience or *importance* of an issue. News reporting "may not be successful much of the time in telling people *what to think,* but it is stunningly successful in telling its readers *what to think about*" (p. 13, emphasis added; see also McCombs & Shaw, 1972). In their study of television, Iyengar and Kinder (1987) defined agenda setting in this way: "Those problems that receive prominent attention on the national news become the problems the viewing public regards as the nation's most important" (p. 16). In other words, the public's perception of what is important influences the media less than media influence the public's priorities (Ader, 1995, p. 300).

The agenda-setting hypothesis has been influential in much environmental communication research on the effects of media, though the results sometimes have been conflicting. On the one hand, Iyengar and Kinder (1987) found firm evidence of the agenda-setting effect in their study of evening news on television, in which viewers rated the importance of the environment higher *after* viewing increased coverage of news of environmental pollution (p. 19). And Eyal, Winter, and DeGeorge (1981) and Ader (1995) discovered that the agenda-setting effect is especially strong for unobtrusive issues. This effect is most apparent in media's enhancement of the public's perceptions of risk or danger from environmental sources.

On the other hand, Gooch's (1996) study of the coverage of environmental issues by Swedish newspapers did not find evidence of an agenda-setting effect. Although reports about water pollution and waste received the greatest amount of news coverage in the press, the public rated other environmental concerns, such as air quality, as more serious. Similarly, Iyengar and Kinder (1987) found no support for the *vividness* of news reports in affecting television viewers' perception of the importance of environmental issues. In this case, a story that featured a link between a toxic waste site and a stormy interview with a mother and her sick child produced no more viewer concern than a pallid version in which a reporter merely discussed a possible connection between the chemical site and catastrophic illness.

Environmental communication scholars, however, caution against a rejection of agenda-setting effects based on these studies. Ader (1995) observes that real-world conditions may affect perceptions of the seriousness of a problem independently of news coverage of these concerns. Anderson (1997) also points out that other influences, such as friends and family, may affect the public's perception of the importance of environmental issues and that agenda-setting research should take these factors into consideration.

In an attempt to refine agenda-setting theory, Ader (1995) investigated the relative influence of real-world conditions, public opinion, and the media's agenda in a study of news reports about the environment in the *New York Times* from 1970 to 1990. She asked two questions: (1) Is the public's concern about environmental problems driven by real-world conditions rather than media reports? And (2) Do public attitudes influence the amount of media coverage of an issue rather than the other way around? Using data from Gallup polls during this period, Ader identified problems that the public periodically rated as the "most important problem facing the nation today." To control for the influence of public opinion and real-world conditions on media coverage, Ader examined the length and prominence of news reports of pollution in the *Times* for three months before and three months after each Gallup poll was conducted, as well as data from independent sources documenting real-world conditions for disposal of wastes, air quality, and water quality in these same periods.

Ader's findings affirmed the presence of a strong agenda-setting effect, even when real-world environmental conditions and prior public opinion both were taken into account. That is, even though objective measures showed that overall pollution had declined for the period studied, the *Times* increased its coverage of news stories about pollution, and the greater length and prominence of these stories correlated positively with a subsequent increase in readers' concerns about this issue. However, the opposite was not true; that is, the media did not appear to be mirroring public opinion. Ader concluded, "The findings suggest that the amount of media attention devoted to pollution influenced the degree of public salience for the issue" (p. 309).

While the agenda-setting hypothesis may explain the importance of an issue to the public, it doesn't claim to account for what people *think* about this issue. Therefore, it is important for us to look at other theories that focus on the role of the media in constructing meaning or ways of understanding environmental concerns.

Narrative Framing and Cultivation Analysis

Media communicate not only facts about the environment but also wider frameworks or guides for understanding and making sense of these facts. Theories of media effects that focus on such sense making emphasize the importance of discourse in coherently organizing our experience of the world and our relationship to the environment. Such theories do not argue that discourse "causes" public opinion; rather, they claim that "media discourse is part of the process by which individuals construct meaning" (Gamson & Modigliani, 1989, p. 2). In this section, we look at two related approaches to the role of media discourse in our sense making: narrative framing and **cultivation analysis**.

Narrative Framing

Unlike the direct transmission model, a narrative model takes seriously the perspective of media frames that provide central organizing themes to connect different elements of a news story into a coherent whole. **Narrative framing** refers to the ways in which media organize the bits and facts of phenomena through stories to aid audiences' understanding and the potential for this organization to affect our relationships to the phenomena being represented. The principal proponents of this approach, James Shanahan and Katherine McComas (1999), observe that environmental media coverage is "hardly ever the simple communication of a 'fact,'" because

> journalists use narrative structures to build interesting environmental coverage. Hence, studies of environmental communication show that media portrayals of environmental issues are presented from the start as stories; because journalists and media programmers must interest audiences, they must present their information in narrative packages. (pp. 34–35)

Such "packages" structure our understanding of the environment along certain lines rather than others, and it is this selective portrayal and its potential impact that interest environmental media scholars.

A case in point is Schlechtweg's (1992) detailed study of framing in a Public Broadcasting Service (PBS) program on Earth First! protesters. In May 1990, the *Earth First! Journal* announced the start of Redwood Summer, a mobilization of activists who would flood into California's northern redwood forests and "nonviolently blockade logging roads, [and] climb giant trees to prevent their being logged" (Cherney, 1990, p. 1). Earth First! organizers stressed that anyone who disagreed with nonviolence would be barred from Redwood Summer. Earth First! also tried to open a dialogue with loggers, suggesting they shared a common interest in sustainable logging from new-growth forests rather than the older-growth areas (Schlechtweg, 1992). Nevertheless, that summer tensions grew among loggers, Earth First! activists, and rural communities. On July 20, 1990, the PBS program *The MacNeil-Lehrer NewsHour* ran "Focus–Logjam," a report about the protests. It is this report and its narrative framing of loggers, Earth First! protesters, community people, and violence that Schlechtweg explored.

In his analysis of "Focus–Logjam," Schlechtweg identified key visual and verbal terms that disclosed the broadcast's thematic frame. These included scenes of pristine forests, references to "small-town economies" that depended on "lumber," close-up shots of an ax or hatchet pounding a spike into a tree, and the PBS reporter's voiceover announcing that "Earth First! has a record of civil disobedience, injuring private timberlands, sabotaging logging machinery, and . . . writing about putting metal spikes in trees so they can't be logged" (pp. 266–267). By the end of the 9-minute, 40-second news report, "Focus–Logjam" had established clear identities for "protagonists" and "antagonists" in a tense confrontation that suggested the real prospect of violence.

Protagonists in the broadcast were portrayed through key identity and value terms: The report introduces "workers, "timber people, and "regular people" who depended on "timber harvests" and "small-town economies" for "jobs," "livelihood," and their "way of life" (p. 273). Conversely, the report identified Earth First! protesters as "apocalyptic," "radical," "wrong people," "terrorists," and "violent" people who engaged in "confrontation," "tree spiking," "sabotage," and "civil disobedience" to save "tall, beautiful" trees (p. 273). Schlechtweg argued that as a result of these and other verbal and visual terms, "Focus–Logjam" implicitly constructed a narrative that pitted "regular people" against a "violent terrorist organization, willing to use sabotage . . . and tree spiking to save redwood forests" (pp. 273-274).

Cultivation Analysis

Akin to narrative theory is a cultivation model of media influence. Shanahan (1993) describes **cultivation analysis** as "a theory of story-telling, which assumes that repeated exposure to a set of messages is likely to produce agreement in an audience with opinions expressed in . . . those messages" (pp. 186–187). As its name implies, cultivation is not a claim about immediate or specific effects on an audience; instead, it is a process of gradual influence or cumulative effect. The model is associated with the work of media scholar George Gerbner (1990), who stated

> Cultivation is what a culture does. That is not simple causation, though culture is the basic medium in which humans live and learn. . . . Strictly speaking, cultivation means the specific independent (though not isolated) contribution that a particularly consistent and compelling symbolic stream makes to the complex process of socialization and enculturation. (p. 249)

Gerbner's own research looked exclusively at the long-term effects of viewing violence on television—the cultivation of a worldview that he called the "mean world syndrome." This is a view of society as a dangerous place, peopled by others who want to harm us (Gerbner, Gross, Morgan, & Signorielli, 1986).

Similarly, environmental communication scholars who use cultivation analysis are interested in the longer term effects of media on environmental attitudes and behavior. Perhaps surprisingly, this research suggests that heavy media exposure is sometimes correlated with *lower levels of environmental concern* (Novic & Sandman, 1974; Ostman & Parker, 1987; and Shanahan & McComas, 1999). In a study of college students' television viewing, Shanahan and McComas (1999) report that heavy exposure to television may retard the cultivation of pro-environmental attitudes:

> Most correlations with amount of television viewing were negative and significant: heavier viewers consistently expressed lower levels of environmental concern. . . . This tends to go against the suggestion that media attention to the environment results in greater socioenvironmental [sic] concern. That television's heavy viewers tended to be less environmentally concerned suggests the opposite: Television's messages place a kind of "brake" on the development of environmental concern, especially for heavy viewers. (p. 125)

Interestingly, Shanahan and McComas (1999) found that the decrease in environmental concern among heavy television viewers is stronger among politically active students. This finding appears to contradict what we said earlier about the effects of agenda setting; that is, the more frequent the coverage of a subject, the more salience it gained. How is this explained? Cultivation researchers explain this pattern as **mainstreaming**, or a narrowing of differences toward a cultural norm. Shanahan and McComas suggested that, in the case of environmental media, television's consistent stream of messages may draw groups closer to the cultural mainstream, with the mainstream (as represented by television programs) being "closer to the lower end of the environmental concern scale" (1999, p. 130).

A second explanation for the decrease in environmental concern among heavy viewers of television is what Shanahan (1993) terms **cultivation in reverse**. This is the media's cultivation of an anti-environmental attitude through a persistent lack of environmental images or by directing viewers' attention to other, nonenvironmental stories. By ignoring or passively depicting the natural environment, television tends to marginalize its importance. Cultivation theorists (Shanahan & McComas, 1999) also call this phenomenon **symbolic annihilation**—the media's erasure of the importance of a theme by the indirect or passive deemphasizing of that theme.

An exception to the general findings of a mainstreaming effect from frequent exposure to television is a recent study by Michael Dahlstrom (2007) of TV viewers' perceptions about environment risks. Dahlstrom sought to improve cultivation analysis by more carefully identifying the types of TV content being viewed, as well as the individual's uses and gratification in viewing. As a result, he found that individuals who watched TV for informational purposes, as well as those who viewed a wider diversity of TV channels, are more likely to be concerned about environmental risks than other groups.

It can be difficult to detect specific effects of media on viewers' beliefs or behaviors, at least in the short run. Nevertheless, theories such as agenda setting and the longer-term cultivation of viewers' outlooks do suggest broader effects. These indirect effects include the increased salience of issues (when spotlighted by media) or the adoption of mainstream views on the environment as a result of frequent exposure to television programs. But these broader influences may be significant. Meisner (2005) concludes that, while it is difficult to pinpoint short-term effects of media on our beliefs or behaviors, there are undoubtedly longer term cultural impacts of environmental media.

SUMMARY

I've noted several times that environmental communication mediates our understanding of the environment. Because few of us encounter directly the problems of global warming, loss of biodiversity, or mercury poisoning, we rely upon the reports and representations of others, especially mainstream media: television, newspapers, radio, and popular Websites, film, and magazines. Yet, these media are neither innocent nor neutral in their representations of the environment. In the first section of this chapter, we discovered that the mainstream media present different and even contradictory images of nature—as both nurturing and treacherous, sublime and dangerous, a problem (threat), and a resource. These differing views may reflect the viewpoint of one or more gatekeepers. However, the content and shape of environmental news also reflect influences associated with the production of news itself.

In the second section, we saw that news coverage of the environment is subject to some of the same powerful constraints that affect news reports generally: (1) the economic interests of owners (political economy), (2) norms and routines of newsrooms (gatekeeping), (3) accepted criteria for newsworthiness, (4) media frames, and (5) the news conventions of objectivity and balance. In some cases, environmental problems are unobtrusive because their invisibility and delayed effects make news coverage difficult. These constraints limit both the ability to present some stories at all, and, if reported, they influence powerfully the selection, angle, shaping, content, and hence the meaning of issues or concerns.

This chapter also observed that the rise of alternative media—blogs, online news services, and Web TV—are starting to challenge conventional media theory. With the broad access and interconnectivity of Internet sites, scholars will need to rethink who, if anyone, controls access and what determines newsworthiness.

Finally, in the third section, we looked at different approaches to the study of media effects—the impact of different media content on audiences' attitudes, perceptions, and behaviors. Whereas some older theories of media effects, such as the direct transmission (hypodermic) model, have gone out of favor, recent approaches have turned up interesting and unexpected results. Most important, agenda-setting theory has enabled researchers to appreciate media's ability to affect the public's perception of the importance of an issue. That is, media may not be successful in telling people *what* to think, but they often are successful in affecting what people think *about,* or the salience of issues.

The future of environmental coverage will depend upon the public's demands for more accurate, thoughtful, and in-depth reporting and environmental programming. Both media professionals and their audiences (you) have a role to play in improving media representation of nature and the environment in the coming decade. In the next chapter, I look at one example of change as I describe some of the reforms in risk communication and efforts to communicate with vulnerable populations about hazards.

KEY TERMS

Communication-Related Concepts

Agenda setting: An alleged effect of media on the public's perception of the salience or importance of issues, whereby news reporting, although it may not be successful in telling people *what* to think, is successful in telling them what to think *about.*

Alternative public sphere: Term used by media scholars Shanahan and McComas (1999) to refer to a space within society, which environmental and other groups articulate for themselves, in which their own discourse can be privileged and their own knowledge pursued.

Cultivation analysis: Associated with the work of media scholar George Gerbner (1990), the theory that repeated exposure to a set of messages tends to produce, in an audience, agreement with the views contained in those messages.

Cultivation in reverse: The media's cultivation of an anti-environmental attitude through the persistent lack of environmental images or by directing the attention of viewers and readers to other, nonenvironmental stories.

Direct transmission model: An early model that describes media effects as the result of a direct transmission of information from a sender (source) to a receiver; viewed audiences as highly susceptible to manipulation; also called the *hypodermic model,* it likened the media to a syringe that "injected" messages into audiences.

Frames: First defined by Erving Goffman (1974) to refer to the cognitive maps or patterns of interpretation that people use to organize their understanding of reality. See also **media frames.**

Gatekeeping: The role of editors and media managers in deciding to cover or not cover certain news stories; a metaphor used to suggest that individuals in newsrooms decide what gets in and what stays out.

Hypodermic effects theory: See **direction transmission model.**

Image events: Actions by environmentalists that take advantage of television's hunger for pictures; such events often succeed by reducing a complex set of issues to (visual) symbols that break people's comfortable equilibrium, inviting them to ask if there is a better way to do things.

Issue-attention cycle: Anthony Downs's (1972) model of the "natural decline" of the public's concern with environmental issues; predicts that the public's attention to environmental issues goes through the same stages as most social problems, from the lack of awareness to active engagement to disinterest.

Mainstreaming: An alleged effect in consistent viewers of media whereby differences are narrowed toward cultural norms represented in media programs.

Mainstream media: Major television and cable news and entertainment programming, commercial film, large-circulation newspapers, magazines, advertising, and radio news and talk shows that carry news and information about the environment.

Media effects: The influence of different media content, frequency, and forms of communication on audiences' attitudes, perceptions, and behaviors.

Media frames: The central organizing themes that connect different semantic elements of a news story (headlines, quotes, leads, visual representations, and narrative structure) into a coherent whole to suggest what is at issue. See also **frames.**

Media political economy: The influence on news content of ownership and economic interests of the owners of news stations and television networks.

Narrative framing: Media's organization of phenomena through stories to aid audiences' understanding.

News hole: The amount of space that is available for a news story relative to other demands for this same space.

Newsworthiness: The ability of news stories to attract readers or viewers; often defined by such criteria for selecting and reporting environmental news as prominence, timeliness, proximity, impact, magnitude, conflict, oddity, and emotional impact.

Objectivity and balance: Norms of journalism for almost a century; the commitment to which is made by news media to provide information that is accurate and without reporter bias and, where there is uncertainty or controversy, to balance news stories with statements from all sides of the issue.

Symbolic annihilation: Media's erasure of the importance of a theme by the indirect or passive deemphasizing of that theme.

Symbolic domestication: The rhetorical construction of nature (by media) as something tame and useful but also fragile and in need of human care and protection.

Unobtrusive events: Events that are remote from one's personal experience, characterized by their invisibility and delayed effects, which individuals seldom notice in their everyday lives, such as contamination by toxins.

Environment-Related Concepts

Anthropocentricism: The belief that nature exists solely for the benefit of humans; closely related to **anthropocentric-resourcist ideology**.

Anthropocentric and resourcist ideology of Nature: A view of nature that primarily serves the interests of those who benefit the most from the exploitation of nature.

Ecotage: Acts such as vandalism and arson that are undertaken for the purpose of protecting nature; while clearly illegal, these acts are specifically intended not to harm humans.

DISCUSSION QUESTIONS

1. Do media frames influence your understanding of environmental issues? Illustrate your answer by describing the different media frames used in news stories in campus or local newspapers and on a local radio or television station.

2. How do you feel about the journalistic norm of objectivity? Do you agree with journalists who argue for reporters' right to evaluate the competing arguments in an environmental controversy? Or should they be objective? Is this possible?

3. What online sites, other than those listed in this chapter, have you relied on for news and information about the environment?

4. Do media affect your attitudes about and behavior toward the environment? Has an online or mainstream news report altered your attitude about a specific issue, such as nuclear power, vegetarianism, or global warming? Can you identify characteristics of this report that particularly influenced you?

5. To what extent are dominant ideologies reproduced by commercial news and entertainment media? Can you identify mainstream media that question or challenge these ideologies?

REFERENCES

Abramson, R. (1992, December 2). Ice cores may hold clues to weather 200,000 years ago. *Los Angeles Times,* p. A1.

Ader, C. (1995). A longitudinal study of agenda setting for the issue of environmental pollution. *Journalism and Mass Communication Quarterly, 72,* 300–311.

Allan, S., Adam, B., & Carter, C. (2000). *Environmental risks and the media.* London: Routledge.

Allen, C., & Weber, J. (1983). How presidential media use affects individuals' beliefs about conservation. *Journalism Quarterly, 60,* 98–104.

Anderson, A. (1997). *Media, culture, and the environment.* New Brunswick, NJ: Rutgers University Press.

Beder, S. (2002). *Global spin: The corporate assault on environmentalism* (Rev. ed.). White River Junction, VT: Chelsea Green.

Boykoff, M. T. (2007). Flogging a dead norm? Newspaper coverage of anthropogenic climate change in the United States and United Kingdom from 2003 to 2006. *Area 39*(4), 470–481. Retrieved December 23, 2008, from http://www.eci.ox.ac.uk.

Boykoff, M. T., & Boykoff, J. M. (2004). Bias as balance: Global warming and the US prestige press. *Global Environmental Change, 14*(2), 125–36.

Brainard, C. (2008, August 27). Public opinion and climate: Part II. *Columbia Journalism Review.* [online]. Retrieved December 22, 2008, from http://www.cjr.org.

Bryant, J., & Oliver, M. B. (Eds.). (2008). *Media effects: Advances in theory and research* (3rd ed.). London: Routledge.

Center for Media Research. (2008, November 26). *Blogs and mainstream media intersect.* Retrieved December 23, 2008, from http://www.numantra.com.

Cherney, D. (1990, May 1). Freedom riders needed to save the forest: Mississippi summer in the California redwoods. *Earth First! Journal,* pp. 1, 6.

Climate Central. (2009). *Climate Central bridges the scientific community and the public.* Retrieved January 2, 2009, from http://www.climatecentral.org.

Cohen, B. C. (1963). *The press and foreign policy.* Princeton, NJ: Princeton University Press.

Corbett J. B. (2006). *Communicating nature: How we create and understand environmental messages.* Washington, DC: Island Press.

Cunningham, B. (2003). Re-thinking objectivity. *Columbia Journalism Review, 42,* 24–32.

Dahlstrom, M. (2007, May 23). *Prime time risks: Effects of channel diversity and exposure purposes on environmental risk perceptions.* Paper presented at the annual meeting of the International Communication Association, San Francisco, CA.

DeLuca, K. M. (2005). *Image politics: The new rhetoric of environmental activism.* London: Routledge.

Dewan, S. (2008, December 27, 2008). Tennessee ash flood larger than initial estimate. *The New York Times,* p. A8.

Downing, J. (1988). The alternative public realm: The organization of the 1980s anti-nuclear press in West Germany and Britain. *Media, Culture, and Society, 28,* 38–50.

Downs, A. (1972). Up and down with ecology–The "issue–attention" cycle. *Public Interest, 28,* 38–50.

Dunlap, R. E. (1992). Trends in public opinion toward environmental issues: 1965–1990. In R. E. Dunlap & A. G. Mertig (Eds.), *American environmentalism: The U.S. environmental movement, 1970–1990* (pp. 89–116). Philadelphia; Washington, DC; & London: Taylor & Francis.

Environmental Graffiti. (2007, October 21). *Top 10 environmental blogs.* Retrieved December 23, 2008, from http://www.environmentalgraffiti.com

Eyal, C. H., Winter, J. P., & DeGeorge, W. F. (1981). The concept of time frame in agenda setting. In G. C. Wilhoit (Ed.), *Mass communication yearbook* (pp. 212–218). Beverly Hills, CA: Sage.

Ferris, B. (2001, February 22). Arctic oil: New technologies but still in the same messy business. *TomPaine.com.* Available at www.tompaine.com.

Friedman, S. M. (2004). And the beat goes on: The third decade of environmental journalism. In S. Senecah (Ed.), *The environmental communication yearbook* (Vol. 1, pp. 175–187). Mahwah, NJ: Erlbaum.

Friedman, T. L. (2008). *Hot, flat, and crowded: Why we need a green revolution—and how it can renew America.* New York: Farrar, Straus & Giroux.

Gamson, W. A., & Modigliani, A. (1989). Media discourse and public opinion on nuclear power: A constructionist approach. *American Journal of Sociology, 95,* 1–37.

Gerbner, G. (1990). Advancing on the path to righteousness, maybe. In N. Signorielli & M. Morgan (Eds.), *Cultivation analysis: New directions in research* (pp. 249–262). Newbury Park, CA: Sage.

Gerbner, G., Gross, L., Morgan, M., & Signorielli, N. (1986). Living with television: The dynamics of the cultivation process. In J. Bryant & D. Zillmann (Eds.), *Perspectives on media effects* (pp. 17–40). Mahwah, NJ: Erlbaum.

Goffman, E. (1974). *Frame analysis: An essay on the organization of experience.* Cambridge, MA: Harvard University Press.

Gooch, G. D. (1996). Environmental concern and the Swedish press: A case study of the effects of newspaper reporting, personal experiences and social interaction on the public's perception of environmental risks. *European Journal of Communication, 11,* 107–127.

"Green" reporting in business news sections. (2007, Fall). Research report. www.Business Journalism.org. Arizona State University, Walter Cronkite School of Journalism and Mass Communication, Donald W. Reynolds National Center for Business Journalism. Retrieved March 1, 2009, from http://www.businessjournalism.org.

Guber, D. L. (2003). *The grassroots of a green revolution: Polling America on the environment.* Cambridge, MA: MIT Press.

Hall, J. (2001, May/June). How the environmental beat got its grove back. *Columbia Journalism Review* [online]. Retrieved December 22, 2008, from http://backissues.cjrarchives.org.

Hansen, A. (1993). *The mass media and environmental issues.* London: Leicester University Press.

Intergovernmental Panel on Climate Change (IPCC). (1996). *The regional impacts of climate change: An assessment of vulnerability.* New York: United Nations.

Intergovernmental Panel on Climate Change. (2007). *Climate change 2007: Synthesis report.* United Nations Environment Program. Retrieved November 2, 2008, from http://www .ipcc.ch/ipccreports.

Iyengar, S., & Kinder, D. R. (1987). *News that matters: Television and American opinion.* Chicago: University of Chicago Press.

Juskalian, R. (2008, June 6). *Launch:* Yale Environment 360: *Roger Cohn endeavors to make ends meet online.* Retrieved December 27, 2008, from http://www.cjr.org.

Korte, D. (1997). The Simpsons as quality television. *The Simpsons archive.* Retrieved April 23, 2004, from www.snpp.com.

LaMay, C. L. (1991). Heat and light: The advocacy–objectivity debate. In C. L. LaMay & E. E. Dennis (Eds.), *Media and the environment* (pp. 103–113). Washington, DC, and Covello, CA: Island Press.

Lee, M. A., & Solomon, N. (1990). *Unreliable sources: A guide to detecting bias in news media.* New York: Carol Publishing Group.

Lippmann, W. (1922). *Public opinion.* New York: Harcourt, Brace.

Mann, B. (Reporter). (2001, May 26). Bringing good things to life? *On the media.* New York: WNYC. Retrieved May 3, 2004, from www.onthemedia.org.

McComas, K., Shanahan, J., & Butler, J. (2001). Environmental content in prime-time network TV's non-news entertainment and fictional programs. *Society and Natural Resources, 14,* 533–542.

McCombs, M., & Shaw, D. (1972). The agenda setting function of the mass media. *Public Opinion Quarterly, 36,* 176–187.

McNair, B. (1994). *News and journalism in the UK.* London and New York: Routledge.

Meisner, M. (2005). Knowing nature through the media: An examination of mainstream print and television representations of the non-human world. In G. B. Walker & W. J. Kinsella (Eds.), *Finding our way(s) in environmental communication: Proceedings of the Seventh Biennial Conference on Communication and the Environment* (pp. 425–437). Corvallis: Oregon State University Department of Speech Communication.

Meister, M., & Japp, P. M. (Eds.). (2002). *Enviropop: Studies in environmental rhetoric and popular culture.* Westport, CT: Praeger.

Miller, M. M., & Riechert, B. P. (2000). Interest group strategies and journalistic norms: News media framing of environmental issues. In S. Allan, B. Adam, & C. Carter (Eds.), *Environmental risks and the media* (pp. 45–54). London: Routledge.

Nisbet, M. C. (2008, April 18). At *Time,* a tale of two global warming covers. *Framing Science.* Retrieved December 27, 2008, from http://scienceblogs.com/framing-science.

Novic, K., & Sandman, P. M. (1974). How use of mass media affects views on solutions to environmental problems. *Journalism Quarterly, 51,* 448–452.

Opel, A., & Pompper, D. (Eds.). (2000). *Representing resistance: Media, civil disobedience, and the global justice movement.* Westport, CT: Praeger.

Ostman, R. E., & Parker, J. L. (1987). Impacts of education, age, newspaper, and television on environmental knowledge, concerns, and behaviors. *Journal of Environmental Education, 19,* 3–9.

Pan, Z., & Kosicki, G. M. (1993). Framing analysis: An approach to news discourse. *Political Communication, 10,* 55–76.

Rodríguez, I. (2003). Mapping the emerging global order in news discourse: The meanings of globalization in news magazines in the early 1990s. In A. Opel & D. Pompper (Eds.), *Representing resistance: Media, civil disobedience, and the global justice movement* (pp. 77–94). Westport, CT: Praeger.

Russell, C. (2008, July/August). Climate change: Now what? A big beat grows more challenging and complex. *Columbia Journalism Review.* The Observatory. Retrieved December 27, 2008, from http://www.cjr.org.

Sachsman, D. B., Simon, J., & Valenti, J. (2002, June). The environment reporters of New England. *Science Communication, 23,* 410–441.

Schlechtweg, H. P. (1992). Framing Earth First! The *MacNeil-Lehrer NewsHour* and redwood summer. In C. L. Oravec & J. G. Cantrill (Eds.), *The conference on the discourse of environmental advocacy* (pp. 262–287). Salt Lake City: University of Utah Humanities Center.

Shabecoff, P. (2000). *Earth rising: American environmentalism in the 21st century.* Washington, DC: Island Press.

Shanahan, J. (1993). Television and the cultivation of environmental concern: 1988–92. In A. Hansen (Ed.), *The mass media and environmental issues* (pp. 181–197). Leicester, UK: Leicester University Press.

Shanahan, J., & McComas, K. (1999). *Nature stories: Depictions of the environment and their effects.* Cresskill, NJ: Hampton Press.

Slawter, L. D. (2008). TreeHuggerTV: Re-visualizing environmental activism in the post-network era. *Environmental Communication: A Journal of Nature and Culture, 2*(2), 212–228.

Soper, K. (1995). *What is nature?* Oxford, UK: Blackwell.

Spiess, B., & Ruskin, L. (2001, November 4). 2,000-acre query: ANWR bill provision caps development, but what does it mean? *Anchorage Daily News.* Retrieved April 13, 2004, from www.adn.com.

Technorati. (2008). *State of the Blogosphere / 2008.* Retrieved December 23, 2008, from http://technorati.com

Todd, A. M. (2002). Prime-time subversion: The environmental rhetoric of the Simpsons. In M. Meister & P. M. Japp (Eds.), *Enviropop: Studies in environmental rhetoric and popular culture* (pp. 63–80). Westport, CT: Praeger.

Vig, N. J., & Kraft, M. E. (2003). Environmental policy from the 1970s to the twenty-first century. In N. J. Vig & M. E. Kraft (Eds.), *Environmental policy: New directions in the 21st century* (5th ed., pp. 1–32). Washington, DC: CQ Press.

Wagner, T. (2008). Reframing ecotage as ecoterrorism: News and the discourse of fear. *Environmental Communication: A Journal of Nature and Culture, 2*(1), 25–39.

Weise, E. (2004a, February 8). Mercury damage "irreversible." *USA Today.* Retrieved December 23, 2008, from http://www.usatoday.com.

Weise, E. (2004b, April 8). Study: Pregnant women eating too much fish. *USA Today,* p. 3A.

West, B. M., Lewis, M. J., Greenberg, M. R., Sachsman, D. B., & Rogers, R. M. (2003). *The reporter's environmental handbook.* New Brunswick, NJ: Rutgers University Press.

White, D. M. (1950). The "gatekeeper": A case study in the selection of news. *Journalism Quarterly, 27*(4), 383–390.

Wilkins, L., & Patterson, P. (1990). Risky business: Covering slow-onset hazards as rapidly developing news. *Political Communication and Persuasion, 7,* 11–23.

Wilson, M. (2008, June 17). Do green issues make green? *Columbia Journalism Review.* Retrieved October 17, 2008 from http://www.cjr.org.

Yopp, J. J., & McAdams, K. C. (2007). *Reaching audiences: A guide to media writing* (3rd ed.). Boston: Pearson Education.

Risk communication, in its simplest form, seeks to inform potentially affected individuals about the existence, nature, severity, or acceptability of an environmental danger.

CHAPTER 6

Risk Communication

Environmental Dangers and the Public

WASHINGTON—The Food and Drug Administration's assurances that a controversial chemical is safe for use in food containers are flawed, an independent panel of scientific advisers concluded.... The chemical, known as bisphenol A, is used to make plastic for ... baby bottles and other goods.... But the FDA recently said there is no harm from the low doses of BPA....

—Associated Press, "Panel Rebukes FDA" (2008, p. 5A)

Those who control the discourse on risk will most likely control the political battles as well.

—Plough & Krimsky (1987, p. 4)

Humans have always faced danger from natural events such as storms, earthquakes, disease, famine, and crop failure. However, with the rise of modern industrial society, we face ever-increasing danger from human sources as well—nuclear radiation, chemical contamination of water and food, asbestos and lead paint in older buildings, secondhand smoke from cigarettes, and more. As a result of growing public concern, since the 1970s federal agencies have begun to evaluate the risk of environmental hazards to the public's health and safety. Risk assessments typically ask such questions as, Will air pollution from this oil refinery affect the health of residents living within a half-mile radius? Can sewage treated to reduce the toxic chemicals in it be used safely as a fertilizer on farmers' fields? How can health agencies communicate information about such risks to residents, pregnant women, and other populations?

In sharing information about these and other potential hazards, health officials, media, scientists, and the general public engage in an important and sometimes controversial form of environmental communication called *risk communication.* The field of risk communication emerged in the 1980s in response to increasing environmental hazards and a growing discord between experts and the general public over what constitutes "acceptable risk." **Risk communication** is defined in its simplest form as "any public or private communication that informs individuals about the existence, nature, form, severity, or acceptability of risks" (Plough & Krimsky, 1987, p. 6).

The chapter begins by describing what German sociologist Ulrich Beck (1992) has termed "risk society"—the growing threats to human health and safety from modern society itself. As we consider what it means to live in a risk society, we will explore the meaning of *risk* both as a technical construct and as a cultural construct. The differences in the meaning of *risk* have consequences for society's handling of its environmental dangers. As risk communication pioneers Alonzo Plough and Sheldon Krimsky (1987) pointed out nearly two decades ago, "Those who control the discourse on risk will most likely control the political battles as well" (p. 4).

The second section of the chapter introduces the practice of risk communication. I take a critical look at some of the assumptions underlying the traditional model, which has been influenced by *technical* meanings of risk. I also discuss recent efforts to reform this model by involving the affected community and their experiences in a cultural model of risk communication. Finally, the third section explores the ways that media reports may shape our perceptions of risks. In that section, I describe demands that news media open up spaces for the voices of residents, parents of sick children, and others who are most affected by environmental dangers.

When you have finished the chapter, you should be able to recognize some of the difficulties in defining "acceptable risk" and to appreciate the different perspectives on risk that are held by agencies such as the Environmental Protection Agency (EPA), by the news media, and by residents of communities themselves. In the end, society's ability to reduce environmental hazards may depend less on the language of technical risk—*parts per billion* and *dose exposures*—than upon the ability of experts and affected communities to speak honestly to one another about fairness and about who benefits (and who suffers) from dangerous environments.

Dangerous Environments: Assessing Risk

Two popular films from the 1990s, *A Civil Action* and *Erin Brockovich*, dramatize the experiences of small towns in Massachusetts and California: Residents had discovered that toxic contamination of their drinking water had caused leukemia, breast and uterine cancer, and other diseases[1]. The films portrayed the disillusionment and anger that many residents felt after they learned that official assurances that their water was safe to drink were untrue. Both films portrayed the experiences of real communities, and both films called our attention to very real dramas about environmental risks. They also ask us to look more closely at the challenges to improving the communication among technical experts, the media, health officials, and the general public.

Risk Society

In his influential book *Risk Society* and recent writings, sociologist Ulrich Beck (1992, 2000) argued that modern society has changed fundamentally in its ability to manage the consequences of its successful technical and economic development. He explained, "The gain in power from techno-economic 'progress' is being increasingly overshadowed by the production of risks" (p. 13). Unlike risks from nature or from 19th-century factories that affected specific individuals or groups, Beck characterizes today's **risk society** according to the large-scale nature of risks and the potential for irreversible threats to human life from modernization itself. These risks include such far-reaching and consequential hazards as nuclear power plant accidents, global climate change, chemical pollution, and the alteration of genetic strains from bioengineering.

In Beck's risk society, rapid scientific and technological changes entail unknown and unintended consequences. In addition, exposure to risks is unevenly distributed across the population. That is because the burden of coping with the hazards of new technologies and environmental pollutants often falls on the most vulnerable elements of the population: elderly people, children with respiratory problems, pregnant women, and residents of low-income neighborhoods with high concentrations of polluting facilities. As a result, serious conflicts occurred in the 1980s between the residents of at-risk communities and the technical experts and officials who assured them that polluting factories or buried toxic wastes posed no harm, when facts later proved such assurances false. Too often, residents of affected communities felt that officials ignored the experiences and concerns of those suffering from environmental hazards. Lois Gibbs (1994), a former resident of Love Canal, New York, expressed the feelings of many: "Communities perceive many flaws in risk assessment. The first is who is being asked to take the risk and who is getting the benefit. From a community's perspective, risk assessments are 'the risks that someone else has chosen for you to take.' What is a life worth . . . but equally important is whose life" (pp. 328-329).

Because many voices struggle to define risk, it is important to distinguish different meanings of risk and what constitutes acceptable risk for different parties. Indeed, there is heated controversy about whether risk is a technical matter that is determined objectively or a social construction that emerges from communication among experts, affected parties, and public agencies. Therefore, we look at both technical and cultural meanings of *risk,* and in the next section we examine the distinct approaches to risk communication invited by these differing meanings.

The Technical Model of Risk

By the 1980s, the public's fear of environmental hazards, along with the Environmental Protection Agency's mishandling of the health risks in high-profile cases such as Love Canal, had led to pressure on agencies to evaluate risk accurately and to do a better job in communicating with affected communities. In 1984, new EPA Administrator William Ruckelshaus proposed the terms *risk assessment* and *risk management* "as a common language for justifying regulatory proposals across the agency" (Andrews, 2006, p. 266). From a technical perspective, **risk assessment** is defined as the evaluation of the degree of harm or danger from some condition such as exposure to a toxic chemical, and **risk management** is defined as the implementation of steps to reduce the danger to the public and the environment.

In the years following Ruckelshaus's proposal, the EPA dramatically increased its technical analysis of the risks from nuclear power, pollution of drinking water, and pesticides and other chemicals in order to justify new health and safety standards for the commercial production, transport, and disposal of hazardous substances. Environmental policy professor Richard N. Andrews (2006) observed that by the end of the 1980s, "the rhetoric of risk had become the agency's primary language for justifying its decisions" (p. 266).

Although the EPA is the major agency responsible for evaluating health and environmental risks, other federal agencies also have roles. Understanding the technical model of risk used by these agencies is important in its own right. Also, the restriction of this model to the technical sphere of experts allows us to appreciate the type of risk communication that occurred in the 1980s and 1990s and why it generated so much controversy among the affected publics.

Risk Assessment

In everyday terms, *risk* is simply a rough estimate of the chances of something negative happening to us, such as an accident while driving on icy roads in the winter. Usually, our willingness to undertake something that may be dangerous suggests that we consider it to be an acceptable risk. For example, I'm still willing to drive in winter storms. However, for agencies such as the EPA or the Centers for Disease Control (CDC), risk is a *quantitative* concept. In this technical sense, **risk** is *the expected annual mortality (or other severity)* that results from some condition, such as exposure to a chemical substance. In other words, risk is a calculation of the probability that a certain number of people will die (usually from cancer) over a period of time (one year) from their exposure to a toxic chemical or other environmental hazard. But risk is not limited to mortality. It may include illness or injury as well. Risk communication scholar Katherine Rowan (1991) has noted that technical analysts view risk as "a multiplicative function of the severity of some hazard and its likelihood of occurrence (Risk = Severity × Likelihood)" (p. 303).

How do such agencies as the EPA, the Toxic Substances and Disease Registry, and the Centers for Disease Control know a risk's severity and its likelihood of occurrence? In such agencies, risk assessment occurs within a technical sphere of research labs and communication among experts such as toxicologists, epidemiologists, and other scientists. This process typically involves a **four-step procedure for risk assessment:** (1) hazard identification, (2) exposure assessment, (3) dose-response assessment, and (4) risk characterization. (See Figure 6.1.)

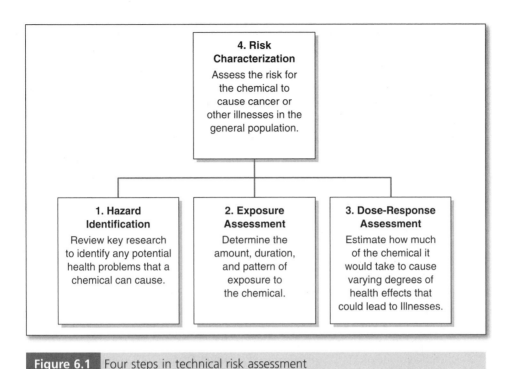

Figure 6.1   Four steps in technical risk assessment

SOURCE: Adapted from the California Environmental Protection Agency's *A Guide to Risk Assessment,* p. 5.

This process initially asks, What is the potential source of danger? For example, does a waste incinerator emit highly toxic dioxins or other hazardous chemicals? Second, it asks, Have any human populations been exposed to this hazard? If so, how much (what dosage) of this substance enters these human bodies? Third, the process seeks to model the effects of this exposure by asking, What is the relationship between the dosage that is received and any harmful responses or illnesses in the exposed population? And, finally, a technical risk assessment *characterizes* the risk, that is, it describes the overall implications of the dose responses for the health of the exposed population: Is exposure to this substance an "acceptable risk"? Or, does such exposure carry "X" likelihood of developing cancer or other illness?

The last step—the characterization of overall risk—usually seeks to combine the prior steps into an estimate of deaths or injuries expected annually from exposure to the hazard. Technical models of risk assessment use the resulting numerical value as the basis for judgments of **acceptable risk.** As we will see when we examine cultural models of risk, a judgment of acceptable or unacceptable risk inevitably involves values. Ultimately, acceptable risk is a judgment of the harms or dangers society is willing to accept (or not) and who is subject to this risk. Judgments of acceptable risk may involve a comparison with other risks, as well as estimates of the costs required to reduce these risks. As we see later, such judgments also involve questions of fairness and justice. For example, who bears the burden of exposure to a toxic waste incinerator, and who receives the benefit? Technical models of risk rarely consider such questions in arriving at an overall risk characterization.

An example of technical risk assessment occurred when the EPA announced that it would not regulate the presence of dioxins in sewage sludge used as fertilizer for farm crops. (Sewage sludge is a by-product of the process that some municipalities use to purify wastewater before releasing the water into local rivers. In the past, wastewater often contained the highly toxic chemical dioxin.) On October 17, 2003, the EPA summarized the results of its risk assessment for dioxins in sewage sludge.

First, the agency characterized the overall risk, announcing that "dioxins from this source [sludge] do not pose a significant risk to human health or the environment" (U.S. Environmental Protection Agency, 2003, para. 1). Second, it described the low probabilities of cancer in the different populations exposed to sewage sludge:

> The most highly exposed people, theoretically, are those people who apply sewage sludge as a fertilizer to their crops and animal feed and then consume their own crops and meat products over their entire lifetimes.
>
> EPA's analysis shows that even for this theoretical population, only 0.003 new cases of cancer could be expected each year or only 0.22 new cases of cancer over a span of 70 years. The risk to people in the general population of new cancer cases resulting from sewage sludge containing dioxin is even smaller due to lower exposures to dioxin in land-applied sewage sludge than the highly exposed farm family which EPA modeled. (U.S. Environmental Protection Agency, 2003, para. 1)

The EPA's decision not to regulate dioxin in sewage sludge set off a fierce controversy and raised questions not only about the limitations in technical risk analysis but also about the (lack of) involvement of the public in judgments about risk. While EPA officials commented that "the risk of new cancer cases from this source is small" (Heilprin, 2003, para. 3), a group of 73 environmental and farm worker groups petitioned the agency (unsuccessfully) for an immediate moratorium on the use of sewage sludge as a fertilizer for farm crops and animal feed (Werner, 2004).

Limitations of the Technical Model

The clash over sewage sludge helps to illustrate some of the difficulties with risk assessment that have surfaced in the past 20 years. This is particularly true when agency officials disagree about which studies to consider in concluding that a substance is an "acceptable" risk. For example, the National Research Council criticized the EPA's reliance on outdated methods of detecting pathogens (harmful substances), and questioned the accuracy of its risk assessment in the case of sewage sludge ("Government May Broaden the Regulating of Sewage Sludge," 2004).

The U.S. Food and Drug Administration's recent assurances that the chemical bisphenol A (BPA), used in plastic bottles and food containers, poses an "adequate" level of safety provides another illustration of the disagreements that are possible, even with the technical characterization of risk. BPA is widely used in hardened plastics for a range of consumer products, including plastic water bottles, baby food containers, and "the lining of nearly every soft drink and canned food product" (Parker-Pope,

2008, p. A21). Exposure to BPA also has been linked with health effects in studies of animals. These, and recent human studies, have caused concern, even for low-level, long-term exposures, especially by infants and babies (Lain, Galloway, Scarlett, Henley, Depledge, Wallace, & Melzer, 2008). The agency, however, has insisted that BPA is safe. Laura Tarantino, director of the FDA's Office of Food Additive Safety, told the *Washington Post* in 2008, "We have confidence in the data we've looked at to say that the margin of safety is adequate" (quoted in Layton, 2008, p. A3).

Despite its assurances, the FDA recently asked an independent scientific panel to review the research on which the agency based its characterization of the risk of low-level exposure to BPA. In September 2008, the panel held a public hearing to receive testimony from the public, other scientists, and health groups. The public comments revealed sharp disagreements with the FDA's risk characterization. A member of the Union of Concerned Scientists complained that the FDA had based its characterization of BPA largely on two studies funded by industry, "while down playing the results of hundreds of other studies" (quoted in Layton, 2008, p. A3). The day before, new research appeared in the *Journal of the American Medical Association* that linked BPA in urine samples of 1,455 men and women to higher rates of heart disease, diabetes, and liver abnormalities. One month later, the panel issued a "blistering report," finding that the FDA had "ignored important evidence in reassuring consumers about the safety" of BPA. Citing new research, the panel concluded that the "margins of safety for BPA exposure used by the agency are 'inadequate'" and urged more research by the FDA (Parker-Pope, 2008, p. A21).

The controversy over the risk characterization of BPA illustrates the role of human judgment in the social/symbolic construction of "risk," even in the four steps of the technical model. In the BPA case, disagreements arose over the sufficiency of scientific studies, over who funded the research, and whether new research contradicted earlier findings. (The uncertainty about the risks from BPA in the public's mind may be one reason plastic bottle makers recently have introduced BPA-free bottles into the market. See Figure 6.2.) Such judgments may also enter other steps in the technical assessment of risk. For example, scientists studying the health problems of residents living near a hazardous facility may find that it is difficult to trace the "pathway" by which individuals may be exposed (for example, via the lungs, skin, and so forth) or to measure with precision the cause–effect relationship between an exposure to toxins and specific damage to the body's respiratory, neurological, or reproductive systems. Gerald Markowitz and David Rosner, in *Deceit and Denial: The Deadly Politics of Industrial Pollution* (2002), observed that "it has often been difficult to show to the satisfaction of government regulators a direct correlation between particular chemicals from smokestacks and sewer pipes and the specific illnesses that clusters of people experience in particular communities" (p. 290).

The book *A Civil Action* and the Hollywood film based on it dramatized this problem in the town of Woburn, Massachusetts. There, the neighbors' exposure to toxic chemicals occurred years before any cases of childhood leukemia and other cancers became known. Yet, the technical sphere of experts and the legal system had difficulty

Figure 6.2	Concerns about potential health risks from the chemical bisphenol A (BPA), used in plastic bottles and food containers, has led some manufacturers to offer "BPA-Free" bottles" to consumers.

© Wild Wing Carving/istockphoto.

determining which of the particular chemicals might have caused these illnesses and how seriously the victims had been exposed (Goldstein & Goldstein, 2002).

I encountered the same problem in the mid-1990s when I worked with the Jesus People Against Pollution (JPAP), a group of African American and white residents of a low-income community in Mississippi who lived next to an abandoned chemical plant. After the plant exploded and burned, the owners closed its doors and buried hundreds of chemical drums on the site and in the nearby countryside. Years later, residents began to complain of skin rashes, headaches, cancers, and reproductive problems. Many had inhaled toxic fumes when the plant caught fire and, later, had drunk water that they believed had been contaminated by chemicals seeping into the community's water source.

The efforts of JPAP to seek medical care for affected residents from state and federal health agencies were frustrated by the absence of any certainty that their illnesses had been caused by their exposure to the chemicals from the abandoned plant. At one meeting with staff from the Agency for Toxic Substances and Disease Registry, a clearly frustrated young African American woman pleaded for more accurate medical studies of the neighborhood, insisting, "The evidence is in our bodies!"

The Cultural-Experiential Model of Risk

The experience of these communities illustrates another difficulty with the technical model of environmental risk. The basic complaint of the individuals and communities that actually experience exposure to chemical hazards is that communication about risks is too often restricted to a technical sphere and thus excludes those who are most affected. That is, technical models equate *numerical risk* (expected annual mortality) with judgments about the experience of those forced to live with imposed or involuntary risks. Yet, as Beck (1998) explained, "There is a big difference between those who take risks and those who are victimized by risks others take" (p. 10). As a result, some public agencies have begun in recent years to solicit the experience and views of affected communities in their assessment of risks and judgments of what is an acceptable and unacceptable risk. It is this **cultural-experiential model of risk** that I now describe, along with the role of a wider public sphere in assessing risk.

Environmental "Hazards" Versus "Outrage"

Political scientist Frank Fischer (2000) notes that experts often make assumptions about environmental risks that are quite removed from the experience of those affected by these risks. As a result, ordinary citizens' understanding of risk may be very different from a technical assessment. This can be rather dramatic in some cases. For example, poverty in some countries of the former Soviet Union has influenced the acceptance of risk in certain situations. A senior adviser for the European Bank for Regional Development told me recently of a controversy over electrical safety in Moldova, "where the price of metal is so high, people are willing to risk electrocution to steal scrap metal and cable" (personal communication, July 22, 2008). In this case, the desperate circumstances of a community may lead some to accept risks that other, more economically well-off, communities would never consider. Fischer explains that the *context* in which a risk is embedded raises a number of questions that may affect one's judgment of whether a risk is acceptable or not: "Is the risk imposed by distant or unknown officials? Is it engaged in voluntarily? Is it reversible?" (p. 65).

Peter Sandman (1987), the former director of the Environmental Communication Research Program at Rutgers University, has made a similar point. Sandman proposed that risk be defined as a combination of technical risk and social factors that people often consider in judging risk. He suggested that what technical analysts call a "risk" instead be called a "hazard" and that other social and experiential concerns be called "outrage." **Hazard** is what experts mean by risk (expected annual mortality), and **outrage** refers collectively to those factors that the public considers in assessing whether their exposure to a hazard is acceptable. "Risk, then, is the sum of hazard and outrage" (p. 21).

Here are some of the main outrage factors that Sandman believed people consider in judging an environmental hazard:

1. *Voluntariness.* Do people assume a risk voluntarily, or is it coerced or imposed on them?

2. *Control.* Can individuals prevent or control the risk themselves?

3. *Fairness.* Are people asked to endure greater risks than their neighbors or others, especially without access to greater benefits?

4. *Process.* Is the agency defining the risk perceived as honest and concerned about the community, or as arrogant? Does the agency listen? Does the agency tell the community what's going on before making a decision?

5. *Diffusion in time and space.* Is the risk spread over a large population or concentrated in one's own community?

Sandman's model of Hazard + Outrage is particularly useful in calling our attention to the experiences of a community that might be left out of technical calculations. This model also suggests the difference that might result from enlarging the public sphere for the assessment of risk to include affected groups. Sandman's definition is not without its critics, however. Some have suggested that this definition subtly characterizes scientific or technical assessments of "hazards" as rational and the emotional "outrage" of communities as irrational. Therefore, they fear that such characterizations can be used to marginalize or trivialize community voices in debates about risk. (See "Another Viewpoint: Irrational Outrage?")

Another Viewpoint: Irrational Outrage?

Journalists Sheldon Rampton and John Stauber write and edit the quarterly newsletter *PR Watch: Public Interest Reporting on the PR/Public Affairs Industry.* In their book *Trust Us, We're Experts!* they take a critical look at the uses of Sandman's well-known formula ("Risk...is the sum of hazard and outrage") by the public relations industry.

Rampton and Stauber (2002) explain: By suggesting that the public's outrage is irrational, companies may be more interested in allaying outrage "rather than focusing on real hazards or harms to the public" (p. 105). They write:

> This deceptively simple formula [risk equals hazard plus outrage] has become a staple in PR industry discussions of risk communication.... By understanding that risk equals hazard plus outrage, [Thomas] Buckmaster [general manager of the public relations firm Hill & Knowlton] says, risk communicators can overcome the fear and hostility of "grassroots members, stakeholders, and the public at large."... Once people are outraged, they don't listen to hazard statistics...don't use numerical risk comparisons." In fact, he says, "managing the outrage is more important than managing the risk." (p. 106, quoting Buckmaster, 1997.)

> Rampton and Stauber suggest that if businesses are more interested in managing the outrage than in focusing on real hazards or harms, they will invest in public relations campaigns rather than in changing the business practices that are causing public concern.

Cultural Rationality and Risk

When judgments about the social context and experience of exposed populations enter definitions of risk, a broader and more complex *cultural rationality* arises. Pioneering scholars in risk communication Alonzo Plough and Sheldon Krimsky (1987) define **cultural rationality** as a type of knowledge that includes personal, familiar, and social concerns in evaluating a real risk event. As distinct from technical analysis of risk, cultural rationality "is shaped by the circumstances under which the risk is identified and publicized, the standing or place of the individual in his or her community, and the social values of the community as a whole" (Fischer, 2000, pp. 132–133). Unlike technical rationality—the valorizing of scientific methods and expertise—cultural rationality includes folk wisdom, the insights of peer groups, traditions, an understanding of how risk impacts one's family and community, and sensitivity to particular events as well as overall patterns. (See Table 6.1.)

Harvard University professors Phil Brown and Edwin J. Mikkelsen (1990) provide a disturbing example of the differences between risk assessments made in a restricted technical sphere and those made in a wider public sphere. In their classic study *No Safe Place: Toxic Waste, Leukemia, and Community Action,* they cite the experience of residents in Friendly Hills, a suburb of Denver, Colorado. In the early 1980s, mothers from the neighborhood wondered why so many of their children were sick or dying. After EPA and state health officials refused to study the problem, the women decided to canvass door to door to document the extent of the problem. They found that 15 children who lived in the neighborhood from 1976 to 1984 had died from cancer, severe birth defects, and other immunological diseases. The mothers suspected that the cause of these deaths was toxic waste discharge from a nearby industrial facility owned by Martin Marietta.

State health officials dismissed the mothers' findings and denied that there was any environmental or other unusual cause of the children's deaths. They insisted that all the illnesses were within "expected limits," and although there were more childhood cancer cases than expected, the officials said that "they might be due to chance" (Brown & Mikkelsen, 1990, p. 143). One week after the officials declared the waste discharges safe, "the Air Force, which runs a test facility on the Martin Marietta site, admitted that the groundwater was contaminated by toxic chemicals" (p. 143). Brown and Mikkelsen describe what happened next: "Residents found that Martin Marietta had a record of toxic spills. . . . Several months later, EPA scientists found serious contamination . . . in a plume, or underground wave, stretching from the Martin Marietta site toward the water plant" (pp. 143–144). The Harvard professors concluded, "The belated discovery of what residents knew long before is eerie and infuriating—and, sadly, it is common to many toxic waste sites" (p. 144).

Table 6.1	Factors Relevant to the Technical and Cultural Rationality of Risk
Technical Rationality	**Cultural Rationality**
Trust in scientific methods, explanations; evidence.	Trust in political culture and democratic process.
Appeal to authority and expertise.	Appeal to folk wisdom, peer groups, and traditions.
Boundaries of analysis are narrow and reductionistic.	Boundaries of analysis are broad; include the use of analogy and historical precedent.
Risks are depersonalized.	Risks are personalized.
Emphasis on statistical variation and probability.	Emphasis of the impact of risks on the family and community.
Appeal to consistency and universality.	Focus on particularity; less concerned about consistency . . .
Those impacts that cannot be uttered are irrelevant.	Unanticipated or unarticulated risks are relevant.

SOURCE: Plough & Kromsky (1987), p. 9.

The Friendly Hills case is not isolated. Environmental communication scholar Tarla Rai Peterson (1997) reported a similar experience among health workers along the Rio Grande River in Brownsville, Texas, and Matamoros, Mexico. This region is known for its high concentration of *maquiladoras,* or manufacturing plants, along the Mexican side of the border, encouraged by the North American Free Trade Agreement (NAFTA). Since 1990, environmentalists and health groups have been concerned about this region because of its polluted air, poor housing and sanitation, unsafe drinking water, and release of raw sewage and chemicals directly into local streams and the Rio Grande River.

Unfortunately, the area also has been known since 1991 for its high rate of anencephalic births. **Anencephaly** occurs during pregnancy, when the end of the fetus's neural tube fails to close, resulting in a partial or complete absence of the brain. "Babies who are born with this condition die within a few hours" (Peterson, 1997, p. 128). A controversial 1992 risk study by the Texas Department of Health (TDH) and the Centers for Disease Control classified the outbreak of the area's anencephalic births as "a long-term incidence" (p. 129) rather than an epidemic. At the same time, the study admitted a major limitation in its findings due to incomplete records of birth defects in area hospitals and a lack of information about nonhospitalized births.

Health workers in Brownsville and Matamoros complained that TDH–CDC investigators' cultural insensitivity to people and their health practices had limited the potential of the study. In addition to use of an English-language survey instrument to interview Hispanic women, the study also overlooked other factors in characterizing the overall risk of anencephaly. Two of Peterson's (1997) informants from the region—Carmen de la Cruz Gomez and Rosa Ramirez—described some of these cultural factors:

Ramirez maintained that the CDC "didn't know our culture" . . . and did not attempt to learn. . . . Although "they're supposed to become sensitive to the particulars of the area, in terms of health care," she pointed out, the CDC, for example, "didn't know about our parturas, our lay midwives" [who deliver a large percentage of the babies in the region]. . . . [Another] irritation, explained Gomez, was that "any environmental concern that we gave them was just completely ignored." . . .

She and Ramirez noted, for example, that all the mothers who had given birth to anencephalic infants during the past year had lived extremely near the Rio Grande during the early part of their pregnancies. When they mentioned this concern and provided THD–CDC with a map, they were told that it was irrelevant to the study. (p. 160)

Peterson (1997) concluded that the reports of CDC epidemiologists and the reassurances of the area's economic boosters conflicted with the stories of mothers and health workers regarding what was and was not relevant to the risk of anencephalic births. Technical risk models fragment "the body into independent pieces, such as 'age' and 'percent of neural tube development,'" whereas health workers such as Rosa Ramirez emphasized the social and cultural contexts in which these families lived (pp. 169–170).

In such cases as Friendly Hills and Brownsville, a cultural-experiential model for evaluating risk challenges the symbolic legitimacy boundaries (Chapter 2) of technical agencies and their methods. That is, the questioning by mothers or community health workers of the limited approaches of these agencies threatens the images of knowledge and authority that usually benefit the agencies. At the same time, I want to stress that *a reliance on cultural rationality does not reject technical assessments of risk.* Indeed, an understanding of the pathways of chemical hazards to the human body and the level of doses experienced is vitally important, even though it is challenging to identify these pathways and effects accurately. But a cultural-experiential approach expands the technical model of risk to include considerations of the contexts in which risks occur and the values of those who are asked to live with environmental dangers.

The differences between technical and cultural models of risk raise important questions about what we consider acceptable risk, how we assess risk, and ultimately how we convey information about risk to others. These differences matter in the larger society's treatment of risk. These differences can be seen clearly in the ways public agencies choose to communicate with affected publics.

Communicating Environmental Risks to the Public

As tensions grew between experts and at-risk communities over environmental pollution, scholars, activists, and agency officials began to pay closer attention to the communication practices of agencies like the EPA in describing these dangers. Although the study of risk communication barely existed before 1986, since then the field has grown steadily in response to increasing complaints about the quality, trustworthiness, and accuracy of experts' risk reports and interactions with affected communities. As we noted at the opening of this chapter, risk communication in its most general form is "any public or private communication that informs individuals about the existence, nature, form, severity, or acceptability of risk" (Plough & Krimsky, 1987, p. 6). However, as practiced by health and environmental agencies, risk communication has come to mean something more specific in its objectives and its assumptions about target audiences.

In this section, we look at two quite different models of risk communication that have emerged since the late 1980s, reflecting the technical and cultural meanings of risk we described in the first section of this chapter. These are (1) the traditional or technical model of risk communication, which seeks to translate numerical assessments of risk to public audiences, and (2) the cultural model of risk communication, which draws upon the experiences and local knowledge of affected communities as well as on laboratory models of risk assessment.

Technical Risk Communication

Early experiences with risk communication grew out of the need of federal managers of environmental projects (such as toxic waste site cleanups) to gain the public's acceptance of risk estimates. Other experiences grew from health agencies' need to communicate about risk to target populations (for example, pregnant women, smokers, or substance abusers). This early model of risk communication was influenced heavily by technical risk assessment. **Technical risk communication** is defined as the translation of technical data about environmental or health risks for public consumption, with the goal of educating a target audience. Communication is usually one-way: Information is channeled from experts to a general audience (Krimsky & Plough, 1988, p. 6). The EPA's press release announcing that "only 0.003 new cases of cancer could be expected each year" from dioxins in sewage sludge is an example of this technical approach to risk communication.

Inform, Change, and Assure

The main goal of technical risk communication is to educate public audiences about numerical risk. As used by the EPA and many health agencies, this goal traditionally has three objectives: to inform, to change, and (sometimes) to assure.

1. *To inform local communities of an environmental or health hazard:* The Environmental Protection Agency's guide for managers, *Risk Communication in Action: The Risk Communication Workbook* (2007), defines risk communication explicitly as "the process of informing people about potential hazards to their person, property, or community" (Reckelhoff-Dangel and Petersen, 2007, p. 1). The agency explains that risk communication is a "science-based approach" whose purpose is to help affected communities understand risk assessment and management by forming "scientifically valid perceptions of the likely hazards" (p. 1). The guide is quite detailed for developing an effective "Outreach Plan," including questions to consider

in "profiling your audience(s)." These questions include, "What is their current level of knowledge about the risk?" and "Are their any organizations or centers that . . . serve the audience and might be avenues for disseminating your outreach products?" (p. 6).

Importantly, technical risk communication occurs after the assessment of the effects of a hazard has been made. It is largely one-way communication (experts to laypeople). In addition to informing target populations, such communication is used in other phases of risk management. For example, managers of a toxic waste cleanup site may need the participation of community members if they are to gain permission to take water samples on private property or mobilize support for specific cleanup strategies at sites near residents' homes.

2. *To* change *risky behavior:* Public health agencies long have had as part of their mission the goal of educating the public about unsafe food products and risky personal behaviors (such as teen pregnancy, substance abuse, and driving without seat belts). This focus on health education has evolved in recent years and now targets at-risk populations with "slick national media campaigns developed by . . . advertising firms in conjunction with science-based strategies in the attempt to change 'unhealthy' behaviors" (Plough & Krimsky, 1987, p. 4). Nevertheless, the objective of health risk communication remains the same: "Don't eat fish from this lake," "Don't drink alcohol while pregnant," and so forth.

3. *To* assure *those exposed to a perceived hazard that the risk is acceptable:* Assuring local residents that a chemical plant or a waste landfill is safe is a controversial chapter in environmental history. The clashes between residents and public officials in Love Canal, Woburn, and Friendly Hills are woven into the memories of many environmental agencies today. As a result, the EPA now cautions its managers to avoid terms such as *safe* or *dangerous* when speaking with affected communities. Its *Risk Communication in Action* guide advises, "Instead, explain risk numbers in ranges: 1–10 ppb [parts per billion] as 'low risk,' for example" (Reckelhoff-Dangel & Petersen, 2007, p. 12).

When chemical contamination was discovered at the nation's Superfund waste sites in 2004, the EPA issued a carefully nuanced statement to media, reassuring the public and, in particular, residents living near the waste sites. An Associated Press report handled the release this way:

> Almost one in 10 of the nation's 1,230 Superfund waste sites lack[s] adequate safety controls to ensure people and drinking water won't be contaminated, according to the Environmental Protection Agency. . . . [An EPA consultant said] the sites . . . "all have some contamination, but none . . . presents an imminent risk to human health" because of either emergency cleanup measures in place or the posting of fish advisories and other official warnings. (Associated Press, 2004, p. A3,)

Despite the EPA's qualifications, the social context of risk communication suggests that there are often symbolic overtones of assurance embedded in the way that scientists and technical experts interact with at-risk communities. This was particularly the case in the tumultuous 1980s and early 1990s, when the EPA and U.S. Army employed a top-down, one-way approach to communicating with communities about environmental hazards. (See "FYI": Risk and the Disposal of VX Nerve Agent.") Plough and Krimsky (1987) noted that in some of these situations, "a scientist speaking to a community about the health risks of a chemical dump may be carrying out a ritual that displays confidence and control. The technical information . . . is secondary to the real goal of the communicator: 'Have faith; we are in charge'" (p. 7).

☞ FYI   Risk and the Disposal of VX Nerve Agent

In her study of environmental risks, Dr. Michelle Simmons (2007) describes an example of the limits of technical risk communication:

In August 1999, the United States Army held a public meeting to inform local residents of Newport, Indiana, about the technology chosen to destroy 1,269 tons of VX nerve agent—the deadliest substance known—onsite at the Newport Chemical Depot. Using a technology called "supercritical water oxidation," the VX nerve agent would be neutralized, and the remaining effluent . . . would be dumped into the nearby Wabash River. Representatives from the Army and the subcontractor hired to dispose of the VX agent stood by posters describing the disposal process. (p. 2)

When Dr. Simmons told an Army representative that she was interested in ways the public participated in such decisions, "she told me that public participation in technical decisions such as this 'goes against [her] way of thinking'" (p. 2). Acknowledging that public response was required, the official described an idea the Army was implementing in which local residents would be invited to a roundtable with two representatives from the Army, familiar with the proposed disposal of VX agent:

"At this roundtable . . . residents were given free pizza and allowed to vent their concerns. 'So these residents don't feel intimidated,' she reported, 'their responses aren't written down; they are completely off the record.' When I asked her how the decision makers learned of the citizens' concerns and feedback, she told me that was not the purpose of the meeting." (p. 2)

SOURCE: Simmons (2007).

Often, during this earlier period, the response of agency officials to concerns about the public's acceptance of technical risk estimates was simply to inject more expertise into the process, "so that *the affected public might more rationally evaluate the risks they face with hazardous wastes or at least respect more the expertise of professional decision makers*" (Williams & Matheny, 1995, p. 167, emphasis added). This belief that the public tends to be irrational in assessing risks contributed to the dominance of the technical model of risk communication for many years.

But is this "elites-to-ignorant" model of risk communication (Rowan, 1991, p. 303) based on an accurate view of the public's judgments of risk? Many risk communication scholars, as well as community activists, argue that the technical model fails to acknowledge the concerns of those individuals who are most intimately affected by environmental dangers. One result has been that, in recent years, many agencies have turned to a more culturally sensitive model of risk communication.

Cultural Approaches to Risk Communication

In his influential essay "Technical and Democratic Values in Risk Analysis," former EPA senior advisor Daniel J. Fiorino (1989) argued that "the lay public are not fools" in judging environmental risks (p. 294). He identified three areas in which the public's intuitive and experiential judgments differed most from technical risk analysis:

1. *"Concern about low-probability but high-consequence events"*: For example, a 1 percent chance that an accident will occur but a terrible death toll if it does.

2. A *"desire for consent and control in social management of risks"*: The public's feeling that they have a say in decisions about risk is the opposite of a coerced or involuntary imposition of risk.

3. *"The relationship of judgments about risk to judgments about social institutions"*: In other words, the acceptability of risk may depend on citizens' confidence in the institution that is conducting a study, managing a facility, or monitoring its safety. (p. 294)

Research since Fiorino's essay confirms that public input into risk assessment often improves the quality of decisions about handling risks. Equally important, it also increases the likelihood that the decisions will be seen as legitimate. In its recent evaluation of public participation in decisions involving substantial amounts of science—as technical risk requires—the National Research Council concluded: Success depends on communication that improves "the ability of interested and affected parties to participate effectively in the risk decision process" (Dietz & Stern, 2008, pp. 9–10). Let's look at what this more interactive (two-way) communication about risk might require.

Citizen Participation in Risk Communication

In recent years, many agencies have begun to recognize the need for a **cultural model of risk communication**, that is, an approach that involves the affected public in assessing risk and designing risk communication campaigns and that recognizes the cultural knowledge and the experience of local communities. A major step toward defining such a model was taken in 1996, when the National Research Council released another report, *Understanding Risk: Informing Decisions in a Democratic Society.* The NRC report acknowledged that technical risk assessment was no longer sufficient to cope with the public's concerns about environmental dangers. It called for greater public participation and use of local knowledge in risk studies, and it pointedly noted that understanding environmental risk requires "a *broad understanding* of the relevant losses, harms, or consequences to the interested and affected parties, *including what the affected parties believe the risks to be in particular situations*" (National Research Council, 1996, p. 2, emphasis added).

Some health and environmental risk agencies have taken this tenet further to develop new practices in risk communication that recognize cultural knowledge and the experience of local communities. For example, communication scholars Jeffrey Grabill and Michelle Simmons (1998) proposed a "critical rhetoric" for risk communication that entails three principles. Such an approach

1. Sees risk as socially constructed and rhetorical. . . . The meaning and value of risk in a given situation is [sic] a function of multiple and sometimes competing discourses. . . .

2. Focuses on the processes of decision making . . . [especially] on the relations of power within decision-making processes, asking questions about who participates and in whose interests decisions are made[,] and . . .

3. Seeks to contextualize and localize risk situations . . . [by encouraging] local participation. (pp. 428–429)

Similar concerns have begun to appear in risk communication, in particular from health agencies that work with vulnerable populations. In each case, the agencies usually identify community partners with whom to collaborate in designing communication campaigns that take a broad approach to the meanings of risk. One example of this model is the ongoing project with the Hmong community in Milwaukee.

Risk Communication and the Hmong Community

A culturally appropriate approach to risk communication has been unfolding in recent years in Milwaukee, Wisconsin. The University of Wisconsin's Marine and Freshwater Biomedical Sciences Center has been a regional leader in sharing knowledge of environmental and health risks with at-risk communities. In association with the National Institute for Environmental Health Sciences (NIEHS), one of the center's objectives has been "to increase the knowledge and involvement of minority communities in environmental health issues, including awareness of the risks and benefits of fish consumption by the Hmong community in Milwaukee" (NIEHS, 2003a, para. 1).

The Hmong are immigrants from Southeast Asia. In Vietnam, the Hmong culture depended heavily upon fish for their diets, and in their new home in the American Midwest they've turned to fishing in local waters and in the Great Lakes. Coming from a rural, relatively unpolluted country, they have little understanding of pollution and contamination of waters and fish in Wisconsin. As a consequence, the center reports that Hmong fishers tend to "ignore the conventional warnings posted by the Department of Natural Resources about eating fish containing methyl mercury, PCBs and other chemicals" (NIEHS, 2003b, para. 2). The center also noted that the federal government recently had recommended lowering the safe level of exposure to methyl mercury in fish. This meant that families who depended upon fish from local waterways should reduce their weekly consumption of certain types of fish.

With the new warnings of the health risks from eating contaminated fish, the center felt that it was important to find effective means to communicate risks and benefits of fish consumption to the Hmong population. However, its approach departed from the traditional (technical) model of risk communication. Although its goal still was to inform the community about the hazards of eating fish contaminated with methyl mercury and polychlorinated biphenyls (PCBs), the university's Marine and Freshwater Biomedical Sciences Center proposed to work in collaboration with the community to design its communication campaign. Collaboration between the center's scientists and the community included the Hmong American Friendship Association and the Sixteenth Street Community Health Center, the major health care provider for these residents.

The communication plan that grew from this interaction of scientists and members of the community relied on the Hmong native language and an awareness of Hmong cultural traditions. It included a classroom module for middle school students, a video, and laminated cards with fish safety information. The main communication vehicle was a bilingual Hmong–English video titled *Nyob Paug Hauv Qab Thu* (*Beneath the Surface*). The video, which features local Hmong residents, "communicates in a simple, understandable, and culturally sensitive way the risks of eating contaminated fish and teaches methods of catching and preparing fish that can reduce these risks" (Thigpen & Petering, 2004, p. A738). And because pregnant women and children were at higher risk, the center and its partners decided to develop approaches relating specifically to these populations. In addition, they relied upon Hmong focus groups to discuss the framing of the content of the communication campaign.

Based on this collaboration, the center's risk communication campaign decided to include information about "the nutritional value of eating fish (benefits), the problems associated with eating contaminated fish (risks), how to recognize different species of fish, safer fishing areas and how to find them, and how to prepare fish to minimize exposure to contaminants" (NIEHS, 2003b, para. 2). The center and its community partners felt that a balanced presentation about pollution and fish consumption was important to gain a respectful hearing and not to alienate the Hmong people.

The center also relied upon volunteers in the Hmong community to distribute the video to households and local stores and to show it at Hmong festivals. Finally, the center and its partners worked with the local middle school to develop a module for its life science class that would educate inner-city students about eating contaminated fish. The risk communication project is ongoing among the Hmong community, largely as a result of the support and participation of local leaders, residents, and professionals in the community itself. As such, the project illustrates well the principal differences between the traditional (technical) form and the cultural model of risk communication.

The University of Wisconsin–Milwaukee's Hmong risk communication approach reflects many of the differences between technical and cultural approaches to risk communication. Whereas technical models of risk reflect numerical probabilities, the affected citizens living near a toxic waste site or fishing from polluted waters may desire to be part of the decision-making process and to have confidence in the social institutions responsible for managing risk. These are reflections of democratic values and agencies increasingly are recognizing that they must be part of any communication among scientists, agency officials, and members of an at-risk community. (For a summary of these differences, see Table 6.2.)

Still, risk warnings do not occur in a vacuum. News reports of oil spills or the effects of eating contaminated fish also influence our perceptions of risk, prompting official actions and influencing the behavior of at-risk communities. I have explored some of the factors that influence media coverage of the environment in general in Chapter 5. Here, I describe some of the major concerns about media reports of environmental risk.

Media and Environmental Risk

With the growing awareness of environmental hazards, multiple interests and voices now compete to characterize risk: Scientists, public health experts, environmental groups, industry, EPA officials, parents of sick children, and others. In a real sense, media have become an important public sphere within which many voices and claims to rationality compete to evaluate and define risks. News reports, TV ads, blogs, and listservs often provide forums for communication about environmental dangers, ranging from breaking news of a fire at a chemical plant to public service announcements (PSAs) warning of an approaching hurricane. Although such communication can be invaluable, it also labors under many of the requirements for "newsworthiness" that I described Chapter 5, such as magnitude, conflict, and emotional impact. And, sometimes media reports may be intended to reassure a frightened public rather than to provide relevant information for public action.

Table 6.2	Models of Risk Communication	
	Technical Model	**Cultural Model**
Type of communication:	Usually one-way (experts-to-laypeople)	Collaborative (citizens-experts-agencies)
Source of knowledge of risk:	Science/technology	Science *plus* local, cultural knowledge and experience
Objectives:	1. To translate/inform	1. To inform by recognizing social contexts of meaning
	2. To change risky behavior	2. To change risky behavior when in the interests of affected groups
	3. To assure concerned groups	3. To involve affected groups in judgments of acceptable and unacceptable risks

A classic illustration of media confusion about serious risk occurred after the accident to the cooling system and subsequent damage to the reactor core at Pennsylvania's Three Mile Island nuclear plant on March 28, 1979. Rhetorical scholars Thomas Farrell and Thomas Goodnight (1981) described communication about the accident by media, government, and industry officials as "conspicuous confusion and failure" (p. 283). In their study of the discourse in response to this accident, they found that "reporters were unable to judge the validity of technical statements. Technicians often could not sense the relevance of reporters' questions. Government sources, frequently at odds with one another, could not decide what information to release. . . . Some representatives of the nuclear power industry made misleading statements" (Farrell & Goodnight, 1981, p. 273).

Finally, media themselves face significant constraints in covering the environment, particularly the more complex news stories about biodiversity, climate change, or energy shortages. Thus, while attempting to provide information about serious hazards, reporters and editors also must negotiate a thicket of journalistic norms: Will the story command the attention and interest of readers or viewers? How should it be framed? Do sensational reports override substantive information? Furthermore, such factors influence not only *what* is reported about environmental risks, but they also affect *who* speaks about risk. For example, are cultural rationality claims of parents and other affected groups included in media reports? Not surprisingly, the answer to such questions is not a simple yes or no. In this section, I describe some of the ways in which risk is represented and factors that contribute to media coverage of environmental dangers, and I point to some of the challenges in raising public awareness of the risks from global climate change and the need for urgent action.

Media Reports of Risk: Accurate Information or Sensational Stories?

A common criticism from scientists and risk managers is that news stories about risk often give readers inaccurate information or sensational images rather than substantive coverage of an environmental danger. For example, accounts of exploding tanker trucks, oil spills off coastlines, or accidents at nuclear power plants call our attention to *low-probability but high-consequence* (acute) occurrences. That is, such risks occur only occasionally, but their effects on the environment and on human safety are significant when they do. Often, in these cases, critics fear that news reports emphasize the victims—sick children, oil-coated sea birds—but fail to explore contributing causes or the steps needed to prevent such dangers. How accurate are these criticisms?

A survey of media coverage of risk by Lundgren and McMakin (2004) found some truth in many of the criticisms of the media. Their chief findings included:

1. "Scientific risk had little to do with the environmental coverage presented on the nightly news. Instead the coverage appeared driven by the traditional journalistic news values of timeliness, geographic proximity, prominence, consequence, and human interest, along with the television criterion of visual impact" (p. 276).

2. "Mass media disproportionately focus on hazards that are catastrophic and violent in nature, new, and associated with the United States. . . . Drama, symbolism, and identifiable victims, particularly children or celebrities, make risks more memorable" (p. 277).

3. "Stories for television, radio, newspapers, and magazines do not generally lend themselves to long discourses. . . . [Hence] concepts important to technical professionals, such as probabilities, uncertainties, risk ranges, acute versus chronic risks, and risk tradeoffs, do not translate well in many mass media formats" (p. 279).

4. "To humanize and personalize the risk story, news organizations often use the plight of an individual affected by a hazard, regardless of how representative the person's situation is" (p. 279).

Lundgren and McMakin stressed that these approaches of simplifying and personalizing information "may make information more accessible to the public, but may result in incomplete and sometimes unbalanced information for making personal risk decisions" (p. 279).

In addition to the criticisms that Lundgren and McMakin report, other studies have pointed to a failure to place risk in a wider perspective. For example, while the EPA warns women who are pregnant about the risks of eating certain types of fish that may contain the mercury (see www.epa.gov/waterscience), such advisories rarely mention the source of the mercury; health officials have long been aware of the dangers from coal-burning power plants that emit mercury into the air that is deposited into lakes and streams where it is absorbed into the fatty tissues of certain fish. Media scholar Sharon M. Friedman (2004) points out that the neglect of technical details and the failure to compare risks with more familiar circumstances means that readers and viewers are unable to "understand and judge their own risk levels" (p. 181).

Finally, scientific research on risk itself may be ambiguous and hence difficult for reporters to interpret fairly or accurately for laypeople. Readers of local newspapers in the town of Teesside in northeastern England experienced the difficulties of media in the competing news headlines about a report linking air pollution possibly to cancer: "Air 'Link' to Cancer: Report Warns Women" and "Illness: It's Not the Teesside Air. Poor Health Cannot Be Blamed on Pollution, Says New Study." Other reports appeared in the environmental health trade press: "Teesside Health Study Links Lung Cancer With Air Pollution"; yet another reported, "Teesside Health Study Takes the Blame Off Industry" (Phillimore & Moffatt, 2000, p. 105).

In fairness, journalists face difficult constraints in reporting risk issues. This is true even at the *New York Times,* "one of the last bastions of serious science journalism" (Brainard, 2008, para. 2). Speaking at a 2008 meeting of the American Association for the Advancement of Science, *New York Times* science reporter Andrew Revkin said, despite the recent interest in the environment, global warming remained a "fourth-tier" story in the press. Among the reasons, he explained, is "the 'tyranny of the news peg,' a dearth of print space, and different learning curves" for complex stories like climate science . . . [Y]ou don't get extra room in a newspaper just because the story's harder . . . [and] the word 'incremental' is the death knell for a story" (quoted in Brainard, 2008, para. 2).

As a result of the limitations on media reporting, especially topics like global warming, other parties have begun to take up the challenge of communicating the risks of climate change.

Communicating the Risks of Climate Change

For the climate scientists and nonprofit groups who have begun campaigns about climate change, communicating the risks of a warming world has proven to be a challenge. There are several reasons for this: Other, more skeptical voices compete with scientists in the public sphere (see Chapter 9), the impacts from global warming are perceived to be distant, and distractions occur daily from war to a worsening economy. Perhaps, the most serious challenge is the lack of a feeling of urgency, even as "large majorities of Americans believe that global warming is real and consider it a serious problem" (Leiserowitz, 2007, p. 44). For example, a recent opinion poll discovered that "while 61% of Americans say the effects of global warming have already begun, just a little more than a third say they worry about it a great deal, a percentage that is roughly the same as the one Gallup measured 19 years ago" (Newport, 2008, para. 1).

As a result, many climate scientists, academic advisers, and environmental groups have begun to rethink their approaches to communicating the risks of global warming. In this section, I explore briefly two of these initiatives, one led by the National Center for Atmospheric Research and, a second, led by Nobel Peace Prize–winner Al Gore's Alliance for Climate Protection.

Global Warming and Interpretive Communities

One important initiative began when the MacArthur Foundation awarded the National Center for Atmospheric Research at the University of Colorado, Boulder, a grant "to help improve the communication between scientists and non-governmental groups about climate change" (Moser & Dilling, 2007, p. ix). Asking what has worked, and what has not worked, more than 40 individuals—academics, business leaders, nonprofit advocacy groups, climate scientists, and others—surveyed the existing knowledge of risk communication and the public's awareness of global warming. Their recommendations are summarized in Moser and Dilling's comprehensive volume, *Creating a Climate for Change: Communicating Climate Change and Facilitating Social Change*. Most directly relevant to this chapter is a series of recommendations for risk communication in the volume that take into account what social scientist Anthony Leiserowitz (2007) calls "interpretive communities" (p. 51).

In his chapter, "Communicating the Risks of Global Warming," Leiserowitz (2007) describes an **interpretive community** as "a group of individuals that share mutually compatible risk perceptions, affective imagery, values, and sociodemographic characteristics" (p. 51). This term derives from his national survey of American risk perceptions of global warming. Among his findings, Leiserowitz discovered that a majority of respondents perceived the dangers from melting glaciers, drought, disease, and other impacts from climate change as impacting primarily "geographically and temporarily distant people, places, and non-human nature" (p. 47). In other words, global warming was not particularly salient to them, their families, or local communities.

Leiserowitz also found substantial variation in these perceptions of risk within the American public—variations that offered a potential opening for rethinking the approach to risk communication. These differences he called "interpretive communities." Importantly, Leiserowitz found that, since "risk perceptions are socially constructed," these different interpretive communities are "predisposed to attend to, fear, and socially amplify some risks, while ignoring, discounting, or attenuating others" (p. 51). He concluded that these differing perceptions strongly suggested that multiple communication strategies were needed to convey the urgency of addressing global warming.

Overall, Leiserowitz recommended five communication strategies whose goal is to address the paradox in American risk perceptions: "While large majorities of Americans believe global warming is real," it remains "a low priority relative to other national and environmental issues" (p. 53). Leiserowitz's five communication strategies:

Strategy 1: Highlight potential local and regional climate change impacts

Strategy 2: [Stress that] climate change is happening now

Strategy 3: Highlight the potential impacts of climate change on human health and extreme weather events

Strategy 4: Talk openly about remaining uncertainties [in climate science]

Strategy 5: Tailor messages and messengers for particular interpretive communities. (pp. 53–57)

Leiserowitz contends that the research behind these strategies suggest strongly that the public as a whole is predisposed to view climate change as "a significant risk" and is willing to support actions addressing it, but "what is lacking is a sense of urgency, strong leadership, and political will" (p. 61). By 2009, it had become clear that some portions of Leiserowitz's recommendations for communicating the urgency of global warming appear to have been widely adopted by educators, climate scientists, and nonprofit advocacy groups like the Alliance for Climate Protection.

Alliance for Climate Protection's Ad Campaigns

A second, quite different initiative communicating about climate change has been the savvy TV and online campaigns by the Alliance for Climate Protection. Started by

Nobel Peace Prize–winner and former U.S. Vice President Al Gore, the initiative is a three-year, multimillion dollar effort "to persuade the American people—and people elsewhere in the world—of the importance and urgency of adopting . . . effective and comprehensive solutions for the climate crisis" (Alliance, 2008, para. 1) (see Figure 6.3). The Alliance's campaign was launched as part of Gore's international "Live Earth" concerts on July 7, 2007. Broadcast and streamed to more than a billion people worldwide, Live Earth showcased more than a hundred pop and rock music acts in eleven nations and urged people to take "the pledge" to demand action on global warming (Live Earth, n.d.).

The goals of the campaign weave together themes of implied risk and solutions to global warming. The Alliance's CEO, Cathy Zoi, stresses that the message of the campaign is twofold: climate change is "urgent and solvable" ("Climate," 2008, para. 7).

Figure 6.3	The message of former Vice President Al Gore's Alliance for Climate Protection Campaign is twofold: The risks from climate change are both "urgent and solvable."

© Jemal Coutess Archive/Getty Images.

By foregrounding *urgency,* the ads largely assume the risks of climate change, and, instead, showcase both ordinary and well-known citizens who, having acknowledged these facts, call upon Americans to be part of the solution. It's an interesting strategy: Whether global warming presents a danger is no longer the real debate; the message of the ads is that smart people (similar to us) are moving forward to solve the problem.

The campaign's core message, in turn, has been woven into a series of well-produced, 60-second ads appearing daily on CNN and other cable TV networks, as well as the campaign's main Website, We Can Solve It (http://wecansolveit.org). The Alliance is sponsoring three different communication projects. Its first project was a series of "We Can Solve It" ads that featured diverse Americans who, while acknowledging the dangers of global warming, exude confidence that Americans can rise to this challenge. Its more recent project, "Repower America," also assumes the facts about the risks of global warming; instead, it foregrounds positive calls from ordinary Americans for wind and solar power to "'repower' our country with 100% clean electricity within 10 years" ("The Plan," 2008, para. 1).

By modeling the behavior of other Americans, both famous and those similar to us, the Alliance ads largely bypass the debate over risk with an alternative vision for America—new jobs, independence from foreign oil, and a healthy planet. As we see in Chapter 7, this approach draws upon the strategy of using *social norms*—our perception of what other people like us are doing—to resolve the gap between the public's awareness that global warming is real and happening now and their lack of urgency about it. (I return to this theme in more detail in Chapter 7.)

Whose Voices Speak of Risk?

Our understanding of environmental dangers depends not simply on information but also on who speaks or interprets information about risk. A growing area of research in environmental communication is the nature of the sources used by media in reports about risks—government officials, scientists, at-risk publics, environmental groups, and so forth. Not surprisingly, the media sometimes echo some of the features of technical models of risk communication, using primarily government officials and experts to provide news about environment risks. As a result, stories too often rely on such sources to provide "objective" accounts of risks but use local residents or environmental groups for the nontechnical aspects of a story such as "color, emotion, and human elements" (Pompper, 2004, p. 106).

In a study of this tendency, Pompper (2004) surveyed 15 years of environmental risk stories in three national newspapers that target different social groups: the *New York Times, USA Today,* and the *National Enquirer.* Her major conclusion: Whereas mainstream media such as the *New York Times* and *USA Today* relied heavily upon government and industry sources, the *National Enquirer* relied mostly on members of the public (individuals, community members, and so forth). This is significant because experts and community members framed the stories quite differently. Government and industry were more likely to frame their accounts of risk in terms of official assessments and assurances of safety. On the other hand, members of the public spoke about environmental and health hazards, such as cancer and industrial accidents.

The study also found that the two mainstream newspapers used frames that supported the status quo: Risk could be controlled, responsible agencies were providing oversight, and so forth. For example, industry sources stressed their ability to manufacture electrical power within a legal framework "designed to preserve natural resources, protect worker safety, and ensure that adequate research had been performed" (Pompper, 2004, p. 114). Pompper's conclusion is stark: "Voices of common people who live with environmental risks every day and voices of groups organized to save the environment from industrialism are drowned out by elites cited most often in environmental risk stories. For non-elites . . . this study's major finding has grim implications, indeed. The news media essentially ignore them" (p. 128).

Voices of the "Side Effects"

The dominance of government and industry spokespersons in environmental risk stories certainly affects the social definition of risk and raises an important question about the opportunities for cultural rationality in media outlets. Indeed, an important debate over media reporting of risk concerns what Beck (1992) has called the **voices of the "side effects"** (p. 61). Beck is referring to those individuals (and their children) who suffer the side effects of risk society, such as asthma and other illnesses from air pollutants, chemical contamination, and the like. Reflecting the tension between technical and cultural rationality that we discussed earlier, these voices of the "side effects" seek media recognition of a very different understanding of environmental dangers and the burdens of risk:

> What scientists call "latent side effects" and "unproven connections" are for them their "coughing children" who turn blue in foggy weather and grasp for air, with a rattle in their throat. On their side of the fence, "side effects" have voices, fears, eyes, and tears. And yet they must soon learn that their own statements and experiences are worth nothing so long as they collide with the established scientific [views]. . . . Therefore people themselves become small, private alternative experts in risks. . . . The parents begin to collect data and arguments. The "blank spots" of modernization risks, which remain "unseen" and "unproven" for the experts, very quickly take form under their . . . approach. (p. 61)

Yet, it is not at all clear that these voices of the "side effects" are given the journalistic space to offer alternative cultural rationality in news accounts of environmental risks. Media communication scholar Simon Cottle (2000) looked at this possibility in a study of environmental news on British television. Unlike Pompper's study of newspapers, Cottle found that for television, "ordinary voices" were more frequently (37%) cited than either government sources or scientific sources. However, he concluded that such ordinary feelings and expressions of "lived experience" are used mainly to provide human interest or a "human face" for stories rather than substantive analysis.

Cottle cites a BBC2 *Newsnight* news story about a proposal for the British government to subsidize the purchase of new cars to reduce harmful emissions from the 7 million cars more than 10 years old that travel Britain's highways. The BBC station aired three reactions from "ordinary" viewers. One voice comes from a music student who expresses his/her personal experience and feelings about continuing to drive an older car: "I wouldn't be free without it; and I think that is the main thing. I wouldn't be able to do my degree, I wouldn't be able to go into work. It's just totally important to me and I do love it as well. It's not just the practical side of it. I love having a car" (p. 36).

The inclusion of personal interviews is important for human interest and thus news value in environmental stories. Nevertheless, these experiences are "sought out and positioned to play a symbolic role, not to elaborate a form of 'social rationality'" (Cottle, 2000, pp. 37–38). That is, they are used to provide color, variety, and human interest rather than to shed insight into a problem. For example, the voice of the British musician speaking about owning a car provides "a private-experiential statement" (p. 36) but does not reflect on the effects of pollution (risk).

In summary, news media, online, and electronic reports constitute a public sphere crisscrossed by competing claims about risk from scientists, government agencies, industry, and (less often) the voices of the "side effects" who are directly affected by environmental dangers. Reporters working in the mainstream media strive to balance not only these differing interests but also journalistic norms for newsworthiness. At times, such constraints push reporters to dramatize specific events and underreport chronic and longer term conditions and causes of environmental and health risks.

SUMMARY

With the arrival of risk society (Beck, 1992), affected communities and government agencies such as the EPA have struggled to assess the dangers of modern hazards. The EPA and other federal agencies dramatically increased their use of technical methods to assess risk in the 1980s. Yet, inaccurate diagnoses and failure to warn the residents of health risks have provoked a firestorm of criticism of technical models of risk assessment. As a result, health workers, residents, scholars, and others have helped develop a cultural model of risk analysis that takes into account broad factors that affect perceptions of the severity of risks.

Differences in technical and cultural assessments of risk also have influenced the practice of risk communication. The technical model of risk communication relies primarily upon one-way communication (experts to lay audiences) and seeks to translate numerical risk estimates for target populations. The cultural model of risk communication expands upon this technical awareness by involving members of at-risk groups in helping scientists and health agencies understand risk in terms of the community's values and cultural experiences. Representatives of affected groups also work with agencies to design communication campaigns that are appropriate for those affected by environmental hazards.

Finally, news media have become a public arena for many voices in evaluating and defining environmental risks—scientists, EPA officials, nonprofit groups, and the voices of the "side effects" (Beck, 1992), those who suffer directly the effects of modern environmental hazards. While mainstream media struggle to convey accurately the scientific findings and official health warnings, newer forms of media, such as the Alliance for Climate protection's online and TV ads, are arising to alert the public, share information, and to provide opportunities for wider engagement with environmental dangers.

The study of risk communication is essentially a study of the differences and conflicts in the struggles to define risk and what is *acceptable risk* by agencies such as the EPA, the news media, nonprofit groups, and residents of communities. At the beginning of this chapter, you read that "those who control the discourse on risk will most likely control the political battles as well" (Plough & Krimsky, 1987, p. 4). I hope, therefore, that this description of the technical and cultural approaches to risk communication has helped you appreciate some of the reasons for conflict among technical experts, public officials, media, and communities exposed to environmental dangers. Equally, I hope you now have some appreciation of the improvements in risk communication that some agencies and universities are attempting today.

KEY TERMS

Communication-Related Concepts

Cultural model of risk communication: An approach that involves the affected public in assessing risk and in designing risk communication campaigns, and that recognizes cultural knowledge and the experience of local communities.

Interpretive community: A group of individuals that share mutually compatible risk perceptions, affective imagery, values, and sociodemographic characteristics.

Risk communication (general): Any public or private communication that informs individuals about the existence, nature, form, severity, or acceptability of risks.

Risk communication (technical): The translation of technical data about environmental or health risks for public consumption, with the goal of educating a target audience.

Environment-Related Concepts

Acceptable risk: From a technical perspective, a judgment based on the numerical estimate of deaths or injuries expected annually from exposure to a hazard. From a cultural perspective, a judgment of what harms society is willing or unwilling to accept and who is subject to this risk; such a judgment inevitably involves values.

Anencephaly: A condition occurring during pregnancy in which the end of the fetus's neural tube fails to close, resulting in a partial or complete absence of the brain and, usually death within a few hours of birth.

Cultural-experiential model of risk: See **risk (cultural-experiential)**.

Cultural rationality: In Plough and Krimsky's (1987) view, a basis for risk evaluation that includes personal, familiar, and social concerns; a source of judgment that arises when the social context and experience of those exposed to environmental dangers enter definitions of risk.

Four-step procedure for risk assessment: Procedure used by agencies to evaluate risk in a technical sense; the four steps are (1) hazard identification, (2) assessment of human exposure, (3) modeling of the dose responses, and (4) a characterization of the overall risk. See **risk (technical)**.

Hazard: In Sandman's (1987) model of risk, what experts mean by *risk* (that is, expected annual mortality). See **risk (technical)**.

Outrage: In Sandman's (1987) model, collective term for factors the public considers in assessing the acceptability of their exposure to a hazard. See **hazard**.

Risk (cultural-experiential): The effort by some public agencies to solicit the experience and views of affected communities in risk assessment.

Risk (technical): The expected annual mortality (or other severity) that results from some condition, such as exposure to a chemical substance; a calculation of the probability that a certain number of people will die (usually from cancer) over a period of time (one year) from their exposure to an environmental hazard; risk may include illness and injuries as well as death.

Risk assessment: The evaluation of the degree of harm or danger from some condition such as exposure to a toxic chemical.

Risk management: The implementation of steps to reduce the danger to the public and the environment from a risk.

Risk society: Term coined by German sociologist Ulrich Beck to characterize today's society according to the large-scale nature of risks and the threat of irreversible effects on human life from modernization.

Voices of the "side effects": Term used by Beck (1992) to refer to those individuals (or their children) who suffer the "side effects" of the risk society, such as asthma and other illnesses from air pollutants, chemical contamination, and so forth.

DISCUSSION QUESTIONS

1. Do you trust government (or industry) warnings about the health risks of smoking, tanning salons, consuming alcohol while pregnant? Are these communications effective? Do they give you useful information? Do they affect your own behavior?

2. Is the public's outrage over environmental hazards rational? Although a toxic waste landfill may inconvenience those living near it, doesn't it have to go somewhere? Or does it? Does society manage fairly the risks associated with our chemical culture?

3. How appropriate is it for governmental agencies like the EPA or Centers for Disease Control, charged with providing accurate risk assessments to the public, to involve affected populations or communities in either assessing that risk or designing a risk communication plan? What are the drawbacks of public involvement? the advantages?

4. Communicating about the risks of climate change faces a dilemma: While the public largely accepts that global warming is happening, many do not feel any urgency to act. How can groups concerned about the risks of climate change resolve this dilemma?

5. Leiserowitz (2007) states that research suggests strongly that the public as a whole is predisposed to view climate change as "a significant risk" and is willing to support actions addressing it, but "what is lacking is a sense of urgency, strong leadership, and political will" (p. 61). Is this accurate? Are U.S. and world leaders today actively addressing the risks of global warming? Are their actions sufficient to this challenge?

6. What precisely do the voices of the "side effects" have to contribute to risk communication? Are these voices merely emotional, or do they have relevant insight into risks in their environment?

NOTE

1. For an account of the real Erin Brockovich's story, see her autobiography, *Take It From Me: Life's a Struggle, But You Can Win* (2002). The story of Woburn, Massachusetts, is told in Phil Brown's and Edwin Mikkelsen's (1990) *No Safe Place: Toxic Waste, Leukemia, and Community Action,* and in Jonathan Harr's (1996) *A Civil Action,* on which the Hollywood movie version is based.

REFERENCES

Allen, S., Adam, B., & Carter, C. (Eds.). (2000). *Environmental risks and the media.* London & New York: Routledge.

Alliance for Climate Protection. (2008). Homepage. Retrieved December 21, 2008, from http://www.climateprotect.org.

Andrews, R. N. L. (2006). *Managing the environment, managing ourselves: A history of American environmental policy* (2nd ed.). New Haven: Yale University Press.

Associated Press. (2004, July 28). New Superfund concerns: Toxic exposure cited; in check at 80 percent of sites, officials say. *Richmond Times-Dispatch,* p. A3.

Associated Press. (2008, October 29). Panel rebukes FDA on safety of chemical in plastic. *The News & Observer* [Raleigh, NC], p. 5A.

Beck, U. (1992). *Risk society: Towards a new modernity.* Newbury Park, CA: Sage.

Beck, U. (1998). Politics of risk society. In J. Franklin (Ed.), *The politics of risk society* (pp. 9–22). London: Polity.

Beck, U. (2000). Risk society revisited: Theory, politics, and research programs. In B. Adam, U. Beck, & J. V. Loon (Eds.), *The risk society and beyond: Critical issues for social theory* (pp. 211–229). London: Sage.

Brainard, C. (2008, February 19). Dispatches from AAAS: A few thoughts on meeting's media-oriented panels. *Columbia Journalism Review* [online]. Retrieved December 9, 2008, from www.cjr.org.

Brockovich, E. (2002). *Take it from me: Life's a struggle, but you can win.* New York: McGraw-Hill.

Brown, P., & Mikkelsen, E. J. (1990). *No safe place: Toxic waste, leukemia, and community action.* Berkeley: University of California Press.

Climate: CEO of Gore-funded group, Zoi, discusses launch of new $300M education campaign. *Energy and Environment News.* Retrieved December 21, 2008, from http://www.eenews.net.

Cottle, S. (2000). TV news, lay voices and the visualization of environmental risks. In S. Allan, B. Adam, & C. Carter (Eds.), *Environmental risks and the media* (pp. 29–44). London: Routledge.

Dietz, T. & Stern, P. C. (2008). *Public participation in environmental assessment and decision making.* National Research Council. Washington, DC: National Academies Press.

Farrell, T. B., & Goodnight, G. T. (1981). Accidental rhetoric: The root metaphors of Three Mile Island. *Communication Monographs, 48,* 271–300.

Fiorino, D. J. (1989). Technical and democratic values in risk analysis. *Risk Analysis, 9,* 293–299.

Fischer, F. (2000). *Citizens, experts, and the environment: The politics of local knowledge.* Durham, NC: Duke University Press.

Friedman, S. M. (2004). And the beat goes on: The third decade of environmental journalism. In S. Senecah (Ed.), *The environmental communication yearbook,* Volume *1,* 175–187. Mahwah, NJ: Erlbaum.

Gibbs, L. (1994). Risk assessments from a community perspective. *Environmental Impact Assessment Review, 14,* 327–335.

Goldstein, I. F., & Goldstein, M. (2002). *How much risk? A guide to understanding environmental health hazards.* New York: Oxford University Press.

Government may broaden the regulating of sewage sludge. (2004, January 2). *The New York Times,* p. A13.

Grabill, J. T., & Simmons, W. M. (1998). Toward a critical rhetoric of risk: Producing citizens and the role of technical communicators. *Technical Communication Quarterly, 7,* 415–441.

Harr, J. (1996). *A civil action.* New York: Vintage.

Heilprin, J. (2003, October 17). EPA won't restrict sludge fertilizer, despite possible cancer-causing dioxins. *SFGate.com.* Retrieved July 20, 2004, from www.sfgate.com.

Krimsky, S., & Plough, A. (1988). *Environmental hazards: Communicating risks as a social process.* Dover, MA: Auburn House.

Lain, I. A., Galloway, T. S., Scarlett, A., Henley, W. E., Depledge, M., Wallace, R. B., & Melzer, D. (2008). Association of urinary bisphenol A concentration with medical disorders and laboratory abnormalities in adults. *Journal of the American Medical Association, 300*(11), 1303–1310. Retrieved December 8, 2008, from http://jama.ama-assn.org.

Layton, L. (2008, September 17). Study links chemical BPA to health problems. *Washington Post*, p. A3.

Leiserowitz, A. (2007). Communicating the risks of global warming: Perceptions, affective images, and interpretive communities. In S. C. Moser & L. Dilling, (Eds.), *Creating a climate for change: Communicating climate change and facilitating social change* (pp. 44–63). Cambridge, UK: Cambridge University Press.

Live Earth. (n.d.). Wikipedia. Retrieved December 21, 2008, from http://en.wikipedia.org.

Lundgren, R. E., & McMakin, A. H. (2004). *Risk communication: A handbook for communicating environmental, safety, and health risks.* Columbus, OH: Battelle Press.

Markowitz, G., & Rosner, D. (2002). *Deceit and denial: The deadly politics of industrial pollution.* Berkeley: University of California Press.

Moser, S. C., & Dilling, L. (Eds.). (2007). *Creating a climate for change: Communicating climate change and facilitating social change.* Cambridge, UK: Cambridge University Press.

National Institute of Environmental Health Sciences (NIEHS). (2003a). *University of Wisconsin Milwaukee Community outreach and education program.* Retrieved July 27, 2004, from www-apps.niehs.gov.

National Institute of Environmental Health Sciences (NIEHS). (2003b). *Fish consumption risk communication in ethnic Milwaukee.* Retrieved July 27, 2004, from www.niehs.gov.

National Research Council. (1996). *Understanding risk: Informing decisions in a democratic society.* Washington, DC: National Academy Press.

Newport, F. (2008, April 21). *Little increase in Americans' global warming worries.* Gallup, Inc. Retrieved December 8, 2008, from http://www.gallup.com.

Parker-Pope, T. (2008, October 30). Panel faults F.D.A. on stance that chemical in plastic is safe. *The New York Times*, p. A21.

Peterson, T. R. (1997). *Sharing the Earth: The rhetoric of sustainable development.* Columbia: University of South Carolina.

Phillimore, P., & Moffatt, S. (2000). "Industry causes lung cancer": Would you be happy with that? Environmental health and local politics. In S. Allen, B. Adam, & C. Carter (Eds.), *Environmental risks and the media* (pp. 105–116). London and New York: Routledge.

Plough, A., & Krimsky, S. (1987). The emergence of risk communication studies: Social and political context. *Science, Technology, & Human Values, 12,* 4–10.

Pompper, D. (2004). At the 20th century's close: Framing the public policy issue of environmental risk. In S. L. Senecah (Ed.), *The Environmental Communication Yearbook, 1,* 99–134. Mahwah, NJ: Erlbaum.

Reckelhoff-Dangel, C., & Petersen, D. (2007, August). *Risk communication in action: The risk communication workbook.* Environmental Protection Agency. Cincinnati, OH: Office of Research and Development, National Risk Management Research Laboratory. Retrieved December 9, 2008, from http://www.epa.gov.

Rowan, K. E. (1991). Goals, obstacles, and strategies in risk communication: A problem-solving approach to improving communication about risks. *Journal of Applied Communication Research, 19,* 300–329.

Sandman, P. (1987). Risk communication: Facing public outrage. *EPA Journal, 13*(9), 21–22.

Simmons, W. M. (2007). *Participation and power: Civic discourse in environmental policy decisions.* Albany: State University Press of New York.

The Plan. (2008). *Repower America.* Retrieved December 21, 2008, from http://www.Repower America.org.

Thigpen, K. G., & Petering, D. (2004, September). Fish tales to ensure health. *Environmental Health Perspectives, 112*(13), p. A738.

U. S. Environmental Protection Agency. (2003, October 17). *EPA makes final decision on dioxin in sewage sludge used in land applications.* (Press release). Retrieved July 20, 2004, from www.epa.gov.

Werner, E. (2004, February 5). Whistleblower says EPA used unreliable data for sludge decision. *The Mercury News.* Retrieved August 1, 2004, from www.mercurynews.com.

Williams, B. A., & Matheny, A. R. (1995). *Democracy, dialogue, and environmental disputes: The contested languages of social regulation.* New Haven: Yale University Press.

PART IV

Voices for Change

Advocacy campaigns against coal-burning power plants have grown in recent years, as a result of concerns about climate change.

CHAPTER 7

Environmental Advocacy Campaigns

S CENE 1: Outside of Bank of America offices, Asheville, North Carolina

Protesters carry placards and banners reading, "Bank of America Stop Funding Climate Change," "Bank of America Stop Mountaintop Removal," and "Bank of America Climate Criminal" (Climate Convergence, 2007, para. 2). An online news site, Asheville Indymedia, shows photos and reports firsthand accounts of the event: Two activists have locked themselves inside the main lobby; other activists are blockading the entrance to the downtown branch of the bank. The event also includes "a large, lively group of concerned citizens dressed as canaries and polar bears" (para. 2). Others are handing out literature and photos of "mountaintop removal," a particularly destructive form of coal mining in West Virginia and other Appalachian states.

SCENE 2: Zuni Pueblo, New Mexico

"It has been a long 20 year struggle . . . but we have had our voices heard," exclaimed Carlton Albert, the Zuni tribe's head councilman (quoted in Seciwa, 2003, p. 2). Albert had learned that a powerful utility company had dropped its plans for a coal mine near the sacred Zuni Salt Lake in western New Mexico. The lake was named for Ma'l Oyattsik'i (the Salt Woman), who, according to legend, for centuries had provided salt from the lake for religious ceremonies and for the well-being of area tribes. A coalition of Native American tribes and local conservationists had waged a successful campaign, including radio ads and tribal runners carrying salt from Zuni Pueblo to the company's headquarters in Phoenix, to halt the coal mine. Reflecting on their success, Albert said, "If there is a lesson to be learned, it is never to give up and [to] stay focused on what you want to accomplish" (quoted in Seciwa, 2003, p. 2).

These scenes illustrate a form of environmental communication known as **advocacy**, the act of persuading or arguing in support of a specific cause, policy, idea, or set of values. The activists outside of the Bank of America were engaging in a form of direct action—civil disobedience and other nonviolent protests—while the Zuni tribe engaged in advocacy by carrying out a strategic campaign to influence the plans of a utility company. Although there are many forms of environmental advocacy, I focus in this chapter on one main form: the **environmental advocacy** campaign.

An **advocacy campaign** can be defined broadly as a strategic course of action, involving communication, that is undertaken for a specific purpose. In the first section of this chapter, I describe advocacy in general, as well as different modes of environmental advocacy, from media events to community organizing. I also introduce and distinguish the advocacy *campaign* from other types of issue advocacy, such as social marketing. And, most important, I contrast advocacy campaigns with *critical rhetorics*. Although critical rhetorics challenge dominant discourses, they often do not engage in strategic action or campaigns on behalf of environmental objectives.

In the second section, I explore more closely the basic questions advocates must address in designing effective campaigns for the environment. The campaign is the form of advocacy most frequently used by local and national environmental groups to accomplish an objective, be it ending logging in a national forest or halting a permit for a coal-burning power plant. After we describe the design of a typical campaign, you'll have an opportunity to "Act Locally!" to apply the principles of the campaign to concerns in your community or on campus.

In the third section, I describe some of the challenges faced by environmental advocates in overcoming the so-called **attitude-behavior gap;** that is, while an advocacy campaign may change peoples' attitudes, it sometimes fails to alter their *behaviors.* We also look at a disputed claim within the environmental movement, the belief that the use of radical tactics such as direct action or even the burning of sport utility vehicles (SUVs) will make mainstream groups appear more reasonable and thus more acceptable in society.

My hope is that, when you have finished this chapter, you'll be more aware of the wide range of communication modes that environmental advocates engage in, and that you'll also appreciate the challenges they face in questioning strongly held values and ideologies and in building public demand for environmental protection.

Environmental Advocacy

The practice of advocacy has a long tradition in the United States. In the 18th century, Samuel Adams's fiery pamphlets stirred colonists' anger against British rule and recruited patriots for the American Revolution. As the nation took form, trade guilds, political parties, charitable groups, and other associations emerged alongside more established institutions as advocates for workers, urban sanitation, women's suffrage, and other social causes.

Today, groups whose goals range from community support for the homeless to the stopping of sweatshop labor provide forums for newly emerging voices and concerns. Groups such as the Children's Defense Fund, the Humane Society, and Behind the Label (a campaign against sweatshop labor) bring a variety of viewpoints to public attention and provide "a collective voice to those who lack the means or expertise to participate on their own" (Richardson & Joe, 1995, p. A19). Such groups hold public institutions accountable to democratic and humane principles and have often achieved significant changes that protect vulnerable populations and interests, such as new medicines for people living with HIV/AIDS, or the agreement by some universities not to buy clothing from companies using sweatshop labor in third world countries.

In providing a voice for those who may have no means of expression, advocacy groups act as intermediaries between individuals and the large, often impersonal institutions of public life. This has been particularly true of environmental groups. Former *New York Times* writer Philip Shabecoff (2000) argues that a chief role of environmental groups is to act as "intermediaries between science and the public, the media, and lawmakers" (p. 152). For example, students at my campus drew on the expertise of economics and physics professors, as well as that of firms working with solar thermal panels, to press the University of North Carolina to change its energy practices by funding a "Green Energy" initiative. As intermediaries, the Green Energy group enabled others students to gain expertise and express their concerns to university administrators.

Modes of Environmental Advocacy

Environmentalists engage in a wide variety of advocacy modes or forms of communication. These modes may differ dramatically in their goals, the media they use, their strategies of persuasion, and the audiences they target. They may include public education, campaigns to influence environmental legislation in Congress, community organizing, boycotts, and direct action protests such as sit-ins and hanging banners from corporate buildings. (See Table 7.1.)

Here and in the following chapter, I describe some of these modes of advocacy in more detail. For example, in Chapter 8 I describe the use of toxic tours, hosted by environmental justice groups who invite people to visit communities that are contaminated by toxic chemicals to see, smell, and feel what daily life is like for those who live there (Pezzullo, 2007). For now, I describe two broad forms of advocacy: advocacy campaigns and critical rhetorics. These, in turn, may draw upon a wide range of more specific types of advocacy, such as public education campaigns, boycotts, direct action, or litigation.

Campaigns Versus Critical Rhetoric

Before an environmental advocacy campaign starts, there is often a period in which existing practices are questioned and a desire to find a better way is expressed. For example, Rachael Carson's classic book *Silent Spring* (1962) sharply criticized the

Table 7.1	Modes of Environmental Advocacy
Mode of Advocacy	**Objective**
Political and Legal Channels:	
1. Political advocacy	To influence legislation or regulations
2. Litigation	To seek compliance with environmental standards by agencies and businesses
3. Electoral politics	To mobilize voters for candidates and referenda
Direct Appeal to Public Audiences:	
4. Public education	To influence societal attitudes and behavior
5. Direct action	To influence specific behaviors through acts of protest, including civil disobedience
6. Media events	To create publicity or news coverage to broaden advocacy effects
7. Community organizing	To mobilize citizens or residents to act
Consumers and the Market:	
8. Green consumerism	To use consumers' purchasing power to influence corporate behavior
9. Corporate accountability	Consumer boycotts, shareholder actions

practices of the pesticide industry and the government agencies that exposed the public to harmful chemicals. As a result of this questioning, public health advocates and groups such as Environmental Action began to campaign for federal legislation to curb the pesticide Dichloro-Diphenyl-Trichloroethane (DDT) and for stronger laws to protect air and water. Although they are different in some ways, campaigns and critical rhetorics can function in complementary ways, and it is therefore important to understand each of these modes of advocacy in more detail.

Critical Rhetoric

Critical rhetoric can be defined as the questioning or denunciation of a behavior, policy, societal value, or ideology; such rhetoric may also include the articulation of an alternate policy, vision, or ideology. Throughout the modern environmental movement, many voices—not part of any particular campaign—have questioned or denounced taken-for-granted views of and behavior toward nature. For example, Greenpeace activists have released *mind bombs* in the media since the 1970s to raise the world's consciousness of the cruelty of modern whaling. Greenpeace cofounder Robert Hunter defines **mind bombs** as simple images, such as scenes of Greenpeace activists on small, inflatable boats interposing themselves between whales and their harpooners, that "explode in people's minds" to create a new awareness (quoted in Weyler, 2004, p. 73).

A critical rhetoric may also include the articulation of an alternate policy, vision, or ideology. The Foundation for Deep Ecology urges such a vision, arguing that the basic economic and technological structures of society must change to the point that "the resulting state of affairs will be deeply different from the present" (Naess & Sessions, n.d.). And advocates for Just Sustainability are initiating a critique of modern development, the burden of whose growth-oriented economies falls most heavily on the poor and disenfranchised. In arguing for a truly "sustainable" society, this critical rhetoric prioritizes justice and envisions "a better quality of life for all, now and into the future, in a just and equitable manner, whilst living within the limits of supporting ecosystem" (Agyeman, Bullard, & Evans, 2003, p. 5). As a result, critical rhetorics frequently serve to expand the range of social choices and visions that are eclipsed in the day-to-day political struggles of a campaign.

Although both the Just Sustainability advocates and the Foundation for Deep Ecology stated their criticisms of society in polite language, critical rhetorics also have gained attention as a result of sharp denunciation and not-so-decorous challenges to existing norms. Sometimes this has taken the form of what communication scholars Robert Scott and Donald Smith (1969) originally termed **confrontational rhetoric**, the use of strident language and actions such as sit-ins and the occupation of buildings to critique racism, war, or exploitation of the environment. Despite the controversy often surrounding such actions, Scott and Smith urge us to take seriously the criticisms they raise. They explain that sometimes the calls for "civility and decorum serve as masks for the preservation of injustice. . . . They condemn the dispossessed to non-being, and . . . they become the instrumentalities of power for those who 'have'" (p. 7).

In the context of environmental advocacy, scholars of confrontational rhetoric have examined marches, demonstrations, sit-ins, and other visual rhetoric, as well as highly symbolic acts such as the destruction of logging equipment, SUVs, and animal research laboratories. Environmental communication scholar Kevin DeLuca (2005) has called these acts of destruction "ecotage" (p. 6). (We return to the idea of confrontation rhetoric later, in exploring the so-called radical flank effect.)

Advocacy Campaigns

Although campaigns, too, may advocate for major social changes, they differ from critical rhetorics in their approach. Most important, campaigns are organized around concrete, strategic actions that move us closer to those larger goals. As I stated earlier, an **advocacy campaign** can be defined broadly as a strategic course of action, involving communication, which is undertaken for a specific purpose. That is, a campaign is waged to win a victory or bring about a concrete outcome; it therefore goes beyond simply questioning a policy. For example, a campaign that aims to block the construction of a toxic waste landfill in a neighborhood might pursue this objective by organizing local residents to attend city council meetings and voice their opposition to the landfill's permit. The difference between a campaign and critical rhetoric, then, is not the goal but the *strategic course of action* by which a campaign pursues such goals.

In contemporary society, the campaign is a mode of communication used by many groups, agencies, and institutions for a wide range of purposes. Sometimes called *information campaigns* or *social marketing,* the basic campaign mode is used, among other purposes, to reduce health risks from smoking, promote family planning, encourage the use of designated drivers, and encourage people to conserve energy by turning down their thermostats. Campaigns are employed by such widely diverse groups as the United Nations, in partnership with civil society groups, to promote peace, human rights, and development, including its "Stand Up and Speak Out Against Poverty" campaign (UN General Assembly, 2008); researchers at Stanford University, who worked to reduce the incidence of heart disease by encouraging at-risk individuals to have medical checkups, alter their diets, and exercise more (Flora, 2001); and the U.S. Forest Service and Ad Council, whose slogan, "Remember, Only You Can Prevent Forest Fires" has warned outdoor users for decades about the danger of forest fires (Rice, 2001, p. 276).

Recently, some groups, particularly in health communication, have adopted an approach to campaigns called **social marketing**. This is "the planning and implementation of programs designed to bring about social change using concepts from commercial marketing" (Social Marketing Institute, n.d., para. 1). Social marketing emphasizes the motives of the target audience in encouraging behavior change, that is, individuals are more willing to take action or change behavior when they believe "the benefits they receive will be greater than the costs they incur" (para. 3; see also Weinreich, 2006). This approach is used especially by health agencies and other entities targeting personal behavior change. On the other hand, Tom Crompton (2008), a strategist for the Worldwide Fund for Nature, in the United Kingdom (WWW-UK), has compiled extensive evidence of the weakness of the social marketing approach in persuading the public to take action on global warming. "A marketing approach to behavioural change," he reports, ". . . insists that we should ask people to take simple and painless steps. But the widening gulf between the cumulative impact of these behavioural changes and the scale of the challenges we confront is openly acknowledged" (p. 2).

Environmental advocacy campaigns share some characteristics of information campaigns and social marketing, and it is important to recognize these similarities before looking at their differences: In their classic study of campaigns, Everett Rogers and Douglas Storey (1987) identified four features shared by most campaigns:

1. *A campaign is purposeful.* That is, "specific outcomes are intended to result from the communication efforts of a campaign" (p. 818).

2. *A campaign is aimed at a large audience.* A campaign's purpose usually requires an organized effort that goes beyond the interpersonal efforts of one or a few people to persuade another person or a small number of others.

3. *A campaign has a more or less specifically defined time limit.* A target audience's response to a campaign—a vote, a change in one's diet, or the purchase of a smoke detector, for example—will be made by some date, and the window for any further response will close.

4. *A campaign involves an organized set of communication activities.* The communication activities in a campaign are particularly evident in message production and distribution. (We return later to the concept of message and its importance in advocacy campaigns.)

Although they share these features with public health and other issue campaigns, environmental advocacy campaigns sometimes differ from them in basic ways. Two differences in particular stand out:

First, most campaigns that aim to reduce risk or influence individual attitudes or behavior are *institutionally sponsored;* that is, they are initiated by a governmental agency such as the Environmental Protection Agency (EPA), a health association, the United Nations, or a university such as the University of Milwaukee's Marine and Freshwater Biomedical Sciences Center (Chapter 6). Environmental advocacy campaigns, on the other hand, are usually waged by *non-institutional* sources—concerned individuals, environmental organizations, or small community action groups.

Second, most public relations and public health campaigns seek to change *individuals' attitudes and/or behaviors* (for example, personal lifestyle, consumer choices, diet, drug or alcohol use, or sexual practices) rather than on system-level changes. Most environmental advocacy campaigns, on the other hand, seek to change *external conditions*—for example, the cleanup of an abandoned toxic waste site—or aim at more systemic change, that is, the policies or practices of a governmental or corporate body.

The campaign mode occurs as part of several of the advocacy forms listed in Table 7.1. For example, the campaign takes a familiar form in both legislative and electoral politics, and it also appears in public education efforts, community organizing, and corporate accountability campaigns. Business groups often launch public relations campaigns to influence the public debate over environmental problems such as global warming. On the other hand, a campaign itself may employ different forms of advocacy, such as education, direct action, and consumer boycott in its efforts to halt a corporation's use of sweatshop labor. The important idea is that a campaign may rely on multiple forms of advocacy as part of a strategic and time-limited course of action for a specific purpose.

Based on my own experience working with advocacy campaigns in the environmental movement, I believe this mode of communication is increasingly important in shaping public debate and decisions about environmental policy. Therefore, in the following sections I describe in more detail the design of advocacy campaigns as "a strategic course of action, involving communication, which is undertaken for a specific purpose." Along the way I also offer several examples of successful advocacy campaigns.

Environmental Advocacy Campaigns

By the time of the first Earth Day in 1970, the environmental movement had begun to change the way that citizens communicated with public officials and with each other. Not content to rely simply on magazine articles, personal testimony, and nature programs on television to educate the public, many environmental groups began to design advocacy campaigns to achieve specific changes. One architect of this strategy was Michael McCloskey, the former executive director of the Sierra Club. In a 1982 interview, McCloskey reflected on his role in the environmental movement's turn to campaigns:

> What I have emphasized has been a serious approach toward achieving our ends. I thought that we were not here just to bear witness or to pledge allegiance to the faith, but in fact we were here to bring that faith into reality. . . . That means we could not rest content with having said the right things, or with having made our convictions known, but we also had to plan to achieve them. We had to know how the political system worked, how to identify the decision makers and how their minds worked. We had to have people concerned with all the practical details of getting our programs accomplished. (Gendlin, 1982, p. 41)

The shift described by McCloskey echoes the tension between critical rhetoric and the advocacy *campaign,* that is, "having said the right things" versus having "to plan to achieve them." It also reflected many environmental groups' interest in a more participatory approach that enabled citizens to take part in decisions affecting their environments. Many campaigns today mobilize their members and the general public to create public pressure for their legislative agendas through citizen lobbying, e-mail and letter-writing campaigns, telephone alerts, and other grassroots involvements. Underlying the different communication channels, however, is a more basic question about the design of an advocacy campaign. The question of **advocacy campaign design** is, "What does a group need to do to implement a strategic course of action, involving communication, undertaken for a specific purpose?" Based on my observations of successful campaigns in the past two decades,[1] I have found that environmental leaders usually ask, and then attempt to answer, three fundamental questions:

1. What *exactly* do you want to accomplish?

2. Which *decision makers* have the ability to respond, and what *constituencies* can hold these decision makers accountable?

3. What will *persuade* these decision makers to act on your objectives?

These three questions ask respectively about a campaign's (1) objectives, (2) audiences, and (3) strategies. I discuss each of these questions in turn.

Advocacy campaigns also pursue three corresponding **communication tasks** in answering these three design questions. First, effective campaigns seek to create broader support or demand for their objectives, whether the objective is to block construction of a hazardous waste incinerator or to get funds approved to build a bicycle path. Second, campaigns strive to mobilize this support from relevant constituencies (audiences) to demand accountability. Third, campaigns develop strategies to influence decision makers to deliver on their objectives. Finally, it is important to be aware that campaigns take place in the context of other, competing voices and counter-campaigns. Successful campaigns adapt their communication in this plural, information environment.

In the remainder of this section, I describe these three questions and their corresponding communication tasks. (See Figure 7.1 for a model of the advocacy campaign.)

Creating Demand: Campaigns' Objectives

Effective advocacy campaigns usually require a focus on concrete objectives. For example, John Muir's famous preservation campaign to protect Yosemite Valley focused on the passage of a single bill in the U.S. Congress in 1890 that designated the mountains around Yosemite Valley as a national park. Thus, the first question in designing an advocacy campaign is about a group's objectives. It asks, first, What *exactly* do you want to accomplish?

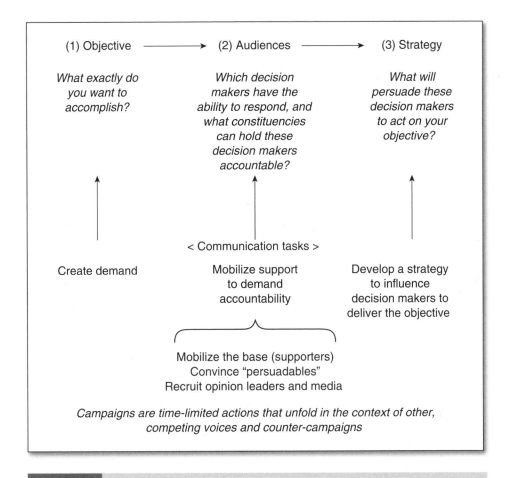

| **Figure 7.1** | Design of the environmental advocacy campaign |

Goals Versus Objectives

Campaigns flounder when their objectives are unclear or when they confuse a broad goal or vision with near-term, achievable, and specific actions or decisions. It is one thing to declare, "The United States should protect all old-growth forests," and quite another to mobilize citizens to persuade the U.S. Forest Service to issue a specific ruling to halt the building of roads into these native forests. While stopping roads in national forests contributed to the broader goal of protecting America's wild lands, it is important to distinguish this objective from the broader effort that is presumably needed to protect permanently the remaining old-growth areas.

What, then, does it mean to answer the first question, "What *exactly* do you want to accomplish?" First, it is important to distinguish between a campaign's long-term goals and its specific objectives. As it is used here, the term **goal** refers to a long-term vision or value, such as the desire to protect old-growth forests, reduce arsenic in drinking water, or reduce the levels of greenhouse gases entering the atmosphere. Critical rhetorics are often important in articulating these broader visions, but they are not campaigns.

On the other hand, the term **objective** refers to a specific action or decision that moves a group closer to a broader goal. An objective is a concrete and time-limited decision or action. For example, the Environmental Protection Agency can issue a regulation imposing stricter limits on the number of parts per billion of arsenic allowed in drinking water. That's why the emphasis in this first question is to ask, What *exactly* do you want? A campaign answers this question by identifying an objective that is a concrete, specific, and time-limited action or decision. Such an objective might be to pass a referendum in support of clean water bonds, persuade a city council to enact a zoning ordinance banning hazardous waste facilities within 10 miles of a school, or convince a state utility commission to deny a permit for a coal-burning power plant.

Creating a Public Demand

A campaign also has an important communication task to perform once it identifies its objective. It must create a broader public demand for its objective. A **public demand** is an active demonstration of support for the campaign's objective by key constituency groups, such as voters in a key swing district, families with small children, persons with respiratory problems, commuters, or members of a sports club. Although the American public generally supports clean air, clean water, and protection of natural resources, particular events and controversies often require the public's attention and active support. (As I cautioned earlier, other voices and constituencies may be competing for the same support.) As a result, many environmental groups' training programs stress that the challenge of a campaign is to translate the public's passive support for environmental values into an active "demand" for action protecting those values (personal communication from Sierra Club training staff, January 6, 2009). Creating such a public demand requires persuading the public that there is a specific and imminent threat to an environmental value, ecosystem, or human community that will motivate people to demand that it be protected and to demonstrate their concern to key decision makers.

Creating public demand forces a campaign to address a second core question, "Who has the ability to respond?" And that, in turn, suggests the relevant constituencies and supporters whom a campaign must educate and mobilize as part of its strategy.

Mobilizing Support

Once a campaign decides what exactly it wants to achieve, it must ask, second, Which *decision makers* have the ability to respond, and what *constituencies* can hold these decision makers accountable? In answering this question, campaign organizers must identify the decision makers who have the authority to act, as well as relevant constituencies (audiences) who are able to hold these leaders accountable.

Primary Versus Secondary Audiences

Here, it is important to distinguish between two different types of audiences: the **primary audience,** which is the decision makers who have the authority to act or implement the objectives of a campaign, and **secondary audiences** (also called "public audiences"), which are the various segments of the public, coalition partners, opinion leaders, and the media whose support is useful in holding decision makers accountable for the campaign's objectives.

A campaign cannot achieve an objective until someone with the ability or authority to decide on the objective responds favorably. These decision makers are a campaign's primary audience. If the objective is to fund bicycle paths along streets in San Jose, California, then the primary audience is most likely to be the members of the San Jose city's Bicyclist and Pedestrian Program. On the other hand, if a campaign wants tighter regulation of emissions of mercury from power plants, then the primary audience is the Environmental Protection Agency, which administers the Clean Air Act.

Mobilizing Support to Hold Decision Makers Accountable

Once a campaign has answered the second question, it faces an important communication task: *to mobilize the support of relevant constituencies to hold the primary audience accountable for its decisions.* The ability to fulfill this second task assumes that decision makers, in fact, are ultimately accountable to voters, to the media, or to other groups. This assumption goes to the heart of the discussion of the nature of legitimacy in Chapter 2. There, I defined *legitimacy* as a right to exercise authority. I observed there that an officeholder's legitimacy may be claimed by that person, but it is granted by others—voters, a group's members, or other constituencies. On the other hand, some decision makers may not be public officeholders and hence may be less susceptible to being held accountable by others. (For example, movements generally find it hard to influence corporate behavior, which is not directly accountable to the public constituencies.)

In mobilizing the support of relevant constituencies to hold decision makers accountable, it is useful to distinguish between the media and opinion leaders, on the one hand, and members of the public, on the other. Opinion leaders are those whose statements often are influential with the media and members of the primary audience. For example, the Natural Resources Defense Council relies upon the well-known environmentalist Robert F. Kennedy Jr. in many of its campaigns, and a grassroots community group may turn to a respected community leader to speak for it publicly.

More often, campaigns turn to members of the public. These may be neighbors, in a local campaign to block construction of a shopping mall in a wetlands area, or students, in a campaign to persuade administrators to adopt a green energy policy on campus. In each case, campaigns often distinguish between three types of public audiences: (1) the campaign's **base** (its core supporters and potential coalition partners), (2) the opponents of a campaign, and (3) **persuadables,** members of the public who are undecided but potentially sympathetic to a campaign's objectives. Persuadables often become important targets in mobilizing support.

It's important to note that, although persuadables potentially may be supporters of a campaign's objectives, they are initially undecided. They may lack awareness and information about the campaign, or they may be conflicted by different arguments. For example, persuadables may be exposed to information from the campaign's opponents and thus are unsure where they stand. Nevertheless, they are viewed as potentially open to information about a campaign's objective and hence are persuadable. Normally, a campaign does not attempt to persuade its opponents, as they are committed already to their own objectives. But persuadables constitute the heart of a campaign's communication because they often make the difference in the outcome of the campaign.

Therefore, a campaign answers the second question by mobilizing a network of supporters—particularly its base and persuadable audiences, opinion leaders, and the media—until sufficient influence is brought to bear on the primary audience of decision makers. At this point, it remains only to ask, What strategy is most likely to persuade this primary audience to act on the group's objective?

Developing a Strategy to Influence Decision Makers

The third question a campaign answers is, What will *persuade* these decision makers to act on your objective? This is a quintessential question of strategy. In the context of the environmental advocacy campaign, we can define **strategy** as a specific plan to bring about a desired outcome; it is the identification of *a critical source of influence or "leverage"* to persuade a primary decision maker to act appropriately. Strategy can be a surprisingly slippery concept, and it is often confused with a campaign's tactics, so let's look more closely at this important term.

Strategy Versus Tactics

In his classic *Ecological Literacy,* David Orr (1992) observed that questions about strategy land us squarely in the realm of *praxis,* the study of efficient action or the best means to achieve an objective. Whereas critical rhetorics may discredit the present and even help us to imagine a desired future, the basic question for a campaign's strategy is, "How do we actually get to this future?" Since social change is not inevitable, we need to ask, How do community and environmental groups go about effecting specific changes in the world?

In this section, I explore three broad types of strategy: democratic politics, education, and the use of market forces. The use of democratic politics in environmental policy involves attempts by advocacy groups to mobilize constituencies to influence public officials accountable to protect the environment. Some campaigns also rely on educating key audiences as part of their strategy. For example, some have used public information campaigns or social marketing to encourage recycling, composting, and proper inflation of tires to increase gas mileage. And we look briefly at the strategic uses of market forces and economic self-interest to influence business performance affecting the environment.

The idea of strategy can be confusing, so it might be best to begin with a brief definition and an example. Simply stated, a **strategy** is *a critical source of influence or leverage* to bring about a desired change. (I expand on this definition in a moment.) **Tactics**, on the other hand, are the specific actions—alerts, meetings, protests, briefings, and so forth—that carry out or implement the broader strategy.

An interesting case of a strategy that relied on both public education and the use of market forces is the case of McDonald's. In 2003, the fast-food chain acknowledged that the use of growth-stimulating antibiotics by large factory farms that raise and sell poultry and beef threatens human health. Many scientists believe that the overuse of these growth hormones in animals encourages the development of resistant strains of bacteria that may affect human immunity to disease. In its 2003 announcement, McDonald's agreed to phase out its purchase of poultry raised in this manner and thus added pressure to the poultry industry to begin to change its practices. (The company's agreement was less specific for hogs and cattle.) (Greider, 2003, p. 8).

What brought about this change, not only at McDonald's, but in the practices of some of the nation's largest providers of meat products? In the McDonald's case, a coalition of 13 environmental, religious, and public health organizations, including Environmental Defense, the Humane Society, and National Catholic Rural Life Conference, did not rely upon a campaign to target public officials; rather, they made innovative use of market forces. Their campaign pursued a strategy that drew on the power of consumers to change industry behavior, "not by one purchase at a time, but on a grand scale by targeting large brands in the middleman position" (Greider, 2003, p. 8). That is, they chose to influence the behavior of the meat industry by targeting one of the largest purchasers of its products: McDonald's.

Journalist William Greider (2003) closely studied the shift in strategy that occurred in this campaign. He observed that traditional "buy green" campaigns that rely on individual consumer purchases have had an exceedingly modest effect on corporate practices. "What has changed is an essential strategic insight" (p. 10). He explained:

> In . . . American capitalism, consumers are in a weak position and have very little actual leverage over the content of what they buy or how it is produced. . . . Instead of browbeating individual consumers, new reform campaigns focus on the structure of industry itself and attempt to leverage entire sectors. The activists identify and target the larger corporate "consumers" who buy an industrial sector's output and sell it at retail under popular brand names. They can't stand the heat so easily, since they regularly proclaim that the customer is king. When one of these big names folds to consumer pressure, it sends a tremor through the supplier base, much as McDonald's has. (p. 10)

In the case of McDonald's, the campaign's strategy sought to use the purchasing power of the fast-food giant itself rather than individual consumers to influence the poultry industry. By targeting the famous brand and familiar logo of this global icon, the campaign was able to leverage the buying power of McDonald's to influence the behavior of its suppliers. If the factory farms that sold meat products to McDonald's wanted to continue to do business, they would have to reduce their use of growth hormones in poultry and perhaps in other animals as well.

The campaign to persuade McDonald's and the poultry industry also clearly illustrates the difference between strategy and tactics. In this case, strategy, as a critical source of influence or leverage, was the use of a powerful corporation's brand and buying power to affect the meat industry's decisions about the use of growth hormones in chicken. The tactics that carried out this strategy included the materials distributed to McDonald's, meetings with company officials, organizing of protests outside the restaurants, and so forth. Each of these was important, but their critical function was to move or implement the wider strategy—using McDonald's vulnerability to public pressure and its purchasing power to affect other changes.

Strategy is often the weak link of an advocacy campaign and is often overlooked. In many cases, campaigns suffer when their strategy is unclear. In his discussion of this problem, Orr (1992) recalled the cartoon shown as Figure 7.2, which appeared in the journal *American Scientist*. He commented, "Most strategies of social change have similar dependence on the miraculous . . ." (p. 61).

Political theorist Douglas Torgerson (1999) suggests that dependence on the miraculous is particularly true of environmental strategies. He explains that a simple, though cynical, notion sometimes underlies green strategic thought: "Environmental problems are sure to get worse . . . and when they do, more and more people will be moved to join the green cause, thus enhancing its power and its chance of making a real difference" (p. 22). Torgerson believes that more is needed. I agree. Most successful advocacy campaigns specify the broader source of influence or leverage required to affect larger powers or decision-makers. That specification of the source of influence or leverage, rather than a reliance on the miraculous, is the meaning of strategy. Let's look at another example of strategy as leverage.

"I think you should be more explicit here in step two."

| Figure 7.2 | A miracle needed? |

Reprinted with permission from Sidney Harris, copyright © www.ScienceCartoonsPlus.com.

Strategy as Leverage: Stopping the "Coal Rush"

Since 2007, growing numbers of citizens, community groups, and environmental organizations have been successful at the local level in blocking or delaying permits for coal-fired power plants, one of the principal sources of CO_2 emissions, a major greenhouse gas. While the U.S. Department of Energy reported that 151 new coal-fired plants had been proposed at the start of 2007, during that year alone, "59 of those proposed plants were either refused licenses by state governments or quietly abandoned. Almost 50 more are being contested in the courts," and, opponents now are challenging the other plants as they come up for approval (Brown, 2008). By early 2009, almost all new coal-burning power plants proposed for the United States have been delayed or halted. At the same time, many states are now mandating that a percentage of energy in these localities come from renewable sources or greater efficiencies.

The movement to "Stop the Coal Rush," as some call it, has had real consequences in the U.S. energy economy. The blocked coal power plants have begun to signal an increased risk for the sources of investment—capital markets—that underwrite our carbon-based energy economy, and this, in turn, has had the potential to shift momentum in investments toward other, renewable energy sources. But, this outcome has not happened by chance. Let me explain.

Construction of a new coal power plant is expensive, and usually the energy company must borrow large amounts of private capital to build the plant. But, the U.S. energy sector is a sensitive arena for private investment. When a bank or Wall Street equity firm invests $2–3 billion in the construction of a power plant, it expects a reasonable return on its investment within a certain period of time. Yet, the U.S. Department of Energy cautioned in early 2007 that "proposals to build new power plants are often speculative . . . based upon the ever changing economic climate of power-generating markets" (National Energy Technology Lab, 2007). Hence, the slowing or cancellations of permits to build coal-fired plants has particular meaning in this business sector: Investment firms may have to wait longer for a return; their capital is tied up in a project that has been delayed or cancelled, and so forth. As a result, environmental groups saw an opportunity to affect larger systems of investment by using (leveraging) the decisions over a permit to alter the signals to the capital markets that coal plants are a risky business (see Figure 7.3).

The objective of the "Stop the Coal Rush" campaign is not simply the cancellation of any one coal-burning power plant, although that is important. Rather, it is the

| Figure 7.3 | Since 2007, students, community groups, and environmental organizations have been successful throughout the United States in blocking or delaying permits for coal-fired power plants, one of the principal sources of CO_2 emissions (a major greenhouse gas). |

Photo courtesy of Sveta McShane.

shifting of the larger energy system itself, from a major source of greenhouse gas to a climate-friendly, renewable source of energy in the United States. As I write, the strategy appears to be succeeding. In 2008, three of the nation's largest investment firms—Citigroup, Morgan Stanley, and J.P. Morgan Chase & Co.—announced they were imposing new requirements for financing construction that "will make it harder for companies to build coal-fired power plants in the U.S." (Ball, 2008, 1). Such reluctance is, itself, "sending *a potent signal to the energy sector* that it views dirty coal as shaky financial prospects and that the smart money is heading toward cleaner, more sustainable energy options" (Beinecke, 2008, 1).

The fights over individual coal plants, of course, are advocacy campaigns in themselves. They have the clear objective of blocking a permit for its construction or operation. But, with each cancelled permit, advocates also saw an opportunity to use or leverage their success in these decisions as a wider strategy. Ultimately, the "Coal Rush" advocates hope, this has the potential, amplified by the continuing efforts at multiple, local battles over coal permits, to build an agenda for a more comprehensive political action on energy in the United States.

A Campaign's "Message" and Other Communication Materials

Finally, in designing its strategy, a campaign also has an important communication task. This is the identification of the appropriate educational and persuasive messages, spokespersons, materials, and media for communicating with the campaign's primary audience of decision makers and its constituencies. These materials help to mobilize a campaign's base and convince its persuadable audiences, opinion leaders, and media to help persuade the primary audience to act on the campaign's objective. For example, in the McDonald's campaign, supporters circulated scientific research on the overuse of antibiotics in farm animals, made persuasive appeals to consumers to protest outside McDonald's restaurants, issued reports to the news media, and briefed officials at McDonald's corporate headquarters.

An important element of a campaign's strategic communication is its message. As developed by many environmental groups, a **message** is usually a phrase or sentence that concisely expresses a campaign's objective and the values at stake in the decision of the primary audience. Although campaigns develop considerable information and arguments, the message itself is usually short, compelling, and memorable and accompanies all of a campaign's communication materials. Messages from the world of advertising are familiar to us for this reason: "Think different" (Apple Computer), "Fly the Friendly Skies" (United Airlines), and "Don't leave home without it" (American Express). A message is not the complete communication, but it opens the door of attention on the part of a target audience to a campaign's other materials.

Messages are only one part of a campaign's communication, but they serve an important purpose. Messages summarize a campaign's objective, state its central values, and provide a frame for audiences' understanding and reception of the details of its other informational materials. In developing such messages, campaigns often attempt to identify values and language that resonate with their base and persuadables—those sympathetic to their objectives but undecided. For example, the message, "Extinction Means Forever" succinctly captured the values at stake in the Center for Environmental Education's campaign for a moratorium on commercial hunting of whales (Center for Environmental Education, n.d.). Also, civil society groups in Asia, Europe, South America, and the United States have joined together in a "Water Is Life" campaign. The campaign opposes the move to turn over the world's water resources to the private sector through commercialization, privatization, and large-scale development. By explicitly identifying water with "life," the message signals the importance of the campaign's work. (I return to the role of values in campaign messages later in the chapter.)

Act Locally!

Design an Environmental Advocacy Campaign for Your Campus

Recently, students at the University of North Carolina (UNC) at Chapel Hill adopted a Green Energy initiative, the result of their well-planned advocacy campaign. The initiative placed the university on a path to the use of alternative, clean energy sources and conservation measures that would lower energy use.

What is one important step that your own campus or community can take to support environmental values? Convert the university's fleet of cars and trucks to biofuels? Reduce the use of paper? Disinvest or sell stock shares in companies that have poor environmental performance?

Working with a small group, design an advocacy campaign plan to pursue a specific objective (for example, the UNC students proposed a raise in student fees to fund the Green Energy initiative). How would you answer the following questions:

1. What exactly do you want to accomplish?

2. Who has the ability to respond?

3. What will influence this person or authority to respond?

What groups are likely to be your base of support? Your coalition partners? Who are your persuadables? What message and other communication materials would be required to perform the related communication tasks of creating demand, mobilizing support to hold decision makers accountable, and designing a course of action to influence these authorities?

As an exercise in drafting a plan, work with several friends or classmates to draft a proposal to submit to a group that is interested in pursuing this campaign.

In summary, advocacy campaigns try to achieve concrete victories by building public demand for an important environmental objective, by mobilizing support, and by holding public officials, corporations, or other decision makers accountable for this objective. When they are designed well, strategic advocacy campaigns have several advantages over unplanned or spontaneous comments, protests, or criticism in general:

- By planning a strategic course of action, campaigns increase the chances of achieving their objectives.

- Campaigns draw on the collective strength of people and resources for both planning and implementing a course of action.

- Campaigns serve as intermediaries between individuals in their private lives and the large, often impersonal, institutions of public life.

Each of these advantages was demonstrated in the campaign of a coalition of Native Americans, religious groups, and environmental groups to oppose plans for a coal mine near sacred tribal lands in New Mexico.

The Campaign to Protect Zuni Salt Lake

On August 4, 2003, the Salt River Project (SRP), the third-largest electric power company in the United States, announced that it was dropping plans for a coal mine located near the Zuni Salt Lake in western New Mexico. The company's announcement was a victory for a coalition of Native American tribes, environmental and religious groups, and the Zuni people themselves, who had waged a multiyear campaign to protect the sacred Zuni Salt Lake and surrounding lands from mining and other environmental threats.

I use this example because it clearly illustrates the three elements of design that advocacy campaigns must consider: (1) a clear objective, (2) a clearly identified decision maker, and (3) a strategy to persuade the primary decision maker to act on its objective. The Zuni Salt Lake campaign also illustrates the ability of a small group, as well as larger environmental organizations, to use the principles of campaign design to carry out successful advocacy.

Zuni Salt Lake and a Coal Mine

The Salt River Project company's plans called for strip mining more than 80 million tons of coal from 18,000 acres of federal, state, and private lands. (**Strip mining** is the removal of surface areas to expose the underlying coal seams.) To settle the coal dust from strip mining, SRP planned to pump 85 gallons of water per minute from underground aquifers (Valtin, 2003). The New Mexico Department of Energy, Minerals, and Natural Resources granted permits for the company to begin construction of the mine in 1996, although work did not immediately begin. By June 22, 2001, opposition to the mine had grown.

To the Zunis and area tribes, the Salt Lake is sacred. It is home to the Zunis' important deity *Ma'l Oyattsik'i*, the Salt Mother, who, Zunis believe, has provided salt for centuries for tribal religious ceremonies. The region surrounding the Zuni Salt Lake is known as the Sanctuary or *A:shiwi A:wan Ma'k'yay'a dap an'ullapna Dek'ohannan Dehyakya Dehwanne*. It has burial grounds and other sacred sites and is laced with trails used by the Zunis, Navajos, Acomas, Hopis, Lagunas, Apaches, and other Southwestern tribes to reach the Zuni Salt Lake. By tradition, the Sanctuary is a neutral zone where warring tribes put their weapons down and share in the gathering of "the salt which embodies the flesh of the Salt Mother herself" (Sacred Land Film Project, 2003, p. 1).

The strip mine would have been located in the heart of the Sanctuary, 10 miles from Zuni Salt Lake. Although the mine itself would not be on Zuni land, tribal leaders feared that the company's plans to pump large volumes of groundwater from the same desert aquifer that feeds the Salt Lake would dry up the lake. Malcolm Bowekaty, former Zuni Pueblo governor, told reporters, "If they vent a lot of pressure that's forcing the water up, we will no longer have the salt" (Valtin, 2003, p. 3).

A Coalition's Campaign

By 2001, Zuni leaders had assembled a coalition that would work together to protect Zuni Salt Lake and the Sanctuary. For two days, the group met informally in the kitchen of a Zuni leader to design a two-year advocacy campaign plan.[2] On November 30, 2001, leaders from the Zuni tribe, Water Information Network, Center for Biological Diversity, Citizens Coal Council, Tonatierra (an indigenous group), Friends of the Earth, Sierra Club, and Seventh Generation Fund for Indian Development publicly announced the formation of the Zuni Salt Lake Coalition. In what follows, I describe how this campaign embodied the core elements of an advocacy campaign.

Campaign Objectives: Creating Demand

From the beginning, the Zuni Salt Lake Coalition saw its long-term goal as to "get SRP to drop its plans for the Fence Lake Coal Mine [and to] protect Zuni Salt Lake for the long-term" (Zuni Salt Lake Coalition [Zuni], 2001). More immediately, the coalition was faced with the prospect of SRP's imminent preparation of the mine site, including plans to drill into the aquifer that fed Zuni Salt Lake.

Therefore, the coalition identified two immediate *objectives:* (1) to "make sure that SRP does not tap Dakota Aquifer" [a key aquifer] and (2) persuade the State of New Mexico and the Department of the Interior to deny the permits needed to open the coal mine and, if these were granted, to appeal the decisions in order to delay actual construction of the mine (Zuni, 2001). Coalition members felt that if they were successful in achieving either of these objectives, they could persuade SRP, in turn, to cancel its plans for the project.

Audiences: Mobilizing Support to Demand Accountability

The Zuni Salt Lake Coalition identified two sets of *primary decision makers.* Ultimately, they sought to persuade the SRP officials to withdraw plans for the coal mine. Related to this goal and the campaign's two objectives, the coalition also targeted the Department of the Interior and New Mexico officials who oversaw the state's permitting process for the mine.

Key to influencing these decision makers was the Zuni Salt Lake Coalition's ability to *mobilize support from the appropriate constituencies* to hold the primary decision makers accountable for their actions. Holding a powerful utility company accountable may seem unrealistic. SRP officials were not elected public figures and therefore were unaffected by voters. Nevertheless, the coalition correctly saw that the company's *legitimacy* (Chapter 2) depended on key constituencies and that these could be mobilized. Most immediately, the coalition had to reach out to its *base*—the Zuni people themselves and their allies among area tribes. In addition, it targeted several *persuadable* groups—area churches, environmental groups, and people of faith generally (Zuni, 2001). In turn, support from these groups would draw support from opinion leaders, the media, and, ultimately, key elected officials.

In creating a demand for its objectives and mobilizing key audiences, the coalition developed communication materials that drew on several sources of persuasion that acknowledged the cultural context and significance of the Zuni Salt Lake. Especially relevant to mobilizing its base and other supporters, the coalition drew upon (1) the spiritual and cultural values associated with the Zuni tribe's history and area indigenous cultures and (2) an appeal to the irreparable nature of the threats to the Zuni Salt Lake. Elsewhere, I defined the **irreparable** as a forewarning or opportunity to act before it is too late to preserve what is unique or rare before it is lost forever (Cox, 1982, 2001). Such a forewarning identifies (1) a threat to something that is unique or rare and therefore of great value; (2) the existence of which is threatened or precarious; (3) and its loss or destruction cannot be reversed; (4) therefore, action to protect it is timely or urgent.

The campaign materials developed by the coalition reflected these persuasive appeals. For the indigenous nations, the Zuni Salt Lake and nearby Sanctuary are very powerful places. Zuni council member Arden Kucate drew on this feeling and the irreparable in urging supporters: "We have to start thinking in the traditional way. It is not the earth, it is Mother Earth. Zuni people will not sacrifice our Salt Woman for cheap coal to serve Arizona or California, because she is irreplaceable" (LaDuke, 2002).

Finally, the Zuni Salt Lake Coalition reached out to other important secondary audiences. Most important, the campaign used the growing support of tribal and public constituencies to gain the attention of the news media and to enlist the support of public officials in New Mexico. I describe the importance of these groups as I identify the coalition's strategy.

Strategy: Influencing the Primary Decision Makers

Given its goal to persuade SRP officials to withdraw their plans for the mine, the Zuni Salt Lake Coalition decided the best strategy would be to *raise the costs* to the company in its pursuit of permits for the mine. At its very first meeting, the coalition pledged to hold SRP accountable by making "it so hard for them that they want to drop it. Make them feel that the Fence Lake project is a fruitless effort" (Zuni, 2001). This core strategy would guide subsequent decisions and activities of the coalition.

Specifically, the coalition sought ways to influence SRP and the federal officials responsible for issuing the mine's permits (1) by introducing scientific evidence of the ecological effects on the Zuni Salt Lake of pumping water from the aquifer and (2) by launching an aggressive outreach to opinion leaders, news media, and New Mexico public officials. By organizing around these actions, the coalition intended to place continual roadblocks in SRP's path and thereby raise the costs to SRP, increasing the pressure on the company to cancel its plans for the coal mine.

The first element of the coalition's strategy was to introduce evidence of environmental damage to Zuni Salt Lake as a basis for challenging the state and federal permits that had been issued.[3] New research was a critical part of the effort to hold the Department of Interior accountable to the National Environmental Policy Act (NEPA) requirement for an environmental impact statement. (I described the importance of NEPA in Chapter 3.) For example, the coalition argued that "every hydrological study, except SRP's own, shows that this pumping will detrimentally affect the lake" (Zuni, 2003). Based on its hydrological information (pumping tests), the coalition requested that Interior conduct a supplemental environmental impact study. Similarly, it appealed the state's water permit pending completion of further pumping tests on the aquifer.

The threat to file a challenge to Interior's failure to consider possible impacts of pumping water from the underground aquifers promised to add delay and therefore more costs to SRP's plans to start construction of the coal mine.

The Zuni Coalition also turned to a second element of their campaign strategy— an aggressive outreach to the news media and New Mexico public officials. In part, this was to respond directly to SRP's counter-publicity. It was also to supplement the coalition's work inside government regarding the permits by keeping the issue of Zuni Salt Lake before the wider public. From the outset of the campaign, the coalition members sought creative ways to keep the issue alive.

At the heart of this effort were efforts to generate publicity, "lots of publicity" (Zuni, 2001). From 2001 to 2003, the Zuni Salt Lake campaign generated thousands of letters to newspapers, public officials, and allied groups; placed multilanguage radio ads and rented a mobile billboard; sent traditional "runners" from Zuni Pueblo to SRP's corporate headquarters in Phoenix; and publicized resolutions of support from the tribal councils and the New Mexico Conference of Churches. It also mounted two "fax attacks"—deluges of fax messages—on the Department of the Interior to press for delays in its approval of the mining plan and won the National Trust for Historic Preservation's listing of the area as one of America's most endangered places ("Victory," 2003, p. 6).

Communication Message

In all their public communication materials, the campaign pressed its *message:* "SRP Is Targeting Our Sacred Lands. Save Zuni Salt Lake." An important tactic was that the campaign was able to adapt this core message to different audiences, such as church members and people of faith. Particularly in the American Southwest, many people are sensitive to the historical mistreatment of Native Americans. One example of such a cultural appeal was the text of a postcard to the SRP president, drawing on the respect for sacred sites and the irreparable nature of any harm to Zuni Salt Lake:

"People of faith don't want any sacred areas to be desecrated by a strip mine and railroad for cheap electricity from dirty coal: Not the Vatican, not Mecca, not Temple Square in Salt Lake City, . . . and **not Zuni Salt Lake**."

One of the campaign's creative tactics was a billboard truck that became a common sight as it drove through towns in Arizona and New Mexico. Valtin (2003) reports that after companies in Phoenix refused to accept the coalition's billboard ad, organizers contacted a mobile company that placed the billboard on the back of a truck. The billboard had a large photo of Zuni Salt Lake with the crosshairs of a rifle superimposed on it, and the campaign's message, "SRP Is Targeting Our Sacred Lands. Save Zuni Salt Lake" (see Figure 7.4). Coalition organizer Andy Bessler explained, "We drove the truck around SRP headquarters and all over Arizona and New Mexico to tribal pueblos, and we got a lot of people to sign petitions" (quoted in Valtin, 2003, p. 3).

In an effort to keep the threat to Zuni Salt Lake before the public, the campaign continually sought creative ways to generate coverage by the news media. Bessler explained:

> Tribal members have a different approach, which made us think "outside the box." Where the Sierra Club might air a radio spot to convey our message, the Zuni suggested sending runners. And where we did run radio ads, we had scripts in English, Spanish, Zuni, Navajo, Hopi, and Apache so the spots could run on tribal radio stations as well as on mainstream stations in Phoenix and Albuquerque. (Quoted in Valtin, 2003, p. 3)

| **Figure 7.4** | Members of the Zuni Salt Lake Coalition pose beside the mobile billboard truck used in their campaign. |

Photo courtesy of the Zuni Salt Lake Coalition.

Examples of such thinking "outside the box" included the use of traditional runners from Zuni Pueblo to SRP's corporate headquarters in Phoenix to generate public pressure for the power company to withdraw its plans for the coal mine. Another example, on July 19, 2003, was the campaign's scheduling of a People's Hearing on Zuni Salt Lake in Zuni Pueblo. The event included the showing of a video, updates on the campaign, and a People's Hearing. More than 500 people attended the informal hearing to offer their testimony. "At the conclusion of the hearing, the sky opened up and let loose a torrential downpour, which the Zuni took as a blessing from heaven" (Valtin, 2003, p. 1).

The campaign's success in framing the news coverage (Chapter 4) of the controversy as a struggle over spiritual and ecological values began to pay dividends. In July 2003, the entire New Mexico Congressional delegation sent a letter to Secretary of the Interior Gale Norton asking her to stop the federal mining permit until new studies of the aquifer could be completed. Their letter also announced that they were planning to bring a lawsuit under NEPA if the department refused to prepare a supplemental environmental impact statement. The prospect of a federal lawsuit threatened to delay SRP's plans even further, carrying out the campaign's strategy of making it "so hard for them that they want to drop" the Fence Lake mine.

Success for Zuni Salt Lake

On August 4, 2003, SRP announced that the company had canceled its plans for the coal mine and would also relinquish its permits and the coal leases it had acquired for the mine. This was a rare victory for both indigenous peoples and environmental groups, as such development projects usually proceed and it is one of the reasons that study of this campaign is noteworthy.

After the announcement by SRP, Zuni tribal councilman Arden Kucate led a delegation to the edge of Zuni Salt Lake to pray and to make an offering of turquoise and bread to *Ma'l Oyattsik'i*, the Salt Mother. Back at Zuni Pueblo, the tribe's head councilman, Carlton Albert, expressed his feelings of relief and appreciation to allies who had worked with the Zuni Salt Lake campaign: "It has been a long 20 year struggle . . . but we have had our voices heard. . . . If there is a lesson to be learned it is to never give up and [to] stay focused on what you want to accomplish" (Seciwa, 2003, p. 2).

The Attitude-Behavior Gap and the Challenges of Advocacy

The Zuni Salt Lake campaign succeeded in mobilizing area tribes, churches, public officials, and others whose support was critical to the campaign. Yet, this is not always possible. In some cases, advocates may succeed in changing beliefs or attitudes, but fail to change the *behavior* of targeted groups. For example, we saw in Chapter 6 that while a majority of the U.S. public believes that global warming is real and happening now, people may not feel any urgency to change their own behavior. Literary critic Stanley Fish (2008) also provides a self-confessed example of this attitude-behavior gap:

Now don't get me wrong. I am wholly persuaded by the arguments in support of the practices I resist. I believe that recycling is good and that disposable paper products are bad. I believe in global warming. . . . But it is possible to believe something and still resist taking the actions your belief seems to require. (I believe that seat belts save lives, but I never wear them, even on airplanes.) I know that in the great Book of Environmentalism my name will be on the page reserved for serial polluters. But I just can't get too worked up about it. (para. 9)

Social scientists who study communication campaigns call this phenomenon the **attitude-behavior gap**. The gap refers to the fact that individuals' *behavior* is often disconnected from the *attitudes* (or beliefs) they hold; that is, they may believe recycling is good or global warming is real, but do nothing to change their behaviors (e.g., recycle, drive a fuel-efficient car).

In this final section, therefore, I describe some of the challenges that advocacy campaigns face in designing messages and other persuasive appeals that actually influence a target audience's behaviors. Particularly important is the role that values play in successful messages. As we will see, campaigns face a choice among very different kinds of values—from self-interest to concern for the biosphere—in designing messages. For example, some advocates believe that appeals to self-interest are a form of compromising or "selling out." I also take up an interesting, but understudied claim: The **radical flank effect** is the belief that radical or even illegal actions such as Earth First!'s tree spiking and the Earth Liberation Front's burning of SUVs make mainstream groups appear more reasonable and thus more acceptable to society.

Attitude-Behavior Gap and the Role of Values

As I noted earlier, the attitude-behavior gap is the failure to find a strong correlation between individuals' attitudes about something and their actual behavior. Obviously, our beliefs and behaviors are related, but the point is that there is not always a strong causal relationship, that is, that our attitudes directly influence our behaviors. In fact, research in this area often finds that it is our *behavior* that influences our opinions, not the other way (Rose & Dade, 2007). Because behavior is generally a strong determinant of peoples' opinions, advocacy campaigns cannot influence behavior changes only by trying to change our attitude toward something.

On the other hand, peoples' *values* do influence their behavior. Indeed, there is a great deal of evidence that pro-environmental behaviors are related to certain values (Crompton, 2008; Schultz and Zelezny 2003). For this reason, WWF-UK has recently urged a rethinking of advocacy campaigns, especially on global warming, to take into greater account the role of values. (See *Weathercocks and Signposts* at wwf.org.uk/strategiesforchange.) Let's look briefly at the different types of values that advocacy campaigns sometimes consider in their messages.

Recent research of values suggests that there are three broad categories of values associated with environmental behaviors:

1. Egoistic concerns focusing on the self (e.g., health, quality of life, prosperity, convenience)

2. Social-altruistic concerns focusing on other people (e.g., children, family, community, humanity)

3. Biospheric concerns focusing on the well-being of living things (e.g., plants, animals, trees) (Farrior, 2005, p. 11; see also Stern, Dietz, & Kalof, 1993)

Thus, some people may be concerned about water pollution because of the dangers to *themselves* (for example, "I don't want to drink polluted water"). Others may be motivated by *social-altruistic* concerns about their children or communities (for example, "I don't want my children to drink polluted water"). A recent ad by the Sierra Club urged parents to take simple steps to help curb greenhouse gases by appealing to social-altruistic concerns. The ad included a photo of television and film star Eva La Rue holding her young daughter Kaya and the message:

> Our kids are counting on us to help protect their world. Scientists say that we can curb the most dangerous effects of global warming if we cut our carbon emissions by 80% by the year 2050. That's an achievable 2% reduction a year—the 2% Solution! LEARN WHAT YOU CAN DO, VISIT www.sierraclub.org/twopercent.

Finally, others may be concerned about the effects of polluted water on plants and animals, that is, *biospheric concerns.*

A recent international survey of values among college students found that social-altruistic values rated the highest. In the United States, a majority rated egoistic concerns higher than biospheric, while students in Latin American countries placed biospheric concerns higher than egoistic (Schultz & Zelezny, 2003, pp. 129–130). The researchers concluded, "A person who scores high on self-enhancement will care about environmental problems when the problem affects them directly" (p. 130).

This finding presents an interesting dilemma for some advocates in choosing the values they will use in their public messages. For example, Earth First! (2005) posed the question, "Why Wilderness?" In arguing for the value of wilderness, Earth First! rejected all self-interested rationales for wilderness, such as recreation or the discovery of medicines from rare plants or other motives that appeal to people's self-interest:

> Is it because wilderness makes pretty picture postcards? Because it protects watersheds for downstream use by agriculture, industry and homes? . . . Because some unknown plant living in the wilds may hold a cure for cancer? (p. 2)
>
> Earth First! proceeds to answer these questions with a firm "No," insisting that, "All natural things have intrinsic value, inherent worth. Their value is not determined by what they will ring up on the cash register. . . . They are. They exist. For their own sake. Without consideration for any real or imagined value to human civilization." (pp. 3–4)

Earth First! therefore faces a dilemma: Can it appeal to biospheric values such as the intrinsic value of nature and still gain a hearing from those it must persuade? Or, must wilderness advocates appeal to the egoistic concerns of individuals or to their social-altruistic values to gain a hearing?

Responses to the dilemma about values have varied. Canadian environmental studies scholar Neil Evernden (1985) has offered the classic defense of biospheric concerns. In *The Natural Alien,* Evernden warned that persuasion based on self-interest ("What is useful to me?") is short-sighted and dangerous: "By basing all arguments on enlightened self-interest . . . environmentalists have ensured their own failure whenever self-interest can be perceived as lying elsewhere" (p. 10). For example, the use of financial value as a rationale for preserving a natural area such as a mountain is risky: Is the mountain worth more as scenery or for the mining of minerals? Evernden cautioned, "As soon as its worth is greater as tin cans than as scenery, the case for the mountain vanishes" (p. 11). On the other hand, the Biodiversity Project (Farrior, 2005) has recommended, based on the Schultz and Zelezny research, that campaigns in support of biodiversity be based on "messages that address socio-altruistic concerns or make biodiversity relevant to everyday life" (egoistic concerns) (p. 11). The key is "targeting audiences and using a 'diversity of messages that will appeal to people with a different range of value orientation'" (Farrior, 2005, p. 11, quoting Schultz & Zelezny, 2003, p. 134).

Still, advocates face very real constraints in trying to persuade audiences whose support is needed to win concrete victories, such as preservation of old-growth forests or protection of sacred tribal lands. How then to do this? Recently, research on the attitude-behavior gap has proposed an overlooked source of appeal: **social norms.** Social norms refer to "the perception of what is commonly done in a situation" or what most people do (Griskevicious, Cialdini, & Gooldstein, 2008, p. 6).

The research on social norms strongly suggests they may serve as a communication *message,* that is, the perception that others are doing the same thing may help to influence a person's behavior. If this is accurate, it would help to overcome the attitude-behavior gap. To test this hypothesis, Griskevicious et al. (2008) designed a study of behaviors in hotel rooms, where guests often encounter a card asking them to reuse their towels. In this experiment, researchers placed three different cards, with different messages, in the guestrooms:

1. Help Save the Environment.

2. Partner With Us to Help Save the Environment.

3. Join Your Fellow Guests in Helping to Save the Environment.

Each message was accompanied by information respectively (1) stressing respect for the environment, (2) urging guests to cooperate with the hotel management, and (3) information that a majority of guests reuse their towels (the social norm message). The outcome? "Compared to the first two messages, the social norms message increased towel reuse by 34% (p. 10).

The hotel experiment also illustrates the two conditions under which social norms appear to be most effective: (1) uncertainty, when people, when unsure, tend to look to others for guidance, and (2) when the "others" are people who are similar to them, and particularly when they are in a similar situation as these others (Griskevicious et al., 2008, p. 11). As a result of their research, Griskevicious et al. argue that "a strategy harnessing social norms provides an effective and low-cost strategy to help reduce our impacts on global warming" (p. 6). Indeed, as I suggested in Chapter 6, the Alliance for Climate Protection's "We" campaign does precisely this, in ads that portray a range of Americans, both famous and those similar to us, who call upon all of us to be part of the solution to "Repower America" ("The Plan," 2008).

Finally, a way to think about the dilemma over idealistic versus pragmatic appeals is to appreciate the differences between critical rhetorics and campaigns. Campaigns inevitably seek support from key audiences to hold public officials and corporations accountable and must therefore be attuned to the pragmatic dimensions of communication. That is, campaigns cannot escape the basic rhetorical task to discover, *in the particular case,* what is most likely to persuade an audience whose support is important to its objectives. On the other hand, critical rhetorics have a different purpose. The contribution of groups such as the Deep Ecology Foundation is precisely their willingness to question existing values and to prod, cajole, or challenge society to go further and imagine a relationship with nature or a society different from what is possible now. Such visions, while questioning our current interests, at the same time hold open the prospect of a society that respects both the human community and the natural world.

Do Radical Actions Help Mainstream Groups Appear Reasonable?

Environmental advocates sometimes face a second and very different question: Do radical tactics—even if unpersuasive—help mainstream groups to appear more reasonable and thus more acceptable? For example, do Earth First!'s use of tree spiking or destruction of logging equipment and Earth Liberation Front's burning of SUVs make the Audubon Society, Sierra Club, or the Wilderness Society appear more reasonable or acceptable? Or do these actions hurt the environmental movement by casting a negative light on all environmental groups? The charismatic environmentalist David Brower came down decidedly on one side of this dilemma, stating: "I founded Friends of the Earth to make the Sierra Club look reasonable. Then I founded Earth Island Institute to make Friends of the Earth look more reasonable. Earth First! now makes us [Earth Island Institute] look reasonable. We're still waiting for someone to come along and make Earth First! look reasonable" (quoted in Strand & Strand, 1993, pp. 59–60).

The claim that actions of radical groups make moderate groups look more reasonable and therefore acceptable is the thesis of what sociologists call a "radical flank effect" (see Gupta, 2002; McAdam, 1996; McAdam, Tarrow, & Tilly, 2001; Tarrow, 1998).

The most common explanation of how the radical flank effect works is provided by social movement scholar Doug McAdam (1992):

> [A] movement stands to benefit when there is a wide ideological spectrum among its adherents. The basic reason for this seems to be that the existence of radicals makes moderate groups in the movement more attractive negotiating partners to the movement opponents. Radicalness provides strong incentives to the state to get to the bargaining table with the moderates in order to avoid dealing with the radicals. (n.p.; quoted in Gupta, 2002, p. 3)

As usually argued, a radical flank effect is presumed to have a positive effect on society's perceptions of the more mainstream groups. Indeed, this has been a basic claim of many writers and scholars sympathetic to radical environmentalism. For example, environmental author Rik Scare (1990) has argued that the effect of radical actions was a major reason behind the formation of Earth First! "Initially, the founders adopted the role of the extremists as a tactic to allow the mainstream groups to look less radical and achieve more protection for the environment" (pp. 6–7). More recently, the radical flank effect seemed to be present when Rainforest Action Network threatened to protest at Staple's for the company's limited offerings of recycled paper, "the company became more inclined to solicit the assistance of an environmental group that was seen as more moderate and therefore more palatable and legitimate for a partnership" (Barnett & HoffmanRoss, 2008, para. 21; Hoffman, 2007).

But this may not always be true. The radical flank effect can work in the other direction as well, that is, the actions of radical groups may produce *negative* views of more moderate groups. Political scientist Devashree Gupta (2002) points out that "there are cases where the presence of radicals in the same movement has deleterious effects on moderates' ability to gain access to decision makers and achieve some measure of success" (p. 6). For example, social movement scholar Herbert Haines (1984/1997) argued in his study of 1960s militant groups that groups such as the Black Panthers, while gaining popular media attention, negatively affected the goals of more moderate civil rights groups.

Whether the radical flank effect occurs at all in the environmental movement—and whether its effect is positive or negative—has been sharply debated. Clearly, some Earth First! leaders believe that their actions do help mainstream groups appear reasonable and thus more acceptable. At the same time, some writers and politicians have tried to paint environmentalism broadly as a movement of "ecoterrorists," as a result of the actions of some. For example, when "an environmental extremist group creates headlines for a terrorist act, all environmental groups may be viewed in the same light, thus limiting their ability to operate as . . . legitimate members of social debates" (Barnett & HoffmanRoss, 2008, para. 20). Indeed, shortly after the terrorism of September 11, 2001, conservative writer Lowell Ponte (2003) asserted, "Once upon a time we tended to regard environmentalists as gentle idealists. . . . But in the wake of 9/11, and as environmental extremism has mutated from this to the tree spikers of Earth First! to the firebugs of ELF [Earth Liberation Front], the laughter has ceased" (n.p.).

In other cases, a few states have considered legislation based on the model Animal and Ecological Terrorism Act drafted by the conservative American Legislative Exchange Council (www.alec.org). The proposed law is concerned with what its supporters refer to as "eco-terrorism," often referring to actions by the Earth Liberation Front. But the suggested language of the Animal and Ecological Terrorism Act appears to define environmental actions other than arson as criminal, and for this reason it has drawn criticism from editorial writers, environmentalists, and civil libertarians for painting environmentalism in general as ecoterrorism. For example, Karen Charman (2003), an investigative journalist writing for online journal *TomPaine.com,* argues that the proposed law "criminalizes virtually all forms of environmental or animal-rights advocacy" and, in one bill, defines "political motivation" meaning any "intent to influence a government entity or the public to take a specific political action" (para. 7).

Despite the attempts by the American Legislative Exchange Council to question environmentalism more broadly, questions of an actual radical flank effect remain unanswered in the environmental movement. To date, there has been no solid research on the impact—either positive or negative—of radical groups on the U.S. environmental movement. Gupta (2002) explains that, in the end, the actual impact of radical groups in a movement "depends on the ability and willingness of moderates to signal their distinctiveness from radical actors," as well as on "the kind of policy change demanded by the moderates" (p. 4). In other words, moderate groups may well be judged on what media and members of the public think of these groups' own actions and objectives.

SUMMARY

In this chapter, I have focused on the environmental advocacy campaign, defined as a strategic course of action involving communication undertaken for a specific purpose. Whereas critical rhetorics stress the questioning or denunciation of a behavior, policy, societal value, or ideology, campaigns strive to win concrete victories. To do this, environmental leaders usually ask, and then work to answer, three basic questions in designing a campaign:

1. What exactly do you want to accomplish?

2. Which decision makers have the ability to respond, and what constituencies can hold these decision makers accountable?

3. What will persuade these decision makers to act on your objectives?

Although similar in many respects to other types of advocacy campaigns, the environmental campaign differs in two respects: It is initiated not by business or government but by local communities and nonprofit groups, and it usually targets a change in governmental policy or corporate behavior rather than individual or consumer behavior. Correspondingly, campaigns face three communication challenges in answering these basic questions. First, campaigns must create *public* support for their objectives (what exactly they wish to accomplish). Second, they must mobilize relevant constituencies to demand accountability from public or corporate decision makers. Third, campaigns must develop strategies that will persuade these decision makers to act on the demands of these constituencies.

I don't want to leave the impression that addressing these communication tasks automatically produces a victory for the campaign. Advocates face many challenges in building public demand to secure protection for the environment. Deeply entrenched and powerful interests often resist change; and sometimes the broader public assumes that corporate or public officials will do the right thing, that there is no need for letter writing, lobbying, or the other communication tools of a campaign. In fact, environmental campaign victories are infrequent, and victories may be impermanent, like the defensive campaigns to protect the Arctic National Wildlife Refuge. Finally, environmental policy can be complex, and the maze of agencies and procedures for public involvement can discourage many citizens from participating in these forums.

Yet, every day many of these same citizens have been willing to speak up for their communities, for natural areas, and for remote wilderness areas that they may never see in their lifetimes. The Zuni people and their allies told the nation's third-largest electric utility company to drop its plans to strip mine coal on lands near the sacred Zuni Salt Lake. Like many community groups, leaders of the Zuni Coalition sat around a kitchen table to consider carefully what steps they needed to take to build public support for their objectives, how they might reach out to potential supporters, and what means of persuasion were available to them to influence a powerful corporation. Similarly, in urban neighborhoods, in rural communities, in the nation's capital, and throughout America, local citizens, environmental groups, and their supporters have protected local green spaces as well as old-growth forests, won victories strengthening the nation's laws for clean air and water, and protected the American bald eagle and thousands of lesser-known plants and mammals. At the same time, they have opened the file cabinets and computers of government agencies to ensure that citizens have the information they need to participate in decisions affecting their environment.

It is my hope that, when you have finished reading this chapter, you will appreciate some of the elements important in designing an advocacy campaign, as well as the challenge of critical rhetoric in questioning existing practices and ideologies. As a result, I hope you will feel inspired to work with others on your campus or in your community to do extraordinary things.

KEY TERMS

Communication-Related Concepts

Advocacy: Persuasion or argument in support of a cause, policy, idea, or set of values.

Advocacy campaign: A strategic course of action, involving communication, which is undertaken for a specific purpose.

Advocacy campaign design: The directions for implementing a strategy that involves communication undertaken for a specific purpose. Campaign design asks three fundamental questions: (1) What *exactly* do you want to accomplish? (2) Which decision makers have *the ability to respond,* and what constituencies can hold these decision makers accountable? (3) What will *persuade* these decision makers to act on your objectives?

Attitude-behavior gap: Individuals' *behavior* is often disconnected from the *attitudes* (or beliefs) they hold; that is, they may believe recycling is good or global warming is real, but do nothing to change their behaviors (for example, recycle, drive a fuel-efficient car).

Base: A campaign's core supporters.

Communication tasks (of a campaign): (1) To create support or demand for the campaign's objectives, (2) to mobilize this support from relevant constituencies (audiences) to demand accountability, and (3) to develop a strategy to influence decision makers to deliver on their objectives.

Confrontational rhetoric: The use of nonconventional forms of language and action, such as marches, demonstrations, obscenity, sit-ins, and other forms of civil disobedience (for example, the occupation of a campus building), to critique social norms or practices such as racism, war, or exploitation of the environment.

Critical rhetoric: The questioning or denunciation of a behavior, policy, societal value, or ideology; may also include the articulation of an alternative policy, vision, or ideology.

Environmental advocacy: Discourse (legal, educational, expository, artistic, public, and/or interpersonal communication) aimed at supporting conservation and the preservation of finite resources; aims also include support for both natural and human environments and the well-being of the life such environments sustain.

Goal (of a campaign): Describes a long-term vision or value, such as protection of old-growth forests, reduction of arsenic in drinking water, or making economic globalization more democratic.

Irreparable, appeal to the: A forewarning or opportunity to act before it is too late to preserve what is unique or rare before it is lost forever. Cox (1982, 2001) identified the four characteristics of an appeal to the irreparable nature of a decision or its consequences: A speaker establishes that (1) the decision threatens something unique or rare and thus of great value, (2) the existence of what is threatened is precarious and uncertain, (3) its loss or destruction cannot be reversed, and (4) action to protect it is therefore timely or urgent.

Message: A phrase or sentence that concisely expresses a campaign's objective and the values at stake in the decision of the primary audience. Although campaigns develop considerable information and arguments, the message itself is usually short, compelling, and memorable and accompanies all of a campaign's communication materials.

Mind bomb: Term coined by Greenpeace cofounder Robert Hunter referring to a simple image, such as Zodiac boats interposing themselves between whales and their harpooners, that "explodes in people's minds" to create a new awareness (quoted in Weyler, 2004, p. 73).

Objective (of a campaign): A specific action or decision that moves a group closer to a broader goal; a concrete and time-limited decision or action.

Persuadables: Members of the public who are undecided but potentially sympathetic to a campaign's objectives; they often become primary targets in mobilizing support.

Primary audience: Decision makers who have the authority to act or implement the objectives of a campaign.

Public demand: Active demonstration of support for a campaign's objective by key constituency groups, such as families with small children, voters in key swing districts, elderly persons suffering from respiratory problems, hunters, anglers, or urban commuters.

Radical flank effect: A result claimed for the actions of radical groups that such actions help moderate groups look more reasonable, rendering the latter more acceptable to the mainstream.

Secondary audience: Various segments of the public, coalition partners, opinion leaders, and the media whose support is useful in holding decision makers accountable for the campaign's objectives; also called public audiences.

Social marketing: The planning and implementation of programs designed to bring about social change using concepts from commercial marketing.

Social norms: The perception of what is commonly done in a situation, or what most people do.

Strategy: A critical source of influence or leverage to bring about a desired change.

Tactics: Specific actions—alerts, meetings, protests, briefings, and so forth—that carry out or implement a broader strategy.

Environment-Related Concepts

Strip mining: The removal of large surface areas of land to expose the underlying coal seams.

DISCUSSION QUESTIONS

1. What mode of advocacy do you believe is most effective in persuading the American public to support environmental proposals? Public education? Campaigns? Image politics? (See Table 7.1.)

2. Do you agree with the claim that relying on the worsening of environmental problems to wake people up is an effective strategy for making real changes?

3. Do you as a consumer have power to affect environmental change? Journalist William Greider (2003) says that consumers are in a weak position and have very little actual leverage over the actions of large corporations. Do you agree?

4. Are corporations or government officials always the responsible parties? Do we share accountability for the greenhouse gases emitted into the atmosphere? For the clear-cutting of forests to supply paper for copiers, newspapers, and junk mail? For storm water runoff that carries oil, paint, and other solvents that we pour on the ground or into the street?

5. Do environmentalists use exaggerated rhetoric to gain attention? How can environmental advocates invite public awareness and concern without crying that the sky is falling?

6. Must environmental advocates appeal to egoist concerns or self-interest to change peoples' actual behaviors? When are groups able to base their messages on biospheric values?

7. Do radical flank attacks help or hurt the mainstream environmental movement? That is, do radical or extreme actions make mainstream groups appear reasonable by comparison and therefore more acceptable, or do these acts harm the credibility of all environmental groups? Do these actions turn people off or invite discussion by interrupting normal but complacent ways of thinking?

NOTES

1. I am indebted to the many leaders in the U.S. environmental movement with whom I've worked, as well as the Sierra Club Training Academy, in describing this approach to the design of an environmental advocacy campaign.

2. In describing the Zuni Salt Lake Coalition's campaign, I am indebted to the meeting notes of the coalition and its campaign materials, and to Andy Bessler, an organizer with the Sierra Club and coalition member who generously shared his recollections of the campaign in a personal interview, September 24, 2003.

3. By May 31, 2002, the Department of Interior had approved SRP's plan for the mine, while New Mexico officials had previously given their permission. Unless challenged, mining at the Fence Lake site was expected to begin by spring 2003.

REFERENCES

Agyeman, J., Bullard, R. D., & Evans, B. (Eds.). (2003). *Just sustainabilities: Development in an unequal world.* London: Earthscan/MIT Press. Retrieved December 19, 2008, from http://www.appropedia.org/Just_sustainability.

Ball, J. (2008, February 4). Wall Street shows skepticism over coal: Banks push utilities to plan for impact of emissions caps. *Wall Street Journal.* Retrieved July 26, 2008, from http://online.wsj.com.

Barnett, M. L., & HoffmanRoss, A. J. (2008). Beyond corporate reputation: Managing reputational interdependence. *Corporate Reputation Review, 11*, 1–9.

Beinecke, F.(2008, February 11). The twilight of dirty coal. *NRDC Switchboard*. Retrieved July 26, 2008, from http://switchboard.nrdc.org/blogs/fbeinecke/the_twilight_of_dirty_coal .html.

Brown, L. R. (2008, February14). *U.S. moving toward ban on new coal-fired power plants.* Earth Policy Institute. Retrieved August 13, 2008, from http://www.earth-policy.org.

Carson, R. (1962). *Silent Spring.* Boston: Houghton Mifflin.

Center for Environmental Education. (n.d.). *Will the whales survive?* [Brochure]. Author.

Charman, K. (2003, May 8). Environmentalists = terrorists: The new math. *Tompaine.com.* Retrieved May 6, 2005, from www.tompaine.com.

Climate Convergence. (2007, August 13). *Activists block Bank of America in downtown Asheville.* Retrieved December 10, 2008, from http://asheville.indymedia.org.

Cox, J. R. (1982). The die is cast: Topical and ontological dimensions of the locus of the irreparable. *Quarterly Journal of Speech, 68*, 227–239.

Cox, J. R. (2001). The irreparable. In T. O. Sloane (Ed.), *Encyclopedia of rhetoric* (pp. 406–409). Oxford and New York: Oxford University Press.

Crompton, T. (2008). *Weathercocks and signposts: The environment movement at a crossroads.* World Wildlife Fund-UK. Retrieved December 17, 2008, from wwf.org.uk/strategies forchange.

DeLuca, K. M. (2005). *Image politics: The new rhetoric of environmental activism.* London: Routledge.

Earth First! (2005). How deep is your ecology? *Earth First! Journal.* Retrieved May 4, 2005, from www.earthfirstjournal.org.

Evernden, N. (1985). *The natural alien: Humankind and the environment.* Toronto: University of Toronto Press.

Farrior, M. (2005, February). *Breakthrough strategies for engaging the public: Emerging trends in communications and social science for biodiversity project.* Retrieved December 18, 2008, from http://www.biodiversityproject.org.

Fish, S. (2008, August 3). *Think again: I am therefore I pollute.* Retrieved August 15, 2008, from http://fish.blogs.nytimes.com.

Flora, J. A. (2001). The Stanford community studies: Campaigns to reduce cardiovascular disease. In R. E. Rice & C. K. Atkin (Eds.), *Public communication campaigns* (3rd ed., pp. 193–213). Thousand Oaks, CA: Sage.

Gendlin, F. (1982). A talk with Mike McCloskey: Executive director of the Sierra Club. *Sierra, 67,* 36–41.

Greider, W. (2003, August 5). Victory at McDonald's. *The Nation,* pp. 8, 10, 36.

Griskevicious, V., Cialdini, R. B., & Gooldstein, N. J. (2008). Social norms: An underestimated and underemployed lever for managing climate change. *International Journal of Sustainability Communication, 3:* 5–13.

Gupta, D. (2002, March 14–16). *Radical flank effects: The effect of radical–moderate splits in regional nationalist movements.* Paper presented at the Conference of Europeanists, Chicago, IL. Retrieved April 2005 from http://falcon.arts.cornell.edu.

Haines, H. (1997). Black radicalization and the funding of civil rights: 1957–1970. *Social Problems 32,* 31–43. In D. McAdam & D. A. Snow (Eds.), *Social movements: Readings on their emergence, mobilization, and dynamics* (pp. 440–449). Los Angeles: Roxbury. (Original work published 1984)

Harris, S. (1977). *What's so funny about science?* Los Altos, CA: Wm. Kaufmann.

Hoffman, A. (2007) *Deconstructing the environmental movement: Structural and perceptual networks and field-level boundaries.* Ross School of Business Working Paper, University of Michigan. Retrieved December 20, 2008, from http://www.palgrave-journals.com.

Hunter, R. (1971). *The storming of the mind.* Garden City, NJ: Doubleday.

LaDuke, W. (2002, November/December). The salt woman and the coal mine. *Sierra,* pp. 44–47, 73.

McAdam, D. (1992). Studying social movements: A conceptual tour of the field. *Program on Nonviolent Sanctions and Cultural Survival.* Weatherhead Center for International Affairs. Princeton, NJ: Princeton University Press. (As cited in Gupta, 2002)

McAdam, D. (1996). The framing function of movement tactics: Strategic dramaturgy in the American civil rights movement. In D. McAdam, J. D. McCarthy, & M. N. Zald (Eds.), *Comparative perspectives on social movements: Political opportunities, mobilizing structures, and cultural framings* (pp. 339–334). Cambridge, UK: Cambridge University Press.

McAdam, D., Tarrow, D., & Tilly, C. (2001). *Dynamics of contention.* Cambridge, UK: Cambridge University Press.

Naess, A., & Sessions, G. (n.d.). *Deep ecology platform.* Foundation for Deep Ecology. Retrieved October 8, 2003, from www.deepecology.org.

National Energy Technology Lab. (2007). *Tracking new coal-fired power plants.* Retrieved August 13, 2008, from http://cmnow.org.

Orr, D. W. (1992). *Ecological literacy: Education and the transition to a postmodern world.* Albany: State University of New York Press.

Pezzullo, P. C. (2007). *Toxic tours: Rhetorics of pollution, travel and environmental justice.* Tuscaloosa: University of Alabama Press.

The Plan. (2008). *Repower America.* Retrieved December 21, 2008, from http://www.Repower America.org.

Ponte, L. (2003, August 4). Eco-terrorism torch. *FrontPageMagazine.* Retrieved May 6, 2005, from www.frontpagemag.com.

Rice, R. E. (2001). Smokey Bear. In R. E. Rice & C. K. Atkin (Eds.), *Public communication campaigns* (3rd ed., pp. 276–279). Thousand Oaks, CA: Sage.

Rice, R. E., & Atkin, C. K. (2001). *Public communication campaigns* (3rd ed.). Thousand Oaks, CA: Sage.

Richardson, E., & Joe, T. (1995, August 29). Reject that gag rule. *Washington Post,* p. A19.

Rogers, E. M., & Storey, J. D. (1987). Communication campaigns. In C. R. Berger & S. H. Chaffee (Eds.), *Handbook of communication science* (pp. 817–846). Newbury Park, CA: Sage.

Rose, C., & Dade, P. (2007). *Using values modes.* Retrieved December 18, 2008, from www.campaignstrategy.org.

Sacred Land Film Project. (2003). *Zuni salt lake.* Retrieved September 24, 2003, from www.sacredland.org/zuni_salt_lake.

Scare, R. (1990). *Eco-warriors: Understanding the radical environmental movement.* Chicago: Nobler Press.

Schultz, P.W., & Zelezny, L. (2003). Reframing environmental messages to be congruent with American values. *Research in Human Ecology, 10,* 126–136.

Scott, R. L., & Smith, D. K. (1969). The rhetoric of confrontation. *Quarterly Journal of Speech, 55,* 1–8.

Seciwa, C. (2003, August 5). *Zuni Salt Lake and sanctuary zone protected for future generations.* [News release]. Zuni Pueblo, NM: Zuni Salt Lake Coalition.

Shabecoff, P. (2000). *Earth rising: American environmentalism in the 21st century.* Washington, DC, and Covelo, CA: Island Press.

Social Marketing Institute. (n.d.). *Social marketing*. Retrieved December 20, 2008, from file:///F:/Social%20Marketing.htm

Stern, P. C., Dietz, T., & Kalof, L. (1993). Value orientations, gender, and environmental concerns. *Environment & Behavior, 25*, 322–348.

Strand, P., & Strand, R. (1993). *The hijacking of the humane movement: Animal extremism.* Sun City, AZ: Doral.

Tarrow, S. (1998). *Power in movement: Social movements and contentious politics.* Cambridge, UK: Cambridge University Press.

Torgerson, D. (1999). *The promise of green politics: Environmentalism and the public sphere.* Durham, NC: Duke University Press.

UN General Assembly. (2008). *United Nations communication campaigns on key issues, partnership with civil society.* Department of Public Information. New York: UN News and Media Division. Retrieved December 19, 2008, from http://www.un.org/News.

Valtin, T. (2003, November). Zuni Salt Lake saved. *Planet: The Sierra Club Activist Resource* [Newsletter], 1.

Victory and new threats at Zuni Salt Lake, New Mexico. (2003, Winter). *The Citizen* [Newsletter of the Citizens Coal Council], 6.

Weinreich, N. K. (2006). *What is social marketing?* Weinreich Communications. Retrieved August 27, 2008, from http://www.social-marketing.com.

Weyler, R. (2004). *Greenpeace: How a group of journalists, ecologists, and visionaries changed the world.* New York: Rodale.

Zuni Salt Lake Coalition. (2001, October 6–7). [Zuni Salt Lake Coalition's campaign plan: Edward's kitchen. Notes from first meeting of coalition members]. Unpublished raw data.

Zuni Salt Lake Coalition. (2003). Retrieved September 23, 2003, from www.zunisaltlakecoalition .org/background.

By late 20th century, citizens in low-income communities had begun to feel themselves surrounded by what environmental historian Samuel Hays (1987) has termed "the toxic 'sea around us'" (p. 171).

CHAPTER 8

Environmental Justice/Climate Justice

Voices From the Grassroots

I heard words like "economic blackmail," "environmental racism." Somebody put words, names, on what our community was experiencing.

—Rose Marie Augustine (1993)

We, representatives of the poor and the marginalized of the world . . . resolve to actively build a movement from the communities that will address the issue of climate change from a human rights, social justice and labour perspective.

—Delhi Climate Justice Declaration (2002)

I n inner cities and Native American reservations, Appalachian communities and villages in poor nations, and in the polluted corridor in Louisiana called "Cancer Alley," grassroots voices have been speaking against "environmental racism" and demanding "environmental justice" and "climate justice." On the front lines of such community struggles are

- Farmworkers in California, who formed El Pueblo para el Aire y Agua Limpio (People for Clean Air and Water) to fight the spraying of toxic pesticides as they worked in the fields
- Activists in Coal River Mountain Watch, who oppose "mountaintop removal," a form of coal mining that threatens the safety of West Virginia communities

- Farmers, fishworkers, Dalits [groups of people traditionally thought of as outcastes], and the displaced in India who marched through the streets of Delhi to protest the impacts of global warming on their livelihoods and communities

Perhaps nowhere have efforts been more evident to redefine the meaning and significance of environment than in these and other community-based, multiracial struggles for environmental justice. As used by community activists and scholars studying the movement, the term **environmental justice** refers to (1) calls to recognize and halt the disproportionate burdens imposed on poor and minority communities by environmentally harmful conditions, (2) more inclusive opportunities for those who are most affected to be heard in the decisions made by public agencies and the wider environmental movement, and (3) a vision of environmentally healthy, economically sustainable communities.

The first section of this chapter[1] examines poor and minority communities' challenging of the U.S. mainstream environmental movement and larger society, which too often define *environment* as a place apart from the places where people live and work. I introduce some of the voices that not only have criticized abandoned toxic waste sites, industrial pollution, unsafe work conditions, contaminated water, and destruction of sacred lands but also have charged that the disproportionate presence of these environmental dangers in low-income neighborhoods and communities of color is **environmental racism**. I also examine the emergence of a discourse that articulates the values and vocabularies of both environmental protection and the struggle for social justice in a vision of environmental justice.

In the second section, I explore some of the impacts of the new movement, including its efforts to build a network, or "a net that works," among grassroots groups facing similar struggles of environmental injustice. The third section of the chapter describes the recurring barriers faced by many residents in these communities. In expressing their opposition, members of low-income communities often are viewed as inappropriate because they fail to speak the official discourse of technical reason. Finally, in the fourth section, I describe the emerging movement for climate justice, whose discourse is framing global climate change ethically, in terms of human rights and environmental justice.

My hope is that when you have finished reading the chapter, you will appreciate a more robust meaning of *environment,* one that includes places where people live, work, play, learn, and, in many indigenous cultures, bury their dead. You will have a better understanding of the barriers that citizens from poor and minority communities often face when they call attention to environmental concerns; and you will understand why, in the end, the movement for environmental justice is also a movement for a more democratically open and inclusive society.

Whose Environment? Whose Voices?

The environmental movement in the United States—historically associated with white, Euro-Americans—had been concerned with wild places and the natural world.[2]

In the 1960s, we saw the beginning of a broadened focus of the movement that included human health and environmental quality. Nevertheless, the movement continued to offer "disjointed and at times contradictory" accounts of humans' place in nature, accounts that assumed a "long-standing separation of the social from the ecological" (Gottlieb, 2002, p. 5). Partly in response, by the 1980s, activists in minority and low-income communities had opened a new antagonism by challenging society's view of nature as a place apart from the places where people live. (In Chapter 2, we defined *antagonism* as the recognition of the limits of an idea or prevailing viewpoint; recognizing a limit creates an opening for alternative voices to redefine a condition or state of affairs.) This opening for new voices also fueled efforts to ensure that processes for environmental decision making are more inclusive, democratic, and just.

Challenging Environment as a Place Apart

By the 1960s, concerns had begun to emerge in the United States about the health and effects related to new developments in large-scale chemical manufacturing and disposal of toxic wastes. Some scientists and citizens were skeptical of public institutions' ability to safeguard citizens' health in this new petrochemical society. Rachel Carson's (1962) best-selling book *Silent Spring* became the most visible text questioning the excessive use of powerful chemicals such as Dichloro-Diphenyl-Trichloroethane (DDT) by agricultural businesses and public health agencies, and it set off a national debate over the practices of the pesticide industry. Two decades later, the small, upstate New York community of Love Canal became a metaphor for the nation's consciousness of the hazards of its chemical culture.[3]

Increasingly, citizens had begun to feel themselves surrounded by what environmental historian Samuel Hays (1987) termed "the toxic 'sea around us'" (p. 171).[4] Many feared that the new synthetic chemicals were having devastating health effects—cancer, birth defects, respiratory illness, and neurological disorders—adding to the public's fears of "an environmental threat that was out of control" (p. 200). It also became clear that certain communities—largely low-income and minority communities—were most affected by toxic pollutants and the resulting health and social problems.

Challenging Traditional Language About Environment

Some attempts to call attention to the specific impacts of these environmental hazards occurred before a movement for environmental justice arose. In the late 1960s and 1970s, a few civil rights groups, churches, and environmental leaders tried to call attention to the particular problems of urban communities and the workplace. Dr. Martin Luther King, Jr., went to Memphis, Tennessee, in 1968 to join with African American sanitation workers who were striking for wages and better work conditions—an event that sociologist and environmental justice scholar Robert Bullard (1993) called one of the earliest efforts to link civil rights and environmental health concerns. Also addressing the workplace environment was Congress's passage of the federal Occupational Safety and Health Act (OSHA) in 1970. This landmark law helped "stimulate the budding workplace environmental movements . . . as well as community-based organizations of activists and professionals such as the various Committees on Occupational Safety and Health . . . that sprang up in the early to middle 1970s" (Gottlieb, 1993, pp. 283, 285).

Other early efforts included the 1971 Urban Environment Conference (UEC), one of the early successful efforts to link environmental and social justice concerns. A coalition of labor, environmental, and civil rights groups, the UEC tried "to help broaden the way the public defined environmental issues and to focus on the particular environmental problems of urban minorities" (Kazis & Grossman, 1991, p. 247). Other attempts to forge diverse coalitions included the 1972 Conference on Environmental Quality and Social Justice at Woodstock, Illinois; the 1976 United Auto Worker's Black Lake Conference, Working for Environmental and Economic Justice and Jobs; and the 1979 City Care conference on the urban environment in Detroit, jointly convened by the National Urban League, the Sierra Club, and the Urban Environment Conference.

Despite these early attempts to bring environmental, labor, civil rights, and religious leaders together to explore common interests, national environmental groups in the 1960s and 1970s largely failed to recognize and address the problems of urban residents or poor and minority communities. Part of the difficulty lay in the prevailing languages about the environment itself. Some community activists— particularly women of color—complained of obstacles when they tried to speak with traditional environmental groups. For example, in her account of efforts to stop the construction of a 1,600-ton-per-day solid waste incinerator in a south central Los Angeles neighborhood in the mid-1980s, Giovanna Di Chiro (1996) reported, "These issues were not deemed adequately 'environmental' by local environmental groups such as the Sierra Club or the Environmental Defense Fund" (p. 299). Di Chiro explained that, when residents of the predominantly African American and low-income community approached these groups, "they were informed that the poisoning of an urban community by an incineration facility was a 'community health issue,' not an environmental one"[5] (p. 299). Activists in other parts of the country similarly complained that "the mainstream environmental community [was] reluctant to address issues of equity and social justice, within the context of the environment" (Alston, 1990, p.23). (For other accounts of such barriers, see Austin & Schill, 1994; Bullard, 1993; Pulido, 1996; and Schwab, 1994.)

Faced with indifference on the part of established environmental groups, in the 1980s residents and activists in some low-income neighborhoods and communities of color started to take matters into their own hands. In the process, they began to redefine the meaning of *environment* to include the places "where we live, where we work, where we play, and where we learn" (Cole & Foster, 2001, p. 16).

"We Speak for Ourselves"

A key event in the beginnings of a movement for environmental justice was the 1982 protest by community members against a PCB (polychlorinated biphenyl) toxic landfill in rural Warren County, North Carolina. In the late 1970s, the state discovered that PCB chemicals had been illegally dumped along miles of highways. To dispose of the toxics-laced soil, officials decided to bury it in a landfill in the predominantly poor and African American Warren County. Rather than accept this, local residents and supporters from national civil rights groups tried to halt the state's plan by placing their bodies in the middle of the roads leading to the landfill, to block 6,000 trucks carrying the PCB-contaminated soil. More than 500 arrests occurred in what sociologists Robert Bullard and Beverly Hendrix Wright (1987) called "the first national attempt by Blacks to link environmental issues (hazardous waste and pollution) to the mainstream civil rights agenda" (p. 32; for background on Warren County as a symbolic birthplace of the environmental justice movement and its continuing struggle against the toxic landfill, see Pezzullo, 2001).

Prompted by protests in Warren County and elsewhere, in the 1980s and 1990s federal agencies and academic scholars began to confirm patterns of disproportionate exposure to environmental hazards experienced by low-income populations and communities of color. For example, the U.S. General Accounting Office (1983) found that African Americans constituted the majority of populations living near hazardous landfills. In a follow-up study, *Toxic Wastes and Race in the United States,* the United Church of Christ's Commission for Racial Justice discovered a similar pattern (Chavis & Lee, 1987). Among its key findings were these:

- Race proved to be the most significant among variables tested in association with the location of commercial waste facilities. . . . Although socio-economic status appeared to play an important role in the location of [these] facilities, race still proved to be more significant. (p. xiii)
- Three out of every five Black and Hispanic Americans lived in communities with uncontrolled toxic waste sites. . . . (p. iv)
- Approximately half of all Asian/Pacific Islanders and American Indians lived in communities with uncontrolled toxic waste sites. (p. xiv)

(A follow-up report, *Toxic Wastes and Race at Twenty, 1987–2007,* revealed that "racial disparities in the distribution of hazardous wastes are greater than previously reported," in the original 1987 study [Bullard, Mohai, Saha, & Wright, 2007, p. x].)

Other research on the racial and income characteristics of communities near environmental hazards soon followed. White (1998) reported that 87 percent of studies of the distribution of environmental hazards revealed racial disparities (p. 63). These studies concluded that minority and low-income populations not only are more likely to live near such hazards but also are "more severely exposed to potentially deadly and destructive levels of toxins from environmental hazards than others" (p. 63). There also appeared to be some disparity in the enforcement of environmental laws. In a study reported in the *National Law Journal,* Marianne Lavelle and Marcia Coyle (1992) found that "there is a racial divide in the way the U.S. government cleans up toxic waste sites and punishes polluters. White communities see faster action, better results and stiffer penalties than communities where Blacks, Hispanics and other minorities live" (pp. S1, S2).

With the heavy concentration of hazardous facilities, especially in low-income neighborhoods or communities of color, there began to appear new narratives of environmental harm. In many cases, such stories spoke of frustration in dealing with local officials and the search for words to express anger and suffering. Reports from community activists with whom I've spoken suggested that people in such circumstances tend to undergo five stages of political awareness:

1. Residents discover that they have been exposed to an environmental hazard and that local authorities withheld this information.

2. They suspect that local health problems may be linked to this exposure and seek answers from local officials.

3. Residents are met with silence, denial, or confrontation on the part of responsible health or public officials.

4. Many residents become angry; their consciousness is politicized.

5. They begin to search for language to explain their situation and for a vocabulary of redress for these grievances.

Many in such communities charged that they were suffering from a form of environmental discrimination. They spoke of being poisoned and complained that their communities were being targeted as human "sacrifice zones" that ignored people and invited sites for polluting industries. Bullard (1993) coined the term **sacrifice zones** to describe two characteristics shared by these communities: "(1) They already have more than their share of environmental problems and polluting industries, and (2) they are still attracting new polluters" (p. 12).

One particularly powerful term used by activists to describe the experience of their communities was **environmental racism**. At a 1991 summit of activists from the environmental justice movement, Benjamin Chavis of the United Church of Christ's Commission for Racial Justice searched for a way to describe "what was going on" in the persistent pattern of locating toxics in poor and minority neighborhoods: "It came to me—*environmental racism*. That's when I coined the term"[6] (quoted in Bullard, 1994, p. 278). Chavis described environmental racism as

> racial discrimination in environmental policy-making and the enforcement of regulations and laws, the deliberate targeting of people of color communities for toxic waste facilities, the official sanctioning of the life-threatening presence of poisons and pollutants in our communities, and the history of excluding people of color from leadership in the environmental movement. (quoted in Di Chiro, 1996, p. 304)

While Chavis highlighted the "deliberate" targeting of people of color communities, others pointed out that discrimination also resulted from the *disparate impact* of environmental hazards on minority communities. The 1964 Civil Rights Act used the term **disparate impact** to recognize discrimination in the form of the disproportionate burdens that some groups experience, regardless of the conscious intention of others in their decisions or behaviors. In other words, racial (or environmental) discrimination results from *the accumulated impacts of unfair treatment,* which may include more than intentional discrimination or deliberate targeting.

Naming the problem as environmental racism was important. Residents in communities that suffered from environmental hazards often search for language to name their experiences. Rose Marie Augustine's experience in Tucson, Arizona, was typical. After trying unsuccessfully to get local officials to recognize the problems of polluted well water and illness in her neighborhood, Augustine attended a workshop for community activists in the Southwest. She said that for the first time, "I heard words like 'economic blackmail,' 'environmental racism.' Somebody put words, names, on what our community was experiencing" (Augustine, 1993, n.p.). In other cases, activists themselves began to call the conditions imposed on low-income communities a form of economic blackmail. For example, Bullard (1993) explained, "The plantation owner in the rural parishes was replaced by the petrochemical industry executive as the new 'master' and 'overseer'" (p. 12–13); "You can get a job, but only if you are willing to do work that will harm you, your families, and your neighbors" (p. 23).

As protests mounted against such patterns and the failure of the mainstream environmental movement to address the problems, activists began to insist that people in affected communities be able to "speak for ourselves" (Alston, 1990). In her book *We Speak for Ourselves,* social justice activist Dana Alston (1990) argued that environmental justice "calls for a total redefinition of terms and language to describe the conditions that people are facing" (quoted in Di Chiro, 1998, p. 105). Indeed, what some found distinctive about the environmental justice movement was the ways in which it transformed "the possibilities for fundamental social and environmental change through processes of redefinition, reinvention, and construction of innovative political and cultural discourses" (Di Chiro, 1996, p. 303). Environmental justice attorney Deehon Ferris put it more bluntly when she said, "We're shifting the terms of the debate" (Ferris, 1993, n.p.).

One important attempt to shift the terms of debate occurred in 1990 when the SouthWest Organizing Project in New Mexico publicly criticized the nation's largest environmental groups, specifically those who belonged to the "Group of Ten."[7] Called "the single most stirring challenge to traditional environmentalism" (Schwab, 1994, p. 388), the letter ultimately was signed by 103 civil rights and community leaders. The letter accused the mainstream environmental organizations of racism in their hiring and environmental policies. A particularly stinging passage stated the signers' grievance with the mainstream groups:

> For centuries, people of color in our region have been subjected to racist and genocidal practices including the theft of lands and water, the murder of innocent people, and the degradation of our environment. . . . Although environmental organizations calling themselves the "Group of Ten" often claim to represent our interests . . . your organizations play an equal role in the disruption of our communities. There is a clear lack of accountability by the Group of Ten environmental organizations towards Third World communities in the Southwest, in the United States as a whole, and internationally. . . . (SouthWest Organizing Project, 1990, p. 1)

Coverage of the letter in the *New York Times* and other newspapers "initiated a media firestorm" and generated calls for "an emergency summit of environmental, civil rights, and community groups" (Cole & Foster, 2001, p. 31).

The First National People of Color Environmental Leadership Summit

A key moment in the new movement came when delegates from local communities and national leaders from social justice, religious, environmental, and civil rights groups met in Washington, D.C., for the **First National People of Color Environmental Leadership Summit** in October 1991. The summit is generally considered to be important for three reasons. First, it was a "watershed moment" in the history of the nascent environmental justice movement (Di Chiro, 1998, p. 113). For three days, activists from local communities shared stories of grievances and attempted to compose a collective critique of the narrow vision of the environment and the exclusion of people of color from decisions that affected their communities. Second, summit participants agreed upon the "Principles of Environmental Justice" that would powerfully shape the vision of the emerging movement. Finally, many viewed the meeting as a declaration of independence from the traditional environment movement. One participant declared, "I don't care to join the environmental movement, I belong to a movement already" (quoted in Cole & Foster, 2001, p. 31).

For the first time, different strands of the emerging environmental justice movement met together and, with leaders in the U.S. environmental movement,[8] challenged traditional definitions of environmentalism and composed a new discourse of environmental justice, articulating or linking the values of social justice and environmental protection. In doing so, summit participants were able to insert their experiences of toxic poisoning into earlier narratives of the U.S. civil rights movement. Running on a monitor during the summit was a powerful example of such a "critical rhetoric" (Chapter 7).

The video showed images of industrial pipes disgorging pollution into the air and water, along with scenes of African American residents of Reveilletown, Louisiana, a community established by freed slaves after the Civil War.[9] The historic community had become so badly polluted by wastes from a nearby chemical factory that it had to be abandoned in the 1980s. Janice Dickerson, an African American activist working with similar communities, provided a running narration as the video showed documentary film images of the Ku Klux Klan burning crosses in the 1960s:

> From the perspective of the African American, it's a civil rights matter; it's interwoven. Civil rights and the environment movement are both interwoven. Because, again, we are the most victimized. . . . There's no difference in a petro-chemical industry locating two, three hundred feet from my house and killing me off than there is when the Klan was on the rampage, just running into black neighborhoods, hanging black people at will. (Greenpeace, 1990)

By drawing on the "morally charged terrain" of the American civil rights movement, summit participants believed that they would be able to insert a powerful moral claim of justice into the public debate about the environment (Harvey, 1996, p. 387). In so doing, many activists believed that they could contest and/or redefine the meaning of environment itself.

Many of the speakers at the summit also urged participants to demand political representation and to speak forcefully to public officials, corporations, and the traditional environmental movement. At the summit, Chavis explained, *"This is our opportunity to define and redefine for ourselves. . . .* What is at issue here is our ability, our capacity to speak clearly to ourselves, to our peoples, and forthrightly to all those forces out there that have caused us to be in this situation" (*Proceedings,* 1991, p. 59). On the last day, participants did so in a dramatic way by adopting 17 **"Principles of Environmental Justice,"** an expansive vision for their communities and the right to participate directly in decisions about their environment.

The principles began with the deeply ethical statement, "Environmental justice affirms the sacredness of Mother Earth, ecological unity and the interdependence of all species, and the right to be free from ecological destruction" (*Proceedings,* 1991, p. viii). The principles developed an enlarged sense of the environment to include places where people lived, worked, and played and enumerated a series of rights, including "the fundamental right to political, economic, cultural, and environmental self-determination of all peoples" (p. viii). (For a copy of the principles, see http://saepej.igc.org/Principles.)

The inclusion of the right of self-determination in the summit's "Principles of Environmental Justice" was especially important to the emerging movement. Many of the summit's participants had criticized the officially sanctioned decision making in their communities for failing to provide meaningful participation "for those most burdened by environmental decisions" (Cole & Foster, 2001, p. 16). In adopting the principles, they insisted that *environmental justice* not only referred to the right of all people to be free of environmental poisons but that at its core is the inclusion of all in the decisions that affect their health and the well-being of their communities. One delegate remarked that the "Principles of Environmental Justice" represented "how people of color define environmental issues for ourselves, as social and economic justice" (*Proceedings,* 1991, p. 54).

In the decade following the First People of Color National Environmental Leadership Summit, the new movement for environmental justice would extend the new antagonism of questioning the view of environment as a place apart from the concerns of those places where people lived and worked. In doing so, the movement also began to see some successes. Urban planning scholar Jim Schwab (1994) observed that "the new movement had won a place at the table. The Deep South, the nation, would never discuss environmental issues in the same way again" (p. 393). But the movement for environmental justice also would confront new obstacles and a need to identify new ways to communicate to pursue the vision put forward in the Principles. The remaining sections of this chapter describe some of these successes and the challenges for an environmentalism that builds healthy, democratic communities.

Act Locally!

What Is Environmental Racism?

The charge of environmental discrimination of racism is a powerful assertion. How is it proved? Does it involve intent, or is evidence of a "disparate impact" on a community or people enough? In answering, it may be helpful to consider the "human face" of the conflicts over environmental racism today. Consider the following exercise:

1. First, watch the video, *A Well of Pain*, a story about Sheila Holt-Orsted, in Dickson County, Tennessee; also, read her story, "Their Water Was Poisoned by Chemicals. Was Their Treatment Poisoned by Racism?" at http://www.washingtonpost.com.

   Holt-Orsted found "documents indicating that Tennessee environmental . . . officials had concerns about the possibility of TCE [trichloroethylene] . . . in the Holt's well water as early as 1988. The Holt's well was left untested for nine years while TCE problems in the wells of white families were tended to with haste, the records showed" (Duke, 2007, p. C1).

   The lawsuits filed by Holt-Orsted are still being considered as this book goes to press in 2009.

2. The story of Sheila Holt-Orsted raises a number of questions. Discuss these questions in class, and then consider another step (no. 3 following).

   - Is this a story of environmental racism? Is there evidence of intentional neglect of the Holt-Orsted well by Tennessee officials? Did officials treat the Holt-Orsteds differently than nearby white families?
   - Holt-Orsted also alleges that the company that dumped drums of TCE in the landfill is liable for her families' illnesses. The company's attorney says, "We have yet to see evidence . . . that the various injuries alleged were the result of TCE contamination." What burden of proof does Holt-Orsted have?

3. Are there cases of environmental racism in your community? Consult with faculty, local officials, and neighborhood advocates to learn about instances of environmental or health harms that are alleged to be the result of intentional or simply the "disparate impact" of practices in the community.

SOURCE: Duke (2007), p. C1.

Building the Movement for Environmental Justice

One year after the 1991 summit, organizers of the large Southern Organizing Conference for Social and Economic Justice in New Orleans alluded to the "new definition of the term 'environment'" and invited community activists "to build a new movement" using the "Principles of Environmental Justice" adopted at the summit (letter, June 2, 1992). Indeed, many community activists and others from national civil rights and social justice groups left the 1991 summit to continue building the communication tools, resources, and networks that would be required to change practices in both their own communities and in government agencies.

Opening the Floodgates

The decade of the 1990s saw clear gains for the growing environmental justice movement. Deehon Ferris (1993) of the Lawyers' Committee for Civil Rights in Washington, D.C., observed that "as a result of on-the-ground struggles and hell-raising, 'environmental justice' [emerged as] a hot issue; . . . floodgates [opened] in the media" (n.p.). Ferris called the early 1990s "a watershed," and the *National Law Journal* reported that the movement—often led by women—had gained "critical mass" (Lavelle & Coyle, 1992, p. 5). A follow-up to the 1991 summit was held, the Second National People of Color Environmental Leadership Summit, in Washington, D.C., October 23–26, 2002. Highlighting women's roles as leaders in the movement, the second event was even larger, attracting more than 1,400 participants. (For information about this event, see http://www.ejrc.cau.edu.)

The "critical mass" of the movement began to be felt: Achievements since the first summit have included expanded media attention, new coalitions with environmental and civil rights organizations, networks offering training and coordination of the growing number of grassroots and community groups, a presidential Executive Order on Environmental Justice, and the beginnings of awareness by state and federal agencies.

In 1993, the movement convinced the Environmental Protection Agency (EPA) to establish a **National Environmental Justice Advisory Committee (NEJAC)** to ensure a voice for environmental justice networks and other grassroots organizations in the EPA's policymaking. The committee—often referred to simply as NEJAC—was chartered to provide advice from the environmental justice community and recommendations to the EPA administrator on environmental justice. For example, NEJAC has produced advisory reports on the cleanup of "brown fields" (polluted urban areas), mercury contamination of fish, and new guidelines for ensuring participation of low-income and minority residents in decisions about permits for industries wishing to locate in their communities. (For more information, see http://www.epa.gov/compliance.)

The movement also achieved an important political goal when President Bill Clinton issued Executive Order 12898, "Federal Actions to Address Environmental Justice in Minority Populations and Low-Income Populations," in 1994. The **Executive Order on Environmental Justice** instructed each federal agency "to make achieving environmental justice part of its mission by identifying and addressing . . . disproportionately high and adverse human health or environmental effects of its programs, policies, and activities on minority populations and low-income populations in the United States" (Clinton, 1994, p. 7629). Although, the succeeding administration of George W. Bush never revoked the executive order, the administration's own EPA Inspector General reported in 2004 that the agency had not adequately carried out the order (Office of the Inspector General, 2004).

Finally, Pezzullo and Sandler (2007) observe that "much has changed within . . . and happened around" the mainstream and environmental justice movements (p. 12). In some cases, vigorous dialogue between leaders of the mainstream green groups and the environmental justice community has led to collaborations between these groups with poor and minority communities.[10] Among the larger, national environmental groups, Greenpeace, Earth Island Institute, Sierra Club, and Earthjustice (a legal advocacy group) have been particularly active in their attempts to support environmental justice concerns.

Toxic Tours and Human Sacrifice Zones

One particularly striking form of communication used more and more by environmental justice groups to connect local communities and wider publics is what grassroots activists call **toxic tours**. Communication scholar Phaedra Pezzullo (2007), in her book *Toxic Tourism Rhetorics of Pollution, Travel, and Environmental Justice*, defines these as "non-commercial expeditions into areas that are polluted by toxins, spaces that Robert D. Bullard (1993) calls 'human sacrifice zones' . . . More and more of these communities have begun to invite outsiders in, providing tours as a means of educating people about and, it is hoped, transforming their situation" (p. 5). (See Figures 8.1 and 8.2, from a toxic tour of "Cancer Alley," in Louisiana.) Unlike other institutional tours of toxic sites, these tours draw on "discourses of uncertainty and contamination, of social justice and the need for cultural change" (pp. 5–6). Although for the past century environmental advocates have taken reporters and others into natural areas such as Yosemite Valley and the Grand Canyon to build support for their protection, this use of toxic tours is more recent.[11]

| Figure 8.1 | Holy Rosary Cemetery, a stop on a toxic tour of "Cancer Alley," Louisiana. Since the towers of the industrial building in the background are so clearly mirrored in the religious icons of the graveyard that are positioned in the foreground, this tour stop rhetorically represents a symbolic elevation of environmental justice by juxtaposing the sacred and the profane, the progress promised by corporate development, and the incommensurable vulnerability of humans. |

I had the opportunity to join Dr. Pezzullo and other environmental leaders on a toxic tour in Matamoros, Mexico, just south of the U.S. border near Brownsville, Texas, in 2001. Part of the *maquiladora* zone, or manufacturing area, this area has large numbers of industrial plants that have relocated from the United States under the North American Free Trade Agreement (NAFTA). Some of the problems associated with this concentration of largely unregulated plants are severely contaminated air and water, unsafe drinking water, poor sanitation, and the prevalence of rare illnesses in the population. (See Chapter 6 for a discussion of the high rate of anencephalic births in the *maquiladora* zone.)

The tour through the crowded, makeshift housing for workers and their families was organized by the Sierra Club and its Mexican allies to introduce some of the leaders from U.S. environmental groups to the threats to human health from pollution in the area. As we walked through the unpaved streets by the workers' homes, we felt overpowered by the sights, smells, and feel of an environment under assault. Strong chemical odors filled the air, children played in polluted creeks by their homes, and young children scavenged in burning heaps of garbage for material they could sell for a few pesos. Speaking of such experiences, Pezzullo (2004) observes that being in a community harmed by such hazards opens our senses of sight, sound, and smell and that this awareness builds support for the community's struggle: "Odorous fumes cause residents and their visitors' eyes to water and throats to tighten . . . , a reminder of the physical risk toxics pose" (p. 248). She shares one toxic tour guide's observation that toxic tours give visitors "firsthand" evidence of "the environmental insult to residents [of having polluters so close to their homes], as well as the noxious odors that permeate the neighborhood" (p. 248). (For more information and a description of a toxic tour in Louisiana's infamous "Cancer Alley," see Pezzullo, 2003 and 2007.)

As toxic tours show, the movement for environmental justice continues to confront real-world, on-the-ground challenges to building sustainable, healthy communities. Indeed, the vision of environmental justice has always been more than simply the removal of the disproportionate burden on communities. Beyond this goal, the National Environmental Justice Advisory Council (1996) insists that the environmental justice movement also embodies "a new vision borne of a community-driven process whose essential core is *a transformative public discourse over what are truly healthy, sustainable and vital communities*" (p. 17).

Important to the nurture of such a "transformative discourse" is the democratic inclusion of people and communities in decisions affecting their lives. Yet, as we will see in the next section, some community groups have fewer resources—for example, less education, time, money, expertise, and influence—with which to participate in such decision making and may face subtle barriers to speaking in official forums.

Indecorous Voices and Democratic Inclusion

An important theme emerging from the discourse of the movement for environmental is the challenge to norms of official decision making and the right of

© Taro Yamasaki/Getty Images.

Figure 8.2   Toxic Tours help visitors to appreciate how close some people live to polluting facilities.

affected communities to be heard. In Chapter 3, I introduced Senecah's (2004) Trinity of Voices (TOV) model of public participation to describe some of the barriers to the ability of citizens to participate and be heard in matters affecting their communities. One important element of the TOV model was a citizen's interpersonal standing—not standing in the legal sense as a plaintiff in court but "the civic legitimacy, the respect, the esteem, and the consideration that all stakeholders' perspectives should be given" (p. 24). It is this sense that often seems at risk as community members struggle to speak and to be respected in official forums. Environmental scholar Robert Gottlieb (1993) has summed up this challenge as the need to embrace "an environmentalism that is democratic and inclusive," as well as one that respects equity and social justice (p. 320).

This section examines one important barrier to a democratic and inclusive environmentalism that arises when agency officials construct the voices of the poor or residents of minority communities as indecorous or inappropriate when they attempt to speak of their concerns in technical forums.[12] We also examine a case study of the barriers placed in the path of a community in southern Mississippi as residents tried to voice their grievances after the explosion of a chemical plant near their homes.

"Hysterical Hispanic Housewives": Constructing the Indecorous Voice

Let me begin by illustrating what I mean by "construction of an **indecorous voice.**" By this, I simply mean the symbolic framing by some public officials of the voices of members of the public as inappropriate to the norms for speaking in regulatory forums and for the level of knowledge demanded by health and government agencies. Believing, for example, that a resident of a low-income community has violated these norms is a way of dismissing the public as unqualified to speak about technical matters. Rose Marie Augustine's story is typical of such dismissal by public officials.

Rose Marie Augustine's Story

On the south side of Tucson, Arizona, where Latino/a Americans and Native Americans are the main residents, chemicals from several industrial plants had seeped into the groundwater table. This contaminated the wells from which some 47,000 residents drew their drinking water. One of the residents, Rose Marie Augustine, described her own and her neighbors' fears: "We didn't know anything about what had happened to us. . . . We were never informed about what happens to people who become contaminated by drinking contaminated water. . . . We were suffering lots of cancers, and we thought, you know, my God, what's happening?" (Augustine, 1991). Environmental Protection Agency officials later confirmed the severity of the toxic chemicals that had been leaching from nearby Tucson industrial plants into their well water and listed this site as one the nation's priority "Superfund" sites for cleanup (Augustine, 1993, n.p.).

Prior to the EPA's official listing, however, residents from the south side struggled to make local officials listen to their fears and concerns. For example, Augustine (1993) reported that when residents met with local officials in 1985, the officials refused to address questions about the health effects of drinking well water. She said that when residents persisted, one county supervisor told them that "the people in the south side were obese, lazy, and had poor eating habits, that it was our lifestyle and not the TC [toxic chemicals] in the water that caused our health problems." Augustine said that one official "called us 'hysterical Hispanic housewives' when we appealed to him for help" (n.p.). (Augustine's account is typical of the narratives I described earlier, as community activists experience a heightened political awareness.)

Dismissal by public officials of community residents' complaints about environmental illness has occurred in other cases. For example, Roberts and Toffolon-Weiss (2001) reported that local officials in Louisiana's "Cancer Alley" dismissed complaints about illness from pollution as due to lifestyle or to eating high-fat food (p. 117). Earlier, Hays (1987) found that when community members offered bodily evidence of illness, they were often "belittled as the complaints of 'housewives'" (p. 200). As we saw in Chapter 1, such notions of the public sphere mistakenly assume a rational or technical mode of communication as the only permissible form of discourse in public forums.

Decorum and the Norms of Public Forums

The Tucson official's dismissal of Rose Marie Augustine's complaints suggests that Augustine had violated a norm or an expectation of appropriateness in speaking with government officials. This may appear strange at first, as it is the official's rudeness that surprises us. But the concerns of poor and minority residents are sometimes treated less seriously due to implicit norms for what counts as appropriate or reasonable in matters of environmental health and regulatory responsibilities. It is precisely this subtle barrier that environmental justice advocates continue to oppose as they work to build more democratic and inclusive communities.

In some ways, the unstated rules that operate in many forums addressing environmental problems pose a challenge to those who speak that reflects something akin to the ancient principle of decorum. **Decorum** was one of the virtues of style in the classical Greek and Latin rhetorical handbooks and is usually translated as "propriety" or "that which is fitting" for the particular audience and occasion. For example, the Roman rhetorician Cicero spoke of the "rare judgment" required for the wise speaker, one who is "able to speak in any way which the case requires" or in ways that are most "appropriate"; following the Greeks, he proposed, "let us call [this quality] *decorum* or 'propriety'" (Cicero, 1962, XX.69).

However, within the context of efforts by members of poor and minority communities to speak about technical matters to public officials, the principle of decorum has taken on a much more constraining, even demeaning, role. The norms for what is and is not appropriate in regulatory forums often construct the lay public's ways of speaking as indecorous or inappropriate to the norms of speaking and the level of knowledge demanded by health and government agencies. Although the members of an environmentally harmed community may speak at public hearings or at meetings with a local official, their standing, or the respect afforded them, may be constrained informally by the rules and expectations of agency procedures and norms for knowledge claims.

At this point, it might be useful to describe some of the informal requirements or expectations for speaking in regulatory and technical forums and the violations that encourage officials to construct an indecorous voice for many members of low-income communities.

Epistemic Standing and the Indecorous Voice

With the threat of exposure to chemical contamination, and with official denial or resistance, affected residents often become frustrated, disillusioned with authority, and angry. Ironically, such responses can be prompted by interaction with the very agencies whose official mandate is to help those who feel themselves to be at risk—for example, state or local health departments, the EPA, or state environmental offices. The individuals who become involved with these agencies often find themselves in a baffling environment of overlapping institutional jurisdictions, technical forums, and a language of risk assessment that speaks of "parts per million" of toxic substances.

These are unfamiliar contexts for most of us, not simply for the residents of low-income communities. Environmental sociologist Michael Edelstein (1988) explained, "What is lost [for residents in these communities] is their ability to participate directly in understanding and determining courses of action important to their lives" (p. 118). They are, in a sense "captured by [the] agencies upon which they become dependent for clarification and assistance" (p. 118).

This "capture" is enabled by many agency officials' tendency to frame the participation of the public within restricted parameters of agency procedures and norms. As we saw in Chapter 1, industry and government officials often try to move the grounding of environmental discussions from the public to the technical sphere, which privileges more "rational" forms of argument. This is also journalist William Greider's (1992) argument in his provocative book *Who Will Tell the People?* Greider wrote that technical forums too often exclude the lay public by their assumptions about what constitutes legitimate evidence in debates about environment and community health.

Nowhere is this more evident than in the very framing of the discourse that surrounds the category of acceptable risk discussed in Chapter 6. The idea of acceptable risk often stands at the center of a rhetorical struggle between aggrieved communities and regulatory authorities. Environmental educator Frances Lynn (1990) explained, "Public concerns may have as much to do with issues of equity, justice, and social responsibility as with a 10^{-6} possibility of contracting cancer" (p. 96). As long as authorities construe citizen testimony on matters of risk in the bipolar terms of expertise versus ignorance, they obscure critical differences between the claims of technical disciplines and the cultural rationality (Chapter 6) of residents' knowledge and experience.

The weight of past practices helps to explain why government agencies are sometimes reluctant to open public hearings or technical panels to more voices of aggrieved communities. Rosenbaum (1983) reported that officials often use technical criteria to restrict the testimony of lay witnesses so that the agency's decision making will not be hampered by what they regard as "an aroused and possibly ignorant public" (cited in Lynn, 1987, p. 359). Under such norms of decorum, for some citizens to speak is therefore to confront a painful dilemma. On the one hand, to enter discussions about toxicology, epidemiology, or the technical aspects of water quality is tacitly to accept the discursive boundaries within which concerns for family health or a sense of caution are seen as private or emotional matters. On the other hand, for worried parents or others to inject such private concerns into these conversations is to transgress powerful boundaries of technical knowledge, reason, and decorum and thus risk not being heard at all.

Indecorous in Mississippi: "The Evidence Is in My Body!"

Charlotte Keyes transgressed such a boundary. Keyes was a young African American woman in the small town of Columbia in southern Mississippi with whom I had worked in my role as president of the Sierra Club in the mid-1990s. Her story continues to motivate my own work now to document the obstacles to citizen involvement in decisions about their environments. Keyes and her neighbors had been living next to an abandoned chemical plant, owned by Reichhold Chemical, that had exploded years earlier. The explosion and fire spewed toxic fumes throughout the neighborhood. The residents also suspected that some of the barrels of chemicals abandoned by the company had leached into the yards of nearby homes and into tributaries of Columbia's drinking water sources. Many of Keyes's neighbors began to complain of unusual skin rashes and illnesses. Officials from the EPA and the mayor of Columbia initially dismissed the residents' complaints as unsubstantiated. No health assessment was conducted. Reichhold spokesperson Alec Van Ryan later acknowledged to local media, "I think everyone from the EPA on down will admit the initial communications with the community were nonexistent" (in Pender, 1993, p. 1).

Ultimately, Keyes organized her neighbors to speak at a meeting with officials from the federal Agency for Toxic Substances and Disease Registry (ATSDR), who had traveled to Columbia to propose a health study of residents. However, the ATSDR officials proposed only to sample residents' urine and test it for recent, acute exposure to toxins. The residents objected. They explained that their exposure had occurred years earlier, when the plant exploded, and had lasted over a period of years. Having done their homework, they insisted that the appropriate test was one that sampled blood and fatty tissues for evidence of long-term, or chronic, exposure. Keyes urged the ATSDR officials to adopt this approach because, she said, "The evidence is in my body!" (Charlotte Keyes, personal correspondence, September 12, 1995).

The officials refused this request, citing budgetary constraints. In turn, the Columbia residents felt stymied in their efforts to introduce the important personal evidence of their long-term exposure to chemicals that they believed was evident in their bodies. The meeting degenerated into angry exchanges and ended with an indefinite deferral of the plans to conduct a health study.[13]

Unfortunately, the tension between the ATSDR and the residents of Columbia, Mississippi, is not unusual. Too often, agency officials dismiss the complaints and recommendations of those facing risk of chemical exposure who are from low-income communities, believing that such people are emotional, unreliable, and irrational. This is one of the dangers of the highly popular Sandman model of risk (risk = hazard + outrage) that I described in Chapter 6: the tendency of industry and government officials to dismiss citizen complaints as outrage or simply the emotional or hysterical reactions of untrained residents. For example, in a study of public comments on the EPA's use of environmental impact analysis, political scientist Lynton Caldwell (1988) found that "public input into the EIA document was not regarded by government officials as particularly useful. . . . The public was generally perceived to be poorly informed on the issues and unsophisticated in considering risks and trade-offs. . . . Public participation was accepted as inevitable, but sometimes with great reluctance" (p. 80). I have overheard agency officials complain, after hearing reports of family illness or community members' fears, "This is very emotional, but where's the evidence?" "I've already heard this story," and simply, "This is not helpful."

Dismissing Indecorous Voices as NIMBYs

In such settings, citizens who object to the construction of an environmentally hazardous facility or who attribute ill health effects to a polluting plant are often constructed as **NIMBYs**, or "not in my backyard" critics. The phrase usually is meant as a dismissal of critics who object to the location of an industrial facility. The NIMBY label implies that such critics are concerned only about their own community and are therefore selfish and irresponsible. Edelstein (1988) observed that public officials view the NIMBY syndrome as "something of a social disease, a rabid and irrational rejection of sound technological progress" (p. 171). This view undercuts the moral authority of communities who object to being dumped upon insofar as it creates the impression that they would not stand up against such polluting industries if the chosen site were somewhere else.

The charge of NIMBY first arose in the early 1980s as a pejorative label to describe the efforts of well-to-do suburban homeowners who wished to exclude low- or moderate-income housing from their neighborhoods (Williams & Matheny, 1995). However, some officials began to apply the label NIMBY to the motives of environmental justice activists who opposed the construction of hazardous facilities in poor or minority communities. Often, those officials retorted that "it has to go somewhere." The charge implies that opponents of such facilities fail to suggest an alternative policy (that is, the facility is just placed somewhere else). In response, some advocacy groups such as the Center for Health, Environment and Justice (formerly called the Citizens' Clearinghouse for Hazardous Wastes) use the term **NIABY,** or "not in anybody's back yard" to describe their approach to environmentally just, sustainable communities.

In short, the construction of an indecorous voice—whether as one who is too emotional or as a NIMBY—functions to dismiss the informal standing of certain citizens and their ability to question the claims of public agencies, industries, or expert consultants. To be clear, I am not suggesting that the indecorous voice is the result of rhetorical incompetence, that is, a failure of marginal groups to find the right words with which to articulate a grievance. Instead, I am suggesting that the arrangements and procedures of power may undermine the rhetorical standing, the respect accorded to such groups, by too narrowly defining the acceptable rhetorical norms of environmental decision making.

The result is that citizens from poor and minority communities sometimes face what environmental sociologist Michael Reich described as **toxic politics** (1991). This is the dismissal of a community's moral and communicative standing, the right of residents to matter within the discursive boundaries in which decisions affecting their fate are deliberated. The phrase refers not only to the politics of locating or cleaning up chemical facilities, but to the "poisonous" nature of such politics on occasions.

The Global Movement for Climate Justice

In recent years, the concern for environment justice has begun to reach beyond the United States as a global movement for **climate justice** views the impacts of global warming from the frame of social justice, human rights, and concerns for labor and indigenous peoples. In ways similar to the criticism of mainstream environmentalism in the United States, social justice activists and advocates for indigenous peoples and the poor in countries throughout Asia, South America, Africa, and the Pacific Island nations argue that climate change is not simply an "environmental" issue. The movement for "climate justice"[14] asserts that global warming not only impacts disproportionately the most vulnerable regions and peoples of the planet, but that these peoples and nations often are excluded from participation in the forums addressing this problem.

Both climate scientists and advocates for climate justice generally agree that "the greatest brunt of climate change's effects will be felt (and are being felt) by the world's poorest people" (Roberts, 2007, p. 295). In 2007, the Intergovernmental Panel on Climate Change (IPCC) predicted that "hundreds of millions of people in developing nations will face natural disasters, water shortages and hunger due to the effects of climate change" (Adam, Walker, & Benjamin, 2007, para. 5). The IPCC chair Dr Rajendra Pachauri stated that "wheat production in India is already in decline, for no other reason than climate change" and that rises in temperatures could affect agricultural crops and spread disease (quoted in Adam, Walker, & Benjamin, 2007, para. 9, 10).

Equally true, the voices of those likely to be most affected by global climate change are usually not part of the conversation about solutions. Environmental studies scholar Dale Jamieson (2007) notes that "seventy million farmers and their families in Bangladesh will lose their livelihoods when their rice paddies are inundated by seawater. Yet despite the vast number of people around the world who will suffer from climate change, most of them are not included when decisions are made (p. 92). For this reason, "participatory justice is also important at the global level" (p. 92). There is also a cruel irony in this exclusion: Members of the European United Left/Nordic Green Left (GUE/NGL) Group in the European Parliament point out that poor nations do not emit high levels of greenhouse gases, the major cause of recent global warming. Yet, "those who emit the least, especially in Africa, will have the greatest burden to bear" (GUE/NGL, 2007, p. 9).

"Climate Justice": A New Discursive Frame

As concerns emerged from local communities and regions that are beginning to feel the effects of climate change—particularly in Asia and Africa—various nongovernmental organizations (NGOs) and informal groups from these areas began to build alliances, as well as coordinate activities with groups in Europe and the United States. One of the most consequential developments of this movement building would be the elaboration of "climate justice" as a new discursive frame.

An initial effort occurred in November, 2000 when thousands of grassroots organizations and climate activists met in the Hague, Netherlands, at the Climate Justice Summit. The summit was an alternative forum to a UN meeting on climate change and was intended as a discursive space "to raise the critical issues that are not being addressed by the world's governments" (Bullard, 2000, para. 5). Two other important organizing efforts occurred when local activists and international NGOs met alongside official UN-sponsored sessions on climate change in Bali, Indonesia, in August 2002, and New Delhi, India, in October 2002.

In Bali, a coalition of international NGOs, including the National Alliance of People's Movements (India), CorpWatch (United States), Greenpeace International, Third World Network (Malaysia), Indigenous Environmental Network (North America), and groundwork (South Africa), crafted one of the first declarations redefining climate change from the perspective of environmental justice and human rights. Meeting alongside the United Nations' preparatory negotiations for the Earth Summit in Bali in June 2002, the coalition developed the **Bali Principles of Climate Justice**, pledging to "build an international movement of all peoples for Climate Justice" (Bali Principles of Climate Justice, 2002, para. 19). The effort would be based on certain principles, echoing the 1991 "Principles of Environmental Justice" (see earlier). For example, the Bali Principles began by "affirming the sacredness of Mother Earth, ecological unity, and the interdependence of all species, Climate Justice insist that communities have the right to be free from climate change, its related impacts and other forms of ecological destruction" (para. 20).

One the consequences of the Bali Principles, as well as other declarations, was to shift "the discursive framework of climate change from a scientific-technical debate to one about ethics focused on human rights and justice" (Agyeman, Doppelt, & Lynn, 2007, p. 121). An important moment in this shift came on October 28, 2002, when more than 1,500 individuals—farmers, fisher people, the poor, Indigenous Peoples, and youth—from more than 20 countries marched for "climate justice" in the streets of New Delhi, India (Roberts, 2007, p. 296). The occasion was a meeting of the grassroots Climate Justice Summit, an effort to organize on an international scale. Representatives from affected communities gathered "to provide testimony to the fact that climate change is a reality whose effects are already being felt around the world" (Delhi Climate Justice Declaration, 2002, para. 1).

The culmination of the summit was the **Delhi Climate Justice Declaration**, which declared that "climate change is a human-rights issue" and expressed the resolve of those at the summit "to actively build a movement from the communities" to address climate change from a social justice perspective (para. 12). (See "FYI: Delhi Climate Justice Declaration.")

Other international gatherings and declarations followed, including the Durban Declaration on Carbon Trading (2004), a critique of proposed market schemes for trading greenhouse gas emissions; and the recent "People's Declaration for Climate Justice" (Sumberklampok Declaration), in Bali, Indonesia (2007), an effort to influence the start of negotiations among the world's nations of a new post-Kyoto treaty. Echoing these declarations in the United States, the Congressional Black Caucus Foundation issued a series of reports in 2004 and 2005 linking climate change and race, including *African-Americans and Climate Change: An Unequal Burden* and *Climate Change and Extreme Weather Events: An Unequal Burden on African Americans*, a response to the impacts of Hurricanes Katrina and Rita.

☞ **FYI** **Delhi Climate Justice Declaration (excerpts)**

October 28, 2002:

Communities from around the world gathered at the Climate Justice Summit in New Delhi on October 26 and 27, 2002 to provide testimony to the fact that climate change is a reality whose effects are already being felt around the world. . . .

- We recognize that the impacts of climate change are disproportionately felt by the poor, women, youth, coastal peoples, indigenous peoples, fisherfolk, dalits, farmers and the elderly;
- We recognize that climate change is being caused primarily by industrialized nations and transnational corporations;
- We recognize that local communities, affected people and indigenous peoples have been kept out of the global processes to address climate change;
- We recognize that market-based mechanisms and technological "fixes" currently being promoted by transnational corporations are false solutions and are exacerbating the problem;
- We recognize that unsustainable production and consumption practices are at the root of this and other global environmental problems; . . .
- We recognize that the impacts of climate change threaten food sovereignty and the security of livelihoods of natural resource-based local economies;

We, representatives of the poor and the marginalized of the world, representing fishworkers, farmers, Indigenous Peoples, Dalits, the poor and the youth, resolve to actively build a movement from the communities that will address the issue of climate change from a human rights, social justice and labour perspective. We affirm that climate change is a human rights issue- it affects our livelihoods, our health, our children and out natural resources. We will build alliances across states and borders to oppose climate change inducing patterns and advocate for and practice sustainable development. . . . Our World is Not for Sale!

Climate Justice "Movement Building": Online and at the Grassroots

As a result of their exclusion from the forums addressing climate change, climate justice groups created alternative structures for communication—at regional summits, as we saw earlier; on online networks to coordinate activities and update activists and organizations across regions and borders; and on the ground, as local activists organized around sites important to climate justice.

At the summits in New Delhi, Bali, and elsewhere, climate activists emphasized the need to create lines of communication across borders and within regions to build a "movement" for climate justice. At the pivotal Bali organizing event in 2002, climate activists resolved "to begin to build an international movement of all peoples for Climate Justice," based on the principles in the Bali declaration (para. 19). The Delhi Climate Justice Declaration similarly concluded, "We, representatives of the poor and the marginalized of the world . . . resolve to actively build a movement . . . that will address the issue of climate change from a human rights, social justice, and labour perspective" (para. 12). And, again, in the Durban Declaration on Carbon Trading in 2004, activists recommitted themselves "to help build a global grassroots movement for climate justice" (para. 9).

The emerging movement itself is sustained largely online but helps to support grassroots actions at sites of importance to climate justice. Some online networks are hosted by existing sites. For example, the India Climate Justice Forum is hosted by the India Resource Center, a project of Global Resistance, whose goal is "to strengthen the movement against corporate globalization by supporting and linking local, grassroots struggles against globalization around the world" (www.indiaresource.org).

On the other hand, the climate justice movement has initiated (and continues to bring online), new networks, blogs, and information sites of its own. An important network is the London-based Rising Tide Coalition for Climate Justice (http://risingtide.org.uk), consisting of environmental and social justice groups from around the world, especially Europe (Roberts, 2007), as well as the Rising Tide North American network (www.risingtidenorthamerica.org). Rising Tide grew out of the efforts of groups who came together to organize events alongside a UN climate conference in The Hague in 2000. Other prominent online networks are the Third World Network (TWN) at http://www.twnside.org.sq; Environmental Justice Climate Change Initiative (EJCC) at http://www.ejcc.org; and Climate Justice Now!, an active blog with links to a wide coalition of climate justice sites, at http://climatejustice.blogspot.com.

A recent site, launched in 2008, in eight languages, is 350.org, at http://www.350.org. The site's name 350 is "the number that is the safe line for our global climate and a start line for a global movement," that is, 350 parts per million of carbon dioxide in the atmosphere. Like many of the other online sites, 350.org provides daily updates, video uploads from local activists, documenting of activities in local communities, and analyses of official proposals. As I was working on this section, I checked 350.org's update for December 12, 2008. It came from the latest UN climate conference in Poznan, Poland:

> Forty five minutes ago Al Gore set the new bottom line for the climate debate— thanks to your hard work for the last year.
>
> Giving the climactic speech at the Poznan global warming conference, Gore set the new bottom line for action on global warming, right where we've been suggesting: 350 parts per million. The old goal of 450 parts per million is "inadequate," he said. We "need to toughen that goal to 350 parts per million."

While the climate justice movement is largely made up of "a series of coalitions, which sometimes appear to exist mostly . . . on a website" (Roberts, 2007, p. 297), it clearly has other important strengths. These include "a 'master frame' in which to claim injustice, substantial but still emergent cross-border links, some key resources in these networking groups, grassroots energy, and academic skills" (p. 297). Much of the "grassroots energy" of the movement comes from the creative, direct actions of local groups as well as the initiatives of larger organizations. Roberts (2007) cites a tactic used by CorpWatch, a San Francisco-based group that is attempting to "redefine the issue of global warming as a question of local and global justice" (p. 294). In 2001, CorpWatch brought together two environmentalists from different countries to the United States for a Climate Justice Tour—Sarah James, a leader of the Gwich'in tribe northern Alaska and Canada, and Oronto Douglas from Nigeria's Niger Delta. The purpose of the tour—which met with oil-affected communities in the San Francisco area as well as in Louisiana and Texas—was to "bring to life the connections between the local effects of oil and the global dynamics of climate change" (quoted in Roberts, 2007, p. 294).

More recently, climate justice activists dramatically publicized the links between global warming and the banks that finance the mining of coal, a major source of greenhouse gases when they blockaded the Bank of America in Asheville, North Carolina. (See Figure 8.3.) An online news site, Asheville Indymedia, reported the event:

> Two activists locked down inside the main lobby and other activists blockaded the entrance to the downtown branch of the Bank of America. The protest included a large, lively group of concerned citizens dressed as canaries and polar bears. Activists carried signs and banners that read: "Bank of America Stop Funding Climate Change," "Bank of America Stop Mountaintop Removal," . . . [and] "Bank of America Climate Criminal." (Climate Convergence, 2007, para. 2)

Figure 8.3   Climate justice activists are dramatically publicizing the links between global warming and banks, corporations, and other institutions that finance or contribute to the human-caused sources of global warming.

As with the Asheville protests, activists often upload reports, photos, and videos of their grassroots actions online. For example, when climate justice activists invaded the Washington, D.C., offices of Environmental Defense (ED), a U.S. environmental organization, in December 2008, the news was quickly spread by Rising Tide of North America and other online sites. The action occurred on the opening day of the UN climate conference in Poznan, Poland, and was intended to protest ED's "key role in promoting the discredited approach of carbon trading as a solution to climate change" (Rising Tide, 2008).

The ultimate effectiveness of the movement for climate justice—and the efforts by some governments—in persuading the United States and China, and other major emitters of greenhouse gases, to change course before it is too late is still uncertain. Climate scientists at the Mauna Loa observatory in Hawaii have sounded new alarms: "CO_2 levels in the atmosphere now stand at 387 parts per million . . . up almost 40% since the industrial revolution and the highest for at least the last 650,000 years" (Adam, 2008, para. 2). As I write, international delegations are still negotiating a post-Kyoto treaty to address future climate-affecting emissions. Further negotiations are planned for Copenhagen in late 2009. The decisions being made there and in the next two to three years will undoubtedly be consequential for future generations.

SUMMARY

As the multiracial, community-based environmental justice and climate justice movements introduce new voices into the public dialogue, they have begun to challenge traditional views of the environment as a place apart—as wilderness or natural areas. In doing so, these movements reveal the limitations of these views, an antagonism that allows other voices to be heard and other relationships to the environment to be voiced. The discourse about the meaning of the environment as including the places where people live, work, play, and learn has nurtured not only a more expansive vision of environment but also a demand for environmental justice: (1) a call to recognize and halt the disproportionate burdens imposed on poor and minority communities by environmentally harmful conditions, (2) more inclusive opportunities for those who are most affected to be heard in the decisions made by public agencies and the wider environmental movement, and (3) a vision of environmentally healthy, economically sustainable communities.

Finally, both environmental justice and climate groups and the traditional environmental movement are beginning to discover ways to work together—a heartening sign. Nevertheless, as Robert Gottlieb (2003) observes, there remains a challenging question: "Can mainstream and alternative groups find a common language, a shared history, a common conceptual and organizational home?" (p. 254). The challenge is complex as diverse groups explore the implications of redefining *environment* not only as human communities and natural spaces, but also as the Earth's climate and its affects on all. In their book *Environmental Justice and Environmentalism: The Social Justice Challenge to the Environmental Movement*, Pezzullo and Sandler (2007) pose similar questions: "Do the events of the past decade signal future directions for . . . [these] movements? Do they adumbrate a collective or unified movement in which there is a widespread appreciation of the importance of social justice to environmentalism and of environmentalism to social justice?" (p. 13).

These are difficult questions for environmental justice and traditional green groups as well as the new movement for climate justice. But even as each addresses these concerns, a more robust meaning of the environment already is emerging in the struggles of these movements, a vision of "transformative alliances" (Gelobter et al., 2005, p. 26). Michel Gelobter, executive director of Redefining Progress, and colleagues recently issued a provocative challenge in *The Soul of Environmentalism* to "break the unwritten gag rule about race and class" in revisioning environmentalism:

> Environmentalism, like poetry, has a soul deeper and more eternal than the one described by its examiners. It's a soul tied deeply to human rights and social justice, and this tie has been nurtured by the Environmental Justice and Sustainability movements for the past 20 years. We are writing to explore this soul . . . and to examine the intermingled roots of social change movements. These roots, these rules and this soul together hold the key to environmentalism's new life. (Gelobter et al., 2005, p. 6)

In the end, nurturing such transformational alliances may offer the best hope for creating a socially just, ecologically sustainable society.

KEY TERMS

Communication-Related Concepts

Decorum: One of the virtues of style in the classical Greek and Latin rhetorical handbooks; usually translated as "propriety" or "that which is fitting" for the particular audience and occasion.

Indecorous voice: The symbolic framing by some public officials of the voices of others as inappropriate to the norms for speaking in regulatory forums and for the level of knowledge demanded by health and government agencies; a way of dismissing the public as unqualified to speak about technical matters.

Toxic politics: Term introduced by sociologist Michael Reich (1991) that refers to the dismissal of a community's moral and communicative standing in deliberations about chemical pollution.

Toxic tours: "Non-commercial expeditions organized and facilitated by people who reside in areas that are polluted by toxics, places that Bullard (1993) has named 'human sacrifice zones' . . . Residents of these areas guide outsiders, or tourists, through where they [residents] live, work, and play in order to witness their struggle" (Pezzullo, 2004, p. 236). (See **sacrifice zones.**)

Environment-Related Concepts

Bali Principles of Climate Justice: One of the first declarations redefining climate change from the perspective of environmental justice and human rights, crafted by a coalition of international NGOs in Bali, Indonesia, in June 2002.

Climate justice: Views the impacts of climate change from the perspectives of social justice, human rights, and concerns for labor and indigenous peoples. The movement for climate justice asserts that global warming not only impacts disproportionately the most vulnerable regions and peoples of the planet, but that these peoples and nations often are excluded from participation in the forums addressing this problem.

Delhi Climate Justice Declaration: Final declaration of Climate Justice Summit, New Delhi, 2002, which declared, "Climate change is a humans-rights issue;" also resolved "to actively build a movement from the communities" to address climate change from a social justice perspective.

Disparate impact: Term used to denote the discrimination resulting from environmental hazards in minority communities; adopted from the 1964 Civil Rights Act, which used it to recognize forms of discrimination that result from the disproportionate burdens experienced by some groups regardless of the conscious intention of others in their decisions or behaviors.

Environmental justice: As used by community activists and scholars studying the environmental justice movement, the term refers to (1) calls to recognize and halt the disproportionate burdens imposed on poor and minority communities by environmentally harmful conditions, (2) more inclusive opportunities for those who are most affected to be heard in the decisions made by public agencies and the wider environmental movement, and (3) a vision of environmentally healthy, economically sustainable communities.

Environmental racism: Term used to denote the persistent pattern of locating toxics in poor and minority neighborhoods; defined by Benjamin Chavis at the 1991 First People of Color National Environmental Leadership Summit as "racial discrimination in environmental policymaking and the enforcement of regulations and laws, the deliberate targeting of people of color communities for toxic waste facilities, the official sanctioning of the life-threatening presence of poisons and pollutants in our communities, and the history of excluding people of color from leadership in the environmental movement" (quoted in Di Chiro, 1996, p. 304). Also refers to the disproportionate impact of environmental harms on communities of color. (See also **disparate impact**.)

Executive Order on Environmental Justice: Issued by President Clinton in 1994, Executive Order 12898, "Federal Actions to Address Environmental Justice in Minority Populations and Low-Income Populations," instructed each federal agency "to make achieving environmental justice part of its mission by identifying and addressing . . . disproportionately high and adverse human health or environmental effects of its programs, policies, and activities on minority populations and low-income populations in the United States" (Clinton, 1994, p. 7629).

First National People of Color Environmental Leadership Summit: A key moment in the new movement for environmental justice, when delegates from local communities and national leaders from social justice, religious, environmental, and civil rights groups met in Washington, D.C., in October 1991.

National Environmental Justice Advisory Council (NEJAC): A federal advisory committee in the Environmental Protection Agency that is intended to provide the EPA administrator with independent advice, consultation, and recommendations related to environmental justice.

NIABY: Acronym for "not in anybody's back yard," a term used to describe the response of environmental justice advocates to the charge of being a NIMBY ("not in my backyard"); used to suggest an alternate approach to environmentally just, or sustainable, communities.

NIMBY: Acronym for "not in my backyard," usually meant to dismiss critics of the location of an industrial facility; implies that critics are concerned only about their own communities and are therefore selfish. (See **NIABY.**)

"Principles of Environmental Justice": Seventeen principles articulating an expansive vision for communities of people of color and the right to participate directly in decisions about their environments, adopted by delegates at the First People of Color National Environmental Summit in 1991.

Sacrifice zones: Term coined by sociologist Robert Bullard (1993) to denote communities that share two characteristics: "(1) They already have more than their share of environmental problems and polluting industries, and (2) they are still attracting new polluters" (p. 12).

DISCUSSION QUESTIONS

1. Does environmental racism exist? What evidence would you regard as compelling proof that it does or does not exist in a particular situation?

2. Should we as a society be willing to accept some dangers, and even deaths, in order to enjoy the benefits of advanced industrial society? Who in society most often accepts these burdens? Who most often enjoys the benefits of industrial society?

3. Gottlieb poses a deeply challenging question: "Can mainstream and alternative groups find a common language, a shared history, a common conceptual and organizational home?" (in Warren, 2003, p. 254). What do you think? How effectively can traditional green groups and activists from poor and minority neighborhoods work together on problems of environmental injustice in the future?

4. Are local opponents to facilities such as hazardous waste incinerators merely NIMBYs who are motivated by a not-in-my-back-yard attitude? If not there, where would they be located? Should society develop alternatives that go beyond simply burning or burying toxic wastes? What might these alternatives be?

5. Should ordinary citizens be permitted to testify at hearings where a decision pivots on technical expertise? Do members of a local community have experience or knowledge that offers a "local expertise," or should they be asked to defer to those with technical expertise?

6. Is global warming a human rights or a social justice problem, as well as an environmental problem?

7. Are world leaders responding quickly enough to address the more severely expected impacts of climate change? To what extent do climate justice online networks or local, direct actions influence nations' official actions?

NOTES

1. I am indebted to Dr. Phaedra Pezzullo of Indiana University for permission to cite material from our unpublished paper, "Re-Articulating 'Environment': Rhetorical Invention, Subaltern Counterpublics, and the Movement for Environmental Justice" (Cox & Pezzulla, 2001).

2. In her excellent history *African-American Environmental Thought*, Kimberly K. Smith (2007) argues that slavery and the racism of the post-Emancipation period set the foundation for African Americans' conflicted relationship to the land "by coercing their labor, restricting their ability to own land, and impairing their ability to interpret the landscape" (p. 8).

3. In 1978, residents of Love Canal discovered "that Hooker Chemical Corporation . . . had dumped 200 tons of a toxic, dioxin-laden chemical and 21,600 tons of various other chemicals into Love Canal. . . . In 1953, Hooker had filled in the canal, smoothed out the land, and sold it to the town school board for $1.00. . . . [Motivated by the harmful health effects that developed as a result of these chemicals, local residents, led by Lois Marie Gibbs] organized and won evacuation . . . in 1980" (Gibbs, 1995, p. xvii). For background on Gibbs's story, see Chapter 1.

4. Hays adapted this phrase from the title of Rachel Carson's first book, *The Sea Around Us* (New York: Oxford University Press, 1950, 1951).

5. Di Chiro (1996) noted, "Eventually, environmental and social justice organizations such as Greenpeace, the National Health Law Program, the Center for Law in the Public Interest, and Citizens for a Better Environment would join [the] Concerned Citizens' campaign to stop [the proposed facility]" (p. 527, note 2).

6. Chavis's claim of having coined the term *environmental racism* has been disputed; some activists in Warren County insist that they used this phrase first.

7. The 10 groups were the Environmental Defense Fund, Friends of the Earth, the Izaak Walton League, the National Audubon Society, the National Parks and Conservation Association, the National Wildlife Federation, the Natural Resources Defense Council, the Sierra Club, the Sierra Club Legal Defense Fund (now Earth Justice), and the Wilderness Society.

8. I was fortunate to have the opportunity to attend and participate in the sessions that included leaders of traditional environmental organizations.

9. The Dickerson video was one of a series of 60-second public service announcements produced by Greenpeace U.S.A. and aired by the VH-1 cable music channel throughout Earth Day 1990. The video ads showcased the stories of individuals of different ages, sex, and ethnicity who had worked to protect their communities and local ecosystems from environmental degradation.

10. For example, see the exchange of views between environmental justice leaders and Sierra Club officials in "A Place at the Table: A Sierra Club Roundtable on Race, Justice, and the Environment," *Sierra* (May/June, 1993), 51–58, 90–91. In the decade following this discussion, the nation's oldest environmental organization would go on to establish a Grassroots Environmental Justice Organizing Program, involving volunteers and a network of environmental justice organizers to work—at the invitation of local communities—with African American, Latino/a, and rural Appalachian communities as well as Native American tribes.

11. Pezzullo (2007) observes that, though not necessarily called "toxic tours," tours of industrial toxic sites have existed since the 1960s (p. 4).

12. Portions of this section are drawn from a paper that I presented at the Fifth Biennial Conference on Communication and Environment (Cox, 2001).

13. Reichhold Chemical ultimately offered to assist community members by helping to fund a health study and a community advisory panel to assist in decisions about the polluted site.

14. Roberts (2007) notes the term *climate justice* apparently was first used in academic literature as early as E. B. Weiss (1989) and H. Shue (1992).

REFERENCES

Adam, D. (2008, May 12). World CO_2 levels at record high, scientists warn. *Guardian.co.uk*. Retrieved December 14, 2008, from http://www.guardian.co.uk/environment/2008/may/12.

Adam, D., Walker, P., & Benjamin, A. (2007, September 18). Grim outlook for poor countries in climate report. *Guardian.co.uk*. Retrieved December 12, 2008, from http://www.guardian.co.uk/environment/2007/sep/18.

Agyeman, J., Doppelt, B., & Lynn, K. (2007). The climate-justice link: Communicating risk with low-income and minority audiences. In S. C. Moser & L. Dilling, (Eds.), *Communicating a climate for change: Communicating climate change and facilitating social change* (pp. 119–138). Cambridge, UK: Cambridge University Press.

Alston, D. (1990). *We speak for ourselves: Social justice, race, and environment.* Washington, DC: Panos Institute.

Alston, D. (1991). Remarks in *Proceedings: The First National People of Color Environmental Leadership Summit.* New York: United Church of Christ Commission for Racial Justice.

Augustine, R. M. (Speaker). (1991). *Documentary highlights of the First National People of Color Environmental Leadership Conference* [Videotape]. Washington, DC: United Church of Christ Commission for Racial Justice.

Augustine, R. M. (Speaker). (1993, October 21–24). *Environmental justice: Continuing the dialogue* [Cassette recording]. Recorded at the Third Annual Meeting of the Society of Environmental Journalists, Durham, NC.

Austin, R., & Schill, M. (1994). Black, brown, red and poisoned. In R. D. Bullard (Ed.), *Unequal protection: Environmental justice and communities of color* (pp. 53–76). San Francisco: Sierra Club Books.

Bali Principles of Climate Justice. (2002). Retrieved December 11, 2008, from http://www.ejnet.org.

Bullard, R. D. (1993). Introduction. In R. D. Bullard (Ed.), *Confronting environmental racism: Voices from the grassroots* (pp. 7–13). Boston: South End Press.

Bullard, R. D. (Ed.). (1994). *Unequal protection: Environmental justice and communities of color.* San Francisco: Sierra Club Books.

Bullard, Robert D. (2000, November 21). Climate justice and people of color. Retrieved May 25, 2009, from www.ejrc.cau.edu/climatechgpoc.html.

Bullard, R. D., Mohai, P., Saha, R., & Wright, B. (2007, March). *Toxic wastes and race at twenty, 1987–2007.* Cleveland, OH: United Church of Christ. Retrieved December 14, 2008, from http://www.ejrc.cau.edu.

Bullard, R. D., & Wright, B. H. (1987). Environmentalism and the politics of equity: Emergent trends in the black community. *Mid-American Review of Sociology, 12,* 21–37.

Caldwell, L. K. (1988). Environmental impact analysis (EIA): Origins, evolution, and future directions. *Policy Studies Review, 8,* 75–83.

Carson, R. (1962). *Silent spring.* Greenwich, CT: Fawcett Crest.

Chavis, B. F., & Lee, C. (1987*). Toxic wastes and race in the United States: A national report on the racial and socio-economic characteristics of communities with hazardous waste sites.* New York: Commission for Racial Justice, United Church of Christ.

Cicero, M. T. (1962). *Orator* (Rev. ed.). (H. M. Hubell & G. L. Hendrickson, Trans.). Cambridge, MA: Harvard University Press.

Climate Convergence. (2007, August 13). *Activists block Bank of America in downtown Asheville.* Retrieved December 10, 2008, from http://asheville.indymedia.org.

Clinton, W. J. (1994, February 16). Federal actions to address environmental justice in minority populations and low-income populations. Executive Order 12898 of February 14, 1994. *Federal Register, 59,* 7629.

Cole, L. W., & Foster, S. R. (2001). *From the ground up: Environmental racism and the rise of the environmental justice movement.* New York: New York University Press.

Cox, J. R. (2001). Reclaiming the "indecorous" voice: Public participation by low-income communities in environmental decision making. In C. B. Short & D. Hardy-Short (Eds.), *Proceedings of the Fifth Biennial Conference on Communication and Environment* (pp. 21–31). Flagstaff: Northern Arizona University School of Communication.

Delhi Climate Justice Declaration. (2002). India Climate Justice Forum. Delhi, India: India Resource Center. Retrieved December 11, 2008, from http://www.indiaresource.org.

Di Chiro, G. (1996). Nature as community: The convergence of environment and social justice. In W. Cronon (Ed.), *Uncommon ground: Rethinking the human place in nature* (pp. 298–320). New York: Norton.

Di Chiro, G. (1998). Environmental justice from the grassroots: Reflections on history, gender, and expertise. In D. Faber (Ed.), *The struggle for ecological democracy: Environmental justice movements in the United States* (pp. 104–136). New York: Guilford Press.

Duke, L. (2007, March 20). A well of pain: Their water was poisoned by chemicals. Was their treatment poisoned by racism? *The Washington Post,* p. C1.

Durban Declaration on Carbon Trading. (2004, October 10). Glenmore Centre, Durban, South Africa. Retrieved March 1, 2009, from http://www.carbontradewatch.org/Durban.

Edelstein, M. R. (1988). *Contaminated communities: The social and psychological impacts of residential toxic exposure.* Boulder, CO: Westview.

Ferris, D. (Speaker). (1993, October 21–24). *Environmental justice: Continuing the dialogue* [Cassette recording]. Recorded at the Third Annual Meeting of the Society of Environmental Journalists, Durham, NC.

Gelobter, M., Dorsey, M., Fields, L., Goldtooth, T., Mendiratta, A., Moore, R., Morello-Frosh, R., Shepard, P., & Torres, G. (2005, May 23). *The soul of environmentalism: Rediscovering transformational politics in the 21st century.* Oakland, CA: Redefining Progress. Retrieved May 26, 2005, from http://www.soulofenvironmentalism.org.

Gibbs, L. M. (1995). *Dying from dioxin: A citizen's guide to reclaiming our health and rebuilding democracy.* Boston, MA: South End Press.

Gottlieb, R. (1993). *Forcing the spring: The transformation of the American environmental movement.* Washington, DC: Island Press.

Gottlieb, R. (2002). *Environmentalism unbound: Exploring new pathways for change.* Cambridge, MA: MIT Press.

Gottlieb, R. (2003). Reconstructing environmentalism: Complex movements, diverse roots. In L. S. Warren (Ed.), *American environmental history* (pp. 245–256). Malden, MA: Blackwell.

Greenpeace. (1990, April). *Ordinary people, doing extraordinary things.* [Videotape]. Public service announcement broadcast on VH-1 Channel.

Greider, W. (1992). *Who will tell the people? The betrayal of American democracy.* New York: Simon & Schuster.

GUE/NGL File. (2007, June 14). *Climate change and developing countries: Who pays the price?* Brussels: Report of the hearing organized by the GUE/NGL European Parliament. Retrieved December 12, 2008, from http://guengl.org.

Harvey, D. (1996). *Justice, nature, and the geography of difference.* Malden, MA: Blackwell.

Hays, S. P. (1987). *Beauty, health, and permanence: Environmental politics in the United States, 1955–1985.* Cambridge, UK: Cambridge University Press.

Jamieson, D. (2007). Justice: The heart of environmentalism. In P. C. Pezzullo & R. Sandler (Eds.), *Environmental justice and environmentalism: The social justice challenge to the environmental movement* (pp. 85–101). Cambridge, MA: MIT Press.

Kazis, R., & Grossman, R. L. (1991). *Fear at work: Job blackmail, labor, and the environment.* Philadelphia: New Society.

Lavelle, M., & Coyle, M. (1992, September 21). Unequal protection: The racial divide in environmental law. *National Law Journal,* S1, S2.

Lynn, F. M. (1987). Citizen involvement in hazardous waste sites: Two North Carolina access stories. *Environmental Impact Assessment and Review, 7,* 347–361.

Lynn, F. M. (1990, April). Public participation in risk management decisions. *Issues in Health and Safety, 1*(2), 95–101.

Moser, S. C., & Dilling, L. (Eds.). (2007). *Communicating a climate for change: Communicating climate change and facilitating social change.* Cambridge, UK: Cambridge University Press.

National Environmental Justice Advisory Council Subcommittee on Waste and Facility Siting. (1996). *Environmental justice, urban revitalization, and brownfields: The search for authentic signs of hope.* (Report Number EPA 500-R-96–002). Washington, DC: U.S. Environmental Protection Agency.

Office of Inspector General. (2004, March 1). *EPA needs to consistently implement the intent of the executive order on environmental justice.* Washington, DC: Environmental Protection Agency. Retrieved March 1, 2009, from http://www.epa.gov/oig/reports.

Pender, G. (1993, June 1). Residents still not satisfied: Plant cleanup fails to ease Columbia fears. *Hattiesburg* [MS] *American,* p. 1.

People's Declaration for Climate Justice (Sumberklampok Declaration). (2007, December 7). Bali, Indonesia. Retrieved March 1, 2009, from http://peoplesclimatemovement.net.

Pezzullo, P. C. (2001). Performing critical interruptions: Rhetorical invention and narratives of the environmental justice movement. *Western Journal of Communication, 64,* 1–25.

Pezzullo, P. C. (2003). Touring "Cancer Alley," Louisiana: Performances of community and memory for environmental justice. *Text and Performance Quarterly, 23,* 226–252.

Pezzullo, P. C. (2004). Toxic tours: Communicating the "presence" of chemical contamination. In S. P. Depoe, J. W. Delicath, & M.-F. A. Elsenbeer (Eds.), *Communication and public participation in environmental decision making* (pp. 235–254). Albany: State University of New York Press.

Pezzullo, P. C. (2007). *Toxic tours: Rhetorics of pollution, travel and environmental justice.* Tuscaloosa: University of Alabama Press.

Pezzullo, P. C., & Sandler, R. (Eds.). (2007)). *Environmental justice and environmentalism: The social justice challenge to the environmental movement.* Cambridge, MA: MIT Press.

Proceedings: The First People of Color National Environmental Leadership Summit. (1991, October 24–27). Washington, DC: United Church of Christ Commission for Racial Justice.

Pulido, L. (1996). *Environmentalism and economic justice: Two Chicano struggles in the southwest.* Tucson: University of Arizona Press.

Reich, M. R. (1991). *Toxic politics: Responding to chemical disasters.* Ithaca: Cornell University Press.

Rising Tide North America. (2008, December 1). *Climate activists invade DC offices of Environmental defense.* Retrieved December 14, 2008, from http://www.risingtide northamerica.org.

Roberts, J. T. (2007). Globalizing environmental justice. In P. C. Pezzullo & R. Sandler (Eds.), *Environmental justice and environmentalism: The social justice challenge to the environmental movement* (pp. 285–307). Cambridge, MA: MIT Press.

Roberts, J. T., & Toffolon-Weiss, M. M. (2001). *Chronicles from the environmental justice frontline.* Cambridge, UK: Cambridge University Press.

Rosenbaum, W. (1983). The politics of public participation in hazardous waste management. In J. P. Lester & A. O. Bowman (Eds.), *The politics of hazardous waste management* (pp. 176–195). Durham, NC: Duke University Press.

Schwab, J. (1994). *Deeper shades of green: The rise of blue-collar and minority environmentalism in America.* San Francisco: Sierra Club Books.

Senecah, S. L. (2004). The trinity of voice: The role of practical theory in planning and evaluating the effectiveness of environmental participatory processes. In S. P. DePoe, J. W. Delicath, & M-F. A. Elsenbeer (Eds.), *Communication and public participation in environmental decision making* (pp.13–33). Albany: State University of New York Press.

Shue, H. (1992). The unavoidability of justice. In A. Hurrell & B. Kingsbury (Eds.), *The international politics of the environment* (pp. 373–397). Oxford, UK: Oxford University Press.

Smith, K. K. (2007). *African-American environmental thought.* Lawrence: University Press of Kansas.

SouthWest Organizing Project. (1990, March 16). Letter to the "Group of Ten" national environmental organizations. Albuquerque, NM. Retrieved March 1, 2009, from http://soa.utexas.edu.

U.S. General Accounting Office. (1983). *Siting of hazardous waste landfills and their correlation with racial and economic status of surrounding communities.* Washington, DC: U.S. General Accounting Office.

Warren, L. S. (2003). *American environmental history.* Malden, MA, and Oxford, UK: Blackwell.

Weiss, E. B. (1989*). In fairness to future generations: International law, common patrimony, and intergenerational equity.* Ardsley, NY: Transnational.

White, H. L. (1998). Race, class, and environmental hazards. In D. E. Camacho (Ed.), *Environmental injustices, political struggle: Race, class, and the environment.* Durham, NC: Duke University Press.

Williams, B. A., & Matheny, A. R. (1995). *Democracy, dialogue, and environmental disputes: The contested language of social regulation.* New Haven: Yale University Press.

PART V

Environmental Discourses of Science and Industry

Climate scientists have become "early warners" in educating the public and public officials about the effects of melting glaciers and a warming planet.

CHAPTER 9

Science Communication and Environmental Controversies

As we stand at the brink of . . . a period of unprecedented climate change, scientists have a special responsibility. . . . As citizens of the world, we have a duty to alert the public to the unnecessary risks that we live with every day, and to the perils we foresee if governments and societies do not take action now.

—Stephen Hawking, physicist (quoted in Connor, 2007)

The scientific debate is closing [against us] but not yet closed. There is still a window of opportunity to challenge the science.

—Frank Luntz, memo to Republican Party leaders
(Luntz Research Companies, 2001)

On December 6, 2005, Dr. James E. Hansen, NASA's chief climate scientist, warned in a speech to the annual meeting of the American Geophysical Union in San Francisco that "the Earth's climate is nearing, but has not passed, a tipping point, beyond which it will be impossible to avoid climate change with far-ranging undesirable consequences." Further warming of more than 1°C (or about 2°F), Hansen said, will leave "a different planet" (quoted in Bowen, 2008, p. 4). Hansen is director of NASA's research center, the Goddard Institute for Space Studies, and it was he who first introduced global warming into the spotlight when he testified before the U.S. Senate nearly two decades earlier (see Figure 9.1).

Hansen's warning in 2005 set off more than just scientific alarm bells. In the days following his speech, NASA officials ordered its public affairs staff to monitor Hansen's lectures, scientific papers, postings on the Goddard Website, and journalists'

| Figure 9.1 | Dr. James E. Hansen, director of NASA's climate research center, the Goddard Institute for Space Studies |

© Brendan Hoffman/Getty Images.

requests for interviews (Revkin, 2006a). When the *Washington Post* reported the story, NASA staff tried to discourage the *Post*'s reporter from interviewing him. They agreed, finally, that Hansen "could speak on the record only if an agency spokeswoman listened in on the conversation" (Eilperin, 2006, p. A1). Other NASA scientists complained to the *New York Times* about similar political pressures on them "to limit or flavor discussions of topics uncomfortable to the Bush administration, particularly global warming" (Revkin, 2006b, A11).

NASA later assured reporters that its scientists could speak freely to the media, but the clumsy handling of the Hansen incident had set off a storm of criticism in the mainstream media and Blogosphere. Dr. Hansen himself defended his actions: "Communicating with the public seems to be essential . . . because public concern is probably the only thing capable of overcoming the special interests that have obfuscated the topic" of global warming (Revkin, 2006a, p. A1). The furor over Hansen's speech and NASA's restrictions raise a number of questions about the role of scientists and science communication in moments of environmental controversies:

- What is the proper role for science (and scientists) in deciding policy in a democratic society?
- Who should control the agenda of science and the uses of scientific research?
- How should the public interpret the significance of scientific claims when science always has some uncertainty?

In this chapter, I explore the environmental sciences as both a source of knowledge and as a site of conflict over symbolic legitimacy. **Symbolic legitimacy** refers to the perceived authority of a policy, source of knowledge, or an approach to a problem. (For a discussion of symbolic legitimacy, see Chapter 2.) Scientific claims are a site of conflict when the legitimacy of science itself is challenged by industry, climate skeptics, and others who seek to influence the public about the meaning and uses of environmental science.

This chapter is organized into four sections. In the first, I trace how science became an important source of symbolic legitimacy in a society beset with complexity and specialized technical knowledge. The second section examines one way in which some propose to manage the problem of uncertainty about environmental dangers: by invoking the *precautionary principle,* an appeal to caution or prudence before taking a step that could prove harmful later. Conversely, some critics, and those skeptical of climate science in particular, play up claims of *uncertainty* as a ploy to delay actions that might be costly to industry. The third section, therefore, looks at attempts by industry and others to challenge the claims of environmental science through what some have called *symbolic legitimacy conflict,* or a challenge to the credibility of science itself. The chapter ends with an examination of recent debates about the role of scientists and recent attempts by some in government to interfere with scientists' communication with the public, particularly about global warming.

Science and Symbolic Legitimacy Boundaries

As I write, climate scientists are trying to resolve a lingering uncertainty in how fast (and high) sea levels will rise with a warming climate. While the Intergovernmental Panel on Climate Change ([IPCC], 2007a) forecast a sea level rise of 1 to 2 feet by the year 2100 (principally from thermal expansion of sea water), other scientists have pointed out that this prediction ignores the likely contribution of melting glaciers in Greenland and West Antarctica (Pfeffer, Harper, & O'Neel, 2008). Rahmstorf (2007), for example, explains that 2 feet "is unfortunately not the 'worst case.' It does not include the full ice sheet uncertainty" by the end of the 21st century (para. 39). Indeed, the Intergovernmental Panel on Climate Change (IPCC) observed that "the last time the polar regions were significantly warmer than present for an extended period (about 125,000 years ago), reductions in polar ice volume led to 4 to 6 metres [13 to 19 feet] of sea level rise" (IPCC, 2007b, p. 8). One problem in forecasting sea level rises from climate change is that scientists are only beginning to model or understand the dynamic and complex processes by which glaciers like Greenland and West Antarctica deteriorate and melt, contributing to greater sea levels.

Similar problems of complexity in scientific research appear in other, major environmental and human health issues: genetically modified organisms, the effect on human fertility of synthetic chemicals that mimic natural hormones, and the amount of critical habitat needed for endangered species. Such complexities in science are not new, nor are the difficulties of communicating these issues to the public. Therefore, it may be useful to look at an earlier era that faced similar concerns, as well as at the emerging role of science and science communication in guiding important decisions about the environment.

John Dewey Redux: Complexity and the Problem of the Public

In the early 20th century, the philosopher John Dewey confronted a similar problem as the American public experienced problems with urban sanitation and industrial safety as well as revolutionary changes in communication technologies. In his book *The Public and Its Problems* (1927), Dewey warned of an "eclipse of the public" that he felt would occur because citizens lacked the expertise to evaluate the increasingly complex issues before them. He wrote that the consequences of the decisions before the public are so large, "the technical matters involved are so specialized . . . that the public cannot for any length of time identify and hold itself [together]" (p. 137). With the growing need for technical expertise in making decisions, Dewey feared the United States was moving from democracy to a form of government that he called **technocracy**, or rule by experts.

The solution favored by the Progressive movement of the 1920s and 1930s was grounded in the reformers' faith in science and technology as a source of legitimacy for state and federal regulation of the new industries. Williams and Matheny (1995) explain that, in regulatory policy, the Progressives wanted to rely on trained experts working within government organizations to discover an objective public interest (p. 12). Legitimacy for political decisions would come from these experts' use of "neutral, scientific criteria for judging public policy" (p. 12).

Although the **Progressive ideal** of neutral, science-based policy would run into difficulty, the legitimacy accorded to science by the public grew steadily stronger. Willis Harman observed that, during the 20th century, popular culture has given "tremendous prestige and power to our official, publicly validated knowledge system, namely science" (1998, p. 116). For example, when the Environmental Protection Agency (EPA) announced in 2001 that the new Bush administration was abandoning a Clinton-era rule requiring lower levels of arsenic in water, EPA administrator Christine Whitman pledged that a new rule would be based on "sound science and solid analysis" (Jehl, 2001, p. A1). (The EPA later reinstated the strict arsenic rule after a review of scientific studies by the National Academy of Sciences.)

The appeals to "sound science" in environmental policy reflected a keen awareness of the cultural norm that policy should be as free as possible of political bias and grounded in reliable and valid knowledge. To some extent, this awareness evolved during the 20th century and continues to do so, as government agencies have sought to incorporate the counsel and findings of scientists in the EPA, the Department of the Interior, and in agencies such as the U.S. Fish and Wildlife Service. Additionally, scientists from the National Research Council, universities, and independent research centers routinely advise policymakers on the scientific implications of environmental proposals.

Still, the Progressive ideal of neutral, science-based policy falls short of its promise in other ways. Agency budgets, pressures from political constituents, ideology, and other factors limit the extent to which policy decisions flow directly from scientific findings. A recent dispute over the use of science in implementing the Endangered Species Act (ESA) illustrates some of the ways in which the Progressive ideal falls short.

In the waning days of the Bush administration, the Department of the Interior and Department of Commerce announced a final rule change in the Endangered Species Act. The new rule overturned an ESA requirement that federal agencies communicate with U.S. Fish and Wildlife Service scientists when making decisions affecting endangered species. The new rule granted federal agencies greater discretion in deciding, without consulting with scientists, if protected species would be threatened by development projects, including roads, dams, and mines (Union of Concerned Scientists [UCS], 2008b, para. 1). Francesca Grifo, director of the Scientific Integrity Program at the Union of Concerned Scientists, charged, "Instead of expert biologists taking the first look at potential consequences, any federal agency, regardless of its expertise, will now be able to make decisions that should be determined by the best available science" (para. 3).

The dispute results from cases in recent years in which developers, agricultural and mining interests, and others have objected to the listing of critical habitat for endangered fish or wildlife, where the protected habitat would impact their economic interests. (For recent court rulings that found that federal officials "limited and skewed" the scientific analyses of the environmental impacts of dams on the Snake and Columbia Rivers, see Barringer, 2005.) (Scientists and environmental groups worked to reverse this rule change in the Obama administration.)

Whatever the outcome, this case illustrates the ongoing tension in federal agencies over whether science will guide policy or whether other factors—such as cost, political pressure, or differences in management philosophy—will prevail.

Questioning Symbolic Legitimacy Boundaries

Even as science has become an important source of symbolic legitimacy in society, science itself is increasingly a site of conflict among disputing parties—industry, public health officials, and environmentalists—as they attempt to influence public perceptions of the scope or severity of problems. For example, environmental historian Samuel Hays (2000) reports that, as the new environmental sciences began to document risks from industrial products in the 1960s and 1970s, affected businesses challenged the science "at every step, questioning both the methods and research designs that were used and the conclusions that were drawn" (p. 222). Regulated industries, such as electric utility companies, oil and gas refineries, chemical manufacturing, and older extractive industries (mining, logging, and ranching), placed tremendous pressure on government agencies to justify the science behind new regulations. Some critics have charged that, in response, agency officials have sometimes ignored or misrepresented scientific findings to placate the criticism from regulated industries (Wilkinson, 1998).

In debates about environmental policies, one source of controversy often is the question of whether there is conclusive proof, something that is often beyond the reach of science. John Fitzpatrick, director of the Cornell Laboratory of Ornithology, observed, "A **paradox for conservation** is that knowledge is always incomplete, yet the scale of human influence on ecosystems demands action without delay" (quoted in Scully, 2005, p. B13). This paradox poses a serious challenge for the public's willingness to support steps to protect the environment. At the same time, it provides the opponents of stronger regulations with an opportunity to contest the scientific claims:

> To the public, the question is usually one of "is there enough proof," an issue that the media takes up in order to bring simplicity out of complexity. . . . This complexity of debate, arising out of the complexity of arguments over proof, generates opportunities for those who wish to slow up application of scientific knowledge and establishes . . . caution on the part of decision makers in public agencies. Their watchword is "insufficient proof." (Hays, 2000, p. 151)

The challenge for government agencies becomes even more acute when the science fails to tell officials how to choose between technical and political questions (for example, What is acceptable risk?) or how to decide among competing values, such as the health benefits to be gained versus the costs to comply with a regulation (for example, the requirement that power plants upgrade their anti-pollution equipment to reduce mercury pollution from the burning of coal.)

Two important questions, therefore, arise for the study of environmental communication: (1) What counts as scientific knowledge? (2) Who controls its production, dissemination, and use? To ask (and answer) these questions is to ask about the symbolic legitimacy boundaries of science itself. It also asks about the types of communication that contending parties use as they challenge, reinforce, or reframe these symbolic boundaries. For example, in the remaining sections of this chapter, I discuss attempts by some opponents of environmental standards to forestall discussion and debate in the public sphere by removing questions about global warming or endangered species to the technical sphere of scientific journals and laboratories as a method of limiting action. (For discussion of the public, personal, and technical spheres, see Chapter 2.)

In the James Hansen case, government officials sought to control the type of information that reached the public about the dangers of global warming. In fact, NASA officials warned Hansen "that there would be 'dire consequences' if such statements continued," according to public affairs officers at the agency (Revkin, 2006a, p. A1). Similar struggles by industry to mobilize science in support of its positions or challenge a policy's legitimacy occur in almost every major new story about the environment. In an infamous case, the EPA felt pressure to delete scientific research on the causes of global warming from its first "report card" on the environment (U.S. Environmental Protection Agency, 2003).

In the "report card" case, White House officials edited the EPA's *Draft Report on the Environment,* deleting a 1999 study showing that global temperatures had risen sharply in the previous decade. In its place, these officials suggested a study funded by the American Petroleum Institute that questioned the 1999 findings on global temperatures (Seelye & Lee, 2003). In the end, the EPA chose to delete the entire section on global warming, "to avoid criticism that they [were] selectively filtering science to suit administration policy" (p. 28A). (For more information on the controversy over the EPA's report card, see Revkin & Seelye, 2003).

The dispute over the EPA's report card also illustrates the importance of the symbolic legitimacy boundaries associated with government uses of science. Earlier, in Chapter 2, I noted that the outcome of arguments between parties over legitimacy depends only partly on the facts. Equally important are the symbolic associations that politicians, business, and the public attach to a proposal, policy, or person (Schulzke, 2000). Symbolic legitimacy boundaries define a particular policy, idea, or institution as reasonable, appropriate, or acceptable. What is often at stake in the disputes between critics of environmental regulations and their supporters is the public's perception of the validity of scientific claims. To understand conflicts over science and the environment, therefore, we need to examine the ways in which the contending parties in society attempt to deal with scientific uncertainty, as well as the communication used in seeking to move scientific knowledge into the public sphere for discussion and as the basis for actions to protect the environment.

Because the symbolic associations of legitimacy boundaries are discursively constituted, they are also open to question and challenge. As far as environmental conflicts go, the fault line for such symbolic legitimacy conflict in a democratic society occurs most explicitly between supporters of an ethic of caution or prudence and others whose economic interests are affected by such caution and who seek to contest the claims of science. We discuss each of these tensions in the following sections.

The Precautionary Principle

Earlier, I noted that knowledge about the effects of human behavior on the environment is always incomplete, yet the scale of our influence on the Earth demands that we take action. Stanford University biologists Paul Ehrlich and Anne H. Ehrlich (1996) once remarked that one of the great ironies in the environmental sciences is that science itself can never provide "absolute certainty or the 'proof' that many who misunderstand science say [that] society needs" (p. 27). Although certainty evokes a powerful pull for social reformers, religious adherents, and popular radio commentators, "it is forever denied to scientists" (p. 27). This is particularly the case in areas like chemical pollution and such large-scale problems like climate change and the loss of biodiversity. The Ehrlichs note with some concern that, in the absence of more precise knowledge of complex environmental systems, "humanity is running a vast experiment on the biosphere and on itself" (p. 29).

Environmental Science and Uncertainty

The absence of scientific certainty also provides openings for some to call for delays before government takes action. For decades, the opponents of the environmental regulation of industry have used the indeterminacy of environmental sciences as a rationale for objecting to new standards to regulate hazardous chemicals such as lead, Dichloro-Diphenyl-Trichloroethane (DDT), dioxin, and polychlorinated biphenyls (PCBs). A classic case, in 1922, involved the introduction of tetraethyl lead in gasoline for cars. Although public health officials thought lead posed a health risk and should be studied more carefully first, the industry argued that there was no scientific agreement on the danger and pushed ahead to market leaded gasoline for the next 50 years. Peter Montague (1999) of the Environmental Research Foundation writes, "The consequences of that . . . decision [to delay standards for leaded gasoline] are now a matter of record—tens of millions of Americans suffered brain damage, their IQs permanently diminished by exposure to lead dust" (para. 3).

Historically, the procedures for assessing risk have given the benefit of the doubt to new products and chemicals, even though these may prove harmful later. (For a description of methods used in risk assessment, see Chapter 6.) For example, existing government standards require only a tiny fraction of the 70,000 or more chemicals in commercial use in the United States today to be "fully tested for their ability to cause harm to health and the environment" (Shabecoff, 2000, p. 149). By the 1990s, however, a number of scientists, environmentalists, and public health advocates had begun to argue that the burden of proof should be shifted to require use of the precautionary principle.

As early as the 1960s, scientists such as René Dubos, Rachel Carson, Barry Commoner, George Wald, and others had begun to warn of possible ecological disaster and danger to human health from new chemicals appearing in water, air, and soil and in the food chain and mothers' breast milk. Rachel Carson's best-selling book *Silent Spring* (1962) became the most visible public warning about the use of chemical agents such as DDT in agricultural spraying and pesticides. (*Silent Spring*'s publication prompted congressional hearings and scientific study of the health effects of massive spraying of chemicals on food crops.) Media stories of nuclear fallout from atmospheric tests and chemical residues on foods also fueled growing public anxieties. And, as I pointed out in Chapters 2 and 8, by the early 1980s, the upstate New York community of Love Canal had awakened the nation's consciousness to the hazards of its chemical culture. Others warned of specific dangers from the new organochlorines (such as PCBs) that can "reduce sperm counts, disrupt female reproductive cycles . . . cause birth defects, [and] impair the development and function of the brain" (Thornton, 2000, p. 6, in Markowitz & Rosner, 2002, p. 296).

The Precautionary Principle and Its Critics

Eventually, scientists and public health officials began to urge that a new approach to regulation of potential environmental risks be adopted, "one that takes science's uncertainty not as a sign that there is no danger but as a sign that serious danger might well exist" (Markowitz & Rosner, 2002, p. 298). This view emphasized an ethic of caution or prudence in evaluating products that, even with low levels of toxicity, could harm populations in the future. In 1991, the National Research Council offered a compelling rationale for the new precautionary approach: "Until better evidence is developed, prudent public policy demands that a margin of safety be provided regarding potential health risks. . . . We do no less in designing bridges and buildings. . . . We must surely do no less when the health and quality of life of Americans are at stake" (p. 270).

An important step toward defining this principle of precaution was taken in January 1998, at a historic gathering at the Wingspread Conference Center in Racine, Wisconsin. The Wingspread Conference on the Precautionary Principle was convened by the Science and Environmental Health Network and several foundations that funded scientific research. The 32 participants—scientists, researchers, philosophers, treaty negotiators, environmentalists, and labor leaders from the United States, Europe, and Canada—shared the belief that "compelling evidence that damage to humans and the worldwide environment is of such magnitude and seriousness that new principles for conducting human activities are necessary" (Science and Environmental Health Network [SEHN], 1998, para. 3).

At the end of the three-day meeting, the participants issued the "Wingspread Statement on the Precautionary Principle," which called for government, corporations, communities, and scientists to implement the precautionary principle in making decisions about environmental and human health (Raffensperger, 1998). The statement provided this expanded definition of the **precautionary principle**: "*When an activity raises threats of harm to human health or the environment, precautionary measures should be taken even if some cause and effect relationships are not fully established scientifically. In this context the proponent of an activity, rather than the public, should bear the burden of proof*" (SEHN, 1998, para. 5; emphasis added).

The new principle is to be applied when an activity poses a combination of potential harm and scientific uncertainty. It therefore requires (1) an ethic of prudence (avoidance of risk) and (2) an affirmative obligation to act to prevent harm. Montague (1999) explains that the principle shifts the burden of proof to the proponents of an activity to show that "their activity will not cause undue harm to human health or the ecosystem." Further, he explains that it requires agencies and corporations to take proactive measures to reduce or eliminate hazards, including "a duty to monitor, understand, investigate, inform, and act" when anything goes wrong (para. 13). (See "FYI: The Wingspread Statement on the Precautionary Principle.")

☞ **FYI**   **The "Wing Spread Statement on the Precautionary Principle"**

The release and use of toxic substances, the exploitation of resources, and physical alterations of the environment have had substantial unintended consequences affecting human health and the environment. Some of these concerns are high rates of learning deficiencies, asthma, cancer, birth defects and species extinctions; along with global climate change, stratopheric ozone depletion, and worldwide contamination with toxic substances and nuclear materials.

(Continued)

(Continued)

We believe existing environmental regulations and other decisions, particularly those based on risk assessment, have failed to protect adequately human health and the environment—the larger system of which humans are but a part.

We believe there is compelling evidence that damage to humans and the worldwide environment is of such magnitude and seriousness that new principles for conducting human activities are necessary.

While we realize that human activities may involve hazards, people must proceed more carefully than has been the case in recent history. Corporations, government entities, organizations, communities, scientists and other individuals must adopt a precautionary approach to all human endeavors.

Therefore, it is necessary to implement the Precautionary Principle: When an activity raises threats of harm to human health or the environment, precautionary measures should be taken even if some cause and effect relationships are not fully established scientifically.

In this context the proponent of an activity, rather than the public, should bear the burden of proof.

The process of applying the Precautionary Principle must be open, informed and democratic and must include potentially affected parties. It must also involve an examination of the full range of alternatives, including no action.

SOURCE: Reprinted with permission from The Science and Environmental Health Network, downloaded from http://www.sehn.org/state.html.

Not all parties rushed to embrace the precautionary principle, however. Some businesses, conservative policy centers, and politicians are concerned that the consequences of using the principle are at odds with assumptions in the dominant social paradigm (Chapter 2) and object that the principle sometimes errs on the side of too much caution. Writing for the libertarian policy center, the Cato Institute, Ronald Bailey (2002) argued that "the precautionary principle is an anti-science regulatory concept that allows regulators to ban new products on the barest suspicion that they might pose some unknown threat" (p. 5). Bailey cites the case of the European Union's (EU) ban on imports of genetically enhanced crops, or what have been called genetically modified organisms (GMOs), from the United States. He argues that scientific panels have concluded that genetically modified foods are safe to eat and that "the EU ban is not a safety precaution, but a barrier to trade" (p. 4). The dispute over the safety of genetically enhanced food and agricultural products is a continuing debate, one that has placed the precautionary principle squarely at the center of the controversy. (For a defense of its use, see Raffensperger & Barrett, 2001; for a skeptical study of the precautionary principle, see Goklany, 2001.)

The controversy over the precautionary principle mirrors a larger conflict over the role of uncertainty in setting environmental policy. It is to this conflict, and attempts to challenge the symbolic legitimacy of science itself, that we now turn.

Science and Symbolic Legitimacy Conflict

Although science and technology have produced "a cornucopia of material abundance for a substantial portion of the human race" (Shabecoff, 2000, p. 138), scientific knowledge about the environmental impacts of industrial actions has been the site of controversy. In their study of business campaigns to shape the public's perceptions of science, Markowitz and Rosner (2002) observe that, during much of the 20th century, industry has argued that there must be "convincing proof of danger before policymakers had the right to intrude on the private reserve of industry in America" (p. 287). Yet, even as new knowledge emerged, some industries challenged the scientific consensus "at almost every step" when that knowledge might lead to new regulations (Hays, 2000, p. 138). The reason for this is not hard to understand. The possibility that some products and industrial pollutants might be linked to cancers, endocrine disruptors, and other health problems, as well as to changes in the Earth's climate, raises not only issues of the financial liability of these companies but also prospects for further regulation of industry itself.

One result has been that the industries at risk of regulation by environmental science—particularly petrochemicals, energy, real estate development, and utilities—have "sought to turn science in their direction and [have] attracted scientists who could help with that objective" (Hays, 2000, p. 138). A look at several of these cases is instructive for understanding the communication used by industry and others to contest the legitimacy of scientific consensus.

Science and the Trope of Uncertainty

In the past two decades, some industries and so-called climate skeptics have used a range of communication to challenge the symbolic legitimacy of the environmental sciences. This includes the funding of friendly scientists, the production of books and media releases by certain think tanks that promote skepticism, and, most important, the use of a rhetorical *trope of uncertainty*. (In Chapter 2, I described a *trope* as a "turn" or reframing of a claim that alters its meaning or changes our understanding of a statement.) Let me describe this trope briefly and then illustrate its use and the related modes of communication some trade associations and climate skeptics have used to challenge the claims of environmental science in recent years.

When skeptics call for further research into the causes of global climate change or the effect of dams in the Pacific Northwest on runs of salmon, they are drawing on a familiar tool in industry's challenge to the legitimacy of science. This **trope of uncertainty** functions to nurture doubt in the public's perception of scientific claims and thereby to delay calls for action. In rhetorical terms, the trope of uncertainty "turns," or alters, the public's understanding of what is at stake, suggesting there is a danger in acting prematurely, a risk of making the wrong decision. For this reason, Markowitz and Rosner (2002) have observed that "the call for more scientific evidence is often a stalling tactic" (p. 10).

A standard reference for the basic strategy for nurturing doubt about the legitimacy boundaries of an issue is public relations expert Philip Lesly's (1992) article,

"Coping With Opposition Groups." Lesly advises corporate clients to design their communication to create uncertainty in the minds of the public:

> The weight of impressions on the public must be balanced so people *will have doubts and lack motivation to take action.* Accordingly, means are needed to get balancing information into the stream from sources that the public will find credible. There is no need for a clear-cut 'victory.' . . . Nurturing public doubts by demonstrating that this is not a clear-cut situation in support of the opponents usually is all that is necessary. (p. 331; emphasis added)

Feeling uncertain about an issue, the advice goes, the public will be less motivated to demand action, and the political will to solve a problem will lessen. For example, in their study of corporations' uses of public relations strategies opposing government regulation, Sheldon Rampton and John Stauber (2002) observe, "Industry's PR strategy is not aimed at reversing the tide of public opinion, which may in any case be impossible. Its goal is simply to stop people from mobilizing to do anything about the problem, to create sufficient doubt in their minds about the seriousness of global warming that they will remain locked in debate and indecision" (p. 271). They note that the group Friends of the Earth International called such attempts to introduce uncertainty in order to dampen the motive for action as "lobbying for lethargy" (p. 271).

Ironically, the trope of uncertainty is an attempt to *reverse* the assumptions of the precautionary principle. Whereas the principle stresses that, when an activity raises threats of harm to human health or the environment, *precautionary measures should be taken even if some uncertainty remains,* critics' calls for further research turn this "precaution" against the principle itself. A striking case of such deliberate introduction of uncertainty into debates over the politically sensitive matter of global warming occurred in the report of a prominent consultant to the Republican Party.

Memo on Global Warming: "Challenge the Science"

Sometimes, the conflict over the legitimacy of scientific consensus may be fought on the terrain of language itself, by engaging in what one political consultant called the "environmental communications battle" (Luntz Research Companies, 2001, p. 136). In a memo entitled "The Environment: A Cleaner, Safer Healthier America," GOP consultant Frank Luntz (2001) warned party leaders that "*the scientific debate is closing [against us] but not yet closed.*" Nevertheless, he advised, "*There is still a window of opportunity to challenge the science*" (p. 138; emphasis in original). The "window of opportunity" to which Luntz referred was the possibility that skeptics could raise enough doubts about the symbolic legitimacy of scientific claims about global warming that the public's uncertainty would delay governmental action in this area.

Luntz's memo offers a rare look into a behind-the-scenes debate over rhetorical strategy in high-level political circles. It is noteworthy especially for its frank assessment of the public relations dilemma that faced many politicians on the eve of the U.S. congressional elections in 2002. For example, Luntz had found that voters particularly distrusted the Republican Party on the environment. Thus, his memo to the party is revealing for his advice on the rhetorical strategy that he believed Republicans needed in order to challenge the growing consensus—the legitimacy boundaries—for many environmental issues, such as safe drinking water, the protection of natural areas, and especially global warming.

In one section of the memo, Luntz asserts that voters currently believe there is no consensus about global warming in the scientific community. "Should the public come to believe that the scientific issues are settled," he writes, "their views about global warming will change accordingly." Advising party leaders, the memo states, "'Therefore, *you need to continue to make the lack of scientific certainty a primary issue in the debate*" (p. 137; emphasis in original). Among the ways to challenge the science, according to the memo, is to "be even more active in recruiting experts who are sympathetic to your view, and much more active in making them part of your message" because "people are willing to trust scientists" more than politicians (p. 138).

☞ **FYI** | **Luntz's Memo on the "Environmental Communications Battle" (excerpts)**

"While we may have lost the environmental communications battle in the past, the war is not over...." (p. 136).

"The scientific debate is closing [against us] but not yet closed. There is still a window of opportunity to challenge the science." ... (p. 138)

"LANGUAGE THAT WORKS"

"We must not rush to judgment before all the facts are in. We need to ask more questions. We deserve more answers. And until we learn more, we should not commit America to any international document that handcuffs us either now or in the future.

You need to be even more active in recruiting experts who are sympathetic to your view, and more active in making them part of your message. People are willing to trust scientists, engineers, and other leading professionals, and less willing to trust politicians." (p. 137)

SOURCE: Luntz Research Companies (2001).

Manufacturing "Uncertainty": Industry and Conservative Think Tanks

Luntz's advice to "make the lack of scientific certainty a primary issue" appears as a major theme in a number of attempts by industry and others to challenge environmental science itself, on issues ranging from chemical contamination to climate change. The objective of these efforts is to encourage the public's questioning of the legitimacy of scientific claims and scientific consensus about environmental problems. Let's look at some examples of this "environmental communication battle" (Luntz Research Companies, 2001, p. 136).

One of the earliest communication efforts by corporations to influence public perceptions of environmental science was disclosed in a *New York Times* report in

1998. The *Times* reporter, John Cushman (1998), had uncovered a proposal by the American Petroleum Institute and other corporations to spend millions of dollars to convince the public that the Kyoto accord on global warming was based on "shaky science" (p. A1). Cushman reported that the proposal included

> a campaign to recruit a cadre of scientists who share the industry's views of climate science and to train them in public relations so they can help convince journalists, politicians and the public that the risk of global warming is too uncertain to justify controls on greenhouse gases like carbon dioxide that trap the sun's heat near Earth. (p. A1)

Other sources noted that the American Petroleum Institute's proposal included a $5 million Global Climate Science Data Center to provide information to the media, government officials, and the public; grant money for "advocacy on climate science;" and fund a Science Education Task Group to put industry information into school classrooms (National Environmental Trust, 1998). Finally, Beder (1999) wrote that other groups also had formed in this period to oppose measures to regulate the emissions contributing to global warming. (I discuss the case of one of these groups in Chapter 10.)

The campaigns of industry to influence public perceptions of the science behind climate change may not be isolated instances. Independent monitoring groups and news accounts have documented a range of practices used by industry to question the consensus—or legitimacy boundaries—for many environmental topics. These have included:

- Corporate-sponsored science symposiums (Rampton & Stauber, 2002)
- Letters to editors and paid message ads in newspapers, including payments to scientists to write letters to influential medical journals that dispute evidence of cigarette smoking as a cause of health problems (Hanners, 1998)
- Funding of "defensive science" or encouragement of research that refutes mainstream science (Hays, 2000)
- Corporate funding of scientists who had published in leading biomedical journals on subjects in which the funders had a financial interest (Krimsky et al., 1998)
- Distribution of materials containing scientific claims sympathetic to industry to schools, journalists, and public officials (Cushman, 1998)

For example, Philip Shabecoff (2000), the founder of the online news source *Greenwire,* reported that the largest study ever conducted on the effects of PCBs on workers' health had been funded by an interested party, General Electric. Published in the *Journal of Occupational and Environmental Medicine,* the industry-funded study "found no evidence of 'significant' links to cancer deaths among workers exposed to PCBs on the job" (p. 142). (As I noted in Chapter 4, the large corporation had been fighting for years to avoid cleaning up the PCBs it had discharged into New York's Hudson River.)

Beyond these attempts, a more basic challenge has emerged in the past decade—a conscious manufacturing of an attitude of "environmental skepticism" that seeks to shape public debates about environmental science and about global warming in particular. Among those engaging in this "climate skepticism" are former (retired) scientists and non-climate scientists, dissident scientists, and most prominently, conservative think tanks and tax-exempt organizations. The message varies somewhat from skeptic to skeptic, but generally the strategy is to sow doubt about climate change, challenging the consensus of mainstream scientists: Is global warming really occurring? Is human activity truly to blame? And are rising temperatures such a bad thing?

The main pillars of support for this skepticism are so-called conservative **think tanks** (CTTs). These are nonprofit, advocacy-based groups, modeled on the image of neutral policy centers (for example, the Cato Institute and the Heartland Institute). In a recent study, "The Organization of Denial: Conservative Think Tanks and Environmental Skepticism," Peter J. Jacques, Riley E. Dunlap, and Mark Freeman (2008) identified a systematic effort to nurture "environmental skepticism" about serious environmental problems—from loss of biodiversity to toxic chemicals and, especially, global warming (p. 349). They found a key rhetorical strategy underlying this effort: The books, press releases, and policy papers published or linked to these conservative think tanks promoted an attitude of **environmental skepticism** that disputed the seriousness of environmental problems and questioned the credibility of environmental science itself (p. 351).

The fundamental theme of environmental skepticism, the authors found, is a rejection of the scientific literature about serious environmental problems. Skeptics charge that the environmental sciences have been "corrupted by political agendas that lead it to unintentionally or maliciously fabricate or grossly exaggerate these global problems" (p. 353). They cite the case of Patrick Michaels, a senior fellow in environmental studies at the Cato Institute, who writes in his book *Meltdown: The Predictable Distortion of Global Warming by Scientists, Politicians, and the Media:* "Global warming is an exaggerated issue, predictably blown out of proportion by the political and professional climate in which it evolved" (2004, p. 5).

Such skepticism, Jacques, Dunlap, and Freeman (2008) argue, "is designed specifically to undermine the environmental movement's efforts to legitimize its claims via science" (p. 364).

The role of the seemingly neutral policy think tanks is particularly important in the strategy of manufacturing environmental skepticism. Many corporations had learned that scientists directly funded by industry lacked the credibility of university scientists in debates on issues such as cigarette smoking, "so providing political insulation for industry has become an essential role for CTTs" (Austin, 2002; Jacques, Dunlap, & Freeman, 2008, p. 362). As a result, the conservative think tanks stepped into this role, using the trope of uncertainty as a major strategy. When it comes to climate change, several think tanks have performed this function for various corporations. Michaels and Monforton (2005) explain that, in doing this, "a *major tactic is to 'manufacture uncertainty,' raising questions about the scientific basis for environmental problems* and thereby undermining support for government regulations" (p. 362; emphasis added).

During the past decade, the conservative think tanks have promoted this uncertainty through a range of communication channels, including the publication of an "an endless flow of printed material ranging from books to editorials designed for public consumption to policy briefs aimed at policy-makers and journalists, combined with frequent appearances by spokespersons on TV and radio" (p. 355). Overall, Jacques, Dunlap, and Freeman (2008) reported an "unambiguous link" between the CTTs and the manufacturing of environmental skepticism: More than 92 percent of the English-language environmentally skeptical books surveyed from 1972 to 2005 were linked to conservative think tanks, while 90 percent of the conservative think tanks that were interested in environmental issues espoused environmental skepticism (p. 364).

For awhile, the efforts by dissident scientists, corporations, and conservative think tanks succeeded in establishing themselves as a kind of counter-intelligentsia on global warming, achieving an "equal legitimacy with mainstream science and academia— . . . [and] providing 'balance'" in the media (p. 356). As a consequence, the U.S. news media have been "significantly more likely than media in other industrial nations to portray global warming as a controversial issue characterised by scientific uncertainty" (Jacques, Dunlap, & Freeman, 2008, p. 356; see also Dispensa & Brulle, 2003; and Grundmann, 2007). (I noted in Chapter 5, however, the trend of major U.S. newspapers resorting to a "balance" of sources—using both climate scientists and skeptics in news articles—has significantly declined in recent years.)

Environmental Science and Public Accountability

In the past decade, a number of groups have begun to scrutinize corporate and CCT funding that might influence scientific claims about cancer, climate change, and other public health and environmental concerns. These efforts were fueled by disclosures such as Cushman's *New York Times* story of the campaign by the American Petroleum Institute to discredit the science of global warming. For example, the Union of Concerned Scientists' (2007) report, *Smoke, Mirrors and Hot Air: How ExxonMobil Uses Big Tobacco's Tactics to "Manufacture Uncertainty" on Climate Change*, details how "ExxonMobil has funneled about $16 million between 1998 and 2005 to a network of ideological and advocacy organizations that manufacture uncertainty on the issue" (p. 1). According to the report, ExxonMobil has

- *Manufactured uncertainty* by raising doubts about even the most indisputable scientific evidence.
- Adopted a strategy of *information laundering* by using seemingly independent front organizations to publicly further its desired message . . . [and]
- *Promoted scientific spokespeople* who misrepresent peer-reviewed scientific findings or cherry-pick facts in their attempts to persuade the media and the public that there is still serious debate among scientists that burning fossil fuels has contributed to global warming . . . (p. 1)

As a result of cases like ExxonMobil, groups such as the Society of Environmental Journalists, the Center for Science in the Public Interest, Union of Concerned Scientists, and others now provide databases to research potential conflicts of interest when reporters read reports by scientists or interview them on controversial public policy topics. For example, the Society of Environmental Journalists maintains one of the most comprehensive and accessible databases on disinformation about climate change for journalists (www.sej.org). The site makes available links on "Skeptics and Contrarians" (identifying industry funding of climate skeptics), "Help for Sifting Disinformation From Information," and others.

One of the most influential groups monitoring the public uses of science is the Center for Science in the Public Interest (CSPI). CSPI has emerged as the leading resource in the United States for scientists, government officials, journalists, and public interest groups seeking to investigate and report corporate funding of scientists and university research projects. Its long-standing goals are "to educate the public, advocate government policies that are consistent with scientific evidence on health and environmental issues, and counter industry's powerful influence on public opinion and public policies" (2009, para. 2).

The CSPI also sponsors the Integrity in Science Project (ISP), whose purpose is to scrutinize federal science advisory committees for undisclosed conflicts of interest and monitor the news media and scientific literature for failure to disclose funding sources. The ISP project (www.cspinet.org/integrity) also publishes a weekly Integrity in Science Watch e-newsletter and maintains a searchable database of public records of more than 4,000 scientists for possible affiliations with chemical, gas, oil, food, drug, and other corporations. The goals of the ISP database are to

- Raise awareness about the role that corporate funding and other corporate interests play in scientific research, oversight, and publication;
- Investigate and publicize conflicts of interest and other potentially destructive influences of industry-sponsored science;
- Advocate for full disclosure of funding sources by individuals, governmental and nongovernmental organizations that conduct, regulate, or provide oversight of scientific investigation or promote specific scientific findings; . . .
- Encourage journalists to routinely ask scientists and others about their possible conflicts of interests and to provide this information to the public. (Integrity in Science, 2009, para. 10–13, 14)

Although it acknowledges the benefits of corporate funding in areas such as genetics, bioengineering, and other cutting-edge research, the Integrity in Science Project seeks to highlight the dangers of commercialization of science and the growing problem of conflicts of interest. The project addresses an important aspect of the debate over the role of science in environmental affairs—the responsibility of journalists, policymakers, and others to scrutinize the possible conflicts of interests in corporate funding of science and other efforts to influence the public's perception of scientific research.

But what should be the role of scientists themselves? In the final section of the chapter, I explore a growing debate within the ranks of environmental scientists: Should scientists, at any point, serve as "first responders" or early warners for environmental dangers such as global warming or enter debates in the public sphere *as scientists*? And, what is the role of scientists employed by the federal government? Should they be free to speak publicly about the implications of their research?

Early Warners: Disputes Over the Public Role of Environmental Scientists

Biologist Paul Ehrlich (2002) has expressed the conflict felt by a number of environmental scientists: Although there is "little dispute within the knowledgeable scientific community today about the global ecological situation and the . . . well-documented environmental danger," he observed that the majority of the public and public decision makers were still unaware of the seriousness of the problem (p. 31). On the other hand, epidemiologist Steve Wing (2002) has recognized the natural reluctance of many academic researchers to interact with the news media, particularly when their research may be misinterpreted. Still, he insisted, public health researchers and epidemiologists who work with at-risk communities have a special responsibility to make their findings public. By doing so, research can help community members "protect themselves, can motivate participation in democratic processes, and can influence public opinion and policy makers" (p. 442).

Dilemmas of Neutrality and Scientists' Credibility

The conflicts that Ehrlich (2002) and Wing (2002) outline springs from the fact that many environmental scientists find themselves asked to choose between two very different and competing identities: Are they laboratory scientists, whose duty is to remain neutral, disregarding the implications of their research? Or are they environmental physicians of a sort, guided by a medical ethic—the impulse to go beyond the diagnosis of problem to a prescription for its cure? This dilemma was heightened by the new discipline of conservation biology that emerged in the late 1980s and a series of provocative essays by one of its founders. Biologist Michael Soulé (1985) insisted that conservation biology was a **crisis discipline**, that is, its emergence was necessitated by a rapid ecological perturbation with irreversible effects on species, communities, and ecosystems (p. 727). He believed that scientists, therefore, cannot remain silent in the face of a "biodiversity crisis that will reach a crescendo in the first half of the twenty-first century" (Soulé, 1987, p. 4). Indeed, scientists have an ethical duty to offer recommendations to address this worsening situation, even with imperfect knowledge, because "the risks of non-action may be greater than the risks of inappropriate action" (Soulé, 1986, p. 6).

Soulé's challenge and the rise of conservation biology have provoked considerable debate within the environmental sciences. Traditionally, scientists have been viewed as neutral parties who rely on objective procedures to investigate problems or questions, with the resulting empirical evidence laying the basis for any policy implications (Mason, 1962). Shabecoff (2000) summarized this traditional view when he wrote, "The scientist, free of preconceived values, seeks the truth and follows it wherever it leads. It is assumed that whatever the outcome of the search, it will benefit human welfare" (p. 140). As a result, many scientists fear that to abandon this identity by entering public arenas to advocate responses to environmental problems would violate an ethic of objectivity and risk the credibility of scientists themselves (Slobodkin, 2000; Wiens, 1997).

Other scientists, especially ecologists, have begun to question the ethical appropriateness of scientists' silence outside their laboratories in the face of worsening environmental problems. Recently, climate scientists, in particular, have spoken out publicly to warn of the dangers in not acting urgently to address global warming. For example, Rajendra Pachauri, director of the United Nations' Intergovernmental Panel on Climate Change, warned, "If there's no action before 2012, that's too late. What we do in the next two to three years will determine our future. This is the defining moment" (quoted in Rosenthal, 2007). Yet, some scientists who have spoken so publicly, particularly scientists working for the federal government, have faced repercussions and have seen their research criticized. The controversy over scientists' identity and their ethical duty in the face of ecological and human challenges has its roots in earlier controversies, and it may be useful to briefly review this history.

Environmental Scientists as Early Warners

The advent of nuclear weapons in 1945 and scientists' pivotal role in their development prompted one of the first major debates over the ethical responsibilities of scientists. Along with nuclear scientists, molecular biologists also began to insist on a greater scientific voice in informing the public and policymakers of the consequences of the new research emerging after World War II (Berg, Baltimore, Boyer, Cohen, & Davis, 1974; Morin, 1993). As a result, scientific associations such as the Federation of American Scientists, along with journals such as the *Bulletin of the Atomic Scientists,* arose to represent scientists in the public realm (Kendall, 2000).

By 1969, the Union of Concerned Scientists had formed to address survival problems in the late 20th century, particularly the dangers of nuclear war. Having since expanded its scope to problems of global warming and the potential dangers of genetic manipulation, the UCS now includes more than 250,000 scientists and citizens. The organization defines its mission as combining "independent scientific research and citizen action to develop innovative, practical solutions and to secure responsible changes in government policy, corporate practices, and consumer choices" (UCS, 2009, para. 1).

Other scientists also began to participate in public debates about the environment. For example, Physicians for Social Responsibility (PSR) brings knowledge of medical science to environmental and health problems caused by new technologies and industrial practices. Its focus most recently on global warming, as well as toxic pollution, includes advocacy for comprehensive energy legislation in the U.S. Congress (PSR, 2009). And, in a joint statement in 2007, officials of the national science academies in the United States, China, India, Japan, and other nations publicly called for all countries of the world to cooperate in responding to global climate change: "It is unequivocal that the climate is changing, and it is very likely that this is predominantly caused by the increasing human interference with the atmosphere. These changes will transform the environmental conditions on Earth unless countermeasures are taken" (Joint Science Academies' Statement, 2007, para. 2).

The Debate Within the Scientific Community

Beyond these groups, a contentious debate has arisen since the 1990s in scientific journals about scientists' responsibilities in their own work. Along with Michael Soulé's earlier essays, James Karr's 1993 letter in the journal *Conservation Biology* ignited a debate over the appropriateness of science advocacy. Stressing the responsibility of scientists to report clearly the ecological consequences of society's actions, Karr equated this duty with the responsibility faced by an engineer who discovers a fatal flaw in a design (p. 8). In 1996, the debate flowered into full bloom when *Conservation Biology* published a special section on "the role of advocacy in the science of conservation biology" (Noss, 1996, p. 904). The gauntlet was thrown down in the opening essay: "Conservation biology is inescapably normative. Advocacy for the preservation of biodiversity is part of the scientific practice of conservation biology. . . . To pretend that acquisition of 'positive knowledge' alone will avert mass extinctions is misguided" (Barry & Oelschlaeger, 1996, p. 905).

Other scientists took a differing view of the role of environmental science, reflecting the traditional belief that advocacy taints a scientist's credibility. In his review of an Ecological Society of America symposium on science, values, and policies, Edward Rykiel (2001) argued that scientists must separate their role as providers of impartial information to the public from the inherently opposite role of advocates, as value-driven campaigners. Other ecologists have agreed, insisting that, although scientists should report their results to the public, they should not recommend outcomes or decisions. Frederick Wagner (1999), for example, pointed to the image problems some ecologists have had with public officials when they advocate specific approaches; in these cases, he warns, the officials "not infrequently discount our scientific message" (para. 12).

More recently, the debate about the scientist as advocate has taken a sharper focus as new voices have spoken up. For example, William Schlesinger (2003), former dean of the Nicholas School of the Environment and Earth Sciences at Duke University, has argued that scientists have a responsibility "to speak out against a toxic impact to our environment, just as we would expect a physician to speak against a carcinogenic substance that might contaminate our food" (p. 23A). And British theoretical physicist Stephen Hawking, author of *A Brief History of Time*, told a gathering of scientists in 2007 that they had a duty of to speak out:

> As scientists . . . we are learning how human activities and technologies are affecting climate systems in ways that may forever change life on Earth. . . . As citizens of the world, we have a duty to alert the public to the unnecessary risks that we live with every day, and to the perils we foresee if governments and societies do not take action now . . . to prevent further climate change. As we stand at the brink of . . . a period of unprecedented climate change, scientists have a special responsibility (quoted in Connor, 2007, para. 5, 6)

But, Michael Soulé, William Schlesinger, and Stephen Hawkins are university scientists, free to speak publicly if they choose. Other scientists, particularly in government, may face interference in their research and even censorship of reports and Web postings intended for public release.

Political Interference in Science Communication

As we saw in the opening of this chapter, NASA officials ordered its public affairs staff to monitor Dr. James Hansen's lectures, scientific papers, and postings on the Goddard Website after Hansen had spoken publicly about the imminent danger from climate change. Similar reports of restrictions on federal scientists began to appear in the news media, books, reports by monitoring groups, and the Blogosphere during the eight years of the Bush administration (for example, Mooney, 2006; Revkin, 2005; UCS, 2004, 2008a).

One case occurred early in the Bush administration. On March 7, 2001, Ian Thomas, a 33-year-old government cartographer, posted a map of caribou calving areas in the Arctic National Wildlife Refuge on a U.S. Geological Survey Website. At the time, Thomas had been working on maps for all of the national wildlife refuges and national parks, using the new National Landcover Datasets (Thomas, 2001). Nevertheless, his timing in posting the new map of caribou calving areas landed him in the center of a national controversy. The U.S. Congress had begun to debate a proposal from President George W. Bush's administration to open parts of the Arctic National Wildlife Refuge (ANWR) to oil and gas drilling, and the calving grounds appeared to be directly in the path.

On his first day at work after posting his map, Thomas was fired and his Website removed. In an official statement, a public affairs officer for the U.S. Geological Survey stated that Thomas had been "operating outside the scope of [his] contract" and had not had his maps "scientifically reviewed or approved" before posting them on the Website (Harlow, 2001). Thomas himself believed that his dismissal was "a high-level political decision to set an example to other federal scientists" who might not support the administration's campaign to open the refuge for oil and gas exploration. "I thought that I was helping further public and scientific understanding and debate of the issues at ANWR by making some clearer maps," Thomas wrote in an e-mail to colleagues (2001).

More comprehensive evidence of political interference in federal science communication soon appeared. In 2004, more than 60 prestigious scientists (including 20 Nobel Prize–winners) issued a report sharply criticizing the misuse and suppression of science by federal agencies. The *Scientific Integrity in Policymaking* report, released by the Union of Concerned Scientists, charged that White House officials had engaged in "a well-established pattern of suppression and distortion of scientific findings" (p. 2). Among its findings, the report claimed that officials had "misrepresented scientific consensus on global warming, censored at least one report on climate change, manipulated scientific findings on the emissions of mercury from power plants and suppressed information on condom use" (Glanz, 2004, p. A21). (For the report's principal conclusions, see "FYI: *Scientific Integrity in Policymaking*.")

☞ **FYI**   **Scientific Integrity in Policymaking**

On February 18, 2004, the Union of Concerned Scientists made public its report, *Scientific Integrity in Policymaking: An Investigation Into the Bush Administration's Misuse of Science*. The principal findings of the investigation into charges of misuse of science by government officials were stated in the report's executive summary:

- There is a well-established pattern of suppression and distortion of scientific findings by high-ranking Bush administration political appointees across numerous federal agencies. . . .

- There is strong documentation of a wide-ranging effort to manipulate the government's scientific advisory system to prevent the appearance of advice that might run counter to the administration's political agenda. . . .

- There is evidence that the administration often imposes restrictions on what government scientists can say or write about "sensitive" topics. . . . [And]

- There is significant evidence that the scope and scale of the manipulation, suppression, and misrepresentation of science . . . is unprecedented. (p. 3)

SOURCE: Union of Concerned Scientists (2004). The complete report is available at http://www.ucsusa.org.

The UCS report defended the importance of scientists' role in the public sphere. It called upon other scientists to "encourage their professional societies and colleagues to become engaged in this issue, discuss their concerns directly with elected representatives, and communicate the importance of this issue to the public, both directly and through the media" (p. 3).

In the following years, more evidence of political interference with science communication would emerge. One of the more egregious instances was the case of Philip A. Cooney, Chief of Staff for the White House Council on Environmental Policy. In 2005, the *New York Times* obtained documents showing that Cooney—the former "climate team leader" and a lobbyist at the American Petroleum Institute—had personally edited several reports intended for public release by the federal Climate Change Science Program in 2002 and 2003. In handwritten notes, Cooney "removed or adjusted descriptions of climate research that government scientists and their supervisors . . . had already approved" (Revkin, 2005, para. 2). *Times* reporter Andrew Revkin (2005) noted that the changes, "while sometimes as subtle as the insertion of the phrase 'significant and fundamental' before the word 'uncertainties,' *tend to produce an air of doubt about findings that most climate experts say are robust*" (para. 3; emphasis added). In other instances, Cooney wrote in the margins, "speculative findings/musings," and he inserted the phrase "reduce the significant, remaining uncertainties associated with human induced climate change" into text, which had otherwise stated, "the role for the CCRI is to [**inserted change**] facilitate full use of this scientific information in policy and decision making . . ." (see Figure 9.2).

Finally, in January 2007, the U.S. House of Representatives Committee on Oversight and Government Reform held hearings into charges that the Bush administration had

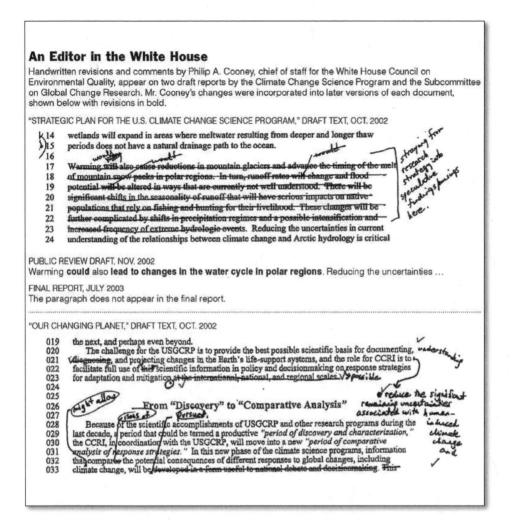

Figure 9.2	Philip A. Cooney, Chief of Staff for the White House Council on Environmental Policy (and former lobbyist at the American Petroleum Institute) personally edited reports intended for public release by the federal Climate Change Science Program in 2002 and 2003.

SOURCE: Revkin, A. (2005, June 8). Bush aide softened greenhouse gas links to global warming. *New York Times*. Retrieved January 6, 2009, from http://www.nytimes.com/2005/06/08/politics/08climate.html?_r=1&hp&ex=1118289600&e

engaged in "systemic tampering with the work of government climate scientists to eliminate politically inconvenient material about global warming" (Goldenberg, 2007, para. 1). At the public hearing, scientists and environmental groups described the efforts of the White House "to remove references to global warming from scientific reports and limit public mention of the topic to avoid pressure on an administration opposed to mandatory controls on greenhouse gas emissions" (para. 2). One witness charged that these efforts discouraged academic inquiry by government scientists: "'If you know what you are writing has to go through a White House clearance before it is to be published, people start writing for the class,' said Rick Piltz, a former senior associate at the US Climate Change Science Programme. 'An anticipatory kind of self-censorship sets in'" (quoted in Goldenberg, 2007, para. 5).

As I write, the Obama administration has taken a sharply different tone toward the role of science in governmental policy making, stating in his January 2009 inaugural address, "We will restore science to its rightful place" ("Obama's Inaugural Address," 2009, para. 16). All signs points to a lessening of ideological battles over science and an elevation of the importance of peer-reviewed science in federal policy making. With the looming threats from rapidly increasing climate change facing the new administration, freedom of federal scientists to speak openly is more important than ever.

Environmental Science and the Public

While I have focused much of this chapter on symbolic legitimacy conflict among scientists, industry, and governmental officials, scientists often work in less controversial ways with citizen groups, the media, and policymakers. Indeed, initiatives have increased in recent years for bringing scientists, the public, and media together to resolve misunderstandings and implement projects.

One example of a successful effort by scientists to bridge the gap between the technical sphere and interested public and environmental groups was the decommissioning of the dam on the Kennebec River in Maine. In his book *Dam Politics: Restoring America's Rivers,* William Lowry (2003) describes the efforts of scientists to educate the public about the ecological importance of rivers, teaching values that go beyond the economic uses of rivers for transportation, irrigation, and hydroelectric power. In the Kennebec case, local and federal officials, scientists, and public interest groups not only cooperated in removing the dam but have begun restoration attempts to aid the return of spawning fish native to the area. And, more recently, groups like the Yale Forum on Climate Change and the Media have begun to bring together reporters and editors with prominent climate scientists for briefings on the latest research on global warming and its impacts (Russell, 2008, para. 11).

Overall, support has been increasing for more ways to bring together scientists, environmental officials, and members of the public. For example, Lach, List, Steel, and Shindler (2003) surveyed the attitudes of scientists, resource managers, and citizens about their preferred roles for research and the involvement of field ecologists in natural resource management in the Pacific Northwest. The study identified five levels of escalating involvement in public communication and decision making that research scientists might have. These levels range from simply "reporting scientific results that others use in making decisions on natural resource management issues," to:

- Interpreting scientific results for others who are involved in natural resource . . . decisions
- Working closely with managers and others in integrating scientific results into management decisions

- Actively advocating for specific . . . natural resource management decisions
- Making decisions about natural resource management policy. (p. 174)

With the exception of scientists, all the surveyed groups preferred the role of integrating scientific results into management decisions; that is, they would support means to ensure that management decisions—such as deciding where logging could occur—reflected the findings of science more directly. Scientists preferred the slightly more cautious role of interpreting scientific results for others, though there was some support among scientists for the integrative role as well (p. 174). In other words, while many scientists preferred to limit their roles in the public sphere to reports and explanations of their findings, members of the public and natural resource managers themselves wanted greater involvement by scientists.

Act Locally!

Science and the Public in the Obama Administration

Arrange for a conservation biologist, a toxicologist, an ecologist, or other environmental scientist on your campus to visit your class to discuss the role of environmental science in the Obama administration as well as the debate about the role of public advocacy in the public sphere. Discuss with your guest these and other questions:

- Who are President Barack Obama's science advisor, Director of the President Council on Environmental Quality (CEQ), and other key environmental science members of his administration?

- What is the status of science in agencies like the EPA, Fish and Wildlife Service, and other environmental agencies?

- Are scientists free to speak to news media about their research with censorship by political appointees?

Finally, what is your guest's own viewpoint? What does he or she believe is the proper role of scientists in the public sphere?

Finally, the ease of research on the Internet has now placed the results of environmental science more easily within reach of anyone with a computer and online access. In some cases, research in the technical sphere has been made available through sites that are easily engaged by the public. For example, in Chapter 3 I discussed the research that is clearly organized and made public by the EPA's Toxic Release Inventory, showing sources of air and water pollution in communities. (See http://www.scorecard.org.) In addition, the requirement under NEPA for environmental impact statements provides additional scientific information about the effects of proposed actions on the environment. With the increased availability of science, the quality of debate within the public sphere has grown immeasurably.

SUMMARY

In this chapter, we have considered several provocative questions about the discourse of science in public controversies over environmental policy. Who should control the uses of scientific research? How should society interpret the meaning of scientific claims when the research is characterized by uncertainty? In disputes over environmental policy especially, access to and command of technical knowledge is an important source of legitimacy. Equally important to the importance of scientific knowledge are the symbolic associations that public officials, industry, and the public attach to the claims of science, which constitute critical symbolic legitimacy boundaries in the public debate. Because such boundaries influence many decisions about business activity, scientific discourse often becomes a site for public debate and controversy.

In the second section, we looked at one way in which some have urged that we manage the uncertainty of scientific claims about environmental dangers. The precautionary principle states that, when an activity threatens human health or the environment, even if some cause-and-effect relationships are not fully established scientifically, caution should be taken. Thus, when deciding what action to take about unsafe products or business activities, it is industry, rather than the public, who should bear the burden of proving that it is safe.

Although it can safeguard against uncertainty, the appeal to caution or prudence also can restrict new products and increase costs to industry. In the third section, we examined the attempts by some industrial and political interests to challenge the claims of environmental science through a trope of uncertainty and other forms of symbolic legitimacy conflict. By funding a series of challenges to scientific claims of global warming and other environmental dangers, political and corporate groups have suggested that there is danger in taking action prematurely, a risk of making the wrong decision. The goal of such legitimacy challenges is to create doubt in the public's minds, thereby lessening the will to political action, particularly action that might harm business or industrial interests.

Finally, we explored recent and sometimes contentious debates about the appropriate roles of scientists, as well as charges of political interference in federal scientists' communication with the public. At stake are both the public's perception of the symbolic legitimacy of science and the growing sense of urgency about loss of biodiversity and climate change that time is running out and that "the risks of non-action may be greater than the risks of inappropriate action" (Soulé, 1986, p. 6).

KEY TERMS

Communication-Related Concepts

Crisis discipline: Term used to characterize the new discipline of conservation biology; coined by biologist Michael Soulé (1985) to refer to the duty of scientists, in the face of a looming biodiversity crisis, to offer recommendations to address this worsening situation, even with imperfect knowledge.

Progressive ideal: Put forth by the 1920s and 1930s Progressive movement, the concept of a neutral, science-based policy as the best approach to government regulation of industry.

Symbolic legitimacy: The perceived correctness, authority, or common sense of a policy or approach to a problem relative to other competing responses. (For a definition of symbolic legitimacy boundaries, see Chapter 2.)

Technocracy: John Dewey's term denoting a government ruled by experts.

Think tanks: Nonprofit, advocacy-based groups, modeled on the image of neutral policy centers.

Trope of uncertainty: An appeal that functions to nurture doubt in the public's perception of scientific claims and thereby to delay calls for action; in rhetorical terms, the trope of uncertainty "turns" or alters the public's understanding of what is at stake, suggesting there is a danger in acting prematurely, a risk of making the wrong decision.

Environment-Related Concepts

Environmental skepticism: An attitude that disputes the seriousness of environmental problems and questions the credibility of environmental science.

Paradox for conservation: Awareness that "knowledge is always incomplete, yet the scale of human influence on ecosystems demands action without delay" (quoted in Scully, 2005, p. B13).

Precautionary principle: As defined by the 1998 Wingspread conference, "When an activity raises threats of harm to human health or the environment, precautionary measures should be taken even if some cause and effect relationships are not fully established scientifically. In this context the proponent of an activity, rather than the public, should bear the burden of proof" (SEHN, 1998, "Wingspread Consensus Statement," para. 5).

DISCUSSION QUESTIONS

1. Is the precautionary principle a clear guide to decision making, or does it leave too much discretion to agency staff or others to determine whether a product is unsafe or should be withdrawn from the market? Should industry carry the burden of demonstrating to the general public that its products or chemical substances are safe *before* releasing them to the marketplace?

2. Does corporate funding of scientific research necessarily taint the credibility or influence the conclusions of scientists' reports?

3. What is the role of the media in disclosing the sources of funding or conflicts of interest for scientific reports when they report an environmental story?

4. Should ecologists and other environmental scientists ever serve as advocates in the public sphere? Where do you draw the line—if at all—in how far scientists should go in entering the public sphere or working with government agencies?

5. What changes from the Bush administration, if any, characterize the freedom of government scientists to communication freely with the public under the Obama administration?

REFERENCES

Austin, A. (2002). Advancing accumulation and managing its discontents: The US antienvironmental movement. *Sociological spectrum, 22,* 71–105.

Bailey, R. (2002, August 14). *Starvation a by-product of looming trade war.* Washington, DC: Cato Institute. Retrieved May 23, 2005, from http://www.cato.org.

Barringer, F. (2005, May 27). Government shirked its duty to wild fish, a judge rules. *The New York Times,* p. A14.

Barry, D., & Oelschlaeger, M. (1996). A science for survival: Values and conservation biology. *Conservation Biology, 10,* 905–911.

Beder, S. (1999, April/March). Corporate hijacking of the greenhouse debate. *The Ecologist,* 119–122.

Berg, P., Baltimore, D., Boyer, H. W., Cohen, S. N., & Davis, R. W. (1974). Potential biohazards of recombinant DNA molecules. *Science, 185,* 303.

Bowen, M. (2008). *Censoring science: Inside the political attack on Dr. James Hansen and the truth of global warming.* New York: Dutton.

Carson, R. (1962). *Silent spring.* Boston: Houghton Mifflin.

Center for Science in the Public Interest. (2009). *About CSPI.* Retrieved January 5, 2009, from http://www.cspinet.org/about.

Connor, S. (2007, January 18). Hawking warns: We must recognise the catastrophic dangers of climate change. *The Independent* [UK]. Retrieved January 1, 2009, from http://www.independent.co.uk.

Cushman, J. H. (1998, April 26). Industrial group plans to battle climate treaty. *The New York Times,* p. A1.

Dewey, J. (1927). *The public and its problems.* New York: Henry Holt.

Dispensa, J., & Brulle, R. (2003). Media's social construction of environmental issues: Focus on global warming—a comparative study. *International Journal of Sociology and Social Policy, 23*(10), 74–105.

Ehrlich, P. R. (2002). Human natures, nature conservation, and environmental ethics. *BioScience, 52*(1), 31–43.

Ehrlich, P. R., & Ehrlich, A. H. (1996). *Betrayal of science and reason: How anti-environmental rhetoric threatens our future.* Washington, DC: Island Press/Shearwater Books.

Eilperin, J. (2006, January 29). Debate on climate shifts to issue of irreparable change. *The Washington Post,* p. A1.

Glanz, J. (2004, February 19). Scientist says administration distorts facts. *The New York Times,* p. A21.

Goklany, I. M. (2001). *The precautionary principle: A critical appraisal of environmental risk assessment.* Washington, DC: Cato Institute.

Goldenberg, S. (2007, January 31). Bush administration accused of doctoring scientists' reports on global warming. *The Guardian.* Retrieved January 6, 2009, from http://www.guardian.co.uk.

Grundmann, R. (2007). Climate change and knowledge politics. *Environmental Politics, 16,* 414–432.

Hanners, D. (1998, August 4). Scientists were paid to write letters: Tobacco industry sought to discredit EPA report. *St. Paul Pioneer Press.* Retrieved September 9, 2003, from http://junkscience.com.

Harlow, T. (2001, March 16). [Message posted on Infoterra listserv]. Retrieved June 17, 2003, from http://www.peer.org.

Harman, W. (1998). *Global mind change: The promise of the twenty-first century.* San Francisco: Berrett-Koehler.

Hays, S. P. (2000). *A history of environmental politics since 1945.* Pittsburgh: University of Pittsburgh Press.

Intergovernmental Panel on Climate Change. (2007a). *Climate change 2007: Synthesis report.* UN Environment Program. Retrieved November 2, 2008, from http://www.ipcc.ch/ipccreports.

Intergovernmental Panel on Climate Change. (2007b). *Climate change 2007: The physical science basis: Summary for policymakers.* UN Environment Program. Retrieved March 2, 2009, from http://www.aaas.

Integrity in Science Project. (2009). *About the Integrity in Science Project.* Retrieved January 5, 2009, from http://www.cspinet.org/integrity.

Jacques, P. J., Dunlap, R. E., & Freeman, M. (2008). The organisation of denial: Conservative think tanks and environmental skepticism. *Environmental Politics, 17*(3), 349–385.

Jehl, D. (2001, March 21). E.P.A. to abandon new arsenic limits for water supply. *The New York Times,* p. A1.

Joint Science Academies' Statement on Growth and Responsibility. (2007, May). *Sustainability, energy efficiency and climate protection.* Retrieved January 5, 2009, from http://www.nationalacademies.org.

Karr, J. R. (1993). Advocacy and responsibility. *Conservation Biology, 7*(1), 8.

Kendall, H. W. (2000). *A distant light: Scientists and public policy.* New York: Springer-Verlag.

Krimsky, S., et al. (1998, July–October). Scientific journals and their authors' financial interests: A pilot study. *Psychother Psychosom, 67*(4–5), 194–201.

Lach, D., List, P., Steel, B., & Shindler, B. (2003). Advocacy and credibility of ecological scientists in resource decision-making: A regional study. *Bioscience, 53*(2), 170–178.

Lesly, P. (1992). Coping with opposition groups. *Public Relations Review, 18*(4), 325–334.

Lowry, W. R. (2003). *Dam politics: Restoring America's rivers.* Washington, DC: Georgetown University Press.

Luntz Research Companies. (2001). The environment: A cleaner, safer, healthier America. In *Straight Talk* (pp. 131–146). Retrieved June 12, 2003, from http://www.ewg.org.

Markowitz, G., & Rosner, D. (2002). *Deceit and denial: The deadly politics of industrial pollution.* Berkeley: University of California Press.

Mason, S. F. (1962). *A history of the sciences.* New York: Collier Books.

Michaels, P. (2004). *Meltdown: The predictable distortion of global warming by scientists, politicians, and the media.* Washington, DC: Cato Institute.

Michaels, D., & Monforton, C. (2005). Manufacturing uncertainty: Contested science and the protection of the public's health and environment. *Public Health Matters, 95*(1), 39–48.

Montague, P. (1999, July 1). The uses of scientific uncertainty. *Rachel's Environment & Health News, 657*. Retrieved August, 25, 2002, from http://www.rachel.org.

Mooney, C. (2006). *The Republican war on science.* New York: Basic Books.

Morin, A. J. (1993). *Science policy and politics.* Englewood Cliffs, NJ: Prentice Hall.

National Environmental Trust. (1998). *Monitor 404: Information missing from your daily news.* [Press release]. Retrieved September 2, 2005, from www.monitor.net.

National Research Council Committee on Environmental Epidemiology. (1991). *Environmental epidemiology: Vol. 1. Public health and hazardous wastes.* Washington, DC: National Academy Press.

Noss, R. F. (1996). Conservation biology, values, and advocacy. *Conservation Biology, 10,* 904.

Obama's Inaugural Address. (2009, January 20). *The Washington Post.* Retrieved March 2, 2009, from http://media.washingtonpost.com.

Pfeffer, W. T., Harper, J. T., & O'Neel, S. (2008, September 5). Kinematic constraints on glacier contributions to 21st-century sea level rise. *Science, 321*(5894), 1340–1343.

Physicians for Social Responsibility. (2009). *Environment and Health.* Retrieved January 5, 2009, from http://www.psr.org.

Raffensperger, C. (1998). Editor's note: The, precautionary principle—a fact sheet. *The Networker, 3*(1), para. 1. Retrieved August 25, 2003, from http://www.sehn.org.

Raffensperger, C., & Barrett, K. (2001, September). In defense of the precautionary principle. *Nature Biotechnology, 19,* 811–812. Retrieved May 23, 2005, from http://www.biotech-info.net.

Rahmstorf, S. (2007, March 27). The IPCC sea level numbers. *RealClimate.org.* Retrieved January 2, 2009, from http://www.realclimate.org.

Rampton, S., & Stauber, J. (2002). *Trust us, we're experts!* New York: Jeremy P. Tarcher/Putnam.

Revkin, A. (2005, June 8). Bush aide softened greenhouse gas links to global warming. *The New York Times.* Retrieved January 6, 2009, from http://www.nytimes.com.

Revkin, A. C. (2006a, January 29). Climate expert says NASA tried to silence him. *The New York Times,* p. A1.

Revkin, A. C. (2006b, February 8). A young Bush appointee resigns his post at NASA. *The New York Times,* p. A11.

Revkin, A. C., & Seelye, K. Q. (2003, June 19). Report by the E.P.A. leaves out data on climate change. *The New York Times.* Retrieved June 19, 2003, from http://www.nytimes.com.

Rosenthal, E. (2007, November 17). U.N. report describes risks of inaction on climate change. *The New York Times.* Retrieved November 3, 2008, from http://www.nytimes.com.

Russell, C. (2008, Climate change: Now what? *Columbia Journalism Review.* The Observatory [online]. Retrieved January 5, 2009, from http://www.cjr.org.

Rykiel, E. J., Jr. (2001). Scientific objectivity, value systems, and policymaking. *BioScience, 51,* 433–436.

Schlesinger, W. (2003, May 18). Academics have right to speak out. [Raleigh, NC] *News & Observer,* p. A23.

Schulzke, E. C. (2000, March 26). *Policy networks and regulatory change in the 104th Congress: Framing the center through symbolic legitimacy conflict.* Paper presented at the meeting of the Western Political Science Association, San Jose, CA.

Science and Environmental Health Network. (1998, January 26). *Wingspread conference on the precautionary principle.* Retrieved August 25, 2003, from http://www.sehn.org.

Scully, M. G. (2005, October 3). Studying ecosystems: The messy intersection between science and politics. *Chronicle of Higher Education,* p. B13.

Seelye, K. Q., & Lee, J. (2003, June 24). E.P.A. calls the U.S. cleaner and greener than 30 years ago. *The New York Times*, p. A28.

Shabecoff, P. (2000). *Earth rising: American environmentalism in the 21st century.* Washington, DC: Island Press.

Slobodkin, L. B. (2000). Proclaiming a new ecological discipline. *Bulletin of the Ecological Society of America, 81,* 223–226.

Soulé, M. E. (Ed.). (1985). What is conservation biology? *BioScience, 35,* 727–734.

Soulé, M. E. (1986). *Conservation biology: The science of scarcity and diversity.* Sunderland, MA: Sinauer Associates.

Soulé, M. E. (1987). History of the Society for Conservation Biology: How and why we got here. *Conservation Biology, 1,* 4–5.

Thomas, I. (2001, March 16). Web censorship. [Email]. Retrieved June 16, 2003, from http://cartome.org.

Union of Concerned Scientists. (2004, February). *Scientific integrity in policymaking: An investigation into the Bush administration's misuse of science.* Cambridge, MA: Union of Concerned Scientists.

Union of Concerned Scientists. (2007, January). *Smoke, Mirrors and Hot Air: How ExxonMobil Uses Big Tobacco's Tactics to "Manufacture Uncertainty" on Climate Change.* Retrieved January 5, 2009, from http://www.ucsusa.org.

Union of Concerned Scientists. (2008a). *Freedom to speak? A report card on federal agency media policies.* Retrieved January 6, 2009, from http://www.ucsusa.org.

Union of Concerned Scientists. (2008b, December 11). *New Interior department rule weakens Endangered Species Act, blatantly disregards rulemaking process.* News Center. Retrieved January 2, 2009, from http://www.ucsusa.org.

Union of Concerned Scientists. (2009). *About us.* Retrieved January 5, 2009, from http://www.ucsusa.org.

U.S. Environmental Protection Agency. (June 23, 2003). EPA announces unprecedented first "draft report on the environment." *EPA Newsroom.* Retrieved June 24, 2003, from http://www.epa.gov.

Wagner, F. H. (1999). Analysis and/or advocacy: What role(s) for ecologists? *EcoEssay Series No. 3.* Santa Barbara, CA: National Center for Ecological Analysis and Synthesis. Retrieved June 12, 2003, from http://nceas.ucsb.ed.

Wiens, J. A. (1997). Scientific responsibility and responsible ecology. *Conservation Ecology, 1*(1), 16. Retrieved June 12, 2003, from http://www.consecol.org.

Wing, S. (2002). Social responsibility and research ethics in community-driven studies of industrialized hog production. *Environmental Health Perspectives, 110*(5), 437–444.

Wilkinson, T. (1998). *Science under siege: The politicians' war on nature and truth.* Boulder, CO: Johnson Books.

Williams, B. A., & Matheny, A. R. (1995). *Democracy, dialogue, and environmental disputes.* New Haven: Yale University Press.

Environmental image enhancement is the use of advertising to improve the image or identity of a corporation, reflecting its environmental concern and performance.

CHAPTER 10

Green Marketing and Corporate Advocacy

Coal industry magnates, who would lose big if new pollution standards are signed into law, spent between $35 million and $45 million on advertising this year—most of it on television ads . . . pitching "clean coal" as a new environmentally friendly fuel.

But the concept of "clean coal" is somewhat nebulous . . . and the most effective technology, carbon sequestration, is still 10–15 years from being built for American plants.

—LoBianco (2008)

The commercial appeared daily on my TV screen: An elderly woman sitting by a pool says confidently, "I believe in the future"; a students repeats, ". . . in the future"; a farmer looks sincere as he says, "I believe in protecting the environment"; a nurse tells us, "I believe that meeting a challenge . . . ," and a young factory worker finishes the sentence, " . . . brings out the best is us." This "I Believe" commercial was the latest ad from the coal industry public relations group, American Coalition for Clean Coal Electricity (ACCCE).

During the same period, a radio ad aired across the United States: "As a single mother, I'm concerned about energy costs." And another voice: "I'm concerned about our growing reliance on imported energy." Then, a reassuring male voice answers: "Whatever the question, American clean coal can be a big part of the answer." The ad continued, assuring listeners that coal is affordable, "plentiful here at home," and most important, *clean* (America's Power, 2009). This ad was also sponsored by ACCCE, a trade group that promotes the interests of coal companies, coal transporters, and electricity producers (SourceWatch, 2009).

The TV and radio advertisements for "clean coal" are just one of many forms of corporate environmental communication within the public sphere. These range from the familiar "green" advertising of products to corporate lobbying aimed at influencing environmental regulations. Corporate lobbying also relies upon media frames such as "economic growth" and the claim that environmental regulations cost jobs. These frames often appear in public relations campaigns and in print or electronic media that carry a message opposing or supporting legislation or other issues affecting the interests of a company or industry.

In general, environmental communication scholars have identified three major types of corporate communication in the public sphere about the environment: (1) the practice of "green marketing," or the construction of an environmental identity for corporate products, images, and behaviors; (2) industry advocacy campaigns aimed at influencing environmental legislation, agency rules, and public opinion, and (3) more aggressive legal strategies to discredit or intimidate environmental critics. In this chapter, I discuss examples of each type of communication. We also, throughout the chapter, describe a skillful and complex dance of identity in corporate communication: the effort by many businesses to appear "green," often while actively opposing environmental protections.

The first section of this chapter provides background for the study of corporate environmental communication by describing the discourse of the free market that underlies much of this communication. Then, the second section examines the first of three major components of corporate communication: the use of public relations and marketing to construct a green identity. I describe not only the advertising of products and corporate images but also the image repair that corporations perform to restore their credibility after environmental accidents such as the spill from the oil tanker *Exxon Valdez* in Alaska. We also look briefly at the discourse of *green consumerism*—marketing that encourages the belief that, by buying allegedly environmentally friendly products, consumers can do their part to protect the planet.

In the third section, I explore another component of corporate environmental communication: the role of corporate advocacy campaigns in the public sphere to influence public opinion and environmental laws. In the final section, I describe a third corporate communication practice, the use of a legal strategy called "Strategic Litigation Against Public Participation," or SLAPP suits, to discredit or intimidate those who criticize industry for harming the environment.

Free Market Discourse and the Environment

As I pointed out in Chapter 1, much of the organized opposition to environmental standards has come from two main sources: (1) older extractive, resource-based industries such as timber, mining, and oil and gas extraction and (2) newer industries such as chemical and electronics manufacturing, transportation, and electric utility companies (which often use coal-fired plants). Second, newer industries also have supported campaigns to persuade the public and Congress to oppose environmental rules that they view as cumbersome or expensive. These rules have included higher fuel efficiency requirements for cars and sport utility vehicles (SUVs), liability of companies under the Superfund law for the cleanup of toxic waste, and curbs on pollutants that contribute to global warming. In each case, opponents of regulations have engaged in communications in the public sphere to influence media, opinion leaders, the general public, and public officials.

Before looking more closely at the diverse forms of corporate communication, it is important to appreciate the ideological premises and sources of persuasion that underlie much of these appeals. Corporate advocacy against governmental regulation does not occur in a vacuum. Instead, it draws upon and furthers a discourse of the "free market" that circulates an ideologically coherent set of meanings about business and the proper role of government.

Behind much of the rhetorical opposition of business and allied groups to environmental standards is a more fundamental belief in the **free market**, a phrase that is usually meant to refer to the absence of governmental restriction of business and commercial activity. As a discourse, the "free market" sustains the idea that the private marketplace is self-regulating and ultimately promotes the social good. As a result, the discourse of the free market constructs an *antagonism* (Chapter 2) with environmental rules, taking such forms as, "We need to get 'big government' off our backs," and "Companies will find the best solutions when left to themselves."

At the core of this rhetoric is the belief held by many corporate leaders that adequate environmental protection can be secured by the operation of the marketplace, through the unrestricted or unregulated buying and selling of products and services. Such faith in the market assumes that "the public interest is discovered in the ability of private markets to transform the individual pursuit of self-interest into an efficient social allocation of resources" (Williams & Matheny, 1995, p. 21). For example, the National Consumer Coalition (NCC) supports market solutions to reduce global warming and solve other environmental problems. The NCC explains, "A market economy benefits consumers by expanding consumer choice and competition and fostering innovation, which lowers costs and improves consumer health and safety" (2004, para. 1).

The assumption that the market is the preferred means for addressing societal problems derives from the Scottish economist Adam Smith's theory of the **invisible hand** of the market. This metaphor is used to name an invisible or natural force of the private marketplace that determines what society values. In his classic book, *An Inquiry Into the Nature and Causes of the Wealth of Nations,* Smith (1776/1910) argued that the sum of individuals' self-interested actions in the marketplace promotes the public's interest, or the common good. He explained that an individual "neither intends to promote the public interest nor knows how much he [sic] is promoting it. . . . He intends only his own gain. And he is in this . . . *led by an invisible hand to promote an end which was no part of his intention*" (p. 400, emphasis added). Business advocacy groups such as the National Consumer Coalition implicitly evoke Adam Smith's premise when they argue that free and open competition in the market leads naturally to innovations that will ensure broader social goods such as cleaner air and safer products.

Not surprisingly, many business leaders argue that, although government requirements to reduce pollution may have been necessary once, such **command-and-control** policies are now outdated. The phrase *command and control* is used by opponents of environmental regulations to refer to government restrictions on business operations. Such regulations specify procedures and technologies for reducing pollution, as well as measurable levels of performance that a company must meet. In their study of business compliance with environmental regulations, Neil Gunningham, Robert Kagan, and Dorothy Thorton (2003) report, "Public policy analysts today often call for a 'second generation' of environmental regulation that relies less on government prescription and more on the imagination and innovativeness of corporate environmental management" (p. 1).

The discourse of the free market has been especially present during recent debates over so-called free trade agreements. Neoliberal economists and supporters of globalization, in particular, believe that by opening global markets and encouraging investment abroad, poor nations not only will grow economically but will foster stronger environmental protections. For example, U.S. trade representative Robert Zoellick (2002) testified before the Congress that "free trade promotes free markets, economic growth, and higher incomes. And as countries grow wealthier, their citizens demand higher labor and environmental standards" (p. 1). And Samuel Aldrich and Jay Lehrwriting (2006), writing for the libertarian think tank, the Heartland Institute, argued that the "nations that have the best track records on environmental protection and improvement are those with the highest amount of free-market capitalism . . . [while] persons living in command-and-control economies, barely surviving on life's necessities of food, clothing, and shelter, use their natural resources to the absolute limit" (para. 4, 6). (For a different view of free market discourse, see "Another Viewpoint: 'The Myth of the Universal Market.")

Another Viewpoint: "The Myth of the Universal Market"

Communication among economists, other social scientists, natural scientists, and lawyers is far from perfect. . . . Economists themselves may have contributed to some misunderstandings . . . about the environment, perhaps through enthusiasm for market solutions, perhaps by neglecting to make explicit all of the necessary qualifications. . . .

Environmental economists, of course, are interested in pollution and other *externalities,* where some consequences of producing or consuming a good or service are external to the market—that is, not considered by producers or consumers. With a negative externality, such as environmental pollution, the total social cost of production may thus exceed the value to consumers. If the market is left to itself, too many pollution-generating products get produced. There's too much pollution, and not enough clean air, for example, to provide maximum general welfare. In this case, laissez-faire markets—because of the market failure, the externalities—are not efficient.

SOURCE: Stavins (2004).

In summary, the discourse of the free market provides a rhetorical and philosophical rationale for corporate opposition to government-imposed standards for environmental performance. As we shall see, this discourse underlies a range of corporate communication practices, including the construction of a green identity and a sophisticated program of political influence.

Corporate Green Marketing

As popular support for the environment increased in the past three decades, many industries have worked to improve their environmental performance. As a result, many corporations now have a twofold goal in their environmental communication programs: (1) to link corporate goals and behavior to the increasingly popular values of environmental quality and (2) to avoid if possible—and, if not, to influence—any additional environmental regulations that will affect their business. In this section, I focus on the first goal: the use of corporate public relations and marketing to construct green identities for corporate products, images, and behaviors. I also look at charges that these marketing efforts are a form of "greenwashing," a pun on "whitewash" that refers to a type of misleading information that is "disseminated by an organization so as to present an environmentally responsible public image" (Pearsall, 1999, p. 624).

Before a corporation organizes an advocacy effort to forestall or shape environmental legislation, it usually has invested heavily in influencing consumers' and the public's perceptions of its identity and business operations Indeed, U.S. businesses spend several billion dollars a year on environmental public relations or what is sometimes called "green marketing." **Green marketing** is a term used to refer to a corporation's attempt to associate its products, services, or identity with environmental values and images. In this section, I use the term *green marketing* to refer to corporate communication used for one of three purposes: (1) product promotion (sales), (2) image enhancement, or (3) image repair. Whatever else green marketing may be, it is principally an attempt to influence the perceptions of consumers, media, politicians, and the public, and it is this function that invites much debate over corporations' behavior.

Green Product Advertising

Perhaps the most familiar form of corporate green marketing is the association of a company's products with popular images and slogans that suggest a concern for the environment. Such **green product advertising** is the attempt to market products as having a minimal impact on the environment and also to "project an image of high quality, including environmental sensitivity, relating both to a product's attributes and its manufacturer's track record for environmental compliance" (Ottman, 1993, p. 48; see also Goldman & Papson, 1996).

The list of such "environmentally sensitive" products can be lengthy: Coffee, cars, water filters, clothing, hair sprays, SUVs, magazines, allergy pills, breakfast cereals, lipstick, and children's toys are but a few examples. These may be visually linked to images of mountain peaks, tropical forests, clear water, or blue skies, or come with labels such as *organic, nontoxic, ozone friendly, biodegradable, phosphate free, fat free, cruelty free;* they may contain the familiar symbol for recycled content (Giuliano, 1999). (See Figure 10.1.)

Of course, as with advertising generally, the company's product is often secondary. What is being sold at the same time is an image or identification with the environment: "An advertisement for a car shows the vehicle outdoors, and . . . ads for allergy medications feature flowers and 'weeds'" (Corbett, 2002, p. 142). In green advertising, the environment offers a seemingly limitless range of possibilities. From Jeep ads

Figure 10.1   What does it mean when a product is advertised as "environmentally friendly" or "natural"? Clorox describes its Green Works line of "natural" household cleaning products as meeting three core principles—made from renewable resources (plant-based), is biodegradable, and is 99 percent free of petrochemicals; in this instance, the product also has been certified by Design for the Environment, a certification by the U.S. Environmental Protection Agency.

encouraging urbanites to escape to mountain ridges to "all-natural" or "organic" breakfast foods, green ads rely on evocative appeals to nature as powerful rhetorical frames.

Examples of green product ads may be unlimited, but the underlying frames for such advertising draw on common themes. What environmental communication scholar Steve Depoe (1991) first identified two decades ago still applies: there are three basic frames for green product advertising: (1) nature as *backdrop* (Jeep ads using mountain terrain), (2) nature as *product* ("all-natural" raisins), and (3) nature as *outcome* (products do not harm and may even improve the environment). Communication scholar Julia Corbett (2002) observes that "using nature merely as a backdrop—whether in the form of wild animals, mountains vistas, or sparkling rivers—is the most common use of the natural world in advertisements" (p. 142).

A classic illustration of the use of nature as backdrop was General Motors (GM) Corporation's full-page, color advertisement on the back cover of the nature magazine *Audubon.* The ad showed a new GM truck in a forest of "old-growth redwoods, with sunlight gently filtering through the trees to the ferns below" (Switzer, 1997, p. 130). A caption accompanying the photo declared, "Our respect for nature goes beyond just giving you an excellent view of it," and noted that GM had made "a sizable contribution to The Nature Conservancy" (quoted in Switzer, p. 130).

In addition to visual layouts, green product advertising also relies on the widespread practice of using environmentally friendly labels on products: "all-natural," "organic," "biodegradable," and so forth. Ottman (2003) reports that "Americans look for eco-labels at the store. . . . Roper's Green Gauge poll shows a growing tendency towards 'pro-cotting'—buying products from companies perceived as having good environmental track records" (para. 4). (The term **pro-cotting** is a play on *boycotting,* or the refusal to buy certain products.) Indeed, environmentally conscious consumers in the United States appear increasingly to be confident in the accuracy of green ads. Burst Media recently reported results of its online survey showing that "the greenest consumer audience is the one that is most accepting and encouraging of green marketing initiatives" (Bulik, 2008, para. 1). Instead of being critical of green product advertising, 44 percent of the self-described "completely green" consumers think that "advertisers are doing an excellent or good job at providing information on green claims, compared to less than 20% of the much larger group of consumers classified as 'aspirationally green'" (para. 4). I return to one of the rhetorical purposes of this type of green consumerism shortly.

A word of caution also may be in order. The field of green advertising is largely unregulated. With the exception of "organic" (which is regulated by the U.S. Department of Agriculture), most environmentally friendly labels and product claims in the United States are governed only by voluntary guidelines. (See "FYI: Guidelines for Environmental Marketing Claims.") As a result, product advertising may signal a range of meaning, from unsubstantiated claims to solid information about the environmental qualities of the product or behavior of the corporation. For example, the business blog, *GreenBiz.com* (2009) recently trumpeted the opportunities opened by "the lack of standards for determining what it means to be a green product—or a green company" (para. 1). It noted that with the growth in consumers who want to buy "green," as well as the popularity of eco-labeling, an opportunity existed "for just about anything to be marketed as green, from simple packaging changes to products and services that radically reduce materials, energy, and waste" (para. 1).

Interestingly, Canada recently banned eco-labels with "vague claims implying general environmental improvement" (Sustainable Life Media, 2008, para. 1). Instead, Canada's Competition Bureau released a new set of guidelines that require companies to stick to "clear, specific, and accurate" claims that have been substantiated. Sheridan Scott, Commissioner of Competition, stated, "Businesses should not make environmental claims unless they can back them up" (Sustainable Life Media, 2008, para. 2).

As a result of the largely unregulated arena of corporate greenwashing, numerous groups have arisen to monitor and/or to verify product advertising claims. While the U.S. Department of Agriculture sets standards for "organic" products (www.ams.usda.gov/nop), there is no uniform standard for other labels such as "free range." In fact, "one company's free range-label might mean that the animal went outside for 15 minutes a day, while another's might mean that the animal roamed a 10-acre field all its life" ("Consumers Beware," 2006, p. 23A). The most prominent independent group is SourceWatch, which monitors corporate funding and behavior generally. (See http://www.sourcewatch.org.)

☞ **FYI** | **Guidelines for Environmental Marketing Claims**

What does it mean to purchase a product that is promoted as environmentally friendly or labeled "recycled" or "nontoxic"? Are businesses required to prove such claims? The Federal Trade Commission's "Guides for the Use of Environmental Marketing Claims" (Section 260.7) states:

General environmental benefit claims: It is deceptive to misrepresent, directly or by implication, that a product, package or service offers a general environmental benefit. Unqualified general claims of environmental benefit are difficult to interpret, and depending on their context, may convey a wide range of meanings to consumers. In many cases, such claims may convey that the product, package or service has specific and far-reaching environmental benefits. . . . Every express and material [sic] implied claim that the general assertion conveys to reasonable consumers about an objective quality, feature or attribute of a product or service must be substantiated. Unless this substantiation duty can be met, broad environmental claims should either be avoided or qualified, as necessary, to prevent deception about the specific nature of the environmental benefit being asserted.

However, the Federal Trade Commission (FTC) guidelines are voluntary. Section 260.2 clearly states, "Because the guides are not legislative rules under Section 18 of the FTC Act, they are not themselves enforceable regulations, nor do they have the force and effect of law." As one critic noted, "Nothing is done unless someone complains" (Giuliano, 1999, p. 1).

Read the complete Federal Trade Commission's "Guides for the Use of Environmental Marketing Claims" at http://www.ftc.gov.

Other groups monitor specific claims, for example, that eggs are "cage free" and that vegetables and meat are "natural," "free range," or "humanely raised." A few animal welfare groups issue their own labels that certify when products meet certain criteria. For example, the American Humane Society has a "free-farmed" label, and Humane Farm Animal Care oversees a "certified-humane" label. And Whole Foods has been developing an "animal-compassionate" program that will require that animals be raised "in a humane manner" (cage-free, and so on), until they are slaughtered (Martin, 2006).

Image Enhancement

Along with the green marketing of products, corporate communication relies on **environmental image enhancement**, the use of advertising to improve the image or identity of a corporation itself, reflecting its environmental concern and performance. As environmental values became increasingly popular in the United States and other countries, many corporations began to expand their communication to link their identities and behaviors with "images of environmentally responsible corporate citizens" (Schumann, Hathcote, & West, 1991, p. 35). This communication takes two important forms: image advertising and corporate environmental reports.

Image Advertising: The Ad Wars Over "Clean Coal"

Corporations must navigate a constantly changing business environment, and doing so often requires an investment of resources in ensuring that the public maintains a positive image of a corporation's identity and performance. This sometimes takes the form of an image advertising campaign. For example, during a period of high gasoline prices in the United States, ExxonMobil (2005) sponsored a series of full-page ads in the *New York Times* promoting its concern for energy and the environment. In one ad, the giant oil company declared:

> Because we take energy seriously, we take our responsibilities seriously too. In how we look for it. How we retrieve it. . . . And why we're now making the largest-ever investment in independent climate and energy research that is specifically designed to look for new breakthrough technologies. (p. A5)

(For an analysis of some of the first corporate environmental image ads by Mobil and Exxon, see Crable & Vibbert, 1983; and Porter, 1992.)

One of the most visible image enhancement efforts has been the coal industry's multimillion dollar "Clean Coal" ad campaign. Since 2002, high-quality-production ads have appeared thousands of times on TV, radio, billboards, and online. (The "I Believe" and "Clean Coal" ads at the opening of this chapter are from this campaign.) Starting in 2002, the coal industry sponsored three TV ads that ran a total of 845 times in Washington, D.C., targeting lawmakers. One of the ads declared that Americans "are learning that advancements in clean coal technologies are effectively making our environment cleaner," while a second ad assured listeners that "new coal-based power plants built beginning in about 2020 may well use technologies that are so advanced that they'll be virtually pollution-free" (quoted in SourceWatch, 2009, para. 4).

These ads are not trying to sell a product—a ton of coal or a new power plant. Instead, they are intended to reassure lawmakers (and other opinion leaders) that the *coal industry* is vital to America's energy future, and that, because coal is "clean"—that is, coal-burning power plants can produce electricity without causing pollution—the industry should not be regulated. Why? Why does the coal industry feel an image campaign is needed? What is the changing business environment that the U.S. coal industry feels it must navigate in order to survive?

Fundamentally, the business environment for coal is changing. While U.S. laws already regulate emissions of pollutants like sulfur dioxide and mercury from coal-burning power plants, the burning of coal also produces carbon dioxide (CO_2), a greenhouse gas. Worldwide, coal-burning power plants are a major source of global warming. As a result, the U.S. Congress is expected to enact new regulations to reduce CO_2 emissions from coal-burning power plants (and other sources) in 2009–2010. At the same time, state governments are mandating that a percentage of energy in these states come from renewable sources like wind or solar, or from greater energy efficiencies.

Already proposals for new coal-based power plants are being rejected in the United States, and major financial institutions have begun to impose stricter requirements on loans for these projects. In 2008, three of the nation's largest investment firms—Citigroup, J.P. Morgan Chase & Co., and Morgan Stanley—announced they were imposing new requirements for financing construction that "will make it harder for companies to build coal-fired power plants in the U.S." (Ball, 2008, 1).

As a result, the coal industry invested heavily in a multimillion "clean coal" ad campaign in an attempt to forestall new regulations on coal-burning power plants. In 2008 alone, industry groups like the American Coalition for Clean Coal Electricity spent $35 million to $45 million on image advertising, "most of it on television ads aired during the 2008 campaigns—pitching 'clean coal' as a new environmentally friendly fuel" (LoBianco, 2008, para. 2; Mufson, 2008). ACCCE, formerly called Americans for Balanced Energy Choices, is a public relations group for coal mining companies, coal transport (railroads), and coal-electricity producers (SourceWatch, 2009). Many of the TV and billboard ads attempt to drive viewers to more detailed information on ACCCE's sophisticated Website, AmericasPower.org.

Chapter 1 featured one of the ACCCE ads. Its "Adios" ad shows an older couple on their front porch, a young woman driving her convertible, two workers going into a factory, kids waving, and a family at the beach. A (male) voice declares:

> We wish we could say farewell to our dependence on foreign energy. And we'd like to say "adios" to rising energy costs. But first, we have to say "so long" to our outdated perceptions about coal. And we have to continue to advance new clean coal technologies to further reduce emissions, including the eventual capture and storage of CO_2. If we don't, we may have to say "goodbye" to the American way of life we all know and love. Clean coal. America's power. (America's Power, 2009)

The ad draws on the strategy of invoking social norms (Chapter 7) to suggest ordinary Americans—like "us"—are saying "so long" to "outdated perceptions about coal," and that coal can continue to power "the American way of life." But, is this image enhancement campaign working?

There is some evidence suggesting the ad campaign may have had an impact on public attitudes about coal. A public opinion poll on the eve of the 2008 U.S. presidential election (sponsored by ACCCE) found that "72 percent of opinion leaders nationwide support the use of coal to generate electricity, a significant increase over the past year and the highest level of support since the group began polling nearly 10 years ago" (*Business Wire,* 2008, para. 3). Joe Lucas, vice president of communications at ACCCE, confidently stated, "The fundamentals of the energy debate have changed. While environmental concerns were the primary driver of the debate in the past, this poll shows that energy concerns are more pressing" (2008, para. 7).

The prospect for new coal plants, however, may not be as bright as ACCCE assumes. Only days after ACCCE released its poll results, the Associated Press (2008) reported, "The fate of scores of new coal-burning power plants is now in limbo over whether to regulate heat-trapping greenhouse gases" (para. 1). The reason was a ruling by an Environmental Protection Agency (EPA) appeals panel that rejected a federal permit for a Utah coal-based power plant, saying the permit had not required controls on carbon dioxide. (The ruling was prompted by the U.S. Supreme Court decision in *Massachusetts v. EPA;* see Chapter 3.) Lawyers for the coal industry conceded, "The ruling puts in question permits . . . of perhaps as many as 100 coal plants" (Associated Press, 2008, para. 6).

More recently, the "clean coal" ad campaign has been met with a counter-image effort by the "Reality" campaign, a coalition of the Alliance for Climate Protection (Chapter 6), League of Conservation Voters, National Wildlife Federation, Natural Resources Defense Council, Sierra Club, and other environmental groups. Its first "This Is Reality" commercial ran on cable TV and its Website (www.thisisreality.org) beginning in late 2008. The scene opens with a male technician in a safety helmet and holding a clipboard. The technician says, "Clean coal. Heard a lot about it. So let's take a tour of this state-of-the-art clean coal facility." The technician opens a door with a sign "CLEAN COAL FACILITY ENTRANCE," and walks through it, into the "facility," which is actually the outdoors, a Western desert scene, with bird sounds and wind. He says: "Amazing! The machinery is kind of loud, but that's the sound of clean coal technology!" ("Reality Coalition," 2008).

The "This Is Reality" commercial relies on irony, appearing to take the coal industry at its word, only to find there is "nothing there." In its press conference on December 4, 2008, the coalition said it was launching the "Reality" advertising effort "to tell a simple truth: in reality, there is no such thing as 'clean coal,'" and said the campaign's purpose was to challenge "the coal industry to come clean—in its advertising and in its operations. Coal cannot be considered clean until its carbon dioxide emissions are captured and stored" ("This Is Reality," 2008, para. 1, 2). As this book goes to press, the ad wars over "clean coal" are continuing, each party attempting to shape the public perception of coal and the U.S. energy future. (See Figure 10.2.)

Figure 10.2	Coal-burning power plants like this are at the center of industry PR campaigns in the United promoting "clean coal," while environmental advocacy groups counter that burning coal causes emissions of carbon dioxide (CO_2), a major greenhouse gas.

© Jan Brons/istockphoto.

Corporate Environmental Reports

As the "clean coal" ads illustrate, the enhancement of a corporation's image is not limited to advertising of its product line. Sometimes the trade association for an industry that has been troubled by a poor environmental image will launch a special program to signal its commitment to environmental values. For example, in the 1990s—following a decade of negative news stories about toxic waste sites—the Chemical Manufacturers Association unveiled its Responsible Care Initiative, which aimed to assure the public of its care in producing and handling chemical products. Many corporations also publish annual reports of their environmental performance. (A company's environmental performance is sometimes included in a broader "sustainability" or "corporate social responsibility" report.)

First issued in the early 1990s, **corporate environmental reports** are documents distributed to shareholders and investors that report the status of a company's environmental performance, actions taken, and commitment to environmental values. In her study of early U.S. corporate reports, environmental communication scholar Wendy Feller (2004) argued that these reports often tended to construct a utopian narrative of a company's environmental progress and values. (A **utopian**

narrative is a story that depicts an ideal future; in this context, especially in its personal, social, and environmental features.) For example, Motorola Corporation's report for 2001 made this bold claim:

> Imagine a world that creates sustainable growth without harming the environment. That is a sustainable world. . . . Imagine a world filled with intelligent devices—devices that think and share information—making people's lives easier, safer, more productive and more fun. That is an amazing world. Now imagine all of it together. That is the world Motorola is bringing to life. (quoted in Feller, 2004, p. 57)

Such reports craft a particular outlook about a company. Apart from documentation of specific actions or achievements, the reports also serve a rhetorical purpose. Feller argued that they "function as narratives that unfold a free-market utopia" in which private corporations are portrayed as protectors of consumers' health and the Earth's environment (p. 59). For example, Canon Corporation offered this promise in one of its reports: "In the years to come, we will continue fostering environmental protection activities with the aim of contributing to world prosperity and the happiness of people everywhere" (quoted in Feller, 2004, p. 65).

More recently, corporate environmental and sustainability reports have become more realistic and transparent, and they are now an annual feature of businesses in the United States, Europe, and other regions. European countries, particularly, have seen a growth in corporate environmental, social, and sustainability reporting, where shareholders expect an increasing level of transparency about environmental performance. An environmental adviser for the European Bank for Reconstruction and Development reported that, in addition to reports, "It is now mainstream that companies have a grievance procedure for the public—whether that be a mechanism, a hotline, a community liaison officer, or other person responsible for managing complaints and responding in a timely manner" (Elizabeth Smith, personal communication, July 22, 2008).

While corporate environmental reporting is sometimes required as a condition for banks lending money to a corporation, especially in Europe, such reporting remains largely voluntary in the United States. Nevertheless, the trend is strongly in the direction of more transparency and reporting of environmental performance. An important development in encouraging voluntary reporting is the Global Reporting Initiative ([GRI] www.globalreporting.org). The mission of GRI is to encourage reporting on economic, environmental, and social performance by corporations as a routine communication practice; it provides businesses with "a universally-applicable, comparable framework in which to understand disclosed information" ("About GRI," 2008, para. 2). Other online services for corporate environmental reporting include the International Corporate Sustainability Reporting Site (www.enviroreporting.com), one of the first online sites providing guidelines for reporting and other resources.

Corporate Image Repairs: Apology or Evasion?

One of the most-studied functions of corporate environmental communication is **image repair:** the use of public relations to restore a company's credibility after an environmental harm or accident. Corporations that engage in wrongdoing often face a crisis of "symbolic legitimacy" (Chapter 2). Corporate image repair, therefore, attempts to minimize the harm and accompanying public perceptions that might otherwise "cause the organization irreparable damage" (Williams & Olaniran, 1994, p. 6). Image repair, also called *crisis management,* is vital to a company's continued operations, but the practice can be controversial, especially when a corporation's communication is viewed as insincere. A much-studied case of ineffectual image repair is the massive oil spill of the *Exxon Valdez* supertanker in Alaska's Prince William Sound in 1989. The tanker hit a reef, spilling nearly 11 million gallons of oil that "wreaked havoc on the immediate environment, despoiling almost eleven hundred miles of shoreline" (Hearit, 1995, p. 4). Called "the nation's worst oil spill" ("Oil Slick Spreads," 1989, p. 1), the pollution killed thousands of seabirds, sea otters, and other wildlife and seriously harmed local fisheries.

Exxon faced a flurry of negative publicity as television, radio, newspapers, and magazines worldwide carried stories of oil-soaked birds and sea lions struggling to move or breathe. One story in the *New York Times* reported:

> On a small pebbled beach on Eleanor Island, what appeared to be a blackened rock turned out to be a seabird befouled with oil. As a helicopter descended, the frightened bird raised its wings to flee but was unable to lift itself into the air. Just off Seal Island, a large group of sea lions swam in a tight knot straining to keep their heads well above the oily surface. (Shabecoff, 1989; quoted in Benoit, 1995, pp. 119–120)

As a result of the tragic accident, Exxon offered to respond with remedial actions—help with the cleanup and cooperation with a federal investigation—and an extensive image repair campaign. In a full-court press, including publication of a full-page "Open Letter to the Public" from Exxon's chairman in major newspapers, the company launched a three-part strategy of image restoration. Communication scholar William Benoit (1995) noted that Exxon first sought to shift the blame for the accident to the captain of the *Exxon Valdez,* who was discovered to have been drinking before his ship hit the reef. The company also tried to lessen the offensiveness of the oil spill through what Benoit called "minimization" and "bolstering" (p. 123). That is, Exxon tried to minimize reports of damage and bolster the company's image by announcing that it had "moved swiftly and competently" to lessen the impact of the oil on the environment and wildlife (quoted in Benoit, p. 126).

In the end, Exxon undoubtedly failed to alleviate public blame and loss of credibility in the immediate aftermath of the *Exxon Valdez* disaster. Although the company sought to portray itself as repairing damage caused by the accident, Benoit concluded that this strategy was undermined by well-publicized delays in the cleanup of the polluted coastlines. Hearit (1995) reported that, as a result of Exxon's bureaucratic handling of the crisis and failure to reestablish legitimacy, the company's public communication did not end with its letter of apology but continued with "a long-term campaign designed to communicate continued concern for, and assessment of, the effects of the *Valdez* spill" (p. 12).

Overall, Exxon's image repair campaign was not particularly successful. The company's promises to correct the damage were vague and were undermined by continued negative publicity in the media. As a result, Benoit concluded that "Exxon's reputation suffered from the *Valdez* oil spill, and its attempts to restore it in the short term appear ineffective" (p. 128).

Due to cases like the *Exxon Valdez,* some environmental critics question the validity of green marketing altogether. Corbett (2002), for example, has argued that "the business of advertising is 'brown'; therefore the idea of advertising being 'green' and capable of supporting environmental values is an oxymoron" (p. 144). Others have made a similar claim about environmental consumerism—the belief that by buying green, consumers can help the environment. It is this debate that I consider next.

"Greenwashing" and the Discourse of Green Consumerism

Corporate practices of image enhancement and image repair have not been without their critics. Let's look at two criticisms in particular: the charge that corporate green marketing is a form of "greenwashing," and a discourse of "green consumerism," the belief that purchasing environmentally friendly products can help save the Earth.

Corporate Greenwashing

In an earlier study of corporate opposition to environmental regulations, Jacqueline Switzer (1997) noted that often corporate "public relations campaigns—called 'greenwashing' by environmental groups—[are] used by industry to soften the public's perceptions of its activities" (p. xv; see also Corbett, 2002). The *Concise Oxford English Dictionary* defines the term **greenwash** as "disinformation disseminated by an organization so as to present an environmentally responsible public image.... Origin from *green,* on the pattern of *whitewash*" (Pearsall, 1999, p. 624). And the environmental marketing firm TerraChoice (2007) describes the term this way: "Green·wash (grēn'wŏsh,' -wôsh')—*verb:* the act of misleading consumers regarding the environmental practices of a company or the environmental benefits of a product or service" (p. 2).

Environmental groups routinely use "greenwash" to call attention to what they believe is deception by a corporation—an effort to mislead or divert attention from a corporation's poor environmental behavior or products. For example, Greenpeace (2008) gave the oil company British Petroleum (BP) its "Emerald Paintbrush" award in "recognition of the company's attempts to greenwash its brand over the course of 2008, in particular its multimillion dollar advertising campaign announcing its commitment to alternative energy sources . . . [and its use of] slogans such as 'from the earth to the sun, and everything in between'" (para. 4). Using internal BP documents, Greenpeace claimed that, in 2008, "the company allocated 93 per cent ($20bn) of its total investment fund for the development and extraction of oil, gas and other fossil fuels. In contrast, solar power (a technology which analysts say is on the brink of important technological breakthroughs) was allocated just 1.39 per cent, and wind a paltry 2.79 per cent" (para. 5). BP, on the other hand, insists that the company is committed to developing new, renewable energy sources (BP, 2009).

How, then, can someone tell if a corporate advertisement is greenwashing or the report of a legitimate environmental achievement? Most critics point to a basic standard of deception. Has the ad conveyed information or an impression that is countered by factual evidence? Many times, the truthfulness of a claim may be difficult for the ordinary consumer to determine. In other cases, there are groups such as SourceWatch (www.sourcewatch.org) that monitor the statements and behavior of corporations, providing information about their compliance with environmental regulations, and even evaluating specific marketing campaigns.

In a more general effort, the environmental marketing firm TerraChoice has identified six patterns, which it called the "Six Sins of Greenwashing," commonly used by companies. For example, TerraChoice (2007) defines the "Sin of Irrelevance" as when a product ad makes "a statement that may be truthful but is unimportant and unhelpful for consumers seeking environmentally preferable products" (p. 4). A typical "Sin of Irrelevance" is the claim that a product, such as an oven cleaner, is "CFC free." CFCs (chlorofluorocarbons) is a chemical linked to depletion of the ozone layer and has been legally banned for more than 30 years. (See FYI: "The Six Sins of Greenwashing.")

☞ FYI "The Six Sins of Greenwashing"

The environmental marketing firm TerraChoice has identified six patterns, which it called the "Six Sins of Greenwashing," used by companies in greenwashing. Here are the "sins," along with brief excerpts from its 2007 report, including guidelines for marketers:

1. **Sin of the Hidden Trade-Off:** Suggesting a product is "green" based on a single environmental attribute (the recycled content of paper, for example) (p. 2)

2. **Sin of No Proof:** "Any environmental claim that cannot be substantiated by easily accessible supporting information, or by a reliable third-party certification" (p. 3)

3. **Sin of Vagueness:** A "claim that is so poorly defined that its real meaning is likely to be misunderstood by the intended consumer" (p. 3)

4. **Sin of Irrelevance:** "Making a statement that may be truthful but is unimportant and unhelpful for consumers seeking environmentally preferable products" (p. 4)

5. **Sin of the Lesser of Two Evils:** "'Green' claims that may be true within the product category, but that risk distracting the consumer from the greater impacts of the category as a whole," such as "organic cigarettes" (p. 4)

6. **Sin of Fibbing:** "Making environmental claims that are simply false" (p. 4)

SOURCE: TerraChoice Environmental Marketing Inc. (2007).

The Discourse of "Green Consumerism"

Green marketing and discourses based on the free market raise another important question for scholars of environmental communication: Can consumers minimize damage to, or even improve, the environment by their purchase of certain products? That is, can we reduce air pollution, reduce the clear-cutting of our national forests, or protect the ozone layer by buying recycled, biodegradable, nontoxic, and ozone-free products? Many people appear to think so. As we saw earlier, Roper's Green Gauge poll has reported consumers' tendency toward pro-cotting, or "buying products from companies perceived as having good environmental track records" (Ottman, 2003, para. 4). Irvine (1989) first referred to this "use of individual consumer preference to promote less environmentally damaging products and services" (p. 2) as **green consumerism**. As we noted earlier, this is the belief that, by buying allegedly environmentally friendly products, consumers can do their part to protect the planet.

Whether green consumerism actually helps the environment is a matter of some debate. As we've seen, eco-labels are often vague, and federal standards for compliance with the content of such labels are unenforceable. Furthermore, as Canadian social theorist Toby Smith (1998) points out, "Some ecologists insist that only a product that has passed a so-called cradle to grave environmental audit can be said to be authentically eco-friendly" (p. 89). For example, a product may be biodegradable but also toxic, and it can still claim to be environmentally friendly under current standards.

Why, then, is the idea of green consumerism popular? Most of us do not wish to harm the environment and believe that we can consciously choose to lessen our impact on the Earth's capacity to sustain life. On the other hand, this belief itself is buttressed by green advertising claims that invite a specific identity through the act of buying. In her provocative book, *The Myth of Green Marketing: Tending Our Goats at the Edge of Apocalypse,* Toby Smith (1998) argues that green consumerism is not simply an act—the purchase of a certain product—but a *discourse* about the identity of individual consumers. (In Chapter 2, I described "discourse" as a *recurring pattern* of speaking or writing whose function is to circulate a coherent set of meanings about an important topic.) Smith explains that our purchasing does not occur in a discursive vacuum but is "an act of faith"; that is, "it is based on a belief about the way the world works" (p. 89). Our actions have effects, and among these is the effect of our purchasing on producers of products. In other words, the discourse of green consumerism assures us that, when we buy green, our buying not only can affect the actions of large corporations such as oil companies but that it also can alter our own relationship to, and impact on, the Earth. In short, one takes on a particular identity as purchaser.

Smith argues that green consumerism communicates because the act of purchasing is cloaked in an aura of other, authoritative discourses that buttress our identity as purchasers. She explains that our belief that we can do well for the environment by green shopping is underwritten by certain discourses that encode our buying with significance. Two discourses in particular assign meaning to our purchasing decisions: the discourses of market forces and participatory democracy.

First, green advertising affirms the belief that the market can be an avenue for change; that is, that by doing our bit, we contribute to the free market's invisible hand, and, as "all the little bits are counted, the consequence will be a net good" (T. Smith, 1998, p. 157). Second, the discourse of participatory democracy nurtures the belief that, in a liberal democracy, each of us is entitled to a voice in deciding about issues that matter to us. Thus, The Body Shop's founder, Anita Roddick, declared, "We can use our ultimate power, voting with our feet and wallets," while another retailer asserted, "Customers vote at the cash register" (quoted in T. Smith, p. 156). In each case, consumers are encouraged to believe that their purchases exercise a democratic will: "Voting" at the cash register affects retailers directly in determining which products succeed and which are in disfavor, and it affirms the consumer's identity as someone who acts responsibly toward the Earth.

The discourse of green consumerism can be an attractive magnet, pulling one toward a persuasive identity as a purchaser. "Green consumerism makes sense," explains Smith. "That is why people are attracted to it; they are not irrational, immoral, or uninformed. Quite the opposite: they are . . . moral in their desire to do their bit" (p. 152). Nevertheless, she believes that green consumerism also poses a danger by co-opting a more skeptical attitude toward the social and environmental impacts of excessive consumption. In a provocative charge, Smith claims that green consumerism serves to deflect serious questioning of a larger **productivist discourse** in our culture, one that supports "an expansionistic, growth-oriented ethic" (p. 10). Indeed, whether green consumerism can be a real force in the marketplace or a subtle diversion from the questioning of our consumer society is a question that invites serious debate in our classes and in research by environmental scholars.

In summary, the practice of green marketing is now widespread. It involves subtly and skillfully associating corporations' products, images, and behaviors with environmentally friendly values. As we saw, this effort to construct a green identity can serve any of three purposes: (1) green advertising or product promotion, (2) corporate image enhancement, and (3) image repair in the aftermath of negative publicity about a company. As we shall see shortly, companies may engage in green marketing even as they oppose stronger environmental protections.

Corporate Advocacy: Three Bites of the Apple

As we saw in Chapter 9, the newer fields of environmental chemistry and toxicology began to document health risks from industrial products as early as the 1960s. As these discoveries led to new requirements for industry, the affected businesses challenged the environmental sciences "at every step, questioning both the methods and research designs that were used and the conclusions that were drawn" (Hays, 2000, p. 222). Regulated industries such as chemical manufacturing, oil and gas refineries, coal-based, electric utility companies, and older, extractive industries (mining, logging, and ranching) put tremendous pressure on federal agencies to justify the science that supported the new regulations. Many corporations mounted advocacy campaigns to alter or defeat environmental laws and regulations for tougher clean air rules, car fuel standards, and disposal of toxic chemicals. Others have sought ways to discredit the symbolic legitimacy of science or silence their critics through public relations and the courts.

Although environmental groups occasionally counter corporate lobbying campaigns, their efforts at the federal level are often stymied by the larger resources of industry and commercial interests. Therefore, in this section I explore two of the most common forms of corporate advocacy: legislative and agency lobbying, and the use of issue ads to frame the terms of public debate. In the next section, I look at a more aggressive tactic: the use of the courts.

Corporate Lobbying and the Environment

Most corporations that are affected by environmental regulations invest considerable sums of money to influence the legislative process in both Washington, D.C., and state legislatures. For example, the coal and electric utility industries' "clean coal" ads aired at a time when Congress was scheduled to consider a new energy policy, including possible requirements that coal-fired power plants curb their CO_2 emissions.

Since the late 1990s, particularly, business groups have grown more influential in shaping environmental policies. Through their trade associations and well-funded public relations groups like the American Coalition for Clean Coal Electricity, as well as professional lobbyists and campaign contributions, U.S. corporations exert a powerful influence on the writing of laws and regulations aimed at protecting the environment. For example, groups such as the Business Roundtable devote substantial resources to legislative lobbying campaigns, press releases, and position papers to oppose environmental policies that would affect their operations or profits. Historians Gerald Markowitz and David Rosner (2002) describe some of these means:

> Organizations such as the Business Roundtable, made up of the CEOs of two hundred of the largest corporations in the country, have intensified their lobbying efforts among government officials and established well-funded and large offices in Washington, D.C. Through political contributions, "message ads," support for pro-industry legislators, and direct contact with members of the executive branch—at the very highest levels—industry attempts to protect its interests. (p. 9)

Corporations' public relations campaigns, political contributions, and direct lobbying serve a number of purposes. Journalist Mark Dowie (1995) has described the communication activities used by many corporations to shape environmental law as the **three-bites-of-the-apple strategy.** He explained, "The first bite is to lobby against any legislation that restricts production; the second is to weaken any legislation that cannot be defeated; and the third, and most commonly applied tactic, is to end run or subvert the implementation of environmental regulations" (p. 86).

Corporate lobbying to affect a law while it is being debated in the legislative arena is the most familiar, but more recently business groups have used their influence inside the bureaucracies of state and federal governments. In this strategy, the "third bite of the apple" is the end run or targeting of agencies that write the rules implementing an environmental law. Switzer (1997) reported that the reason for this interest by business is that "by removing an environmental issue from the legislative arenas to the less visible and more difficult to track bureaucratic arena, organized interests can better control the debate" (p. 154). For example, Chapter 9 presented an example of the third "bite of the apple," in which developers, agricultural and mining interests, and others objected to the Bush administration about the listing of critical habitat for endangered fish or wildlife when the protected habitat would affect their economic interests. As a result, the administration announced a rule change in the Endangered Species Act, overturning a requirement that federal agencies must communicate with U.S. Fish and Wildlife Service scientists when making decisions affecting endangered species. The new rule gave agencies greater discretion in deciding, without consulting with scientists, whether protected species would be threatened by development projects, including roads, dams, and mines.

To better understand Dowie's "three-bites-of-the-apple" strategy, let's look at two examples of corporate advocacy: (1) first, how one industry coalition helped to defeat a key international treaty that dealt with global warming and (2) industry's successful behind-the-scenes efforts to redefine a coal mining regulation that allowed the destructive practice of mountaintop removal to continue.

The Global Climate Coalition

One of the most effective corporate lobbying efforts against new international standards to curb the emissions that cause global warming was the Global Climate Coalition (GCC). Established in 1989, the GCC billed itself as "a leading voice for business and industry" (Global Climate Coalition, 2000, para. 1). Its early members included corporations and business associations such as the U.S. Chamber of Commerce, Texaco, Shell Oil, General Motors, and the American Forest and Paper Association. The coalition stated that its role was to coordinate the participation of business in public debates about global warming: "The GCC represents the views of its members to legislative bodies and policymakers. And it reviews and provides comments on proposed legislation and government programs" (para. 1). In reality, the GCC commanded a potent war chest that was used to wage aggressive public relations campaigns to protect its members' interests.

In 1997, the Global Climate Coalition launched a well-funded and extensive advocacy campaign to dispute the science behind the theory of global warming and to influence the terms of a new treaty that the United States and other nations had been negotiating in Kyoto, Japan. The Kyoto Protocol, signed in 1997, set international standards requiring governments to reduce emissions of carbon dioxide (CO_2) and other gases that fuel climate change. The GCC's advocacy campaign included the publication of reports suggesting uncertainty in the science of climate change, "aggressive lobbying at [the] international climate negotiation meetings, and raising concern about unemployment that it [claimed] would result from emissions regulations" (PR Watch, 2004, para. 6).

Although the United States signed the Kyoto Protocol when international negotiators completed it in 1997, then-President Bill Clinton still had to submit the treaty to the Senate for ratification under the Constitution. As a result, the Global Climate Coalition conducted a separate advertising campaign in the United States, objecting to the treaty's requirements. One of the GCC's major criticisms was that the United States would be required to meet stringent timelines for reducing so-called greenhouse emissions, yet many developing countries, along with China, would be exempt.

As a result of the questions raised by the Global Climate Coalition and other critics, the Senate voted 97–0 against the Kyoto Protocol in an advisory vote. As a result, President Clinton ultimately decided not to submit the treaty to the Senate for ratification. As the GCC continued its efforts at the first bite of the apple, its campaign claimed victory when newly elected President George W. Bush formally withdrew the United States from the list of signatories to the treaty in 2001.

In 2002, the GCC disbanded. Its sponsors believed that the lobbying campaign had served its purpose. A prominent statement on its deactivated Website announced, "The industry voice on climate change has served its purpose by contributing to a new national approach to global warming. . . . At this point, both Congress and the Administration agree that the U.S. should not accept the mandatory cuts in emissions required by the [Kyoto] protocol" (Global Climate Coalition, 2004). Perhaps another reason for the GCC's deactivation may have been that many corporations no longer accepted one of its main premises, that climate change was not a serious threat. Major companies such as BP-Amoco, DuPont, Ford Motor Company, Daimler-Chrysler, Texaco, and General Motors all had left the GCC within three years of its creation, many announcing initiatives that promised to develop alternative, cleaner sources of energy.

Weakening Mountaintop Coal Mining Regulations

A dramatic example of the three-bites-of-the-apple strategy has been the coal industry's campaigns to weaken federal rules regulating mountaintop removal in the Appalachian region of the United States. **Mountaintop removal** is the removal of the tops of mountains to expose the seams of coal that are buried in the mountain. Environmentally, it is a particularly destructive form of mining. "Miners target a green peak, scrape it bare of trees and topsoil, and then blast away layer after layer of rock until the mountaintop is gone" (Warrick, 2004, p. A1). In the past decade, hundreds of mountain peaks have been flattened in West Virginia, eastern Kentucky, and Tennessee. (See Figure 10.3.) The EPA estimates that 2,200 square miles of Appalachian forests will be cleared for mountaintop removal sites by the year 2012 (Parker, 2007, para. 19). Adding to the damage, the mining operations dump tons of rocky debris from the blasts over the sides of the mountain into the valleys below, "permanently burying more than 700 miles of mountain streams" (p. A1).

| Figure 10.3 | The towering dragline, center, is dwarfed by the size of the mountaintop removal operation. |

Photo by Vivian Stockman, May 30, 2003. Photo courtesy of Vivian Stockman/www.ohvec.org.

Although the rules implementing the Clean Water Act expressly forbid the dumping of mine waste into streams, lax enforcement by the Army Corps of Engineers officials who administered the law had allowed the practice of mountaintop removal to continue for years. Environmental attorneys, however, had succeeded by 2000 in challenging this illegal practice, and the number of permits granted for mountaintop removal started to decrease. It was at that point that industry decided to take a third bite of the apple by quietly lobbying federal agencies to change the regulation defining waste, the dumping of which is forbidden by the Clean Water Act.

In 2001, with a change of presidential administration in Washington, D.C., the coal industry saw an opportunity. On April 6, 2001, lobbyists from the National Mining Association met with EPA officials to argue for "a small wording change" (Warrick, 2004, p. A1) to the regulations that prohibit dumping of soil and rocks from mountaintops into valley streams. (The EPA is the federal agency responsible for implementation of these rules.) As a result of this lobbying, officials "simply reclassified the [mining] debris from objectionable 'waste' to legally acceptable 'fill'" (p. A1). This change in the definitions of *waste* and *fill* "explicitly allows the dumping of mining debris into streambeds" (p. A6). For its part, administration officials insisted that the rule change merely clarified existing policies.

In late 2008, before the Bush administration left office, its EPA and Office of Surface Mining also gave approval for another rule change for mountaintop mining operations. The "Stream Buffer Zone Rule" had prevented coal operators from dumping mining waste within 100 feet of a stream. The new rule, however, would not apply to "permanent excess spoil fills and coal waste disposal facilities" (Straub, 2008, para. 6). In other words, the revised wording allows the mining operations to push the dislodged soil and rocks from mountaintops into massive "valley fills" that directly cover miles of mountain streams. The revised mountaintop coal mining regulations represent both a case study of the three-bites-of-the-apple strategy and also the way that the Bush administration attempted to reshape environmental policy. *Washington Post* reporter Joby Warrick (2004) explained, "Rather than proposing broad changes or drafting new legislation, administration officials often have taken existing regulations and made subtle tweaks that carry large consequences" (p. A1).

Corporate Issue Ads: Framing the Terms of Debate

Although the ultimate goal of a corporate campaign may be the defeat or weakening of a particular law, the battle may be fought initially in the media and in the court of public opinion. Often accompanying an advocacy campaign is an extensive public relations effort aimed at persuading key opinion leaders and other members of the public. Business advocates attempt to influence the direction of environmental policy and legislation not only by placing advertisements in print and electronic media but also by feeding press releases and other information to reporters.

One of the most frequently used methods of influencing public perceptions of an environmental issue is the message or issue ad. An **issue ad** is a purchased advertisement in print, visual, or other media that carries a message opposing or supporting particular legislation or other issue affecting a company or industry's interests. Such ads often set the terms of debate by successfully framing an issue in terms of economic growth, jobs, a commitment to sustainability, and so forth. Let's look briefly at the growing use of issue ads and some of the framing devices that help to shape debate about the environment.

Issue Ads

In 1976, in the *Buckley v. Valeo* case, the U.S. Supreme Court distinguished issue ads from election campaign ads. Whereas election campaign ads clearly are intended to influence the election of a candidate, issue ads address a concern, such as the environment, health care, taxes, drunk driving, or education reform. Issue ads, which may be sponsored by corporations, by labor unions or other organizations, or by individuals, cannot endorse candidates for public office.

The Annenberg Public Policy Center at the University of Pennsylvania explains that the purpose of issue ads is "to mobilize constituents, policymakers, or regulators in support of or in opposition to legislation or regulatory policy" (2003a, para. 1). For example, the Global Climate Coalition successfully used issue ads and lobbying to mobilize opinion leaders and key members of Congress in its advocacy campaign to scuttle the Kyoto Protocol on global warming. More recently, the industry-funded group American Coalition for Clean Coal Electricity ran the series of "clean coal" ads on television throughout the 2008 election, not only to enhance the image of the industry but to mobilize broad public support for coal as a source of clean energy.

Often the purpose of such ads is to frame the debate over an issue by structuring the discussion in terms favorable to industry. (We discussed the role of media frames in Chapter 5.) According to Australian media scholar Sharon Beder (2002), Mobil Oil Corporation (now ExxonMobil) pioneered the use of issue ads to explain their business concerns without the media's filters. In an early issue ad, Mobil introduced the primary media frame that it would use in the future: A free and unfettered business climate is the American way. The ad explained:

> Business, generally, is a good neighbor. . . . From time to time, out of political motivations or for reasons of radical chic, individuals try to chill the business climate. On such occasions we try to set the record straight. . . . And the American system, of which business is an integral part, usually adapts. . . . So when it comes to the business climate, we're glad that most people recognize there's little need to tinker with the American system. (Mobil Oil ad, quoted in Parenti, 1986, p. 67)

Although corporations use issue ads to address many concerns, the environment is clearly one of the main subjects. By 2002, the amount of money spent on issue ads to influence environmental policy had become enormous. For example, during the debates over the Bush administration's energy policy (including the proposed opening of the Arctic National Wildlife Refuge), the Annenberg Public Policy Center estimated that about $15.4 million was spent on issue ads to influence the energy policy, most supporting the Bush proposals. Annenberg (2003b) reported, "Roughly 94% (about $14.5 million) of this spending was sponsored by energy/business interests, with environmental interests spending the remaining 6%" (para. 7).

Framing the Terms of Debate

Issue ads are critical to corporate communication primarily because they help to frame the terms of debate in ways favorable to the sponsoring group. As discussed in Chapter 5, a *frame* is a cognitive map or pattern of interpretation that people use to organize their understanding of reality. Skillful framing of issues is a robust feature of corporate advocacy during public debates over environmental policy. For example, as I write, business groups are arguing that any major effort to address climate change in the U.S. Congress during the near future "will drive up energy costs and put more people out of work" (Gannett News Service, 2008, para. 4). The "environment versus jobs" frame is a long-used appeal in controversies over the environment.

Some corporations also have used environmental values themselves to frame their support or opposition to a particular policy. Indeed, in opposing stricter environmental protection, some corporations have framed their message in the vocabulary of a concern for "sustainability," as well as jobs and economic growth. Let's look more closely at two different frames that often appear in corporate issue ads: "sustainability" and "economic growth" (and its related theme of "jobs versus the environment").

The terms *sustainability* and *sustainable development* appeared on the scene initially in the 1980s as concerns grew for the future of the Earth's environment and its resources. The phrase *sustainable development* entered popular use when the UN World Commission on Environment and Development (1987) published its report, *Our Common Future.* In a frequently quoted passage, the report defined **sustainable development** as "development that meets the needs of the present without compromising the ability of future generations to meet their own needs" (p. 43). As a metaphor for a new ethic toward the environment, the idea gained considerable public support, with ecologists and businesses also embracing the term (Peterson, Peterson, & Peterson, 2005).

Nevertheless, with little agreement over the concrete meaning of the phrase, sustainable development was interpreted in disparate ways by the parties who rushed to embrace the term. Many ecological scientists viewed the term as a road map for environmentally sensitive policies that would usher in a new orientation for society. On the other hand, some corporate interests used the term to denote sustainable *economic* growth. Such diverse uses of *sustainability* and *sustainable development* have led inevitably to confusion and a growing skepticism on the part of environmental leaders, scientists, and activists. Ironically, with its inherent ambiguity, the idea of sustainable development "fell from grace among ecologists as rapidly as it had become popular" (Peterson, Peterson, & Peterson, 2005, p. 674). Business interests have retained an enthusiasm for the term and have appropriated its rich but ambiguous meaning as a powerful frame in marketing claims and issue ads.

"Economic growth" is an equally popular frame for issue ads. Since the 1970s, efforts by environmental supporters to reduce acid rain, to raise the miles-per-gallon requirement for cars, and to impose strict safety rules for nuclear plants all have met criticism that such actions would cost jobs or damage the economy. Indeed, no more damaging charge has been brought against environmental progress over the years than the claim that such progress costs American jobs.

One reason this frame has been so influential is that it is a conflict-oriented frame and, as such, fits well with typical "newsworthiness" standards in mainstream journalism (Chapter 5). It also taps a reservoir of concern about job security felt by many people. An example was the charge, prominently made in the early 1990s, that the preservation of the Pacific Northwest's old-growth forests as critical habitat for the endangered spotted owl would cost jobs. Bumper stickers and signs reading "Save a Logger, Eat an Owl" and "This Family Supported by Timber Dollars" (Lange, 1993, p.251) dotted pickup trucks and storefront windows in logging communities throughout Oregon and Washington State. Environmental communication scholar Jonathan Lange (1993) reported that the timber industry "succeeded in creating an 'owl versus people' scenario in the media" (p. 250) with stories about threatened job losses in *Time*, the *Wall Street Journal*, and other national media.

The "jobs-versus-environment" frame also is used frequently by businesses in response to attempts by Congress to raise the average fuel standard for cars. In a study of framing these disputes, communication scholar John Bliese (2002) notes claims by U.S. automakers that raising fuel standards to 40 miles per gallon "would devastate the industry, putting 300,000 auto workers out of their jobs" (p. 22). Is this accurate? Where did the figure 300,000 come from? Bliese pointed out that the claim was based on a faulty study. He explains the industry's study "simply add[ed] up all of their employees currently making cars that get less than forty miles per gallon and assume that every single one of them would lose his or her job!" In other words, the study assumed that "the industry would not even attempt to build a single new car that met the proposed gas mileage standard" (p. 22).

The warning that environmental protection will cost workers their jobs, however, may be losing its almost mythic status in contemporary culture. A poll conducted by the Rockefeller Foundation and *Time* magazine in 2008, while finding significant economic anxiety among U.S. workers, also reported the emerging popularity of *environmental regulation* as a positive factor for the economy. It found, "Stricter pollution limits and tax credits for alternative energy development were supported by 84 percent of all respondents, the highest of any proposal. Increasing the minimum wage, expanding public works projects were nearly as popular, with 83 percent and 82 percent approval respectively" (Adler, 2008, para. 13). Certainly, the Obama administration has framed the shift to a "green economy" (investments in solar, wind, and other renewable energy sources) as a source for the creation upward of 5 million jobs rather than job loss (Dickerson, 2009).

SLAPP Lawsuits: Strategic Litigation Against Public Participation

While corporations and industry trade groups routinely engage in issue advertising and advocacy campaigns, they have not been shy about responding aggressively to their critics in the environmental movement in other ways. In this final section of the chapter, we look at a particularly chilling strategy used by some businesses to silence, discourage, or intimidate critics—a legal action known as the SLAPP lawsuit.

Consider the case of Colleen Enk: Shortly after Enk started to question a sand and gravel mine proposed for the Salinas River, near her neighborhood in San Luis Obispo County, California, she found herself the target of a lawsuit by the developers for libel and defamation, among other charges. The lawsuit also sought money damages. "It's pretty transparent why they did it," her attorney, Roy Ogden, said. "They wanted to shut her up" (Johnston, 2008, para. 12). Ultimately, Enk was forced to pay several thousand dollars in attorney fees and court costs.

The sand mining in the Salinas River proposed to dig and haul away sand and gravel from the river over a 20-year period. After Enk and her neighbors questioned the plans, a process server appeared at her door one evening in May 2008. She was not at home. The next day, Enk voiced her opinion again at a meeting of the San Luis

Obispo County Planning Commission. "My heart was pounding," she said (quoted in Johnston, para. 11). The next morning, the server caught her at home and served the papers summoning her to court. "Colleen has been sued for exercising the right of free speech in America. She's been stomped," her attorney explained.

Enk found herself faced with a strategy that "developers used against their opponents for years, a lawsuit known as a SLAPP" (Johnston, para. 3). SLAPP is the acronym for Strategic Lawsuit Against Public Participation. Pring and Canan (1996) define a **SLAPP** as a lawsuit involving "communications made to influence a governmental action or outcome, which, secondarily, resulted in (a) a civil complaint [lawsuit] . . . (b) filed against nongovernmental individuals or organizations . . . on (c) a substantive issue of some public interest or social significance" such as the environment (pp. 8–9). Such lawsuits have become common. California's State Environmental Resource Center (2004) reported that every year thousands of people are hit with SLAPP suits.

University of Denver professors George Pring and Penelope Canan (1996) co-direct the university's Political Litigation Project, an effort to document cases similar to Enk's. They reported in their influential study, *SLAPPs: Getting Sued for Speaking Out*, that lawsuits have been brought against citizens and environmental groups for writing letters, speaking at public hearings, publicly protesting, filing complaints, and circulating petitions to government:

> An anthropology professor fought to preserve an ancient Indian village found on his California State University campus before the university buried it in apartment buildings and retail stores. He wrote letters to government officials complaining . . . and was sued for $570,000 by the university's consulting firm for "negligent interference with contractual relations," "libel," [and] "slander." . . .
>
> In 1992 a North Kingston, Rhode Island, homeowner reported to government authorities her concern that a local landfill was contaminating the area's drinking water. The owners sued her for "defamation" and "contractual interference." . . .
>
> Peaceful demonstrators protested a California nuclear power plant. The county responded with a $2,891,000 lawsuit, demanding that demonstrators repay its costs for arresting and jailing them. (pp. 6–7)

In the end, most SLAPP lawsuits are dismissed because of First Amendment protections of citizens' rights to speak and petition government. But the mere act of filing a lawsuit that alleges libel, slander, or interference with a business contract can be financially and emotionally crippling to defendants. Pring and Canan explain that corporations or even government units that file SLAPP suits "seldom win a legal victory—the normal litigation goal—yet often achieve their goals in the real world. . . . Many [of those who are sued] are devastated, drop their political involvement, and swear never again to take part in American political life" (p. 29). Even if the group or citizen wins, he or she most likely "has paid large sums of money to cover court costs and has been thrown into the public eye for months or even years. This unlawful intimidation pushes people into becoming less active and outspoken on issues that matter" (California State Environmental Resource Center, 2004, para. 7).

The purpose of a SLAPP is not necessarily to win the lawsuit but to cause the corporation's critics to spend time, energy, and money defending themselves and to discourage others from participating in public life. Yet, some have decided to fight back. In fact, many states are providing remedies for cases in which a court determines that a lawsuit against an individual is a SLAPP action. That is, some courts may agree quickly to dismiss a lawsuit if it appears to be motivated by the unconstitutional purpose of silencing speech and to require the plaintiffs to pay court costs.

Over the years, two principal sources of defense have arisen in response to SLAPP lawsuits—one based in constitutional guarantees of democratic rights and the other in personal injury law. Pring and Canan refer to these two sources of defense as the "one-two punch" that has characterized successful defense against SLAPP lawsuits.

The core defense against a SLAPP suit is derived from the basic rights granted to citizens in the First Amendment to the U.S. Constitution, particularly the rights of freedom of speech and the right of the people to petition the government for redress of grievances. Often, a court will grant expedited hearings to dismiss a SLAPP if the citizen's criticism was part of a petition to the government. In such cases, the plaintiff (the party bringing the lawsuit) must show that the citizen's petition is a "sham" in order to proceed with the original lawsuit.

The second part of the defense involves what is known as a **SLAPP-back** suit against the corporation or governmental agency bringing the initial allegations against a citizen. Here, the defendant "SLAPPs back" by filing a countersuit alleging that the plaintiff infringed on the citizen's right to free speech or to petition government. It is important that a SLAPP-back suit allows for the recovery of attorneys' fees as well as punitive damages for violating constitutional rights and inflicting damage or injury on the defendant (malicious prosecution).

Environmentalists, labor, individual citizens, and others have won monetary awards in fighting SLAPP actions. Pring and Canan report that awards in SLAPP-backs occasionally have been large—jury verdicts of $5 million to a staggering $86 million were awarded against corporations that brought SLAPP suits in the 1980s and 1990s. Increasingly, developers, polluters, and others have had to weigh the chances of a SLAPP-back before bringing a SLAPP action. Pring and Canan observed, "Even though SLAPP-backs are not a panacea, this risk of having to defend against them may prove to be the most effective SLAPP deterrent of all" (p. 169).

SUMMARY

In this chapter, we identified three major types of corporate environmental communication in the public sphere: (1) green marketing, or the construction of an environmental identity in corporate products, images, and behaviors; (2) industry advocacy campaigns aimed at influencing legislation, agency rule making, and public opinion; and (3) an aggressive communication strategy known as SLAPP lawsuits, used by some businesses to silence or intimidate their environmental critics. We also observed that a broader discourse of the free market underlies much of corporate communication and helps to explain much opposition to government regulation of business. In the view of its proponents, a free-market discourse offers a powerful ideological rationale for determining the value that a society assigns to environmental protection as well as the best way to secure that value.

Despite such communication approaches, many U.S. businesses have come to appreciate the environmental values embraced by the general public, consumers, and the media. As a consequence, much of corporate communication illustrates a skillful dance of corporate identity—an attempt to associate its products and identity with "green" values while at the same time continuing to oppose selected environmental regulations. This intricate effort plays out in the midst of the public sphere—a crucible of diverse voices, each seeking to speak for "nature" or the nature of the relationship between society and the environment.

KEY TERMS

Communication-Related Concepts

Corporate environmental reports: Documents, distributed to shareholders and investors, that report the status of a company's environmental performance, actions taken, and commitment to environmental values.

Environmental image enhancement: The use of advertising to improve the image or identity of a corporation, reflecting its environmental concern or performance.

Green consumerism: Marketing that encourages the belief that, by buying allegedly environmentally friendly products, consumers can do their part to protect the planet.

Green marketing: A corporation's attempt to associate its products, services, or identity with environmental values and images; generally used for (1) product promotion (sales), (2) image enhancement, or (3) image repair. Recently defined to include communication about environmentally beneficial product modifications.

Green product advertising: The marketing of products as having a minimal impact on the environment and to "project an image of high quality, including environmental sensitivity, relating both to a product's attributes and its manufacturer's track record for environmental compliance" (Ottman, 1993, p. 48).

Greenwashing: "Disinformation disseminated by an organization so as to present an environmentally responsible public image. . . . Origin from *green* on the pattern of *whitewash*" (Pearsall, 1999, p. 624).

Image repair: The use of public relations to restore a company's credibility after an environmental harm or accident.

Issue ads: Purchased advertisements in print, visual, or other media that contain a message opposing or supporting particular legislation or other issues affecting a company or industry's interests.

Pro-cotting: Buying products from companies perceived to have good environmental track records; the opposite of *boycotting.*

Productivist discourse: A discourse in our culture that supports "an expansionistic, growth-oriented ethic" (T. Smith, 1998, p. 10).

SLAPP-back: A lawsuit against the corporation or governmental agency bringing an initial SLAPP suit against a citizen. The defendant "SLAPPs back" by filing a countersuit alleging that the plaintiff infringed on the citizen's right to free speech or to petition government; a SLAPP-back suit allows for the recovery of attorneys' fees as well as punitive damages for violating constitutional rights and/or inflicting damage or injury on the defendant (malicious prosecution).

SLAPP lawsuits: Strategic Litigation Against Public Participation. As defined by Pring and Canan (1996), a SLAPP is a lawsuit involving "communications made to influence a governmental action or outcome, which, secondarily, resulted in (a) a civil complaint [lawsuit] . . . (b) filed against nongovernmental individuals or organizations . . . on (c) a substantive issue of some public interest or social significance" such as the environment (pp. 8–9).

Three-bites-of-the-apple strategy: Phrase used by journalist Mark Dowie (1995) to describe the communication activities used by many corporations to shape environmental law: "The first bite is to lobby against any legislation that restricts production; the second is to weaken any legislation that cannot be defeated; and the third, and most commonly applied tactic, is to end run or subvert the implementation of environmental regulations" (p. 86).

Utopian narrative: A story depicting an ideal future; in this context, especially in its personal, social, and environmental features.

Environment-Related Concepts

Command and control: Phrase used by opponents of environmental regulations to refer to government requirements that impose restrictions on business operations; these specify procedures and technologies for reducing pollution as well as measurable levels of performance that a company must meet.

Free market: Usually, the absence of governmental restriction on business or commercial activity.

Invisible hand (of the market): Scottish economist Adam Smith's theory of the working of the market; a metaphor for an invisible or natural force of the private marketplace that determines what society values. In his classic book, *An Inquiry Into the Nature and Causes of the Wealth of Nations,* Smith (1776) argued that the sum of individuals' self-interested actions in the marketplace promotes the public's interest, or the common good.

Mountaintop removal: The removal of the tops of mountains in the Appalachians to expose seams of coal buried in the mountain; a particularly destructive form of mining environmentally.

Sustainable development: Defined by the UN World Commission on Environment and Development (1987) in its report, *Our Common Future,* as "development that meets the needs of the present without compromising the ability of future generations to meet their own needs" (p. 43).

DISCUSSION QUESTIONS

1. Do advertising labels on products, such as "organic," "biodegradable," or "recycled" affect your purchases? Are these labels always accurate?

2. Do you believe that government regulation of business activities are needed to prevent harm to the environment? Or do you side with Adam Smith's theory that there is an "invisible hand" in the activities of the private marketplace that naturally leads to the public good?

3. Can green consumerism help to protect the environment? That is, can we reduce air pollution, lessen the clear-cutting of our national forests, or reduce global warming by buying products that are biodegradable, nontoxic, recyclable, and so forth? Or does green consumerism simply reinforce consumption?

4. Are all corporate marketing claims about their environmental products or values merely greenwashing or deceptive? How can you tell? Can you give an example of an accurate "green" label or commercial about a product?

5. Are the corporations that file SLAPP lawsuits merely a few bad apples, or do corporations have a right to sue individuals that they believe defame or libel the company's activities?

REFERENCES

About GRI. (2008). *Global Reporting Initiative.* Retrieved January 9, 2009, from http://www.globalreporting.org.

ACCCE. (2008, April 16). I believe. [TV ad]. Retrieved January 8, 2009, from http://www.youtube.com.

Adler, B. (2008, July 17). Poll: Deep economic insecurity. *Politico.* Retrieved January 12, 2009, from http://www.politico.com.

Aldrich, S., & Lehrwriting, J. (2006). *Free enterprise protects the environment.* Retrieved January 8, 2009, from http://www.heartland.org.

America's Power. (2009). *Ad archive.* Retrieved January 8, 2009, from http://www.americaspower.org.

Annenberg Public Policy Center. (2003a). *About issue advertising.* University of Pennsylvania. Retrieved October 16, 2004, from http://www.annenbergpublicpolicycenter.org.

Annenberg Public Policy Center. (2003b). *Energy/environment.* University of Pennsylvania. Retrieved October 16, 2004, from http://www.annenbergpublicpolicycenter.org.

Associated Press. (2008, November 14). Coal plants jeopardized over climate. *International Herald Tribune.* Retrieved January 9, 2009, from http://www.iht.com.

Ball, J. (2008, February 4). Wall Street shows skepticism over coal. *Wall Street Journal.* Retrieved July 26, 2008, from http://online.wsj.com.

Beder, S. (2002). *Global spin: The corporate assault on environmentalism* (Rev. ed.). White River Junction, VT: Chelsea Green Publishing Company.

Benoit, W. L. (1995). *Accounts, excuses, and apologies: A theory of image restoration strategies.* Albany: State University of New York Press.

Bliese, J. R. E. (2002). *The greening of conservative America.* Boulder, CO: Westview Press.

BP. (2009). *Alternative energy.* Retrieved January 10, 2009, from http://www.bp.com.

Bulik, B. S. (2008, April 16). Green ads call attention, but raise doubts. *EcoAmerica. News and Events Blog.* Retrieved January 8, 2009, from http://ecoamerica.typepad.com.

Business Wire. (2008, November 6). *New poll data reveals 70 percent public opinion approval for coal-fueled electricity.* Retrieved January 9, 2009, from http://biz.yahoo.com.

California State Environmental Resource Center. (2004). *"Eco-SLAPPs" are a frequent occurrence.* Retrieved October 31, 2004, from http://www.serconline.org.

Consumers Beware: What labels mean. (2006, November 19). *Raleigh News & Observer,* pp. 23A–24A.

Corbett, J. B. (2002). A faint green sell: Advertising and the natural world. In M. Meister & P. M. Japp (Eds.), *Enviropop: Studies in environmental rhetoric and popular culture* (pp. 141–160). Westport, CT: Praeger.

Crable, R. E., & Vibbert, S. L. (1983). Mobil's epideictic advocacy: "Observations" of Prometheus-bound. *Communication Monographs, 50,* 380–394.

Depoe, S. P. (1991). Good food from the good earth: McDonald's and the commodification of the environment. In D. W. Parson (Ed.), *Argument in controversy: Proceedings from the 7th SCA/AFA Conference on Argumentation* (pp. 334–341). Annandale, VA: Speech Communication Association.

Dickerson, M. (2009, January 4). Why Obama's green jobs plan might work. *The Los Angeles Times.* Retrieved January 12, 2009, from http://www.latimes.com.

Dowie, M. (1995). *Losing ground: American environmentalism at the close of the twentieth century.* Cambridge, MA: MIT Press.

ExxonMobil. (2005, May 9). Energy and the environment. [Advertisement]. *The New York Times,* p. A5.

Federal Trade Commission. (n.d.). Guides for the use of environmental marketing claims. Section 260.7. *Environmental marketing claims.* Retrieved November 25, 2004, from http://www.ftc.gov.

Feller, W. V. (2004). Blue skies, green industries: Corporate environmental reports as utopian narratives. In S. L. Senecah (Ed.), *The environmental communication yearbook* (Vol. 1, pp. 57–76). Mahwah, NJ: Erlbaum.

Gannett News Service. (2008, December 25). *Environment versus economy: 2009 poised to be a green year, but. . . .* Retrieved January 12, 2009, from http://www.tucson citizen.com.

Giuliano, J. (1999). Green advertising claims—to heal or deceive? *Healing our world weekly commentary.* Retrieved October 15, 2004, from http://www.spiritual endeavors.org.

Global Climate Coalition. (2000). *About us.* Retrieved October 4, 2004, from http://www .globalclimate.org.

Global Climate Coalition. (2004). [Statement]. Downloaded October 30, 2004, from http://vwww.globalclimate.org.

Goldman, R., & Papson, S. (1996). *Sign wars: The cluttered landscape of advertising.* New York: Guilford.

GreenBiz.com. (2009, January 8). *Marketing and communications.* Retrieved January 8, 2009, from http://www.greenbiz.com.

Greenpeace. (2008, December 22). *BP wins coveted "emerald paintbrush" award for worst greenwash of 2008.* Retrieved January 10, 2009, from http://weblog.greenpeace.org.

Gunningham, N., Kagan, R. A., & Thorton, D. (2003). *Shades of green: Business, regulation, and environment.* Stanford, CA: Stanford University Press.

Hays, S. P. (2000). *A history of environmental politics since 1945.* Pittsburgh, PA: University of Pittsburgh Press.

Hearit, K. M. (1995). "Mistakes were made": Organizations, apologia, and crisis of social legitimacy. *Communication Studies, 46,* 1–17.

Irvine, S. (1989). *Beyond green consumerism.* London: Friends of the Earth.

Johnston, K. (2008, October 29). Shut down for speaking up: SLAPP suits continue to chill free speech, despite legislated remedies. *New Times, 23*(13). Retrieved January 12, 2009, from http://www.newtimeslo.com.

Lange, J. I. (1993). The logic of competing information campaigns: Conflict over old growth and the spotted owl. *Communication Monographs, 60,* 239–257.

LoBianco, T. (2008). Groups spend millions in "clean coal" ad war. *The Washington Times.* Retrieved January 8, 2009, from http://www.washingtontimes.com.

Markowitz, G., & Rosner, D. (2002). *Deceit and denial: The deadly politics of industrial pollution.* Berkeley: University of California Press.

Martin, A. (2006, October 24). Meat labels hope to lure the sensitive carnivore. *The New York Times.* Retrieved March 2, 2009, from http://www.nytimes.com.

Mufson, S. (2008, January 18). Coal industry plugs into the campaign. *The Washington Post,* p. D1. Retrieved October 4, 2008, from http://www.washingtonpost.com.

National Consumer Coalition. (2004). *Proclamation of the NCC.* Retrieved November 15, 2004, from http://www.consumeralert.org.

Oil slick spreads toward coast: FBI begins probe. (1989, April 2). *The Los Angeles Times,* Sec. 1, p. 1.

Ottman, J. A. (1993). *Green marketing: Challenges and opportunities for the new marketing age.* Lincolnwood, IL: NTC Business.

Ottman, J. A. (2003). *Hey, corporate America, it's time to think about products.* Retrieved October 14, 2004, from http://www.greenmarketing.com.

Parenti, M. (1986). *Inventing reality: The politics of the mass media.* New York: St. Martin's.

Parker, L. (2007, April 19). Mining battles marked by peaks and valleys. *USA Today.* Retrieved January 12, 2009, from http://www.usatoday.com.

Pearsall, J. (Ed.). (1999). *Concise Oxford English dictionary* (10th ed.). Oxford, UK: Oxford University Press.

Peterson, N. M., Peterson, M. J., & Peterson, T. R. (2005). Conservation and the myth of consensus. *Conservation Biology, 19*(3), 762–767.

Porter, W. M. (1992). The environment of the oil company: A semiotic analysis of Chevron's "People Do" commercials. In E. L. Toth & R. L. Health (Eds.), *Rhetorical and critical approaches to public relations* (pp. 279–300). Hillsdale, NJ: Erlbaum.

Pring, G. W., & Canan, P. (1996). *SLAPPs: Getting sued for speaking out.* Philadelphia: Temple University Press.

PR Watch. (2004). *Global climate coalition.* Retrieved October 4, 2004, from http://www .prwatch.org.

Reality Coalition. (2008, December 4). *"Reality" coalition launches campaign debunking "clean coal" myth.* Retrieved January 10, 2009, from http://acp.3cdn.net.

Schumann, D. W., Hathcote, J. M., & West, S. (1991). Corporate advertising in America: A review of published studies on use, measurement, and effectiveness. *Journal of Advertising, 20*(3), 35–56.

Shabecoff, P. (1989, March 31). Captain of tanker had been drinking, blood tests show. *The New York Times,* pp. A1, A12.

Smith, A. (1910). *An inquiry into the nature and causes of the wealth of nations: Vol. 1.* London: J. M. Dent & Sons. (Original work published 1776)

Smith, T. M. (1998). *The myth of green marketing: Tending our goats at the edge of apocalypse.* Toronto: University of Toronto Press.

SourceWatch. (2009, January 5). *American Coalition for Clean Coal Electricity. [ACCCE].* Retrieved January 8, 2009, from http://www.sourcewatch.org.

Stavins, R. N. (2004). The myth of the universal market. *The Environmental Law Institute.* Retrieved January 8, 2009, from http://john-whitehead.blogs.com.

Straub, N. (2008, December 4). EPA approves mountaintop removal rule changes. *Earth News.* Retrieved January 12, 2009, from http://www.earthportal.org.

Sustainable Life Media. (2008, June 26). Canada bans "green" and "eco-friendly" from product labels. Retrieved January 8, 2009, from http://www.sustainablelifemedia.com.

Switzer, J. V. (1997). *Green backlash: The history and politics of environmental opposition in the U.S.* Boulder, CO: Lynne Rienner.

TerraChoice Environmental Marketing Inc. (2007, November). *The six sins of greenwashing.* Retrieved January 8, 2009, from http://www.terrachoice.com.

This Is Reality. (2008). [Facilities video.] Retrieved January 10, 2009, from http://www .thisisreality.org.

Warrick, J. (2004, August 17). Appalachia is paying the price for White House rule change. *The Washington Post,* pp. A1, 6–7.

Williams, B. A., & Matheny, A. R. (1995). *Democracy, dialogue, and environmental disputes.* New Haven: Yale University Press.

Williams, D. E., & Olaniran, B. A. (1994). Exxon's decision-making flaws: The hypervigilant response to the *Valdez* grounding. *Public Relations Review, 20,* 5–18.

World Commission on Environment and Development. (1987). *Our common future.* Oxford, UK: Oxford University Press.

Zoellick, R. B. (2002, February 6). *Statement of U.S. trade representative before the Committee on Finance of the U.S. Senate.* Washington, DC: Office of the U.S. Trade Representative.

Epilogue

Imagining a Different World

In a world that is getting hot, flat, and crowded, the task of creating the tools, systems, energy sources, and ethics that will allow the planet to grow in cleaner, more sustainable ways is going to be the biggest challenge of our lifetime.

—Thomas L. Friedman, *Hot, Flat, and Crowded* (2008, pp. 5–6)

In February 2009, I joined thousands of people from the United States, Canada, and other nations in Washington, D.C., for a "Good Jobs, Green Jobs in 2009" conference. The task before the many speakers, workshops organizers, and participants was no less than a reimagining of our future. We were seeking to transform society by creating a new generation of "green" jobs and exploring green technologies—wind, solar, biomass, geothermal, and more—that reduce global warming and increase clean, renewal sources of energy ("Good Jobs, Green Jobs," 2009). There was no doubt that this challenge was daunting, but also inspiring: *to imagine a different world.*

William McDonough and Michael Braungart (2002) issued a similar call at the start of their inspiring book *Cradle to Cradle: Remaking the Way We Make Things*. They invited readers to *think*—to imagine new ways to confront the challenges facing us today—toxic poisoning of the Earth's ecosystems, global climate change, and the rapid loss of biodiversity. In some ways, the task of environmental communication in the years surrounding Earth Day 1970 was more straightforward than the task facing us today. The challenges then had "tangible, local, and immediate consequences for the public. Lake Erie was dying under the boats of fishermen, the Cuyahoga River could be seen to burn by Clevelanders . . . and children in Los Angeles could not go out and play hundreds of days of a year" (Pope, 2004, p. 7). In response, scientists, environmentalists, editorial writers, students, and others sounded an alarm and rallied individuals to protect not only the nation's rivers and air but also the places where people lived, attended school, and worked. State and federal officials responded with laws to clean up rivers, reduce air pollution, and regulate the disposal of toxic waste.

By contrast, the challenges that alarm scientists, environmentalists, and many government leaders today are less tangible but are global in scale. As James Speth (2008), Dean of the School of Forestry and Environmental Studies at Yale University, recently put it:

> All we have to do to destroy the planet's climate and biota and leave a ruined world to our children and grandchildren is to keep doing what we are doing today. . . . Just continue to release greenhouse gases at current rates, just continue to impoverish ecosystems and toxic chemicals at the current rate, and the world in the latter part of this century won't be fit to live in. (p. x)

Gradual heating of the Earth's climate, invisible chemicals, the disappearance of biological diversity, loss of tropical forests—the Earth's "lungs"—require more from us than business as usual and more than environmental communication as usual. They require us not only to imagine a different world but to compose a compelling way of speaking to each other and to broader publics about our planet's possible futures.

In this book, I have surveyed many different forms of environmental communication: advocacy campaigns, blogs, news stories, risk reports from Environmental Protection Agency (EPA) officials, and the courageous testimony of the residents of "sacrifice zones," among others. Building on these, some environmental leaders are now calling for a **language of aspiration**—that is, an ethically compelling narrative, grounded in core values, to address these new global challenges (Werbach, 2004). Such a language would speak more urgently of our values and the vision we hold for the future, an urgent, convincing appeal that addresses both planetary warming and what some ecologists warn could be the "sixth great extinction," "an extinction of plant and animal species that matches the catastrophe of the dinosaurs 65 [million] years ago" (Radford, 2001, para. 1).

In ancient Greece, communication that addressed a community's values was called **epideictic rhetoric,** speech that celebrated the accomplishments and values of a community as well as the character of its citizens and leaders. Orators praised the achievements of Athenian athletes, warriors, and others, as well as the virtues of Athens and other city-states. But they also condemned shortcomings, criticizing leaders for failure in governance or the community itself for selfishness or lack of courage. Most important, epideictic orators encouraged citizens to step back from everyday routines and the press of business to remember the norms and behaviors that bound them together and consider their actions within a longer arch of history. They asked, "What matters to us as a community?" "What does our future hold?" and, "Are we, as a people, behaving in ways that ensure our well-being, honor, and prosperity?" Some Native American cultures had a similar tradition. Before taking an important action, tribal leaders would deliberate and ask what the effects would be "unto the seventh generation," a reminder that their choices would have lasting consequences for many generations after their own.

Similarly, I suggest that you and I, as well as public officials, scientists, business leaders, and environmentalists, need to nurture, more urgently than ever, a language of aspiration or epideictic rhetoric for today. What would constitute a compelling, ethical narrative about our future, one that would mobilize public concern about the intangible and long-term consequences of our fossil fuel economy and our consumption of the Earth's biological heritage and future? Are there stirrings of such rhetorics today? In what forums are they occurring, and what are they saying?

Warnings of danger, dire as they may be, are not enough. Danger can paralyze as well as motivate. If we believe that nothing can be done, we are more likely to turn aside or divert ourselves with daily cares and work. Instead, what is needed is the ability to imagine a different future and the values and principles that can help us design pathways to it, the ability to envision other possible ways of living and doing business. Many believe that this requires new cognitive maps, new ways of thinking. For example, business entrepreneur and environmentalist Paul Hawken thinks that the prevailing mental model of human behavior toward the environment—the assumption that the natural world of rivers, plants, animals, and air are there simply for our use or abuse—should be abandoned. This model, Hawken believes, "usurps language and meaning, nullifying vision, reason, and perception" (quoted in Lertzman, 2002, p. 193).

In the end, however, the prospects for such ideas will depend on more than the breakthrough discoveries in the lab or the inspiration of books such as *Cradle to Cradle*. No imagined future is possible without an informed and mobilized public that is willing to demand it and work to achieve it. As the Sierra Club's executive director Carl Pope (2004) put it, without such popular demand, "decision makers have not been forced to confront the need for fundamental changes in the way our society uses carbon (and other greenhouse gases)" (para. 3).

Building popular demand for fundamental changes will require all of us to become involved—in public conversations, online conversations, documentary filmmaking, at community meetings and in public hearings, and in other forums of the public sphere. Yet, Paul Hawken says, "This is heartening because it means that farmers, teachers, mechanics, parents, architects, and people in every other vocation have a role to play" (Lertzman, 2002, pp. 191–192). That also includes you and me. What will be our role? The conversation about the future of our cities, about our forests, water, air, and wildlife, and about the life of our planet itself has started. The debate is under way. Will you join this already-in-progress conversation and help imagine a different world "unto the seventh generation?"

KEY TERMS

Communication-Related Concepts

Epideictic rhetoric: Speech that celebrated the accomplishments and values of a community as well as the character of its citizens and leaders.

Language of aspiration: An ethically compelling narrative, grounded in core values that address environmental challenges.

REFERENCES

Good Jobs, Green Jobs in 2009. (2009, February 4–6). Good jobs/green jobs national conference. Retrieved January 13, 2009, from http://www.greenjobsconference.org.

Lertzman, R. (2002). Down to business: Paul Hawken on reshaping the economy. In A. H. Badiner (Ed.), *Mindfulness in the marketplace: Compassionate responses to consumerism* (pp. 185–200). Berkeley, CA: Parallax Press.

McDonough, W., & Braungart, M. (2002). *Cradle to cradle: Remaking the way we make things.* New York: North Point Press.

Pope, C. (2004, December). *Carl Pope response to "the death of environmentalism": There is something different about global warming.* Retrieved July 7, 2005, from http://www .sierraclub.org.

Radford, T. (2001, November 29). Scientist warns of sixth great extinction of wildlife. *The Guardian* [United Kingdom]. Retrieved August 26, 2005, from http://www.guardian.co.uk.

Speth, J. G. (2008). *The bridge at the edge of the world: Capitalism, the environment, and crossing from crisis to sustainability.* New Haven and London: Yale University Press.

Werbach, A. (2004, December 19). *Is environmentalism dead?* Speech presented to the Commonwealth Club of San Francisco. Retrieved August 4, 2005, from http://www .3nov.com.

Index

About the Author

Robert Cox (PhD, University of Pittsburgh) is Professor of Communication Studies and the Curriculum Ecology at the University of North Carolina at Chapel Hill. His principal research and teaching areas are environmental communication, rhetorical theory, and critical study of the discourse of social movements. Considered one of the nation's leading scholars in environmental communication, he has been president of the Sierra Club three times (2007–2008, 2000–2001, and 1994–1996) and has served on the Sierra Club's board of directors for 14 years. His published work includes critical studies of the discourse of civil rights, peace movement, labor, and the environmental movement. Cox currently serves as a board member of *Environmental Communication: A Journal of Nature and Culture*, and previously served as associate editor for the *Quarterly Journal of Speech*. In addition to his teaching activities, Cox advises environmental groups and is called upon regularly to participate in numerous initiatives concerning the environment. In 2000, he campaigned with former Vice President Al Gore and singer Melissa Etheridge in the U.S. presidential election.